Y0-CBB-207

# Orientation

A provincial settlement on the edge of the civilized world; a trading district dominate by merchants and aldermen; a royal stronghold; a center of politics, power, and culture . . . London has had almost as many faces as it has years of histo England's capital and Britain's seat of government has evolved over the centuries from an area covering just 677 acres into a vast 620-square-mile metropolis along the north and south banks of the **River Thames**, home to seven million citizens.

Indeed, London is not one but several cities coexisting in the same space. Lo up at **Big Ben** on a bright autumn morning, or stroll along the **Embankme** on a warm summer evening at sunset and you'll find the London of film se complete with red double-decker buses, chunky black cabs, bicycle-riding bobbies, and umbrella-toting politicians. Look closer, and catch a glimpse c local London, comprised of 32 highly individual boroughs, each with its ov mayor and council, not to mention its own special quirks and charms. An elegant town-house atmosphere permeates **Mayfair**, for example, while th literary legacy of **Virginia Woolf's** era clings to **Bloomsbury**. To the east, finance still dominates the original **City**, or Corporation, of London; meanwhile, law and politics rule sober **Westminster**.

Of course, there is also historic London, seat of cathedrals and kings. The city was established roughly 2,000 years ago, first as a Celtic settlement, then as Londinium, a lonely Rom outpost that eventually grew into an empire extending around the globe. The city is survivor, having weathered the brazier history: **Queen Boadicea** of the Celts burned the city to the ground in AD 6 but within a few years it had risen fro the ashes; the **Great Plague** swept through in 1665, followed by the **Gre Fire** of 1666, but neither disaster nor t 20th-century **Blitz**, centuries later, cou annihilate the city's collective soul or the souls of its inhabitants p and present. Famous ghos from every epoch cohab here—in just one day you may happen upon **Henry VIII** in the **Tower of London, William**

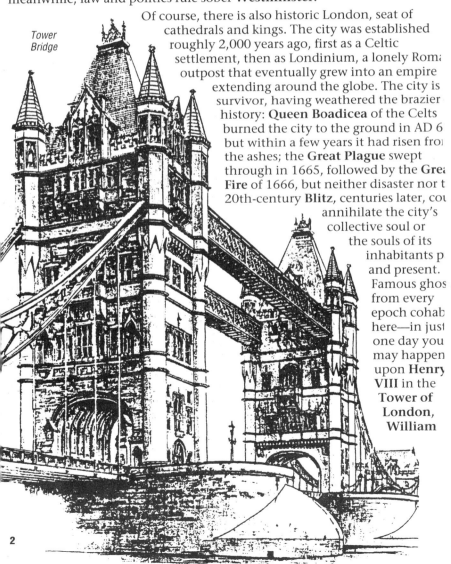

*Tower Bridge*

**Shakespeare** in **Southwark**, and **Charles Dickens** in **Tavistock Square**. Even modern redevelopment plans have failed to tarnish London's grandeur: **St. Paul's Cathedral** retains its majesty, despite the glass-and-steel structures that now crowd it on **Paternoster Square**.

But no city thrives on its past alone. Modern London stands tall, in the space-age 1986 **Lloyd's of London Building**, in the high-tech **Docklands** developments, and in the best of contemporary art and theater, as well as in the fast-food joints that have cropped up on various corners. And, to be honest, London possesses a dark side, with an undercurrent of racial tension in the **East End**; a class system that produces its own special problems, including stereotypes perpetuated by something as simple as an accent or dialect; the homeless, who huddle under railway bridges; and, of course, crime. The infamous pea-soup fogs have disappeared, but they've been replaced by noxious exhaust fumes and grime—mostly from cars jamming narrow streets and alleyways never meant to cope with modern-day traffic.

For all its problems, however, the magic of London acts as an elixir for tourists: 17 million of them visited in 1993 alone. Some come for the **West End** musicals; some for the fashion of **Regent Street** and **Knightsbridge**; some to wander the spacious parks and meet history face-to-face; others to explore the modern street culture that thrives in tiny art galleries and pulsates in clubs and discos. Whatever the reason, visitors to London share an affection for a city that is at once ancient and modern, reserved and tempestuous—an ever-changing kaleidoscope of a metropolis. "London," wrote **H.G. Wells** in *The New Machiavelli*, "is the most interesting, beautiful, and wonderful city in the world to me, delicate in her incidental and multitudinous littleness, and stupendous in her pregnant totality."

## Getting to London

*Country code: 44. City codes: 71 (inner London) or 81 (outer London).*

### Airports

Two major airports serve London from North America: **Heathrow,** roughly 15 miles west of the city's center, and **Gatwick,** some 28 miles to the south. Three smaller airports take incoming flights from continental Europe: **Luton,** 35 miles to the northwest; **Stansted,** 34 miles to the northeast; and **London City Airport,** located to the east in the Docklands development.

### Heathrow Airport

Heathrow is the world's busiest airport, and the closest to London proper. Most major North American airlines (with the exception of **Delta**) fly into Heathrow's four terminals; U.S. transatlantic arrivals and departures generally use Terminal 3, although **British Airways** uses Terminal 4. Each terminal has its own **Travel Information Centre,** bank, currency exchange bureau, post office, and hotel booking desk. The **London Tourist Board** (daily 8:30AM-6PM) has an office at the Underground station serving Terminals 1 through 3; ask for free travel and tourist information.

### General Information

| | |
|---|---|
| Emergencies | 081/745.7047 |
| Airport Information | 081/759.4321 |
| Airport Police | 081/897.7373 |
| Customs and Excise | 081/750.1515 |
| First Aid | 081/745.7211 |
| Lost and Found | 081/745.7727 |

### Airlines

| | |
|---|---|
| Air Canada | 081/897.1331 |
| American Airlines | 081/572.5555 |
| British Airways | 081/897.4000 |
| KLM Royal Dutch Airlines | 081/750.9820 |
| United Airlines | 0426/915500 |
| Virgin Atlantic | 0293/511581 |

### Business Facilities

The **Heathrow Business Centre** (081/759.2434), located at the end of Terminal 2, offers use of conference rooms and boardrooms, a lounge, telephones, telex, fax, word processors, secretarial services, and car parking.

### Parking

Heathrow has short-term, long-term, and business parking facilities. For general information, call 081/745.7160.

### Rental Cars

| | |
|---|---|
| Alamo | 081/759.6200 |
| Avis | 081/897.9321 |
| Budget | 081/759.2216 |
| Eurodollar | 081/751.6466 |
| Europacar | 081/897.0811 |
| Hertz | 081/897.3344 |

### Traveler's Aid

All terminals at Heathrow have trained medical staff, and there is a 24-hour **Medical Centre** located in the Queen's Building between Terminals 1 and 2. Drugstores, or "chemists," are situated in all four terminals. **Travel Care** (M-Sa 9:30AM-4:30PM), an independent social work agency, is also located in Room 1214 of the Queen's Building, and provides information, advice, and counseling to travelers. Contact it through the information desks.

For assistance with visas, passports, documents, cars, flight delays, and transfers, contact **Airport Assistance Ltd** (081/897.6884) or **Air Welcome** (081/979.8774).

### Getting from Heathrow to London

There are two **Underground** (subway) stations: one serving Heathrow Central (Terminals 1-3), the other serving Terminal 4; both are on the **Piccadilly Line** and are the quickest and cheapest way to get to and from central London. Trains leave approximately every five minutes during weekday peak hours (7-9:30AM, 4:30-7PM), and approximately every 10 minutes during other times and on weekends. The trip takes 40 to 55 minutes, depending upon the destination, and trains operate Monday to Saturday from 5:08AM-11:49PM (5:26AM-11:33PM in Terminal 4), and on Sundays from 6:01AM-10:57PM (5:52AM-10:46PM in Terminal 4). For more information about schedules and fares, call 071/222.1234.

Two **Airbus** (071/222.1234) services connect Heathrow with central London: the A1 goes to **Victoria Station** via Hyde Park Corner, and the A2 runs to **Russell Square** via Euston Station. Buses depart every 30 minutes, cost a bit more than the tube, and usually take a lot longer; if you can keep from nodding off after the long flight, however, you can sightsee along the way.

**Speedlink** (081/668.7261), a luxury bus service, provides service between Heathrow and Gatwick airports; travel time is about one hour.

**Taxis** accept passengers from the authorized ranks located outside each terminal. Fares can be steep, however, so it's best to share with others in your group (if you have one), or with fellow travelers headed your way.

### Gatwick Airport

Besides serving major North American airlines, Gatwick also receives the bulk of charter flights into its North and South Terminals, which are linked by a free rapid-transit system that runs every three minutes. Both terminals have 24-hour information desks located in the international arrivals concourse; the North Terminal also operates a separate **British Council** desk to provide assistance to passengers. Each terminal operates banks, exchange bureaus, post offices, and hotel booking desks.

### General Information

| | |
|---|---|
| Emergencies | 0293/505444 |
| Airport Information | 0293/535353 |
| Airport Police | 0293/531122 |
| Customs and Excise | 0293/517711 |
| Lost and Found (South Terminal) | 0293/503162 |
| Tourist Information Centre (South Terminal Arrivals Concourse) | 0293/560108 |
| 24-Hour Information Line | 0293/567675 |

### Airlines
**North Terminal**

| | |
|---|---|
| British Airways | 0293/525555 |
| Delta Airlines | 0800/414767 |
| Lufthansa | 0293/535353 |

**South Terminal**

| | |
|---|---|
| American Airlines | 081/572.5555, 0800/010151 |
| Canadian Airlines International | 081/667.0666 |
| Continental Airlines | 0293/776464 |
| Northwest Airlines | 0293/567955 |
| TWA | 071/439.0707 |
| USAir | 0800/777333 |
| Virgin Atlantic | 0293/538222 |

### Business Facilities

Business services are available in the **Forte Crest Hotel** (0293/567070), located in the North Terminal, and in the **Gatwick Hilton Hotel** (0293/518080), located in the South Terminal.

### Traveler's Aid

**Travel Care** (M-F 9:30AM-5:30PM; Sa-Su 9:30AM-4:30PM), in the South Terminal, offers help to anyone at the airport, whether or not the problem is travel-related.

**Medical emergencies** (0293/505444 in the North Terminal and 0293/503725 in the South Terminal).

### Rental Cars:

| | |
|---|---|
| Alamo | 0293/547671 |
| Avis | 0293/529721 |
| Budget | 0293/540141 |
| Eurodollar | 0293/513031 |
| Europacar | 0293/531062 |
| Hertz | 0293/530555 |

### Getting from Gatwick to London

The fast and easy **Gatwick Express** (071/928.2113) train leaves the South Terminal station for Victoria Station every 15 minutes (every 30 minutes during late-night hours); travel time runs about half an hour.

There is also the **Thameslink** (071/928.5100) train service, which runs from Gatwick to King's Cross, Blackfriars, and London Bridge rail stations every half-hour during the day, every hour at night; travel time: 35 minutes.

The **Flightline 777** (081/668.7261) bus operates a daily service between Gatwick and Victoria Coach station; buses leave both terminals approximately every hour, and the travel time takes at least an hour and 20 minutes. Though it isn't nearly as fast or as efficient as the Gatwick Express, Flightline does accept American and Canadian dollars as payment.

---

"There is in the Englishman a combination of qualities, a modesty, an independence, a responsibility, a repose, combined with an absence of everything calculated to call a blush into the cheek of a young person, which one would seek in vain among the Nations of the Earth."

Mr. Podsnap in **Charles Dickens'** *Our Mutual Friend*

# Getting around London

## Bicycles

For the intrepid only. Bicycling is an enchanting but exceptionally dangerous way to get around London unless you're a seasoned cyclist. You must remember to stay on the left side of the street and to lock your bike. Try to avoid the main routes where you will be subjected to traffic fumes as well as lorries thundering past, often too close for comfort. Regardless of these deterrants, seeing London from a bike is one of the best ways to savor it—slowly enough to take in the beauty and find hidden ways through the back streets and across London's greenswards, and easy to park (lamp-posts and meters are free). **The London Cycling Campaign** (3 Stamford Street, 071/928.7220) is an excellent source of cycling information. You can rent wheels at the following shops:

Mountain Bike & Ski
   18 Gillingham Street .......................071/834.8933
F.W. Evans
   77-79 The Cut, Waterloo.................071/928.4785
Portobello Cycles
   69 Golborne Road............................081/960.0444

## Double-Decker Buses

If speed is not a priority, take a London bus. The view from the top is unbeatable, and the bus itself—a fire-engine-red double-decker, with its roller-coaster movements and friendly atmosphere—offers a quintessential London experience. Bus stops have signs indicating the numbers of the buses that stop there, outlines of the bus route, and sometimes a map of the route. Have your fare or **Travelcard** ready to show the driver as you board, and remember to enter at the front of the bus. Like on the tube, the fare is tied to zones, but the bus is sometimes cheaper. Strange but true: the bus driver cannot sell you a one-day bus pass; look for them at newsstands and in the tube stations.

### Bus Etiquette

1. Don't cut in the bus line, or "queue," as it's called here; doing so may tee off the locals.

2. You may be the only person at the stop waiting for your particular bus, so keep your eyes open. Buses do sail past, even when they're supposed to stop. Don't feel silly flagging your bus down; you'll have to in any case if the stop is marked "Request."

3. Smoking is not permitted on any bus.

4. There is no standing on the upper deck or on the platform.

5. Even though the English do it, don't jump off—or onto—a moving bus.

6. Avoid buses at rush hour (weekdays 7:30-9:30AM, 4:30-7PM), as you may have to wait a long time to get one.

7. Some of the larger one-man buses can be very dangerous, as they travel fast and brake suddenly. If possible, stay in your seat, and hold on tight at all times, as people do get thrown around.

## Scenic Bus Routes

The numbers refer to bus routes and are displayed on the front of each bus.

**11**—King's Road, Sloane Square, Victoria Coach Station, Victoria, Westminster Cathedral, Westminster Abbey, Westminster, Whitehall, Horse Guards, Trafalgar Square, National Gallery, The Strand, Law Courts, Fleet Street, St. Paul's Cathedral.

**12**—Bayswater, Hyde Park, Marble Arch, Oxford Street, Oxford Circus, Regent Street, Piccadilly Circus, Trafalgar Square, National Gallery, Horse Guards, Whitehall, Westminster, Millbank, Tate Gallery, Vauxhall Bridge.

**15, 15b**—Paddington, Marble Arch, Oxford Street, Oxford Circus, Regent Street, Piccadilly Circus, Trafalgar Square, The Strand, Aldwych, Fleet Street, St. Paul's Cathedral, Tower of London (look for a yellow sticker on the destination board at the front of the bus that says: "Via Tower").

**53**—Oxford Circus, Regent Street, Piccadilly Circus, National Gallery, Trafalgar Square, Whitehall, Horse Guards, Westminster, Westminster Bridge, Imperial War Museum, Elephant and Castle.

### Night Buses

Special night buses (marked with an "N" sign) run from London to the suburbs through the night until 6AM. Buses leave from Trafalgar Square and the Central London restaurant, theater, and cinema districts. One-day Travelcards are not valid.

## Driving

If you can avoid driving in London, by all means do so. If you're determined to try it, however, remember that driving in the U.K. is a left-hand/left-lane experience. Given that London traffic is also getting increasingly aggressive and more congested each year, and that city parking is nearly nonexistent during working hours, you could be in for some hair-raising moments. Also bear in mind that gasoline ("petrol" this side of the Pond) is substantially more expensive than it is in the U.S.: about $2 to $2.50 per gallon.

That said, here are some tips to make the ride smoother: As long as you have been driving for at least a year, and are over the age of 18 (21 in some cases), your U.S. or Canadian driver's license is valid for 12 months in the U.K. However, getting an **International Driving Permit**—available for a small fee through the **American Automobile Association (AAA)** or the **Canadian Automobile Association (CAA)**—isn't a bad idea since, if you're unlucky enough to have an accident, it could help placate the police. Seat belts—in both front and back seats—are mandatory in Britain. Speed limits in urban areas are technically 30mph, but most Londoners tend to ignore this. When approaching a "roundabout," a circular junction that is the bane of those who are unfamiliar with it, *always, always* yield to the traffic approaching from your right.

Renting a car in Britain isn't cheap (£85 to £220 and up per week for a midsize car), but rental companies such as Hertz, Avis, and Budget frequently offer sizable discounts if you arrange to rent a car when purchasing your airline ticket. Charges usually include unlimited mileage, insurance, and temporary **Automobile Association (AA)** membership, but be sure you understand exactly what type of insurance is included in the package. If you want a car simply to take you *out* of London, then hold off and rent one from a local company rather than from the bigger, more expensive names at the airports.

For the fainthearted and the wise, chauffeur-driven cars may be an appealing alternative. Most major car rental agencies, including those listed below, offer this service.

Avis Chauffeur Drive or Car Rental
  8 Balderton Street ...........................071/917.6703
Camelot Chauffeur Drive
  Headfort Place Garage .....................071/235.0234
Europcar Chauffeur Drive
  Division or Car Rental
  Davis House, Wilton Road ...............071/834.6701
Hertz Chauffeur Drive Office
  24-28 Oval Road .............................071/485.3344

**Parking**
Unless you want to carry a hefty (and heavy) supply of change and risk being clamped by a Denver boot or towed away, look for one of the multistory **National Car Parks (NCPs)** sprinkled around central London; some are marked on the larger-scale city maps. These car parks may be more expensive than meters, but they save hassles, headaches, and a lot of precious time.

**Public Transportation**
The only way to become a bona fide Londoner—even temporarily—is to use public transport. Mastering the tube or the bus eases the pressure on the wallet and orients you in a way that taxi rides never will. You can pick up a free visitor's guide at a **London Transport Information & Travel Centre** at the following tube stations: Heathrow Central, Euston, Paddington, King's Cross, Liverpool Street, Charing Cross, Victoria, St. James's Park, Piccadilly Circus, and Oxford Circus. Or go to the **British Travel Centre** (12 Lower Regent Street, 081/846.9000). Ask for a free Underground map at any tube station.

A word of advice for surviving urban London: don't be afraid to carry a map. Londoners do so because it's essential, and the "A-Z" series (Z pronounced "zed") is by far the best; you can pick up a copy at most newsstands and bookstores. The best source for tourist information, though, is the **London Tourist Board Information Centre** in Victoria Station.

---

"London thou art the flower of citties all!
Gemme of all joy, jasper of jocunditie."

**William Dunbar**

**Taxis**
Who has not been in love at one time or another with a black London cab? Capacious, timeless, and honorable, these shiny vehicles—nearly all are Austins—are icons of British dependability and integrity. Taxi ranks can be found in front of hotels and main tourist areas; otherwise, flag down a black cab if its yellow "For Hire" sign is lit. If your destination is under six miles and within London boundaries, drivers are obligated to take you where you want to go. London taxi drivers are the best and most knowledgeable cabbies around by virtue of having learned a huge amount of London geography, and then passing an incredibly tough exam to prove it. Tip between 10 and 15 percent. If you have any problems with a particular driver, contact the **Taxi Drivers' Association** (071/286.1046).

While minicabs are another option, it's wise to rely on recommendations from hotels or friends, since these cabs must be ordered by telephone. Many "bucketshop" cab drivers also operate a cheaper service in the central London area, but they are often unlicensed, under-insured, and, because they haven't had to take the exam, frequently get lost.

**Tours**
**Boat Tours** The best way to see London if you are blessed with a warm, sunny day is by boat. You can cover 28 twisting miles of the Thames from Hampton Court to Greenwich Palace on one of the passenger boats that spend their days cruising up- and downstream from central London. For information, call 0839/123.432.

**Bus Tours** A good way to get a sense of the lay of the land is on a bus tour. There are two basic types of tours: the panorama, which is a 18- to 20-mile nonstop sightseeing tour; and the full- and half-day guided tours, which cover Westminster Abbey and the Changing of the Guard in the morning, and St. Paul's and the Tower of London in the afternoon.

**Harrods Tours** This excellent whole-day tour leaves from Harrods on Thursdays only; call 071/581.3603 for more details. Two-hour tours leave Harrods daily at 10:30AM, 1:30PM, and 4PM, and include tea, coffee, biscuits, and a taped commentary.

**London Coaches** London Coaches, a.k.a. **The Original Round London Sightseeing Tour,** is a traditional red double-decker bus, open-topped in summer. Tours depart every half-hour and on the hour from Piccadilly Circus, Victoria, and Baker Street stations. They start at 10AM and finish at 5PM in the summer, 4PM in the winter. There's no need to book, just show up and wait; call 081/877.1722 for more information.

**Note:** For those who love castles, abbeys, palaces, stately homes, gardens, and historic sites, a **British Heritage Pass** will give you access to 600 of them dotted around the country. The pass is available through the British Travel Centre, from the Tourist Information Centres at Heathrow and Gatwick airports, or your travel agent.

# Trains

Although somewhat less than punctual, trains are a great, civilized way to travel. If you use trains all the time, you realize how unreliable they really are, but occasional travelers need not fear. The whole country is linked to London via **British Rail,** and there is a circular network of train stations that leads you into the English countryside, or at least as far as the suburbs.

Most long-distance trains have buffet or restaurant facilities, but check when you buy your ticket. All have toilets and all are accessible to the disabled, but some of the stations are difficult to negotiate, and on some routes you might need to change trains (which can be nightmarish), so find out beforehand.

Even if you do not have a BritRail pass, you may be able to get cheap British Rail fares. To get the cheapest fare (this depends on how full the train is likely to be, not on your bargaining skills) for rail travel in Britain, and rail and sea journeys to the Continent and Ireland, visit the **British Travel Centre** (12 Lower Regent Street) or one of these mainline station travel centers: Charing Cross, Victoria, Paddington, Euston, King's Cross, or Liverpool Street.

On long-distance InterCity journeys, you can book **Apex** tickets (seven days before departure) or buy a **Saver** or **Super Saver** ticket if you book in advance and travel on any day except Friday, a summer Saturday, Easter, or on a bank holiday weekend. Those who buy Savers or Super Savers will find there are early morning and some evening travel restrictions on the trains they can use. Children under 16 pay half-price and those under 5 ride free when accompanied by an adult.

London has 15 major British Rail train stations, each of which serves a different part of Britain and is accessible by tube or bus. For information about trains and schedules, call the following numbers (but don't be surprised if you get a busy signal!):

East and Northeast England,
  Scotland East Coast .........................071/278.2477
East and West Midlands,
  North Wales, Northwest England,
  Scotland, and Ireland ......................071/387.7070
South of England ..............................071/928.5100
West of England, South Midlands .......071/262.6767

**Note:** When booking your flight, ask the travel agent about BritRail passes. British Rail maintains that if you take three trips out of London to big cities or major attractions, then you will have covered the cost. A BritRail pass allows you to travel on any train, although on particularly busy routes, such as London to Edinburgh, you should reserve a seat. Check when you book the ticket.

---

"To be an Englishman is to belong to the most exclusive class there is."

**Ogden Nash**

## Train Timetable Information:

British Rail International .....................071/834.2345
  Credit card reservations ...................071/828.0892
London, Southern England,
  East Anglia, Essex...........................071/928.5100
Luxury Days Out ...............................071/388.0519
North London,
  East and Northeast England,
  Scotland via East Coast....................071/278.2477
Northwest London and England,
  East and West Midlands, North Wales,
  Scotland via the West Coast,
  Northern Ireland and
  Republic of Ireland via Holyhead......071/387.7070
West London, South Midlands,
  West of England, South Wales,
  Republic of Ireland via Fishguard.....071/262.6767

# Underground

The tube, as it's known, is by far the easiest, the most efficient, and the most economical way to get around London. It is fast, fairly clean, and relatively safe until around 9 or 10PM. Tube stations are marked by circular red and blue **London Transport** signs. There are 11 lines (or routes), each designated by a different name and color. Large-scale maps of the Underground network are displayed in each station, and each compartment of the train *should* have a map of the route the train follows. Be forewarned: Some trains, such as those on the District and Circle lines, use the same platforms, so be sure to check the lighted platform signs and the destination board on the front of the train before boarding. Smoking is not permitted anywhere on the Underground.

Service starts at 5AM, and ends around midnight Monday through Saturday, and runs from 7AM to 11PM on Sunday. Restricted hours apply on bank or public holidays. If you travel after 9:30AM on weekdays, you'll save heaps with a one-day **Travelcard,** which is good for unlimited travel on the tube, the buses, the Docklands Light Railway, and the British Rail Network Southeast trains throughout the Greater London area. Travelcards are good at all times on weekends. Alternatively, if you have a passport-size photograph, you can purchase a weekly or monthly Travelcard—a cheaper option if you plan to travel extensively. London is divided into six travel zones, and all tube tickets and Travelcards are sold according to zone; most major attractions are located in zones one and two.

You can now purchase tickets and Travelcards from ticket machines in most Underground stations, as well as from the usual ticket counters, but you need to know which zones you want to visit beforehand. If in doubt, ask a friendly native; half of them are still getting used to the machines themselves, and will be sympathetic to your confusion. Be sure to hold onto your ticket: You'll need it to pass through the entry/exit turnstiles, and once in a while, a plainsclothes inspector will ask to see it during your journey. In London, 24-hour travel information about the Underground is available at 071/222.1234.

**Note:** London Transport has a special **Visitor Travelcard**, which you can buy from your travel agent before leaving home. The advantage is that you won't need a photograph, and you won't have to buy a new one every day or week. Although it is slightly more expensive, the Visitor Travelcard offers a discount on standard tube fares, and on tickets to major tourist attractions. It allows you to travel on central Underground and bus routes, the Docklands Light Railway, and some suburban train services, such as Network Southeast.

## Walking
You only really know and love a city through your eyes and feet, and London offers marvelous rewards to the walker. Such distinguished feet as those of **Daniel Defoe, Samuel Johnson, James Boswell, John Gay, Thomas Carlyle,** and **Sir Anthony Hopkins** made walking the streets of London part of their life's work. Some advice: Look both ways before crossing the street. In addition to regular traffic, there's the added hazard (and one not to be underestimated) of cyclists cutting swathes through pedestrians on the pavement. Walking tours are listed in the back of the *Times* and in the weekly *Time Out* magazine, and include the City, the Great Fire and Plague, and the London of the Romans, Victorians, Shakespeare, and Dickens. It is now almost possible to walk from the Thames Flood Barrier back to the source in the Cotswolds—a very long walk, indeed!

# FYI

## Business Services
Almost every hotel and an increasing number of shops and newsstands offer fax and photocopy services for a small charge. Sending a fax to the U.S. at peak time (3-8PM), however, will cost roughly $3.50 or more per page. **Chesham Executive Centre** (150 Regent Street, 071/439.6288) has fax, telex, and photocopy facilities.

## Climate
Believe it or not, London's climate is relatively moderate and mild, although it is prone to change at a moment's notice. Whatever the season, you'd be well advised to bring sweaters and jackets for evenings, as well as raincoats, umbrellas, and, above all, shoes that are kind to the feet and can endure the occasional puddle.

## Customs and Immigration
All foreign visitors to the U.K. must have a valid passport, which will be stamped by immigration officials at each entry point. Although there is rarely a problem, it might help speed things along if you can provide the address where you'll be staying while in the U.K.

## Disabled Travelers
**Artsline** (M-F 9:30AM-5:30PM. 071/388.2227; fax 071/383.2653) advises on theater, cinema, museum, and other art center access for those with disabilities and special needs. It also has minicoms for the deaf, but is not a drop-in service. Most cinemas, theaters, and public places (including restaurants) do cater to the disabled. Always call and check when booking or visiting, as this guarantees special help when you arrive and an appropriate seat. A monthly magazine, *Disability Arts in London,* is available free to any disabled person in the U.K.; call 071/916.6351.

**Evan Evans** (daily 24 hours; 26-28 Paradise Road, Richmond, Surrey, 071/930.2377), which runs daily coach tours of London, takes a number of disabled passengers as long as someone able-bodied travels with the disabled person. Specify the nature of the disability before booking.

**Holiday Care Service** (2 Old Bank Chambers, Station Road, Surrey, 0293/774535; fax 0293/784647) is a charity offering free information and advice on vacations for people with special needs—the elderly and the disabled. It is not a booking service. Call or write explaining the problem and what sort of holiday you are looking for, and provide a rough estimate of your budget. Holiday Care has details on inclusive or specialized holidays, accommodations, transportation, publications, and guides for U.K. destinations, plus it can find people who will drive elderly and disabled people around, too.

**London Transport** (55 Broadway, 071/222.5600) runs a daily **Stationlink** service every hour on a clockwise circular route that goes past all of London's mainline stations (except Charing Cross and Cannon Street), starting at 8:30AM at Victoria. These buses connect with the wheelchair-accessible **Airbus** services to Heathrow Airport at both Victoria and Euston. Buses are specially designed and drivers are specially trained.

**National Trust** (36 Queen Anne's Gate, 071/222.9251; fax 071/222.5097), which owns places of historic interest or natural beauty all over the country, publishes a free annual booklet, *Information for Visitors with Disabilities,* showing those sights accessible to people with disabilities, including scented gardens for the blind.

## Embassies
**Canadian High Commission** (McDonald House, Grosvenor Square, 071/258.6600).

**U.S. Embassy** (24 Grosvenor Square, 071/499.9000). For emergencies of all types, ask for extensions 570 or 571 for the American Aid Society, a registered charity that helps Americans in distress.

## Health
Because the U.S. and the U.K. have no reciprocal health agreement, be sure to take out medical insurance before leaving home. You will be treated without question, but you'll be charged at the private patient rate, which can prove expensive. In

emergencies, dial 999, and you will be connected to an operator who will inquire about the nature of the problem, then arrange for an ambulance, police, or a fire engine. Although patients who arrive at a hospital by ambulance get priority, horror stories about delays abound. If possible, head for the nearest hospital "casualty department" (i.e., emergency room), then be prepared to have someone make a fuss until you're seen by a doctor; otherwise, you could be in for a long wait.

The following London hospitals have 24-hour emergency rooms:

Charing Cross Hospital
Fulham Palace Road ........................081/846.1234
Guy's Hospital
St. Thomas Street ...........................071/955.5000
Royal Free Hospital
Pond Street ......................................071/794.0500
St. Bartholomew's Hospital
West Smithfield ...............................071/601.8888
University College Hospital
Gower Street.....................................071/387.9300

## Hostels
Your wallet is virtually empty, but you'd like to stay a few days longer. The cheapest place to find lodging (for youngish people only) is at youth hostels. They're very primitive and you must be prepared to share rooms and facilities. If you are, ring ahead to check if they've got space. The best two (location-wise) are **Holland House** (Holland Walk, 071/937.0748), in the middle of Holland Park, in Kensington, and **City of London** (36 Carter Lane, 071/236.4965), right by St. Paul's.

## Money
Banking hours have been extended to 4:30PM and many branches are now open on Saturday mornings. Traveler's checks can be cashed at major banks (**Midland, National Westminster, Lloyds,** and **Barclays**), or at the **American Express Office** (M-Tu, Th-F 9AM-5:30PM; W 9:30AM-5:30PM; Sa 9AM-4PM; 147 Victoria Street. 071/828.4567). You can also cash personal checks for up to $1,000, depending on the type of AMEX card you have. Avoid exchange bureaus and hotel cashiers, as they charge more for the service.

While inflation has been brought under control for the time being, some things—hotels, gasoline, and good restaurants—still seem hideously expensive. The exchange rate varies daily, and is listed in major newspapers such as the *Times* or *Financial Times.*

British currency consists of pounds sterling. There are 100 pence to the pound. Pound coins are small, thick, and golden; 50p coins are silver and hexagonal, while the 20p coin is similar but smaller; the 10p coin is small, silver, and round; and the 5p coin is minuscule; tuppences (two penny pieces) and pennies are both copper. Five pound notes are greenish blue; £10 ones are orange; £20 notes are light purple, and £50 ones are greenish gold. Credit cards are used as widely as in the U.S., the most popular being VISA and ACCESS (same as Mastercard).

## Pharmacies
**Bliss Chemist** (daily 9AM-midnight; Marble Arch, 071/723.6116)
**Boots** (M-F 8:30AM-8PM; Sa 9AM-8PM; Su noon-6PM; Piccadilly Circus, 071/734.6126)
**Boots** (M-Sa 9AM-10PM; Su 10AM-10PM; 114 Queensway, 071/229.4819)

## Phone Book
**Ambulance/Police/Fire** ................................**999**
American Embassy ............................071/499.9000
American Express Travel Service........071/221.7190
British Hotel Reservations Centre .......071/828.2425
Directory Information...............................192
International Operator ..............................155
International Telegrams .....................0800/190.190
London Transport Lost Property........071/486.2496
London Transport Travel
Information.....................................071/222.1234
Lost or Stolen Credit Cards:
American Express ...........................071/222.9633
Mastercard.....................................0383/621.166
VISA................................................071/937.8111
Operator Services
(if you have trouble getting through) ...............100
Time.....................................................123
U.S. and International Directory Information ......153
Recorded Information (dial 0891/505, then the following numbers):
Changing of the Guard .........................452
Current Exhibitions ..............................441
Day Trips.............................................469
Museums.............................................462
Palaces................................................466
River Trips/Boats for Hire ...................471
Rock and Pop Concerts.......................447
Sporting Events...................................442
Sunday in London...............................444
Victoria Coach Station....................071/823.6567
Weather Forecast .........................0839/500.951
What's on this Week ...........................440

## Post Office
The **Trafalgar Square Post Office** (24 William IV Street) offers full postal service and collectors' items, such as stamps, coins, and cards; the hours are Monday through Saturday 8AM-8PM. Local post offices, which may double as newsstands, are usually open Monday through Friday 9AM-5PM, and Saturday 9AM-noon.

## Publications
By far the most comprehensive guide to all types of entertainment in both central and greater London is the weekly magazine *Time Out,* available at most newsstands. *The Guardian* newspaper also has a good entertainment listing in its "Guardian Weekend" edition.

## Public Holidays
In addition to the Christmas and Easter holidays, Britain rests on Boxing Day (December 26), Easter Monday, May Day (first Monday in May), Spring

Bank Holiday (last Monday in May), and the August Bank Holiday (last Monday in August). These are called "bank holidays" because banks close on those days. Many businesses stay open, but you'll never know which ones unless you happen to wander past.

### Pubs

The pub (short for "public house") is to Britain what cafes are to France. To complete the British experience, you should have at least one drink, and preferably a meal, in a pub. The minimum age for drinking in the U.K. is 18. Pubs are usually open from 11AM-11PM Monday through Saturday, and from noon-3PM and 7-10:30PM on Sunday. However, some still operate the old licensing times every day and close during the afternoon. Ten minutes before closing time, you'll hear the barman call for "last orders." Although many pubs are getting more adventurous, your best bet is to opt for standards in terms of drinks: beer, ale, or lager, all served by the half (pint) or pint. There is no waitress service, even in pubs that serve food. Most pubs worth their salt now serve a variety of dishes, including vegetarian meals, but some traditional terminology is worth noting: "bangers" are sausages; "bangers and mash" is sausage with mashed potatoes; "chips" are french fries, while "crisps" are potato chips; "Cornish pasties" consist of meat and vegetables wrapped in dough; a "plowman's" is a cheese and salad plate; a "pork pie" is chopped spiced pork wrapped in dough; "sausage rolls" are just what they sound like—tiny sausages rolled up in dough; and "shepherd's pie" consists of ground beef covered in mashed potatoes.

### Restrooms

There never seem to be enough public toilets, or "loos" as they're called here, especially when you need one. However, all public buildings, including museums and department stores, have them, and if you're poised and surreptitious, you can take advantage of those in the larger hotels. Pubs and restaurants generally expect you to be a customer for the privilege. For the daring, there are automated, French-style toilets, located in public parks; these, however, can often be a chilling experience!

### Street Smarts

Keep a close eye on your bags and valuables at all times. Many pickpockets operate around the Underground system, in the main British Rail stations, and on the busiest tourist streets. If possible, use a closed or zipped purse and hang on to it. Some pickpockets travel in gangs during the summer, so be particularly careful when people are crowding onto buses or tubes.

Accommodations hustlers work the areas around the main train stations, especially Victoria. Consult the Tourist Information Centre at the station or find your own accommodations, since many of the places offered by these room touts are overcrowded, uninsured, and have little or no fire protection—not to mention the fact that they are usually pretty dreadful.

### Tax/VAT

At 17.5 percent of the marked price, the **Value Added Tax (VAT)** can be substantial. But if you are leaving the U.K. within three months, you can claim back the VAT on many of the items you buy if you have spent more than £100. Make sure the shop operates the over-the-counter export scheme, which involves filling out a VAT 707 form. (The shop will give it to you along with a stamped, addressed envelope.) You must carry as hand luggage the goods for which you intend to collect a VAT refund and present them to U.K. customs as you leave the country. Customs will stamp the forms, which you will then mail back to the shop before leaving the country. If you forget and pack the goods, or simply cannot carry them, then you have to show them to the officials when you arrive in the U.S., get the form stamped there, and mail it to the shop. After about six weeks, the shop will send you a check in sterling, which can end up costing a lot to process through your bank.

### Telephone

Although London's traditional red phone booths have all but disappeared, telephone "boxes" have improved enormously and now accept a variety of change: 5p, 10p, 20p, 50p, and £1 coins. **British Telecom (BT)** phone cards can be obtained from most newsstands and sweet shops in units of 10 to 200 for £1 to £20 and used like credit cards to make phone calls. If you'll be making a lot of calls, dial after 1PM (standard rate charge), or preferably after 6PM when the rates are cheapest. A premium rate means that you'll pay between 36p and 48p per minute for a call, usually for recorded information. Most premium rate numbers have a four-digit prefix, such as 0891. The cheapest time to phone the U.S. is after 8PM or during weekends. Telephoning from hotels or the Mercury-type phone booths is expensive, so stick to the British Telecom boxes; if you'll be making a long-distance call, have a phone card or lots of change on hand. To call into the U.K., dial 44 (the country code), followed by either 71 or 81 (the zero is dropped), then the number. To phone the U.S., dial 0101, then your area code and the number.

"An Englishman is never so natural as when he is holding his tongue."

**Henry James,** *The Portrait of a Lady*

O, the Grand Old Duke of York, he had ten thousand men,

He marched them up to the top of the hill and he marched them down again,

And when they were up, they were up, and when they were down, they were down,

And when they were only halfway up they were neither up nor down!"

Popular during the Duke's lifetime but first published in **Arthur Rackham's** *Mother Goose* in 1913

## Theater Tickets

Ticket touts are ubiquitous, operating along theater queues and from supposedly reputable ticket offices scattered throughout the city. Beware of gross overcharging for tickets and/or fake tickets. Aim instead to get a normal price and stand-by tickets directly from theater box offices, your hotel, or the **Society of West End Theatres'** half-price-ticket booth in Leicester Square; at the latter, you'll have to stand in line on the day of the performance, but it's worth it to get a legitimate seat at a reasonable price. Also, be adventurous: some excellent performances at lower prices can be found at smaller theaters outside the West End, as well as in the larger arts complexes such as the Barbican or South Bank; check *Time Out* for details. (For more information, see "That's the Ticket: How to Get Theater Seats in London" on page 173.)

## Tipping

In restaurants, check whether service is included or not, especially if you find the amounts you are expected to pay left blank on the credit card slip (as it quite often is) because they just want a bit more money. If service is not included and the service and food have been good, then go ahead and tip between 10 and 15 percent. When you collect your bill at your hotel, again check whether service has been included. Taxi drivers hope for between 10 and 15 percent, but nowadays seem grateful for anything you give them. Porters, cloakroom attendants, and hairdressers also expect a small tip. If you are invited to a large house for a weekend in the country and there is a certain standard of grandeur (dressing for dinner) and evidence of a housekeeper or maid, you can leave money on your dressing table just before your departure (a couple staying two nights usually leaves about £5).

## Tourist Information

The **London Tourist Board Information Centre** (daily 8AM-7PM; shorter hours during winter months) in Victoria Station offers free information on travel within London and the U.K., theater, concert, and tour bookings, and accommodations, as well as good maps and guidebooks for sale. The staff is very friendly and helpful, but they do charge a nominal fee for arranging a place to stay. Other LTB information centers are in the basement of Selfridges department store on Oxford Street, at the Liverpool Street Underground Station, and, of course, at Heathrow Airport. For hotel and bed-and-breakfast reservations, call 071/824.8844 (credit card holders only).

## How to Read this Guide

**LONDON** ACCESS® is arranged so you can see at a glance where you are and what is around you. The numbers next to the entries in the following chapters correspond to the numbers on the maps. The text is color-coded according to the kind of place described:

**Restaurants/Clubs:** Red          Hotels: Blue

Shops/ 🌳 **Outdoors:** Green          **Sights/Culture:** Black

## Rating the Restaurants and Hotels

The restaurant star ratings take into account the quality, service, atmosphere, and uniqueness of the restaurant. An expensive restaurant doesn't necessarily ensure an enjoyable evening; however, a small, relatively unknown spot could have good food, professional service, and a lovely atmosphere. Therefore, on a purely subjective basis, stars are used to judge the overall dining value (see the star ratings above at right). Keep in mind that chefs and owners often change, which sometimes drastically affects the quality of a restaurant. The ratings in this guidebook are based on information available at press time.

The price ratings, as categorized above at right, apply to restaurants and hotels. These figures describe general price-range relationships among other restaurants and hotels in the area. The restaurant price ratings are based on the average cost of an entrée for one person, excluding tax and tip. Hotel price ratings reflect the base price of a standard room for two people for one night during the peak season.

*Conversion rate here is $1.50 to £1.*

### Restaurants

| | | |
|---|---|---|
| ★ | Good | |
| ★★ | Very Good | |
| ★★★ | Excellent | |
| ★★★★ | An Extraordinary Experience | |
| $ | The Price Is Right | (less than $10) |
| $$ | Reasonable | ($10-$15) |
| $$$ | Expensive | ($15-$20) |
| $$$$ | Big Bucks | ($20 and up) |

### Hotels

| | | |
|---|---|---|
| $ | The Price Is Right | (less than $100) |
| $$ | Reasonable | ($100-$175) |
| $$$ | Expensive | ($175-$250) |
| $$$$ | Big Bucks | ($250 and up) |

### Map Key

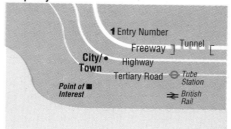

Entry Number
Freeway
Tunnel
City/Town
Highway
Tertiary Road
Tube Station
Point of Interest
British Rail

# The London Ledger of Annual Events

For the London traveler who wishes to take in more than just the sights, the following calendar of events offers suggestions. Also consult listings in magazines such as *Time Out* or *What's On* during your stay, or visit any tourist information center for details on other events.

## January

### Lord Mayor of Westminster's New Year's Day Spectacular

Beginning at noon on 1 January, a parade complete with marching bands, floats, classic cars, and clowns makes its way from Parliament Square along Whitehall to Trafalgar Square, then west along Cockspur Street and Pall Mall, north along Lower Regent Street to Piccadilly Circus, west along Piccadilly, then north along Berkeley Street to finish in Berkeley Square. A gala performance is usually held at the **Royal Albert Hall** in conjunction with the festivities.

### International Boat Show

This 10-day display of all types of boats and boating equipment, including a specially created indoor harbor, takes place at the **Earl's Court Exhibition Center** the first week of January.

### Commemoration Ceremony of Charles the Martyr

At 11:30AM on the last Sunday of the month, the **King's Army** (members of the **English Civil War Society**) in period dress progresses from St. James's Palace to Banqueting House. There, at noon, a wreath is laid beneath the window through which **Charles I** stepped onto the scaffold. The parade continues to Trafalgar Square to the base of the statue of Charles I, then returns through Admiralty Arch back down The Mall to St. James's Palace.

## February

### Chinese New Year

In late January or early February, usually on the Sunday closest to the actual New Year date, celebrations, including the famous **Lion Dance,** take place throughout London. The best places to watch the festivities include the areas around Gerrard Street in Soho, where streets are decorated with streamers and garlands, and Newport Place.

## March

### Head of the River Race

Held on the Thames around 20 March, this race is a processional contest for eight-oared racing shells. The course extends from Mortlake to Putney; 420 crews—one behind the other—start at 10-second intervals, and the one that returns in the fastest time wins. The best place for viewing is from the Surrey bank, just above Chiswick Bridge. Arrive about 30 minutes before the race begins (starting times will vary according to the tides), then walk along the towpath toward Putney.

### The Oxford and Cambridge Boat Race

The two universities first raced each other on the Thames in 1829, and have continued competing annually since 1845. The race takes place around the last week of March, and its present course is from the University Stone, Putney, to Mortlake. Good views can be had from the Putney and Chiswick bridges, from the **Dove Inn** (19 Upper Mall, Hammersmith) or from the **Ship Inn** (Ship Lane, Mortlake).

## April

### The Easter Show

This children's show, held every Easter at Battersea Park, is the best known in London. Live entertainment ranges from magic shows to music and dance groups, and performances by stunt teams. There is a special children's village, an arts and crafts tent, and a traditional egg roll down grassy slopes. Contact **The London Tourist Board** (call 0839/123418 starting in mid-January) for full details of all Easter events.

### London Harness Horse Parade

Easter Monday presents a rare opportunity to see working horses of all kinds compete for prizes at **The Inner Circle,** Regent's Park. Festivities begin around 9:30AM with a veterinary inspection, followed by a parade, a judging of classes (such as Heavy Horses, Single Horsed Commercial Vans, and Private Turnouts), and a **Grand Parade of Winners** at noon sharp.

### The London Marathon

More than 25,000 runners compete in this grueling 26.2-mile race, which takes place the third week of April. It begins at 9AM at Blackheath/Greenwich, and ends on Westminster Bridge, under the shadow of Big Ben.

## May

### The London Dollhouse Festival

Growing more popular each year, this children-oriented event takes place at **Kensington Town Hall,** just off High Street Kensington between Campden Hill Road and Hornton Street, during the second or third week of the month.

### The Chelsea Flower Show

*The* event for gardeners the world over takes place at **The Royal Hospital Grounds,** Chelsea, for four days during the last week of May. Plants, flowers, garden furniture, tools, theme gardens, and greenhouses are all on display. The first two and a half days are reserved for members of the **Royal Horticultural Society** only; the last two are for the public (excluding children under five years of age). Advance tickets may be purchased with a credit card: 071/379.4443.

# June

## Derby Day

Held on the first or second of the month at **Epsom Racecourse,** Epsom, Surrey, this is one of the greatest horse-racing events in the world, featuring the **Derby,** the main race, at 3:45PM. Tickets can be ordered starting in January from The Secretary, The Grandstand, Epsom Downs, Surrey, KT18 5LQ; call 372.726311 for more information.

## Beating Retreat

Mounted bands, trumpeters, massed bands (several bands performing as one group), and pipes and drums of the Household Division display their marching and drilling prowess in two floodlit performances at 9:30PM at **Horse Guards Parade.** The event occurs on two of the first three days of the month. Tickets go on sale at the end of February at the Premier Box Office, 1b Bridge Street (opposite Big Ben); call 071/839.6815 for more information.

## Sounding Retreat: Light Division

During the second week of the month, **Horse Guards Parade** stages a follow-up to Beating Retreat. The Sounding Retreat display takes place over three consecutive days, beginning at 6:30PM nightly. See "Beating Retreat" for ticket details.

## Royal Academy Summer Exhibition

The **Royal Academy of Arts,** Piccadilly, the venue for the largest contemporary art show in the world, features works by painters, sculptors, printmakers, and architects—well-knowns alongside the undiscovered. The show begins in early June and lasts through mid-August. Admission is charged.

## Trooping the Colour

Also known as the **Queen's Birthday Parade,** this ceremony celebrates the sovereign's official (but not actual) birthday on 12 June. The Queen leaves **Buckingham Palace** at around 10:30AM and travels down The Mall to Horse Guards Parade, where massed bands greet her with the national anthem and a gun salute in Green Park. After the Queen's troop inspection, the parade begins. At 12:30PM, Her Royal Highness returns to Buckingham Palace where she appears on the balcony to witness the Royal Air Force fly past at 1PM. Tickets for outdoor seats on Horse Guards Parade (behind the Horse Guards building) are available at a nominal charge by lottery only, and are limited to two per person. If you can't get ceremony tickets, try for tickets to one of the two rehearsals (without the Queen, however). Apply in writing before the end of February to The Brigade Major (Trooping the Colour), Headquarters, Household Division, Chelsea Barracks, SW1H 8RF.

## Royal Ascot

This famous horse race at **Ascot Racecourse** in Berkshire (roughly 25 miles west of London), immortalized in *My Fair Lady,* is well known for the fashions—especially the hats—of those who attend. The Queen and other members of the Royal Family arrive from Windsor each day in open carriages. They then drive down the course at 2PM before the first race begins. Admission to the Grandstand for the four-day mid-June event is by ticket only, obtainable well in advance from The Secretary, Grand Stand, Ascot, Berkshire; call 0344/22211 for details.

## Wimbledon Lawn Tennis Championships

Top players from all over the world converge on the **All England Club** in Wimbledon (about nine miles south of London) from the last week of June to the beginning of July to compete for one of the most coveted titles in tennis. Though some tickets are available on the day of play, it's advisable to apply for tickets between October and December. Send a self-addressed, stamped envelope to All England Lawn Tennis & Croquet Club, P.O. Box 98, Church Road, Wimbledon, SW19 5AE, or call 081/946.2244. The London Tourist Board provides Wimbledon information starting in June; call 0839/123417.

# July

## Hampton Court Palace International Flower Show

In the past few years, this show has become almost as well-established as the one at Chelsea. Held during the second week in July at **Hampton Court,** the show also features musical entertainment and crafts displays. Call 081/977.0050 for more information.

## BBC Henry Wood Promenade Concerts

The "Proms" have taken place at the Royal Albert Hall, Kensington Gore, every year since they were begun in 1895 by **Sir Henry Wood.** The nightly concerts, which range from jazz to classical, begin in mid-July and run until September. Season and individual tickets are available in advance from the Promenade Concert Ticket Shop, Royal Albert Hall; call 071/823.9998 for further details. You can also pick up the *Proms Guide,* available in early May, for a nominal charge; call 091/222.0381 to order a copy.

## August

### Notting Hill Carnival
The carnival—a sort of midsummer Mardi Gras—takes place during the last weekend of August (a bank holiday) in Notting Hill Gate, a London area that has a strong Caribbean tradition. Lovers of steel bands and *soca* (a fusion of soul and Calypso music that originated in the West Indies) will be in their element. There are fabulous costume parades, and hundreds of street vendors sell food and crafts from all over the globe. Festivities kick off at 11AM.

## September

### The Great River Race
Around the 25th, more than 150 traditional boats sail 22 miles on the Thames, from Richmond to the Docklands. The flotilla includes gigs, skiffs, Chinese dragonboats, Hawaiian war canoes, Irish curraghs, and whalers. The race begins just below Ham House, Richmond, at 10AM and finishes at Greenwich Pier around 1PM.

## October

### Pearly Harvest Festival Service
Cockney fruit and vegetable hawkers, known as costermongers, have a reputation for being snappy dressers. The leading costermongers were called the Pearly Kings and Queens, in recognition of their characteristic pearl-button-studded outfits. The titles of Pearly King and Queen were handed down from generation to generation, and this religious service, held around 3 October at **St. Martin-in-the-Fields**, is probably the only place you'll see their sartorial splendor. During the service, the altar is arrayed with fruits and vegetables, and a Pearly King or Queen, dressed in full regalia, reads from the bible. The service starts at 3PM.

### Horse of the Year Show
Top names in equestrian circles compete in show jumping, dressage, shire, hunter, and hacks at **Wembley Arena,** Wembley, northwest London. The event usually takes place during the first week of the month. Call the box office at 081/900.1919 for ticket information.

### Trafalgar Day Parade
On or around 21 October, the anniversary of **Lord Nelson's** victory at the **Battle of Trafalgar** in 1805 is commemorated with a parade and service performed by 500 Sea Cadets (boys and girls aged 12-18) from all over the country. A wreath is laid at the foot of **Nelson's Column,** and Nelson's Prayer is read by a young cadet. The ceremony starts at 11AM in Trafalgar Square.

## November

### Bonfire Night
On 5 November 1605, a man called **Guy Fawkes** was arrested as one of the conspirators in the so-called "Gunpowder Plot" to kill **King James I** and blow up **Parliament.** Since then, fireworks and bonfires have been lit throughout the country on this date. For details of displays in the London area, contact the London Tourist Board's Fireworks Service at 0839/123410.

### London to Brighton Car Run
Held on the first Sunday of November, this gathering attracts more than 400 entrants from all over the world, who subject their veteran and classic cars to grueling 58-mile stretch of road. Cars leave from Hyde Park Corner between 8-9AM and follow the A23 to Brighton, where they begin arriving at Madeira Drive around 10:45AM.

### Lord Mayor's Show
This tradition, which dictates that the **Lord Mayor** ride in the gilded State Coach to the **Law Courts** for the declaration of office, dates from the 13th century. Today, there's also a parade featuring floats, military bands, and units of the armed services, and a fair at Paternoster Square. The event is usually slated for the 12th or 13th of November. For more information call 0839/505453.

### Remembrance Sunday
On a date between the 11th and the 14th of November, a memorial day service is held at the **Cenotaph,** Whitehall, to honor all those in the military who gave their lives in the two World Wars and other conflicts. The Queen arrives at 10:59AM, and a two-minute silence begins at 11AM, ended by a gun fired from Horse Guards Parade. The Queen lays a wreath at the Cenotaph, and the **Bishop of London** conducts a short service.

### Christmas Lights
Christmas lights are switched on daily from dusk to midnight in Bond, Jermyn, Oxford, and Regent streets from mid-November until Twelfth Night (6 January). Check with the London Tourist Board's Christmas Service at 0839/123418.

## December

### Trafalgar Square Christmas Tree
Since 1947, the city of Oslo, Norway, has presented London with a Norwegian Christmas spruce in gratitude for help given by the British during World War II. The tree is set up in Trafalgar Square in early December and decorated with white lights. It is lit daily from 3PM to midnight until Twelfth Night (6 January), and carols are sung each evening until Christmas Eve.

Bests

## n Follett
thor

perfect day in London might begin with a
ditative hour in **Southwark Cathedral** on the south
nk of the Thames near London Bridge: it is as
eresting architecturally as Westminster Abbey, but
eter.

favorite museum is the **Bank of England Museum**
Threadneedle Street.

lunch, I would have the best pizza in London at
**Spuntino** on King's Road.

he afternoon, I would order a new suit at
**derson & Sheppard** on Savile Row and a dozen
rts at **Hilditch & Key** on Jermyn Street, then call in
**Hatchard's** bookshop in Piccadilly to make sure
y have sufficient stock of my books. I would have
and scones at **Claridge's Hotel** on Brook Street.

ight call in at the only club I have ever joined, the
**oucho,** for a glass of champagne on my way to the
**rbican Theatre,** where I would see the matchless
**yal Shakespeare Company** perform. I would end
day with a late supper at the **Red Fort** on Dean
eet, the best Indian restaurant in London.

## rlene Winfield
licy Analyst/Writer

e view from the center of **Waterloo Bridge** by day
night. After 21 years of living in London, it still
ills me. At night, I would combine the view with a
lk along the **Embankment** to **Parliament Square,**
an evening of chamber music played on ancient
truments at **St. John's Church** in Smith Square.
e snack bar there is excellent.

reading your way through **Clerkenwell,** finding
y hidden gardens and ancient churchyards along
way. Finishing up with a snack at **The Eagle** pub
Farringdon Road.

tching the meat being bought and sold at
**ithfield Market** at 6AM on weekdays. Afterward, a
English breakfast with the porters and butchers,
me still in their blood-stained aprons, at the **Fox**
**d Anchor** or at one of the cafes nearby. Not for
getarians.

**rmondsey Market** in South London before
0AM, when the real bargains are to be had. There
s been a market there for hundreds of years.

criminal case at the **Old Bailey** in the morning; then
lking up **Fleet Street** (stopping in at **Christopher**
**en's** lovely **St. Bride's Church**) to the **Middle and**
**er Temples.** Here, where judges have their flats
d barristers their offices, you are transported back
Dickensian London. Finish with a sandwich and a
ss of sherry at **El Vino's** on Fleet Street and
rhaps a stroll to **Sir John Soane's Museum** in
ncoln's Inn.

unny summer's day at **Lord's Cricket Ground** in
John's Wood with a very full picnic basket and a
lkman to listen to the commentary. Lord's is the

most English of all experiences. The uninitiated
would be advised to take along an idiot's guide to
cricket.

A real English "fry up" for lunch, including bubble
and squeak (mashed potatoes and vegetables that
are fried together), with half of London's taxi drivers
at **Buscot's Dairy** on Molyneaux Street, Marylebone.
Basic and cheap, it's my mother's favorite restaurant
in London. You'd be wise to follow with a brisk walk
to Hyde Park or up Oxford Street.

A vegetarian Indian meal at the **Mandeer,** hidden
away in Hanway Place near Tottenham Court Road
Station. Ask the proprietor, poet **Ramesh Patel,** to
show you his book of love poems in nine languages.

Dim sum on Sunday afternoon at the **Chuen Cheng**
**Ku** on Wardour Street in Soho.

**The Ivy** in the theater district and **Le Caprice** near
Green Park. The **Museum Street Cafe,** which is tiny
and wonderful, near the British Museum. For an extra
special evening, **Bibendum** on Fulham Road.

## Peg Hailey
Hypnotherapist/Psychotherapist

**Kew Gardens**—A favorite place anytime, but
especially after a new snowfall. Exquisite gardens
blending with birds and waterfowl. Jazz concerts on
the lawn in late July. Take a picnic supper.

**Wallace Collection**—Magnificent works of art,
porcelain, furniture, and armor displayed in a
splendid old home. Perfect for those short of time:
you can enjoy it all in a couple of hours.

**Neal's Yard**—Trendy, good for lunch, and charming
atmosphere. Unique gift items. Close to Covent
Garden but not as "slick."

The **Old Bailey**—Fascinating to spend a few hours
watching the English judicial system in action,
followed by lunch at **Ye Olde Cheshire Cheese** in
Wine Office Court, just off Fleet Street.

**Marks and Spencers**—Don't miss the Marble Arch
store during midday. A retailer's dream, not for the
claustrophobic. May well be the highest volume of
sales per square foot in the world.

**Chiquito's Leicester Square**—A margarita and
Mexican buffet at midday always brings fond
memories of Southern California.

**Richmond**—Only 30 minutes from central London at
the end of the District Line. Walk along the river, then
enjoy an early supper in the basement of the **Orange**
**Tree Pub** on Kew Road or **The Racing Page** on Duke
Street before an evening performance at the
**Richmond Theatre.**

A Sunday dim sum lunch at the **Dragon Inn** on
Westbourne Grove in Bayswater, or at the **Jade**
**Garden** Chinese on Wardour Street any day. Get
there early or you'll have to wait.

People-watching almost anywhere in central London
is good, but you can be sure of interesting variety in
**Leicester Square** or **Covent Garden.**

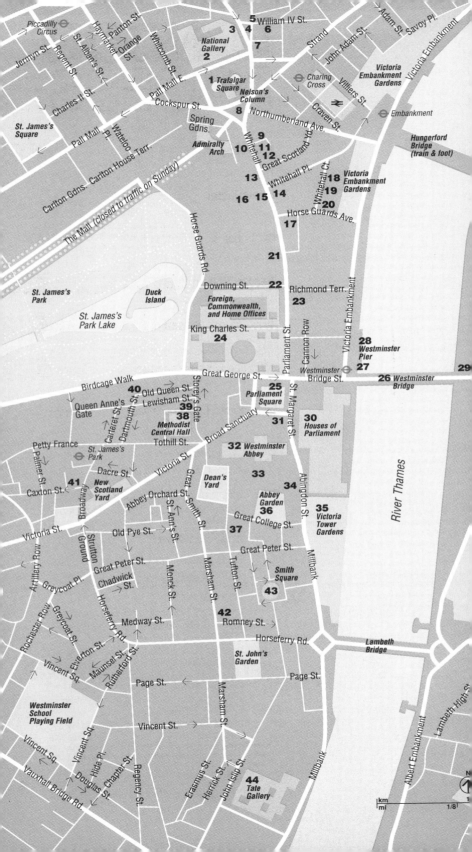

# Westminster

A walk through the City of **Westminster** forms a kind of pilgrimage, a journey that parallels the River Thames, covers one and a half acres of hallowed ground, embraces 900 years of history, and provides a first-rate view of history in the making. Without question, Westminster is Britain's seat of power: kings and queens are still crowned here and the process of democracy continues to unfold before public scrutiny. The **Palace of Westminster**, better known as the **Houses of Parliament**, is where the House of Commons and the House of Lords conduct the sometimes tempestuous, sometimes snoozy day-to-day business of government. Neighboring **Westminster Abbey** occupies the seat of spiritual power and, with its sepulchres of famous Britons, serves as a reminder of the ultimate end to all struggles, death. Your tour of Westminster Abbey could be delayed by a wedding or a funeral—this cathedral is not a museum; indeed, people still make vows, pray, and mourn the dead here.

About a mile north of Westminster Abbey is **Trafalgar Square**, where London's citizens regularly gather (like so many excitable pigeons) to celebrate or protest; through it all, this English *grande place* casts an impartial eye on the legislation passed down the road by Parliament and administered next door by officials in **Whitehall**.

The **National Portrait Gallery** is a who's who of English history, while the splendid **Tate Gallery** can restore your soul with the paintings of **Turner** and your body with the cafe's scrumptious tea and scones. After perusing the collections, contemplate the Thames with London as a backdrop, a scene that could have been painted by the pre-Raphaelites or **Whistler.** You may also decide to stop for a concert at **St. John's** in **Smith Square**, unless you prefer to sample English ale in a pub next to an MP or two.

The ideal time to visit this area is Monday through Thursday when Parliament is in session. On weekends, Westminster and Whitehall are all but abandoned—MPs return to their constituencies, civil servants stay home, and many of the restaurants, pubs, and shops that exist primarily to serve the governing elite are closed. On Sunday, the most interesting parts of Westminster Abbey are closed, and the galleries don't open until noon.

**1 Trafalgar Square** A testament to England's victory over **Napoléon's** fleet in the decisive battle off the coast of Spain in 1805, the **Battle of Trafalgar,** Trafalgar Square is London's grandest place. It is even more monumental testimony to the defeat of anything like Napoléonic vision in town planning. If this were Paris, **Haussmann's** ruthlessness would have you looking down heart-stopping vistas of Buckingham Palace and Westminster Abbey; broad avenues would connect the square to Regent Street and the British Museum; and the square itself, instead of sunken and treeless, would be green, elevated, and uniform. The triumph of the English at Trafalgar, and seven years later at Waterloo, was likewise a triumph of Englishness. Trafalgar Square's honesty reflects the victory of democratic style over dictatorial grandeur: the military, architectural, and dramatic defeat of what the English dislike most—ostentation.

Until 1830, the site was occupied by the **Royal Mews,** when mews were reserved for mewing: the molting of birds of prey. **Edward I** (ruler from 1272 to 1307) kept his hawks here, and **Richard II** (who reigned from 1377 to 1399) kept his falcons and goshawks, a rather distinguished legacy for the famous pigeons and starlings who mew monotonously in the square today. By the reign of **Henry VII** (King of England from 1485 to 1509), horses were kept in the Royal Mews. In 1732, landscape gardener, architect, and painter **William Kent** built the Royal Stables on this site, then known as "Great Mews," "Green Mews," and "Dunghill Mews." The stables stood until 1830, when the site was leveled to prepare for the construction of the square and **Nelson's Column.**

The original designs for Trafalgar Square were made by architect **John Nash,** who had already brought elegance and grandeur to London with **Regent Street, Regent's Park,** and **Marble Arch,** under the aegis of the Prince Regent, later **George IV.** With Regent Street, Nash provided the first north-south axis to connect London's three main east-west routes (Oxford Street, Piccadilly, and the Strand). In his early sketches of Trafalgar Square, Nash saw the site as the medieval turning point in the road leading from **Westminster Abbey** to **St. Paul's Cathedral.**

There was no open space, only a widening where the bronze statue of **Charles I** had stood since 1675, marking the spot where the three roads met. Nash designed the square as a grand axis connecting government (Parliament), finance (the City), and aristocracy (St. James's and the Royal Parks). Unfortunately, Parliament accepted Nash's site and rejected his designs.

Trafalgar Square, as it appears today, is largely the work of **Charles Barry,** the distinguished architect of gentlemen's clubs, including the **Reform Club** and the **Traveller's Club** in Pall Mall, and that club of clubs, the **Houses of Parliament.** Barry favored the Italian palazzo style for this war memorial and he created in Trafalgar Square an economic, Victorian interpretation of the piazza. ♦ Bounded by Pall Mall and the Strand, and Whitehall and Charing Cross Rd

At Trafalgar Square:

**Nelson's Column** Born in 1758, **Horatio Nelson** entered the service of his country at the age of 12, suffered from seasickness all his life, lost his right eye at the Battle of Calvi, his right arm at Santa Cruz, and his life at Trafalgar. The hero now stands in perpetuity atop **William Railton's** 170-foot-high granite column, which was erected in 1843. The statue of Lord Nelson is by **E.H. Bailey.** The figure of the naval hero is 17 feet high and his sword measures 7 feet 9 inches. Together with the column, the monument is as tall as an 18-story building, a gratifying reward for a man who measured just 5 feet 4 inches in real life.

In a city where the sun is no incentive and the past is all-pervasive, there seems to be no need to rush things, and, by and large, Londoners do not: almost 40 years went by from the time of Nelson's funeral at St. Paul's in 1805 to the raising of his column in Trafalgar Square. Railton's design of a massive Corinthian column won the competition for the monument in 1837. The capital is of bronze cast from cannons recovered from the wreck of the *Royal George.* On the sides of the pedestal are four bronze bas-reliefs cast from the metal of captured French cannons, representing incidents in the battles of St. Vincent, Aboukir, Copenhagen, and Trafalgar.

Guarding the column are four vast (20 feet b 11 feet) and lovable lions by **Queen Victoria** favorite animal painter, **Sir Edwin Landseer.** Late arrivals (they were installed in 1868), it these magnificent, tender-faced creatures th humanize the square. When Landseer died in 1871, the public put wreaths around the lion necks. Four octagonal oil lamps, which have been converted to electricity, occupy the corners of the square; they are reputedly fro Nelson's flagship, *HMS Victory.* One likes to think so, anyway.

Every year on 21 October, the anniversary of the Battle of Trafalgar, a parade and service are held in the square by members of the Royal Navy. Officers from modern ships of t fleet lay wreaths at the bottom of the column and descendants of those who fought at Trafalgar contribute an anchor of laurels. Nelson, a genius for naval battle, was a hero with a gift for inspiring devotion.

The highlights of the year for the square are Christmas and New Year's Eve. An enormou Christmas tree, a gift from the Norwegians, erected and carols are sung most December evenings. On New Year's Eve, thousands congregate in the square and welcome in the New Year to the chimes of nearby Big Ben.

**Statue of George IV** Standing out among the many notables in the square is **George I** (ruler from 1820 to 1830), who worshiped **Nelson** (though the feeling was not mutual) and under whose auspices **John Nash** first conceived the square. After the Battle of Trafalgar had established Britain's command of the seas, George IV commissioned **Turner's** great battle piece, *The Battle of Trafalgar* (hanging in the **National Maritime Museum,** Greenwich). But George IV's obsession was architecture. As Prince Rege he built the **Brighton Pavilion;** as King he rebuilt **Buckingham Palace** and transforme **Windsor** into the finest of all the palaces of t British monarchy. An expert horseman, he commissioned most of the equestrian paintings by **George Stubbs** in the Royal Collection. Hence, it is baffling that this statu by **Sir Francis Chantrey,** commissioned by George IV to surmount Marble Arch, shows the King in Roman dress, riding bareback without stirrups. As he had not finished paying for it, the statue was not completed

*Trafalgar Square*

and placed in the square until 12 years after his death. An inscription that reads "King George IV" had to be added because no one knew who it was.

**Statue of James II** Another king in Roman dress, **James II,** whose reign lasted from 1685 to 1688, seems less affected, mainly because he had the good luck to have the 17th-century artisan **Grinling Gibbons** as a sculptor. Impulsive and bullheaded, James II annoyed Parliament with his pro-Catholic wife and politics. He was succeeded by his Protestant daughter, **Queen Mary II,** and spent the last 11 years of his life in exile in France. The naval influence in Trafalgar Square continues with busts of three modern heroes: **Admirals Beatty** and **Jellicoe** of World War I, and **Admiral Cunningham** of World War II. Carved into the stone of the north wall between Jellicoe and Cunningham are the **Imperial Standards** for length, showing the exact measurements of an imperial inch, foot, yard, rod, chain, pole, and perch.

**Fountains** In a city blessed with rain, fountains are few. **Charles Barry's** original fountains and their large pools were part of a design to break up the large, unruly crowds that the government of the day was perceptive enough to realize would congregate. Even with the fountains and their pools, 50,000 people can and do congregate in the square when the cause of democracy calls. The original fountains designed by Barry now face Parliament in Ottawa, Canada. **Sir Edwin Lutyens** designed the fountains in the square to commemorate Admirals Jellicoe and Beatty. They have first-rate water power, and every morning at 10AM the mermaids and mermen respond to the repetitive booms of Big Ben by democratically christening nearby Londoners and visitors, people and pigeons.

**Buildings** The late **Sir John Betjeman,** poet laureate and passionate defender of Victorian architecture, saw the weighty stone buildings that surround Trafalgar Square as a historic backdrop. Looking left in the direction of Whitehall are **Herbert Baker's South Africa House,** built in 1935, its somber classical facade indifferent; the rounded **Grand Buildings** and **Trafalgar Buildings,** designed by the **Francis** brothers and built in 1878 and 1881, respectively; **George Aitchison's Royal Bank of Scotland,** erected in 1885; **Reginald Blomfield's Uganda House,** built in 1915; and **Canada House,** the most handsome building on the square, designed by **Sir Robert Smirke** and completed in 1827. Originally the **Royal College of Physicians,** this building of warm Bath stone has suffered from conversion and extension of the upper parts but nonetheless remains a dignified presence.

# THE NATIONAL GALLERY

**2 The National Gallery** Built in 1838 by **William Wilkins,** the most important building in Trafalgar Square anchors the north side. Architects complain that the scale of the neoclassical building is weak in relation to the square, but the blame should fall on a parsimonious Parliament, which compelled Wilkins to use the columns from the demolished **Carlton House** in the portico. The original building was only one room deep, more a facade than a gallery. But the National Gallery's limited size at its debut had little effect on its destiny: today, it houses one of the most comprehensive surveys of Western art in the world.

Unlike most of the great national galleries of Europe, the National Gallery is not built upon the foundations of a former royal collection, nor did it inherit a nationally based collection. It began late; in 1824, **George IV** persuaded the government to buy 38 paintings from the collection of Russian émigré and marine insurance underwriter **John Julius Angerstein.** The government paid £57,000 for the pictures—which included five paintings by **Claude Lorraine,** Hogarth's *Marriage à la Mode* series, and works by **Raphael, Reynolds,** and **Van Dyck**—then opened the gallery to the public in Angerstein's former town house at 100 Pall Mall. Two other collectors, **Sir George Beaumont** and the **Reverend William Howell Carr,** promised important paintings to the nation if a suitable building were provided to house them. In 1838, the National Gallery opened, and the **Beaumont** and **Howel Carr** paintings, along with **Angerstein's,** formed the nucleus of the national collection.

As the collection grew, so did the National Gallery. The dome and additional rooms were added in the 1870s, followed by the central staircase and further additions in 1911. In 1975, the excellent northern extension was added and **Robert Venturi's** controversial Sainsbury Wing was opened by the Queen in 1991. The 2,000-plus pictures in the National Gallery are predominantly by the old masters. They represent one of the finest histories of Western European painting in existence, from **Duccio** in 14th-century Italy to **Klimt** in the early 20th century. Even in their native countries, painters such as **Holbein, Van Dyck,** and **Velázquez** are not represented with masterpieces of such greatness.

When the **Tate Gallery** opened in 1897, it took on the dual role of modern art museum and home of British art. Many of the British paintings in the National Gallery were transferred to the Tate, leaving the National with a small but choice British collection that consists of two paintings by **Stubbs,** *The Milbanke* and *Melbourne Families;* six by **Reynolds,** including *General Banastre Tarleton,* a portrait of the young general during the American War of Independence; five by **Constable,** including the evocative *Hay Wain;* 10 by **Gainsborough,** including *Mr. and Mrs. Andrews* and *The Morning Walk;* and seven by **Hogarth,** six of which are part of the *Marriage à la Mode* series.

There is no substitute for beholding the paintings, and one of the bonuses of a free museum is being able to look at only a few at a time, guiltlessly. No one has to see it all in one visit, and no one should. A lifetime spent looking at these paintings seems about right, starting with old favorites and acquiring new loves along the way. If you are daunted by the size of the collection or pressed for time, the National Gallery has made a kind of "Hit Parade" of the 20 most famous pictures. *The Twenty Great Paintings* booklet describes them and is well worth its small price. The 20 masterpieces:

*The Wilton Diptych,* English or French school (circa 1395). ♦ Room 53

*The Battle of San Romano,* **Paola Uccello** (circa 1397-1475). ♦ Room 55

*The Baptism of Christ,* **Piero Della Francesca** (active 1439, died 1492). ♦ Room 66

*Cartoon: The Virgin and Child with Saint John the Baptist and Saint Anne,* **Leonardo Da Vinci** (1452-1519). ♦ Room 51

*The Doge Leonardo Loredan,* **Giovanni Bellini** (active circa 1459, died 1516). ♦ Room 61

*Bacchus and Ariadne,* **Titian** (active by 1510, died 1576). ♦ Room 9

*Equestrian Portrait of Charles I,* **Anthony Van Dyck** (1599-1641). ♦ Room 30

*Le Chapeau de Paille (The Straw Hat),* **Peter Paul Rubens** (1577-1640). ♦ Room 22

*The Arnolfini Marriage,* **Jan van Eyck** (active 1422, died 1441). ♦ Room 56

*A Lady with a Squirrel and a Starling,* **Hans Holbein the Younger** (1498-1543). ♦ Room 5

*Self Portrait aged 63,* **Rembrandt** (1606-69). ♦ Room 27

*A Young Woman Standing at a Virginal,* **Johannes Vermeer** (1632-75). ♦ Room 16

*The Hay Wain,* **John Constable** (1776-1837) ♦ Room 40

*The Fighting Temeraire,* **J.M.W. Turner** (177 1851). ♦ Room 35

*The Toilet of Venus (The Rokeby Venus),* **Diego Velázquez** (1599-1660). ♦ Room 29

*Bathers, Asnières,* **Georges Seurat** (1859-9 ♦ Room 44

*Landscape With Psyche outside the Palace Cupid (The Enchanted Castle),* **Claude Gellé (Le Lorrain)** (1604/5-82). ♦ Room 9

*The Stonemason's Yard,* **Canaletto** (1697-1768). ♦ Lower Galleries

*Madame Moitessier,* **Jean-Auguste-Dominique Ingres** (1780-1867). ♦ Room 41

*Bathers at La Grenouillère,* **Claude Monet** (1840-1926). ♦ Room 43

On the lower floor of the gallery is an art lover's dream attic, with stacks of minor masterpieces, damaged paintings by great artists, and good fakes. It is fun to try and figure out what's what.

The **National Gallery Mosaics,** by Russian-born artist **Boris Anrep,** on the floors of the vestibules and halfway landing, are works o art that usually go unnoticed. In the west vestibule, the theme is *The Labors of Life,* with 12 mosaics completed in 1928, includin *Art,* which shows a sculptor at work; *Sacred Love,* which depicts a father, mother, child, and dog; and *Letters,* which shows a child's slate with two favorite children's books, *Robinson Crusoe* and *Alice in Wonderland.* the north vestibule, the theme is *The Moder Virtues,* with 15 mosaics completed in 1952 *Compassion* shows the Russian poet **Anna Akhmatova** saved by an angel from the horrors of war; *Compromise* has the actress **Loretta Young** filling a cup with wine to symbolize American and British friendship; *Defiance* portrays **Winston Churchill** on the white cliffs of Dover, defying an apocalyptic beast in the shape of a swastika; and *Leisure* is **T.S. Eliot** contemplating the kindly Loch Ness monster and Einstein's formula.

In the east vestibule are 11 mosaics completed in 1929 representing *The Pleasures of Life:* a Christmas pudding; a conversation, with two girls gossiping; *Mudpie,* with three mud pies, a bucket, and spade; and *Profane Love,* showing a man an two girls with a dog. In the halfway landing i *The Awakening of the Muses,* an illustrative archive of London's *beau monde* in the '30s portrays the **Honorable Mrs. Bryan Guinnes** (one of the Mitford girls and later **Lady Dian Mosley**) as Polyhymnia, Muse of Sacred Song; **Christabel, Lady Aberconway** as Euterpe, Muse of Music; **Clive Bell** as Bacchus, God of Wine; **Virginia Woolf** as Cl Muse of History; **Sir Osbert Sitwell** as Apoll

God of Music; and **Greta Garbo** as Melpomene, Muse of Tragedy.

Special exhibitions at the National Gallery include **Brief Encounters,** an annual event in which two paintings by one artist are compared; one work comes from the National Gallery, the other from another well-known collection. The **Making and Meaning** exhibition provides an in-depth analysis and presentation of a major work in the collection. **Art in the Making** is a new exhibition in which artists explain the technical side of their work. Guided tours leave from the vestibule weekdays two or three times daily. ◆ Free. M-Sa 10AM-6PM; Su 2-6PM. Trafalgar Sq. Tube: Charing Cross. Recorded information: 071/839.3321. General information: 071/389.1785

Within the National Gallery:

**The National Gallery Shop** Its contents may not be as "with it" as those of other museum shops, but the gallery publications are outstanding. For a general survey of the collection, *The National Gallery* by **Homan Potterton** is excellent. It contains a chapter on conservation techniques, a brief history of the collection, a list of 2,050 pictures, and fresh and lively discussions of the major paintings. The shop carries a fine range of art history books, color slides, and black-and-white photographs of every picture in the collection. ◆ M-Sa 10AM-5:40PM; Su 2-5:40PM. 071/839.3321

**The Cafe** ★★$ Cheerful, cafeteria-style service may be found downstairs, with healthy soups and salads, hot meals at lunchtime, wine and cheese, coffee, tarts and cakes, and Indian, Chinese, and herbal teas. ◆ Cafe ◆ Breakfast, lunch, and tea; tea only on Sunday. 071/839.3321

**The Sainsbury Wing** At the height of his popularity, **Prince Charles** complained that the proposed designs for the National Gallery extension, which incorporated an office block, were "a monstrous carbuncle on the face of Trafalgar Square." People listened. Plans were dropped. Enter the supermarket barons, **Lord Sainsbury of Preston Candover,** and **Simon** and **Timothy Sainsbury,** with funding for the Sainsbury Wing in its entirety. A second competition for designs was won by the Philadelphia firm **Robert Venturi, John Rauch,** and **Denise Scott Brown.** The result is a building of Portland stone that changes before your eyes from the neoclassical architecture of Wilkins' gallery to a clean, ultramodern style that complements both the gallery and Trafalgar Square perfectly. The Sainsbury Wing houses the National Gallery's Early Renaissance painting collection of nearly 250 paintings from 1260 to 1510, including **Duccio's** *The Virgin and Child* triptych (Room 52), *The Battle of San Romano* by **Uccello**

(Room 55), **van Eyck's** *The Arnolfini Marriage* (Room 56), and *The Ansidei Madonna* by **Raphael** (Room 60).

Within The Sainsbury Wing:

**The Micro Gallery** This computerized visual information system offers background information on every painting in the collection as well as the artists, periods, subjects, and genres.

**The National Gallery Shop** The main National Gallery shop is now in the Sainsbury Wing and is vastly superior to its predecessor. Art lovers should definitely make time to browse among the prints, posters, greeting cards, stationery, and postcards (more than 500) developed from the collection. ◆ M-Sa 10AM-5:40PM; Su 2-5:40PM

**The Brasserie and Cafe** ★$ After nourishing the soul with the works of the early masters, drop by the Sainsbury Wing's own brasserie/cafe: waiters offer an à la carte menu in the brasserie, while in the bar/cafe you'll find light snacks. Afternoon teas start at 3PM. ◆ Cafe ◆ Lunch and afternoon tea; afternoon tea only on Sunday. 071/839.3321

**3 National Portrait Gallery (NPG)** After getting your bearings in Trafalgar Square, this is the place to begin a day in London, a stay in England, or a trip to Europe. Built in 1895 by **Ewan Christian** and **J.K. Colling,** the NPG is not a typical art gallery. Here eminence of the subject, not the artist, is what counts. More eloquent than words, the faces in the portraits tell the history of England: history as poetry, biography, and prophecy. Resist the temptation to wander through the bookshop first or amble up the stairs. Instead, begin on the top floor and walk a few steps down to the upper mezzanine, where you will find a royal procession in which art, history, and British civilization converge.

The great age of portraiture began with the Tudors when **Hans Holbein** became court painter to **Henry VIII.** Brought to England from Holland by **Erasmus,** Holbein was the greatest 16th-century artist to work in England. His portraits show a profound perception of character, at once powerfully direct and full of nuance. Through Holbein, Henry VIII is indelibly fixed in the viewer's mind, although unfortunately for Henry, the artist arrived in England after the King was no longer young, thin, and handsome.

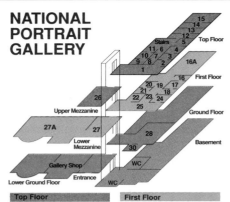

**NATIONAL PORTRAIT GALLERY**

The most celebrated, acclaimed, and painted monarch of all time is **Elizabeth I,** who was virtually an icon during her reign (1558 to 1603). In many of her portraits, even the decorations on her clothes are emblematic—an ermine on a sleeve symbolizes chastity, pearls represent purity. Elizabeth I's legendary ability to rule was enhanced by her being a living idol to her people, in essence a living work of art.

Alongside the kings and queens are the writers who captured the ages in words: a portrait of **Shakespeare** (1564-1616) attributed to **John Taylor,** the best likeness of the playwright that exists. While Elizabeth I was proclaiming herself Gloriana (more than mortal), **Donne** wrote of a heaven "where there shall be no darkness nor dazzling, but one equal light; no noise or silence, but one equal music; no fears nor hopes, but one equal possession; no ends nor beginnings, but one equal eternity." As the paintings in the 25 rooms make brilliantly clear, England would not come close to such a heaven on earth for several hundred years.

Don't miss:

The **Holbein** cartoon of **Henry VIII** in black ink and colored washes on paper, part of a wallpainting for Whitehall Palace (now lost). Still visible are the hundreds of tiny pinpricks the artist used to transfer his designs to the wall. ♦ Level 4

The portrait of **Elizabeth I,** by **Marcus Gheeraedts the Younger,** which was completed soon after the defeat of the Spanish Armada. The Queen is standing triumphantly on her kingdom of England, storm clouds behind and a brilliant sky before her. ♦ Level 5, Room 1C

**Charles I** and **Sir Edward Walker** after the campaigns in the West Country in 1644-45. A look of serenity and sadness shows on the face of the King, as though to presage the tragic future. ♦ Level 5, Room 2

**Oliver Cromwell** with an unknown page, by Walker (circa 1649). The painting shows a man aware of the tragedy around him. ♦ Level 5, Room 2

**Admiral Horatio Viscount Nelson,** an unfinished study for a full-length commission, is a quite brilliant portrait painted from life by **Sir William Beechey** in 1800-01, showing all the passion and fire of the hero who destroyed **Napoleon's** sea power and of the man, brave, tender, and honest. ♦ Level 5, Room 12

Portraits of visionary poet/artist **William Blake,** born in 1757, painted by **Thomas Phillips** in 1807; **John Keats,** one of England's most beloved poets who died in Rome of tuberculosis at age 25, painted by his friend **Joseph Severn** in 1821-23; and finally, **Lord Byron,** that ultimate Romantic, painted by **Thomas Phillips** in 1835. Born in 1788, Byron captured the poetic imagination of the age, and died in Greece during 1824, fighting for Greek independence.

The tiny drawing of **Jane Austen** (1775-1817), by her sister **Cassandra,** is the only likeness that exists of the beloved and acute observer of the human heart. ♦ Level 5, Room 15

**Anne, Emily,** and **Charlotte Brontë** (circa 1834) are here, looking young and serious. The ghost in the background is their brother, **Branwell,** who painted himself out of the portrait. Also by Branwell is the beautiful, cracked portrait of Emily Brontë. ♦ Level 3, Room 20

**Charles Darwin** (1809-82), painted by **John Collier** in 1883. The artist created a haunting, spiritual portrait of the man who used science to destroy the myth of creation. ♦ Level 3, Room 16

**Elizabeth Barrett** and **Robert Browning,** painted by **Gordigiani** in 1858, occupy the same room as a portrait by **Ballantyne** of the artist **Landseer** sculpting the lions now in Trafalgar Square. ♦ Level 3, Room 20

**Henry James** (1843-1916), the American writer who loved London and settled in England, was painted by **John Singer Sargent** on his 70th birthday in 1913. The American artist lived in London and became the most fashionable portrait painter of his generation. ♦ Level 3, Room 25

The **Royal Landing,** Level 2, still has the controversial painting *Queen Elizabeth, the Queen Mother,* by **Alison Watt,** which was hung in 1989 to mixed response. You'll either love it or hate it. Royal portraits include *Prince Charles* wearing his polo clothes and *Princess Diana* when she was still plump and girlish. The **Early 20th-Century Galleries,** Level 2, include First World War Portraits and the War Poets. Political portraits include **Sickert's** *Churchill;* artist's portraits include *James Joyce,* by **Blanche,** and *T.S. Eliot, Somerset Maugham,* and *Virginia Woolf.* As if all this weren't enough, the NPG expanded in 1993, opening an **Education Centre and Studio Gallery,** the **Heinz Archive and Library** (entrance on Orange Street), the **Wolfson Gallery** (a new temporary exhibition space), a new **Photography Gallery,** and the **New Galleries of 20th-Century Portraits.** ♦ Free; occasional charge for special exhibitions. M-Sa 10AM-6PM; Su noon-6PM. 2 St. Martin's Pl (enter opposite St. Martin-in-the-Fields). Tube: Charing Cross. 071/306.0055

Within the National Portrait Gallery (NPG):
**National Portrait Gallery Bookshop** The bestseller postcard here is the melancholy portrait of **Virginia Woolf.** All the heroes and heroines upstairs are down here in alphabetical order. Like museum shops the world over, this one has cleverly expanded. It stocks all the books you are in the mood to read after gazing at the portraits above. ♦ Ground floor

**4 Statue of Edith Cavell** In the small island next to the National Portrait Gallery and behind Trafalgar Square is a monument to **Edith Cavell,** a nurse shot and killed by the Germans in 1915 for spying and helping British prisoners escape. The statue was created by **Sir George Frampton** and unveiled in 1920 by **Queen Alexandra.** Four years later, the Labor Government added her famous words "Patriotism is not enough," a sentiment that would have shocked Nelson, who thought patriotism was everything.

Whitehall, which was originally the home of Cardinal Thomas Wolsey, became a royal residence for 160 years, from the reign of Henry VIII to that of James II. The royal palace that gave the area its name was destroyed by fire in 1698. Today, the name Whitehall is used to designate one of London's widest and busiest streets connecting Trafalgar Square with Parliament Square. Behind the high, impenetrable facades and tall cupolas of its stately buildings, thousands of civil servants act on government decisions. The air of power is almost palpable. In addition to a political thoroughfare, this is also the road of kings and queens, who use it for coronation, marriage, and burial en route to Westminster Abbey.

**5 The Chandos** ★★$ A cooked English breakfast (try the kippers!) is served from 9AM to 10:30AM in The Opera Room on the first floor of this handsome ale pub, which was licensed in 1647, across the street from the Trafalgar Square Post Office. ♦ Pub ♦ Breakfast, lunch, and dinner. 29 St. Martins Ln (at William IV St). 071/836.1401

**6 Trafalgar Square Post Office** Built in the 1960s, this is one of the busiest buildings around. It used to be open 24 hours a day, and is still London's only post office with relatively late hours. ♦ M-Sa 8AM-8PM. 24 William IV St. 071/930.9580

**7 St. Martin-in-the-Fields** John Nash's design for Trafalgar Square was never realized, but his role in it endures because of his idea to open up the vista that brings St. Martin-in-the-Fields into the square. The church is not actually part of the square, but it is its single source of pure loveliness. Built in 1726 by **Christopher Wren's** disciple, **James Gibbs,** its steeple rises 185 feet from the ground, almost the same height as Nelson's Column. The steeple, which was added in 1824, has been an inspiration for many American churches. The interior is light and airy, with a lovely ceiling of Italian plasterwork. The porch offers shelter to passersby on rainy days and the steps a resting place for tired tourists. On Monday, Tuesday, and Friday at 1:05PM, and Thursday through Saturday at 7:30PM, you can enjoy concerts of chamber and choral music in the church where **Charles II** was christened and his mistress, **Nell Gwyn,** was buried. ♦ M-F, Su 8AM-9PM; Sa 9AM-5PM. Trafalgar Sq. Tube: Charing Cross. Concert bookings: 071/930.0089. General information: 071/930.1862; fax 071/839.5163

Within St. Martin-in-the-Fields:
**The Cafe in the Crypt** ★★$ Hidden within the crypt of St. Martin is this treasure of a restaurant still known to those in the know as Field's. It's used by theater stars for private parties and by office workers to meet their friends for lunch and snacks. Try the spinach and cheese pancakes or the celery soup. The floors (gravestones), the walls (16th-century stone), and the black furniture are made less sepulchral by the strains of Bach and the busy clatter of china. ♦ Cafe ♦ Lunch and dinner. 071/839.4342

**Brass Rubbing Center** Here, you can rub effigies of medieval brasses (mostly facsimiles), creating your own knight in shining armor. If you feel pressed for time, buy one ready-made. This is a nice place to spend time with children, who love making copies of the effigies. ♦ M-Sa 10AM-6PM; Su noon-6PM. 071/437.6023

**8 Statue of Charles I** Whitehall physically begins on the south side of Trafalgar Square, with the equestrian statue of **Charles I,** who reigned from 1625 to 1649. The statue, created in 1633 by **Hubbert Le Sueur,** shows the monarch gazing onto the scene of his tragic execution at **Banqueting House** on 30 January 1649, with Parliament looming in the distance. It was his quarrel with Parliament that led to his downfall. In 1642, civil war erupted between the Parliamentarians (the Roundheads, led by **Oliver Cromwell**) and the Royalists (known as the Cavaliers) over Parliament's demand to approve the King's choice of ministers. Charles was tried for treason to the realm and died on the scaffold.

Now stranded in an islet, unreachable except by the most intrepid pedestrian, *Charles I* is the oldest, finest, and most poignant statue in London. The horse's left foot bears the date 1633 and the sculptor's signature. When the Civil War broke out in 1642, the statue was hidden in the churchyard of **St. Paul's,** Covent Garden. After the King's execution, Cromwell sold the statue for scrap to a resourceful brazier named **John Rivett,** who kept the statue intact but enjoyed a brisk trade in candlesticks, thimbles, spoons, and knifehandles supposedly created from it. This Charles I Souvenir Shop thrived until the Restoration, when the statue miraculously reappeared. **Charles II** rewarded the Royalist brazier with £1600. (The Banqueting House, one of the most fabulous buildings of its time, had cost just under £16,000.) The statue finally found its home here at the beginning of Whitehall in 1675.

**9 Walkers of Whitehall** ★$ For a civilized setting for a drink, lunch, or snack, turn into tiny Craig Court and look to the left for this pub/wine bar. You can try cask-conditioned ales or premium lagers with a smoked salmon sandwich, or, if you prefer, a glass of wine with a platter of paté. ♦ Pub/Wine bar ♦ Lunch. Closed Saturday and Sunday. Craig Ct, 15 Whitehall. Tube: Charing Cross. 071/976.1961

**10 Whitehall Theatre** On the other side of Whitehall, opposite Craig Court, stands Whitehall Theatre, built in 1930 on the site of the original **Ye Old Ship Tavern. Edward Stone's** clean, simple lines led one newspaper to comment that the theater made the surrounding government buildings look as if they needed a shave. The Whitehall, which seats 662, usually stages farces and comedies, and its comfy air-conditioning makes the laughter flow easier in summer. ♦ Box office: M-Sa 10AM-8PM. Whitehall (near The Mall). Tube: Charing Cross. General information: 071/867.1119. Credit card bookings: 071/867.1111

**11 Silver Cross** ★★$ Charles I licensed this establishment as a brothel and pub in 1647. The facade is Victorian, but the building dates back to the 13th century, with a wagon-vaulted ceiling, ancient walls sheathed in lead, and, in the bar, a plaster ceiling embossed with vine leaves, grapes, and hops made while Charles I was still living down the street. For the past 250 years, it has been the local for the Old Admiralty next door, and for nearly as long as that, it has been the pub of journalists who report on Whitehall. A warm and special pub, it serves English breakfasts, home-cooked lunches, afternoon teas, and excellent evening buffets. On its upper floors purportedly lives a ghost, said to be of the Tudor maiden whose portrait hangs over the fireplace. ♦ Pub ♦ Breakfast, lunch, and dinner; lunch and dinner only on Sunday. 33 Whitehall. 071/930.8350

**12 Garfunkel's** $ Americans looking for familiar fast food (but not **McDonald's**) will feel at home here. The menu ranges from burgers and omelets to fajitas and chicken kiev, and lo! there is even a half-decent salad bar. Not the place to go for London tradition, but this spot and its compatriots around the city offer reliable fare. ♦ American ♦ Lunch and dinner. 43 Whitehall. 071/930.5678

**12 Clarence** ★★$ A Whitehall institution, this 18th-century pub has gaslights inside and out, oak beams overhead, sawdust on the floor, and wooden tables and pews. The old farm equipment on the beams may be in deference to the regulars from the Ministry of Agriculture next door, but this is also a pub for connoisseurs of real ale—choose among seven served with full bar meals twice daily. ♦ Pub ♦ Lunch and dinner; lunch only on Sunday. 53 Whitehall. 071/930.4808

**13 Old Admiralty** The **Robert Adam** stone screen adorned with sea horses that leads into the cobbled courtyard is all that can be seen of the place that for 200 years ruled the waves. The building was designed in 1725 by **Thomas Ripley.** In the **Board Room** upstairs is a wind dial, dating from 1708, that still records each gust over the roof, even though no one waits here for a sign that the wind will carry the French across the English Channel. The present Admiralty, or Royal Navy, still meets in the building. Smoking has never been allowed, a rule even **Churchill** humbly obeyed. Here **Nelson** both took his orders and returned five years later to lie in state, awaiting his funeral at St. Paul's. **Bailey's** original model for Nelson's statue in Trafalgar Square is kept here. ♦ Whitehall

**14 Ministry of Defence** In this more pacifist age, the **Old War Office,** built in 1898 by **William Young & Son,** is called the Ministry of Defence. Inevitably, it lacks the romance of the Old Admiralty across the street, but the

---

**Restaurants/Clubs:** Red

**Shops/ 🌳 Outdoors:** Green

**Hotels:** Blue

**Sights/Culture:** Black

baroque domes above its corner towers, visible from Trafalgar and Parliament Squares as well as from St. James's Park, have a certain grandeur. ♦ Whitehall

**15 Horse Guards** William Kent, George II's chief architect, designed this long, picturesque—if uninspired—building (shown here) as the headquarters of the King's military General Staff. It replaced a similar dilapidated structure, dating from the reign of **Charles II,** which had been built on the site of **Henry VIII's** tiltyard. Begun in 1750, the building was completed in 1758 by **John Vardy,** who took over its construction after Kent's death. Today, the Horse Guards is a favorite attraction for young visitors, who come to watch the pair of mounted sentries within the central archway.

The two troopers, who change duty every two hours, are drawn from the Cavalry Regiments of the Household Division, which protects the sovereign, better known to military buffs as the Life Guards, and the Blues and Royals. They sit, magnificent and impassive, on their horses, their uniforms elegant compositions of tunics and plumes. (The red tunics and white plumes belong to the Life Guards, while the blue tunics and red plumes belong to the Blues and Royals.)

In addition to the sentries in the archway, the entire Household Division is on daily duty, and the guards are changed daily in a ceremony many Londoners and visitors prefer to that which takes place at Buckingham Palace. At approximately 10:30AM (9:30AM on Sundays), the new guard of the Household Division leaves Hyde Park Barracks to ride down Pall Mall, arriving at the Horse Guards building about half an hour later, at which point the old guard returns. The soldiers are not allowed to talk, but, once in position—if you don't touch their swords or their mounts—you can take photos or be photographed with them. ♦ Changing of the House Guards: M-Sa 11AM; Su 10AM. Mounted guards on duty 24 hours. Whitehall. Recorded information: 0891/505.452 (premium rate call)

**16 Horse Guards Parade** Go through the arch at Horse Guards and you will be in Horse Guards Parade. Ignore, if you can, the cars and dwell on the white stone and splendid Palladian building with arches, pediments, and wings, architecturally one of the finest buildings in London. The parade ground, now so ingloriously used as a parking lot for Whitehall's high and mighty, used to be the Whitehall Palace tiltyard. In 1540, **Henry VIII** invited knights from all over Europe to compete in a tournament on this site.

Every year on the second Saturday in June, the Queen leaves Buckingham Palace in her carriage to drive down Horse Guards Parade for **Trooping the Colour.** This is the most spectacular military display of the year in a country that has no rival in matters of pomp. An annual event dating back to medieval times, it was originally an exercise to teach soldiers to recognize their regimental flags. Now it is the sovereign's official birthday, ceremonial acceptance that English weather does not guarantee a successful outdoor occasion before June. Crowds line the Mall to watch the procession, but it is possible for the lucky few to get tickets. Write from the beginning of January to the end of February to the Brigade Major, Trooping the Colour, HQ, Household Division, Chelsea Barracks, SW1H 8RF. ♦ Behind Horse Guards, Whitehall

**17 Banqueting House** On a bitter winter's day in 1649, a small procession left St. James's Palace and walked through the park to Whitehall. A king of England was going to his execution. Crossing Whitehall, **Charles I** may have gotten his first glimpse of the scaffold built outside the central windows of Banqueting House and his last look at the perfectly proportioned Palladian building commissioned by his father, **James I.**

Banqueting House and the fate of Charles I are inextricably bound. The proportions of the hall, one of the grandest rooms in England, create a perfect double cube at 110 feet long and 55 feet high. This design, created by **Inigo Jones** in 1622, represents the harmony of the universe, of peace, order, and power—the virtues of divine kingship instilled in Charles I by his father. The building, possibly London's first with a facade of Portland stone, so inspired writer **Horace Walpole** that he dubbed it "the model of the most pure and beautiful taste." The magnificent ceiling, which Charles commissioned from **Peter Paul Rubens,** represents the glorification of James I, a visual statement of James' belief in the absolute right and God-given power of kings. If you follow the panels from the far end of the room, you see James rising up to heaven, having created peace on earth by his divine authority as King: peace reigns, the arts flourish, and the King is defender of his realm, the faith, and the Church.

When Charles I tried to impeach five members of Parliament, Civil War broke out between the Parliamentarians and the Royalists. Seven years later he was tried in Westminster Hall and convicted of treason to the realm. On the day of the execution, Charles I wore a second shirt so that he would not shiver in the cold and have his people believe he was afraid. He was a sad and courageous king in death: "I go from a corruptible to an incorruptible crown where no disturbances can be." With one blow, England was without a king, and severed with Charles' head was the belief in the divine right of kings. Until this moment, kings were the chosen representatives of God on earth. Now men would choose princes.

Three centuries later, England still has her kings and queens, and Banqueting House still stands. Despite being one of the most important buildings in all of English architecture, it is almost always empty. Empty but not haunted; there is no feeling that the ghost of Charles I lingers under the newly cleaned ceiling. A bust of Charles I over the staircase entrance (added by **Wyatt** in 1798) marks the site of the window through which he stepped onto the scaffold. ♦ Admission. M-Sa 10AM-5PM; last entry 4:30PM. Whitehall. 071/930.4179

**18 Royal Horse Guards Hotel** $$$ Once the apartments of the influential, the 376 rooms and suites, some with panoramic views overlooking the Thames, are now for the affluent. The reception rooms and the restaurant, **The Granby** (★★★$$$$), have the feel of an elegant country house, but the guest rooms are light and surprisingly grand—some even have marble bathrooms! At lunchtime, the hotel bar and restaurant fills with civil servants from the Ministry of Defence, a quieter breed than that which fills the pubs nearby. Try to sit in the outdoor courtyard, which overlooks an ornamental garden. ♦ Coffee shop: Breakfast, lunch, and dinner. 2 Whitehall Ct. 071/839.3400; fax 071/925.2263

**19 Whitehall Court** This massive Victorian attempt at a French château was a grand apartment building, constructed in 1884 by **Archer and Green.** Both **H.G. Wells** and **George Bernard Shaw** had flats here, and it was the home of several clubs, including the **Farmers'** and the **Liberal Club.** ♦ Whitehall Ct

**20 New Ministry of Defence** Designed by **Vincent Harris** and completed in 1959, these vast buildings were placed behind Whitehall on Horse Guards Avenue out of respect for the scale and proportions of **Inigo Jones'** Banqueting House. Begun just after World War II, this is where the real problems of war and peace are handled—with a few exceptions. In the basement is all that survives of the original Whitehall Palace: **Henry VIII's** wine cellar. The Tudor brick-vaulted roof is 70 feet long, 30 feet wide, and weighs 800 tons. Because the wine cellar interfered with the line of the new building, it was moved 40 feet to one side, lowered 20 feet, and then pushed back to its original site. A huge excavation was made, a mausoleum of concrete and steel built around the cellar to protect it, and a system of rollers devised to shift the cellar a quarter of an inch a time until it had completed its journey of 43 feet. The whole operation cost £100,000, a va sum at the time. ♦ Horse Guards Ave and Whitehall

**21 Cabinet Office** From 1733 to 1844, several great architects had their hands in the design this building, including **William Kent, Sir Joh Soane,** and **Sir Charles Barry.** The lengthy facade exudes Victorian self-confidence and weightiness. At the north end is the office of th Privy Council, the Queen's private council comprising "princes of the blood," high office of the state, and members of Parliament appointed by the Crown. It seems fitting that a statue of **Sir Walter Raleigh,** created in 1959 by **William Macmillan,** stands opposite. Onc a member of **Elizabeth I's** Privy Council, he may look a happy man today, but his fate was grim enough. Raleigh exhibited a very stiff upper lip on the scaffold. Testing the ax for its sharpness, he remarked, "This is a sharp medicine, but it will cure all diseases." ♦ Whitehall

COURTESY DAVID GENTLEMAN

**22 Downing Street** History and television have made this street (shown here) one of the mos famous and familiar in the world. But modern politics and terrorism have shut it off from the public. Named after its builder, **Sir George Downing,** the street lost its quiet, residential a in 1735, when **No. 10** became the official residence of the first prime minister, **Sir Robe Walpole.** Some of the women who have lived the house have complained about the lack of space and light. But **Margaret Thatcher,** Britain's first woman prime minister and one c No. 10's longest residents, made few complaints. **No. 11** is the official residence of the Chancellor of the Exchequer. **John Major** once lived here; now he's moved next door. **N 12** is the office of the Chief Party Whips, the title for the members of Parliament responsible for stirring up party support for various bills and issues.

**23 Cenotaph** Rising in the center of Whitehall is **Sir Edwin Lutyens'** austere memorial to "The Glorious Dead" of World Wars I and II. Erected in 1920, the simple structure of Portland stone shows no sign of imperial glory or national pride or religious symbolism; it is not a monument to victory but a monument to loss. Between the wars, men would take off their hats whenever they passed. Now hats have gone out of style and memories have faded, but once a year, on **Remembrance Sunday** (the second Sunday of November), a service is held to remember the dead of these wars. It is attended by the Queen, the royal family, representatives of the Army and Navy, the Prime Minister, and leading statesmen, and wreaths are placed at the monument. At 11AM, a two-minute silence is observed in memory of the dead.

**24 Cabinet War Rooms** Winston Churchill masterminded the British war effort from this complex 17 feet underground, and now six of the rooms are open to the public, including the one where the War Cabinet met from August 1939 to September 1945. The control room is still crammed with phones and maps covered with marker pins showing the positions of military defenses. Churchill made his stirring wartime broadcasts from the room behind the door marked "Prime Minister." You can almost hear that steadfast, bearlike growl, "Let us therefore brace ourselves to our duties and so bear ourselves that if the British Empire and its Commonwealth last for a thousand years men will still say, this was their finest hour." It is amazing to think that he brilliantly conducted a global war from these poky little rooms. ♦ Admission. Daily 10AM-6PM (last entry 5:15PM). Clive Steps, King Charles St. 071/930.6916

# Afternoon Tea: A Tradition Steeped in History

Tea, the drink so intimately associated with the English, didn't find its way from China to British shores until the mid-1600s. High import taxes meant that only the very wealthy could afford it (in 1706, for example, a pound of tea cost the equivalent of a week's wages for a skilled craftsman). It wasn't until 1784—when Parliament reduced the tax burden after the **Boston Tea Party**—that tea reached a more democratic audience.

Many of the traditions connected with tea grew out of its early association with the upper class. The ladies of the house, not the servants, brewed and served the drink themselves using the best teapots, made of silver. The custom of "afternoon tea" is credited to the **Duchess of Bedford,** who began serving something to eat with her tea in the middle of the afternoon to stem hunger pangs—or so legend has it. In the latter part of the century, tearooms, teahouses, and, in the early 1900s, tea dances sprang up in the finer London hotels and restaurants, and afternoon tea became an institution. The onset of World War II shuttered many of these establishments, but most have made a comeback.

Today, etiquette has loosened its hold on the custom, and tea (plus the beverage and edibles to go along with it) can be enjoyed at just about any time in the afternoon in tearooms or tea shops, although hotels and restaurants still hold to the hours between 3 and 5:30PM. Be sure to work up an appetite beforehand, since chefs—particularly pastry chefs—like to show off their skills for afternoon tea. Food often follows the seasons: summer sandwiches are likely to contain smoked salmon, egg, or cucumber, while in winter, sandwiches are filled with meat. Summer sweets include sponge cakes, éclairs, and Swiss rolls, with fruitcakes, ginger cakes, and hot teacakes served in colder months. Scones, cream, and jam are fairly ubiquitous. In more expensive places, a glass of madeira, sherry, or champagne might be added to the tea trolley. Wherever you take your tea, expect to pay a flat fee for the delectable offerings.

Here is a guide to hotels in central London noted for their afternoon teas, along with the hours during which tea is served:

**Brown's Hotel** ♦ Daily 3-6PM. Albemarle Street/Dover Street. Tube: Piccadilly Circus. 071/493.6020

**The Conservatory in the Lanesborough Hotel** ♦ Daily 3-6PM. 1 Lanesborough Place, Hyde Park Corner. Tube: Hyde Park Corner. 071/259.5599

**Palm Court in the Langham Hilton** ♦ Daily 3-5:30PM. 1C Portland Place. Tube: Oxford Circus. 071/636.1000

**Park Room at the Hyde Park Hotel** ♦ Daily 4-6PM. 66 Knightsbridge. Tube: Knightsbridge, Hyde Park Corner. 071/235.2000

**The Ritz** ♦ Daily 3PM, 4PM (two seatings). 150 Piccadilly. Reservations recommended. Tube: Green Park. 071/493.8181

**The Savoy** ♦ Daily 3-5:30PM. The Strand. Tube: Charing Cross. 071/836.4343

Several patisseries located outside of central London are likewise known for their afternoon tea. Some possibilities include:

**Louis** ♦ 12 Harben Parade, Finchley Road. Tube: Swiss Cottage, Finchley Road. 071/722.8100. Also at: 32 Heath Street. Tube: Hampstead. 071/435.9908

**Forget-Me-Not-Teas** ♦ 45 High Street. Tube: Wimbledon. 081/947.3634

**The Maids of Honour** ♦ 288 Kew Road, Richmond. Tube: Kew Gardens. 081/940.2745

**25 Parliament Square** Sir Charles Barry conceived the square as a kind of garden foreground to his new Houses of Parliament, and it was thus laid out in 1850. Today, it forms a kind of open-air sculpture gallery for prime ministers and other statesmen. The first monument you see is a determined-looking **Winston Churchill** standing on the corner gazing at the House of Commons, which he loved with all his heart. Unveiled in 1973, this 12-foot bronze statue by **Ivor Robert Jones** has not transformed the landscape or led to the renaming of Parliament Square. But it is the memory of Churchill, more than that of **Nelson** or **King Charles I**, that dominates Whitehall. Among the many other brooding statesmen in the square are **Disraeli (Lord Beaconsfield),** by **Raggi,** erected in 1883, and **Abraham Lincoln,** tall and rumpled. His statue is a copy of the **St. Gaudens** in Chicago. ◆ St. Margaret and Victoria Sts

**26 Westminster Bridge** Designed by **Thomas Page,** who rebuilt it to complement **Barry's** Houses of Parliament, Westminster Bridge is one of the best-loved vantage points in the whole of London. You really must walk out on it to get the most splendid view of the seat of British government. The Gothic buildings, rising almost vertically from the Thames, are an inspiration for poets, painters, and believers in democracy. The 810-foot cast-iron bridge is not the one that inspired **Wordsworth** to write his sonnet. But the view surpasses by far what Wordsworth noted that early morning in 1803. He would not have seen the highly wrought Houses of Parliament with the imposing Victoria Tower. He could not have set his watch by the clock lovingly, if wrongly, called Big Ben. Looking down the river, he would not have seen Whitehall Court, the Shell-Mex House, the Savoy, or Somerset House in the background. Standing on the "new" Westminster Bridge, however, stirs up the same poetic feelings Wordsworth must have felt.

**27 Queen Boadicea** This symbol of liberty is well placed at the Westminster end of the bridge, looking out onto the Houses of Parliament from her chariot. In AD 61, under the rule of the **Emperor Nero,** a savage revolt broke out in the newly conquered province of Britain when Roman soldiers forced their way into the palace of the recently widowed Celtic Queen Boadicea. They flogged the Queen for refusing to surrender the lands of the Iceni and raped her two daughters. In her fury, Boadicea led a savage but justifiable rebellion, massacring the inhabitants of the Roman capital at Colchester, then turning south to the undefended port of Londinium. No mercy was shown, and the flourishing town was quickly destroyed. Some 70,000 people lost their lives. But the revenge of the Queen of Iceni was short-lived. The Romans led by **Suetonius Paulinus,** met the Britons in a formal battle and annihilated them. Boadicea is alleged to have poisoned herself. In this bronze statue, erected in 1902 by **Thomas Thorneycroft,** Boadicea has her two half-naked daughters at her side.

**28 Westminster Pier** Perhaps the only thing better than seeing London by foot is seeing London from the river. Westminster Pier is the main launching point for boat trips, either downstream to the Tower, Greenwich, and Thames Barrier, or upstream to the delights Kew Gardens, Richmond, and Hampton Court Palace. Daily cruises are available upstream from April to October, and downstream throughout the year. There are also circular cruises. ◆ Recorded information: 0891/505.471 (premium rate). Circular Cruises: 071/936.2033. Westminster Passenger Service: 071/930.4097. Catamaran Cruises (for trips to Thames Barrier): 071/839.3572. Westminster Tower Boats: 071/237.5134

**29 County Hall** Look across the Thames from Westminster Pier, and you're sure to be taken aback by the palatial sweep of crescent-shaped County Hall—well, the *former* County Hall, at any rate. Designed by **Ralph Knott** for the London County Council, and built between 1911-22 and 1931-33, the building eventually formed the headquarters of the **Greater London Council** (known as the **GLC**) in 1965. In 1986, however, the GLC was abolished by the Tory government, and thus the 2,390 rooms and 10 miles of corridors became empty. In 1992, a Japanese consortium finally purchased the splendid site, complete with 700 yards of river frontage; in the future, it will become a hotel, and when it does, it will have some of the best views of London at its command. Trivia buffs will be pleased to learn that in the early 18th century, a stoneworks on the site of County Hall took out a patent on a particular type of terracotta; this was later improved by **Mrs. Eleanor Coade,** who took over the works and gave the terracotta the name of Coade stone. Strong, appealing, and amazingly weatherproof, the stone was used on The Royal Opera House, Somerset House, and the Bank of England, among other buildings. Yet when the stone yard closed in 1840, the secret Coade stone died with it, and subsequent attempts to analyze its composition failed. ◆ South Bank (off York Rd)

**29 South Bank Lion** The 12-foot-high lion that guards the southern end of **Westminster Bridge** was originally created for the **Lion Brewery.** The regal beast weighs in at 13 tons

---

Restaurants/Clubs: Red          Hotels: Blue

Shops/ 🌳 Outdoors: Green          **Sights/Culture:** Black

Houses of Parliament

**30 Houses of Parliament** To the modern world, no single view so powerfully symbolizes democracy as this assemblage of Gothic buildings, which look as if they have been here throughout the 900 years this has been the site of British government. In fact, these buildings have been standing just over 100 years, but their Gothic style powerfully represents the aspirations and traditions of those nine centuries. The "Symbol of Democracy" and the "Mother of Parliaments" remains a royal palace; it is officially called the "New Palace of Westminster," a name that goes back to the 11th century, when this was the site of the **Palace of Westminster.** First occupied by **Edward the Confessor,** the building was the principal London residence of the monarchs until 1512, when **Henry VIII** moved down the street to Whitehall Palace. Parliament continued to sit here until the palace burned to the ground in the disastrous fire of 1834. All that is left of the ancient Palace of Westminster is the crypt and cloisters of **St. Stephen's Chapel,** the **Jewel Tower,** and **Westminster Hall,** the long Norman hall that is the greatest window into the history of Britain's parliamentary heritage.

After the fire, **Sir Charles Barry** and **Augustus Pugin** won a design competition for a new and enlarged Houses of Parliament building (to occupy the same site) in either the Gothic or Tudor style. Barry gave the buildings an almost classic body; Pugin created a meticulous and exuberant Gothic design. Built between 1840 and 1860, the Houses of Parliament are laid out on an axial plan that reflects the hierarchical nature of British society: **House of Commons, Commons Lobby, Central Lobby, Lords Lobby, House of Lords, Princes Chamber,** and **Royal Gallery.** The complex of buildings covers an area of eight acres and has 11 courtyards, 100 staircases, almost 1,200 rooms, and 2 miles of passages. The House of Commons is in the northern end (MPs enter from **New Palace Yard** on the corner of Bridge Street and Parliament Square) and the House of Lords is in the southern end. (The Peers entrance is in **Old Palace Yard,** where **Guy Fawkes** was hung, drawn, and quartered in 1606 for trying to blow up Parliament, and where **Sir Walter Raleigh** was beheaded in 1618.) ♦ Bridge and St. Margaret Sts. Tube: Westminster

Within the Houses of Parliament:

**Westminster Hall** Built in 1097 by **William Rufus,** son of **William the Conqueror,** this vast, barnlike room is where Parliament began and where **Simon de Montfort** marched in and enforced it. At the end of the 14th century, **Richard II** had the hall rebuilt by **Henry Yevele,** who added the massive buttresses that support 600 tons of oak roof. The hall contains the oldest surviving example of an oak hammerbeam roof, created by **Hugh Herland;** it was a miracle of engineering in its day, marking the end of supporting piers.

The austere and venerable room has witnessed earthshaking moments of history almost since its beginning. Under the benevolent eyes of the carved angels in the arches of the beams, Richard II was deposed the year the work was completed, and **Henry IV** was declared king. In 1535, **Sir Thomas More,** former Speaker of the House of Commons, stood trial here for treason against his former friend and tennis partner, **Henry VIII,** and was beheaded on Tower Hill. Seventy years later, on 5 November 1605, England's most famous terrorist, **Guy Fawkes,** was accused of trying to blow up **King James I** and Parliament. **Charles I** stood trial in his own hall in 1649 and was convicted of treason. **Oliver Cromwell,** the most formidable parliamentarian who ever lived, signed the King's death warrant and had himself named Lord Protector here in 1653. After the restoration of **Charles II** to the throne, Cromwell was brought back to the hall—or rather his skull was cut from his skeleton and stuck on a spike on one of the oak beams, where it rattled in the wind for 25 years before finally blowing down in a storm. And it was here, in Westminster Hall, that **Churchill** lay in state for a fortnight while a grateful nation paid its last respects.

**Crypt/St. Mary's Undercroft** Though once abused and desecrated, and even used as the Speaker's coal cellar, the chapel was richly restored by **Charles Barry** and has a wonderful pre-Raphaelite feeling. The main walls, vaulting, and bosses have withstood at least five fires. Members of both Houses of Parliament use the chapel for weddings and christenings.

**St. Stephen's Porch** The public enters the Houses of Parliament through the porch and hall. Be prepared for the airport-style security check, with metal-detecting arches right next to Westminster Hall, an understandable but inglorious entrance to the Central Lobby.

**Central Lobby** The crossroads of the Palace of Westminster connects the House of Commons with the House of Lords. Citizens meet their MPs in this octagonal vestibule. The ceiling, 75 feet above the floor, contains 250 carved bosses with Venetian mosaics that include the patron saints of England, Ireland, Scotland, and Wales. Above the ceiling is the central spire of the palace, a feature imposed on **Charles Barry's** original plans by **Dr. Reid,** a ventilation expert who insisted that it be built as a shaft to expel "vitiated" air. In fact, the spire has never been needed or used for anything. In the floor of encaustic tiles, **Augustus Pugin** inscribed the Latin text from Psalm 127: "Except the Lord keep the house, they labour in vain that build it."

**Members' Lobby** Off the Central Lobby is the Piccadilly Circus of Commons life, where members gossip and talk to the lobby journalists. Known as the Members' or Commons Lobby, it is architecturally rather bleak (most often described as "neo-Gothic"), and was never fully restored after the 1941 German bombing that left it in ruins. A moving reminder of the destruction is the **Churchill Arch,** made from stones damaged in the fire of 1941. Churchill proposed that it be erected in the lobby in memory of those who kept the bridge during the dark days of the war. Above the main door of the Commons Chamber hangs the family crest of **Airey Neave,** placed here after he was assassinated by terrorists in New Palace Yard in 1979.

**House of Commons** Each day the House opens with a procession in which the **Speaker** enters (wearing a wig, knee breeches, and a long black gown), preceded by the **Sergeant-at-Arms,** who carries a mace (the symbol of authority), and followed by the **Train-Bearer, Chaplain,** and **Secretary.** The day begins with prayers, and no strangers (journalists or visitors) are ever admitted. MPs face the seats behind them—an extraordinary sight—because in the days when they wore swords it was impossible to kneel on the floor; therefore, they turned to kneel on the benches behind them. Every member has to swear loyalty to the Crown (a problem for Irish MPs for the past 100 years), although no monarch has been allowed to enter the House of Commons since 1642, when **Charles I** burst in to arrest his parliamentary opponents.

The House of Commons was completely destroyed in the air raid of 10 December 1941, and was rebuilt in 1950 by **Sir Giles Gilbert Scott,** simply and without decoration and,

## HOUSES OF PARLIAMENT

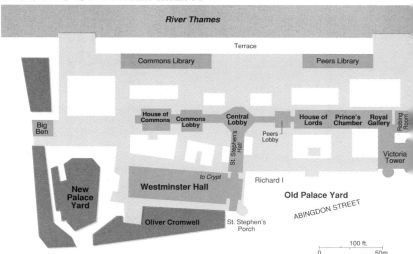

WESTMINSTER BRIDGE

BRIDGE STREET

River Thames

Terrace

Commons Library

Peers Library

Big Ben

House of Commons

Commons Lobby

Central Lobby

St. Stephen's Hall

Peers Lobby

House of Lords

Prince's Chamber

Royal Gallery

Robing Room

Victoria Tower

New Palace Yard

Westminster Hall

to Crypt

Richard I

Old Palace Yard

ABINGDON STREET

Oliver Cromwell

St. Stephen's Porch

100 ft.
0      50m

under **Churchill's** influence, in the exact proportions of the prewar House. It is impressively small: only 346 of the 650 members can actually sit down at any one time; the rest are forced to crowd around the door and the Speaker's chair. The lack of space is considered to be fundamental to the sense of intimacy and conversational form of debate that characterize the House. Equally important is the layout of the **Chamber,** with the party in office (called the Government) and the Opposition facing each other, their green leather benches two swordlengths apart and separated by two red lines on the floor, which no member is allowed to cross. The **Press Gallery** and the **Public Gallery** are at opposite ends of the Chamber. ♦ Sessions: M-Th 2:30PM-closing (often very late); F 9:30AM-3PM. Prime Minister's question time: Tu, Th 3:15PM. 071/219.4272

**House of Lords** This is the most elaborate part of **Charles Barry's** design and **Augustus Pugin's** ultimate masterpiece: Victorian, romantic, and stunning. At 80 feet long, it is not grand in size, but it is extravagantly ornate. Stained-glass windows cast a dark red light, and 18 statues of the barons of Magna Carta stare down from the walls. Their saintlike demeanor emphasizes the sacred look of the room, but the long red-leather sofas on either side suggest a chapel of sorts. Between the two sofas is the "Woolsack" (the traditional seat of the Lord Chancellor), a huge red pouffe stuffed with bits of wool from all over the Commonwealth. Under an immense gilded canopy is the ornate throne of the Queen. ♦ Sessions: M-W 2:30PM-closing; Th 3PM-closing; occasionally on F. 071/219.3107; fax 071/219.5979

Outside the Houses of Parliament:

**Big Ben** The most beloved image in all of London is Big Ben, towering 320 feet over the Thames and lighting up the London sky. Every guidebook will tell you that Big Ben is not the clock but the bell. However, in people's hearts, the **Clock Tower,** or **St. Stephen's Tower** as it is rightfully known, is, and always will be, Big Ben. The tower itself now leans 9½ inches, and the clock's four dials are 23 feet wide. The minute hands are each as tall as a red London double-decker bus. The pendulum, which beats once every two seconds, is 13 feet long and weighs 685 pounds. Besides being endearing, the clock is a near-perfect timekeeper. After spending three years under scaffolding, the Clock Tower has emerged several shades lighter and glistening—4,000 books of gold leaf were used to regild the gold surfaces. Plans were made to restore the hands to their original color, but when it was found that they were blue (the color of the Conservative party), it was felt that Big Ben could not be partisan and they were painted black instead. The hours are struck on the

13½-ton bell, named Big Ben allegedly after **Sir Benjamin Hall,** the first Commissioner of Works when the bell was hung. Since 1885, a light has been shining in the tower at night when Parliament is sitting.

**Victoria Tower Charles Barry** saw the Palace of Westminster as a legislative castle and this was to be its keep, its great ceremonial entrance. When it was built in 1860, the 336-foot tower was the tallest in the world—taller than early American skyscrapers—and it is still the world's highest square masonry tower. (Technologically far ahead of its time, the tower later had to be massively reconstructed to save it from collapse.) It is now an archive of more than three million parliamentary documents dating back to 1497, including the death warrant of **Charles I** and a master copy of every Act of Parliament since 1497. During the day, the Royal Standard flies when the Queen is present, the Union Jack when Parliament is sitting. On a clear day, the flag can be seen by the naval men in Greenwich.

**Statue of Cromwell** The godlike statue of **Oliver Cromwell** caused so much controversy when **Sir Hamo Thorneycroft** finished it in 1899 that Parliament refused to pay for it (mainly due to protests from the Irish Party). Eventually, **Lord Rosebery,** who was Prime Minister at the time, paid for it personally.

---

Queen Elizabeth arrives in the Irish State Coach at the Houses of Parliament once a year for the State Opening of Parliament. In a ceremony that has changed little since the 16th century, she delivers her speech (a policy statement written by the party in office) in the House of Lords. She enters through the Sovereign's Entrance, a gate beneath the Victoria Tower that she alone may use. She proceeds to the Norman Porch and into the Robing Room, where she puts on the Imperial State Crown (which has arrived in its own coach) amid the astonishing splendor of Pugin's decoration. Every inch of the room is covered in gemlike Gothic and Tudor frescoes, and hung with pictures depicting the Legend of King Arthur. The procession continues into the Royal Gallery, which is 110 feet long, 45 feet wide, and lined with paintings, including *The Death of Nelson* and *The Meeting of Wellington and Blucher at Waterloo.* Both paintings measure 45 feet long and 12 feet high. They took the artist, Daniel Maclise, six years to complete, an appropriate recognition of two events without which this grand, Gothic, and democratic place would not exist. Finally, the Queen passes through the Prince's Chamber, the anteroom to the House of Lords and a celebration of Tudor style, with dark paneling and full-length portraits of Henry VIII, five of his six wives, and his mother.

**31 St. Margaret** A few of St. Margaret's historical highlights: **Sir Walter Raleigh,** who was beheaded out front in 1618, is supposedly buried beneath the altar; **Samuel Pepys** married a vivacious 15 year old here in 1655; **John Milton** married here a year later; and **Winston Churchill** married here in 1908. Recently restored, St. Margaret was completed in 1523 by **Robert Stowell** (with the tower added in the 18th century), and has been the parish church of the House of Commons since 1614. The magnificent Flemish glass window was commissioned by **Ferdinand** and **Isabella** of Spain to celebrate the engagement of their daughter **Catherine of Aragon** to **Prince Arthur,** the older brother of **Henry VIII.** By the time the window arrived, Henry had become King and married Catherine—by then his brother's widow. On an ordinary day, this would be quite enough to get one's attention, but St. Margaret's has the bad luck of being wedged in between the Houses of Parliament and Westminster Abbey; most passersby think it's an extension of the latter.

Treasures in the church include the font, created by **Nicholas Stone** in 1641; stained-glass windows in the south aisle, done by artist **John Piper** in 1967; the west windows, given to the church by Americans; the **Milton** window, with the blind poet dictating to his daughter; a memorial to Sir Walter Raleigh, the colonizer of Virginia, with lines from the American poet **John Greenleaf Whittier:** "The New World honours him whose lofty plea for England's freedom made her own more sure"; and a tablet near the altar where Raleigh may be buried urges:

"Reader—
Should you reflect on his errors
Remember his many virtues
And that he was a mortal."

**William Caxton,** the father of modern printing, is buried somewhere in the church or the churchyard, but, ironically, his grave is unmarked. ♦ Daily 9:30AM-4:30PM. St. Margaret St, Parliament Sq

"The well-bred Englishman is about as agreeable a fellow as you can find anywhere—especially, as I have noted, if he is an Irishman or a Scotchman."

**Finley Peter Dunne,**
*Mr. Dooley Remembers*

"You will recognise, my boy, the first sign of old age: it is when you go out into the streets of London and realise for the first time how young the policemen look."

**Sir Seymour Hicks**

**32 Westminster Abbey** This is one of the finest French/English Gothic buildings in the world. Officially called the **Collegiate Church of St. Peter,** it is also the most faithful and intimate witness of English history. Westminster Abbey (depicted above) has survived the Reformation, the Blitz, and, requiring even more miraculous tenacity, nine centuries of visitors, pilgrims, worshipers, wanderers, and tourists. Today, it can be likened to a medieval Heathrow, with windows, vaulting, and buttresses taking flight while the traffic below watches in awe.

It is almost impossible to see the abbey without being surrounded by thousands of tourists, either moving aimlessly down the aisles or purposefully following a raised umbrella beneath which a voice reels off *Abbey Highlights.* If possible, come here for a service, when the abbey empties of gawkers and regains some of its serenity. In any case, try to avoid it in the morning—unless you attend a blissfully quiet 8AM communion service—when all the guided bus tours in London combine Westminster Abbey with the Changing of the Guard.

Once upon a time, this really was an abbey, a monastic community designed for the monkish life of self-sufficient contemplation, with cloisters, refectory, abbot's residence, orchards, workshops, and kitchen gardens. According to legend, the first church was built in the seventh century by **Sebert,** King of the East Saxons, and **St. Peter** himself appeared at the consecration. A Benedictine abbey was also founded; it was called Westminster (West Church) because it was west of the City of London. The existence of the abbey today is credited to the inspired determination of **Edward the Confessor,** who in 1050 set to work on a great monastery to promote the glory of God. In order to supervise the progress of the abbey and efficiently preside over his kingdom of England, he moved his palace next door—hence, the **Palace of Westminster**—and established the bond between Church and State that has endured for more than 900 years.

Edward the Confessor was brought up in Normandy and built his abbey in a Norman style, advanced and unlike anything that had ever been seen in England. Ill and unable to attend the consecration of his church, which took place on 28 December 1065, the King died a week later. No one knows if his successor, **Harold,** was crowned here or at St. Paul's, but after Harold's death at the Battle of Hastings, **William the Conqueror** was crowned here on Christmas Day 1066—the ceremony was written down in the 14th century and is preserved in the abbey. Since 1066, the kings and queens of England have all been crowned at Westminster Abbey, with two exceptions: **Edward V** (presumed murdered) and **Edward VIII** (abdicated).

In 1245, **Henry III** rebuilt the now canonized St. Edward's church in a more magnificent style. Influenced by the French Gothic style of the cathedrals of Amiens and Reims (La Sainte Chapelle in Paris was being built at the same time), Henry started to build, at his own expense, the soaring and graceful church that is here today. The King's architect, **Henry de Reyn** (i.e., "of Reims"), worked with great speed in cathedral terms. By 1259, the chancel, transepts, part of the nave, and the chapter house were complete, giving the medieval church a remarkable unity of style. The nave, continued in the late 14th century by **Henry Yevele** (the master mason who built Westminster Hall), was built in the style originally planned by Henry of Reims. The only important additions to Henry III's church have been the **Henry VII Chapel,** begun in 1503 and believed by many to be the most beautiful and most perfect building in England, and the towers on the west front, built in the 18th century from the designs of **Wren** and **Hawksmoor.**

The best way to enter the abbey is under the towers by the **West Door,** where you can take in the majestic height of the roof: 102 feet to the exalted vault, the pale stone touched with gold and tinted by the colored glass of the aisle windows. The eye is pulled upward by the sheer beauty of it all, then immediately distracted by the chaos of the white-marble figures. You understand at once that any tour of Westminster Abbey will have to be two tours, even if taken simultaneously: one, a tour of the plan and beauty of the building, serene; the other, a survey of the haphazard and wonderful confusion of the more than 5,000 former greats who are buried here. It requires real presence of mind to deal with both at the same time.

Standing at the entrance, you see the impressive length of the stone-flagged nave, the decorated choir screen in front of the nave (too gold, too gaudy, too late; it was created by **Edward Blore** in 1834), and, above, the 16 Waterford chandeliers presented by the **Guinness** family in 1965 to mark the 900th anniversary of the consecration of the abbey. Criticized for being more Mayfair than Gothic, they have since come under the spell of the abbey and now look superbly right.

Immediately in front of you, beyond the green marble slab honoring **Winston Churchill,** is the **Tomb of the Unknown Warrior,** a nameless British soldier brought to the abbey from France on 11 November 1920. The flag that covered the coffin hangs nearby, alongside the Congressional Medal of Honor. The poppy-filled coffin contains earth and clay from France, a terrible and moving reminder of a whole generation lost. His was the last full-bodied burial in the abbey.

To your right is **St. George's Chapel,** the "Warrior's Chapel," with an altar by **Sir Ninian Comper** and a tablet on the west wall commemorating the one million men from the Empire and the Commonwealth who died in World War I. A memorial to **Franklin D. Roosevelt** hangs here. Just outside the chapel is a haunting portrait of the young **Richard II.** It is the first genuine portrait of a king painted in his lifetime. The sad brevity of Richard's life seems to show in his face. Blore's choir screen jolts a bit. Its bright goldness drains the color from **Lord Stanhope** and **Sir Isaac Newton,** who are framed within the arches. Near Newton, a Nobel bevy of scientists are gathered, including **Charles Darwin,** who used science to destroy the myth of creation, and **Lord Rutherford,** who unsettled creation by splitting the atom.

Behind the screen is the choir. The choir stalls are Victorian, but the choir itself has been in this position since Edward the Confessor's own abbey stood on the site. The organ was installed in 1730, but it has been uplifted, rebuilt, and enlarged. Organists at the abbey have been quite distinguished, including **Orlando Gibbons, John Blow,** and his pupil, the English composer **Henry Purcell.**

Because the **North Transept** has **Solomon's Porch,** one of the main entrances to the abbey, it is thick with people coming and going, adding confusion to the mixed bag of the distinguished who are here permanently. Still, persevere until you reach **St. Michael's Chapel** in the east aisle and **Roubiliac's** monument to **Lady Nightingale.** The poor woman was frightened by lightning and died of a miscarriage. She collapses into her husband's arms, while he, frantic and helpless with fear, watches Death, a wretched skeleton, aim its spear at his wife. Maddeningly, this aisle is frequently used for storing chairs. Ask an attendant for permission to visit.

Kings and queens have been crowned in the sanctuary itself since the time of **Richard II** in 1377. A platform is created under the central space (the lantern) between the choir and the sanctuary. The **Coronation Chair** is brought from the **Confessor's Chapel** and placed in front of the high altar. Since the coronation of **Charles I,** the anthem "I was glad when they said unto me, We will go into the House of the Lord" is begun as soon as the sovereign enters the West Door. When **Queen Elizabeth** entered the choir for her coronation in 1952, under the eyes of God and the television cameras, a chorus of "Vivat, vivat, vivat regina Elizabetha" rang out from the voices of Westminster School's scholars. At the sanctuary, she was presented by the Archbishop of Canterbury to the people four times in turn on all sides, who then acclaimed her with loud cries of "God Save the Queen." After an elaborate ceremony of oaths, a service of holy communion, and anointment with special oil, robed in gold and delivered of ring, scepter, and orb, the Archbishop performed the act of crowning.

To the north are the three finest medieval tombs in the abbey: **Edmond Crouchback,** Earl of Lancaster and youngest son of Henry III, and his wife, the rich and pretty **Aveline of Lancaster.** Theirs was the first marriage in the new abbey in 1269. The third grave belongs to **Amyer de Valence,** Earl of Pembroke.

Behind the high altar is the **Shrine of Edward the Confessor.** This is the most sacred part of the abbey, the destination of pilgrims, particularly on St. Edward's Day, 13 October. The Purbeck marble tomb contains the body of the saint. Beside him lie Henry III, who built the church in homage to the Confessor; Henry's son **Edward I,** the first king to be crowned in the present abbey; and his beloved **Queen Eleanor,** for whom he set up what became known as the Eleanor Crosses (the original Charing Cross was one); these marked the places where her funeral cortège stopped to rest along the way from Lincoln to the tomb where she is buried.

The Coronation Chair, when not in use for coronations, stands behind the high altar. Built in 1300, the chair was designed to incorporate the **Stone of Scone.** The stone, part of the Scottish throne since the ninth century, was captured and brought back from Scotland by Edward I in 1297. The **Stone in the Throne** represents the union of the two countries, a union that, even 600 years later, is not without resistance. The stone has been stolen from the abbey by Scottish nationalists several times, most recently in the 1950s, but it has always been recovered. The graffiti on the chair's back was done by 18th-century schoolboys from Westminster School.

If you are able to see one and only one part of the abbey, make it the **Henry VII Chapel.** Because you pay a small admission fee, the abbey suddenly becomes quieter and emptier—a blessing, as this is one of the most beautiful places you may ever lay eyes upon. Notice the exquisite tracery of the fan vaulting, miraculous intricacies, and ecstasies of stone, Matisse-like in their exuberance; the high, wooden choir stalls that line the nave—and their misericordes, carvings located beneath the seats, including a woman beating her husband, and mermaids, mermen, and monkeys; the black-and-white marble floor; and throughout, the royal badges, a kind of illustrated Shakespeare of Tudor roses, leopards of England, the fleur-de-lys of France, the portcullis of the Beauforts, greyhounds, falcons, and daisy roots. This is the Renaissance in England, and Heaven is on Earth in a world alive with confidence, harmony, beauty, and art. The chapel is the grand farewell to the great Gothic style, and forms the perfect setting for the **Order of the Bath,** the chivalrous knights whose tradition was reviewed by **George I** in 1725, and whose order still exists today. (The most recent installation of a Knight of the Bath was in 1982.) In the aisles on both sides of the chapel are a few unforgettable tombs. In the south aisle rests *Lady Margaret Beaufort* by Torrigiani. She was the mother of Henry VII, and was a remarkable Renaissance woman devoted to education, the arts, and the journey of her soul. Her effigy, one of the finest in the abbey, shows a delicately lined face with the gentle sensitivity that, in time, becomes beauty.

"Having restored religion to its original sincerity, established peace, restored money to its proper value. . . ." Most world leaders would die for an epitaph like that, but it seems rather an understatement for **Queen Elizabeth I.** Her four-poster tomb in the north aisle reflects Gloriana more gloriously, although how she feels about being buried with **Mary, Queen of Scots,** whom she had beheaded, God only knows.

In **Innocent's Corner,** at the end of the aisle, are effigies of the two infant daughters of **James I: Sophia,** under her velvet coverlet, died at birth; and **Mary,** leaning on one elbow, died at age two. Both, looking like small dolls, bring tears to parents' eyes and fascinate young children. In another tomb close by lie the bones of two children found in the Tower of London and brought here by order of **Charles II** in 1674. They are believed to be **Edward V** and his brother **Richard,** sons of **Edward IV** and allegedly murdered by their uncle **Richard III** in 1483.

In 1889, **Henry James** came to Westminster Abbey for the memorial service of **Robert**

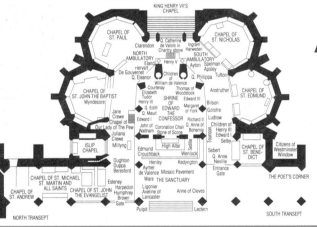

# PLAN OF HENRY VII'S CHAPEL

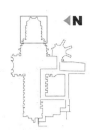

**◀N**

Altar
Dowding
Battle of Britain
Chapel  Trenchard
Cromwell Vault

Buckinghamshire
Q. Anne of Denmark
Anne Mowbray

Montpensier
Wolsey
Stanley
Stanley

Portland
Schomberg
Ormond
Lothian and
Descendants
of Charles II

James I
Henry VII
Q. Elizabeth
of York

Buckingham

Richmond
and Lennox

Edward V
Richard D. of York
Sophia  Mary

Altar

Charles II
Mary II
William III
George of
Denmark Anne

Edward VI

Claypole

Monk

Walpole
Richmond
Lovell

Mary I
Elizabeth

George II
Q. Caroline

Halifax

Frederick
P. of Wales
and Augusta

Louisa and
Edward

Children of
Frederick P. of
Wales

Sandwich

Elizabeth
and
Frederick

Amelia and
Caroline

Mary
Queen of Scots

Stuart
Vault

Lennox

Halifax

Children of Frederick
P. of Wales

Daughters of
George II

Addison

William D. of
Cumberland
Son of George II

Henry D. of
Cumberland
Son of Frederick
P. of Wales

Craggs

Curzon
Cromer

Rhodes
Milner

---

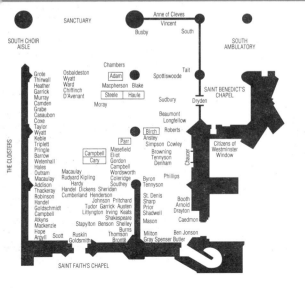

# PLAN OF SANCTUARY AND CHAPELS

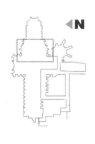

**◀N**

KING HENRY VII'S
CHAPEL

CHAPEL OF
ST. PAUL

CHAPEL OF
ST. NICHOLAS

Clarendon
Q. Catherine
de Valois in
Chantry above

Ingram
Harweden

NORTH
AMBULATORY
Eland
Hervart
De Gouvernet
Q. Eleanor

Henry V
Children
of
William de Valence

SOUTH
AMBULATORY
Ayton
Spelman
Apsley

Q. Philippa

Tufton

CHAPEL OF
ST. JOHN THE BAPTIST
Wyndesore

Courtenay
Elizabeth
Tudor
Henry III
Edward I
Q. Edith
Q. Maud

Thomas of
Woodstock
SHRINE
OF
EDWARD
THE
CONFESSOR

Edward III
Margaret
of York

Anstruther

CHAPEL OF
ST. EDMUND

Bilson
Golofre
Ludlow
Children of
Henry III
Edward I
Selby

Jane
Crewe
Chapel of
Our Lady of The Pew
Juliana
Crewe
Millyng

John of
Waltham

Richard II
Q. Anne of
Bohemia

ISLIP
CHAPEL

Oughton
Duppa
Beresford

Coronation Chair
Stone of Scone

Edmund
Crouchback

High Altar

Sebilla
Wenlock

Touraco

Sebert
Q. Anne
Neville

CHAPEL OF
ST. BENE-
DICT

CHAPEL OF ST. MICHAEL
ST. MARTIN AND
ALL SAINTS

Esteney
Harpeden
Humphrey
Brown

Henley
Aymer
de Valence
Ware

Kedyngton

THE SANCTUARY

Entrance
Gate

Citizens of
Westminster
Window

CHAPEL OF
ST. ANDREW

CHAPEL OF ST. JOHN
THE EVANGELIST

Gate

Ligonier
Aveline of
Lancaster

Anne of Cleves

THE POET'S CORNER

NORTH TRANSEPT

Pulpit

Lectern

SOUTH TRANSEPT

---

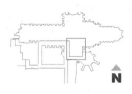

**▲N**

# PLAN OF SOUTH TRANSEPT AND POET'S CORNER

SANCTUARY

Anne of Cleves
Vincent

Busby

South

SOUTH
AMBULATORY

SOUTH CHOIR
AISLE

Chambers

Tait

Grote
Thirwall
Heather
Garrick
Murray
Camden
Grabe
Casaubon
Coxe
Taylor
Wyatt
Keble
Triplett
Pringle
Barrow
Wetenhall
Hales
Outram
Macaulay
Addison
Thackeray
Robinson
Handel
Goldschmidt
Campbell
Atkyns
Mackenzie
Hope
Argyll

Osbaldeston
Wyatt
Ward
Chiffinch
D'Avenant

Adam

Macpherson  Blake

Steele  Haule

Moray

Spottiswoode

SAINT BENEDICT'S
CHAPEL

Dryden

Sudbury

Beaumont
Longfellow

Birch

Roberts

Anstey
Simpson  Cowley

Citizens of
Westminster
Window

Parr

Campbell
Cary

Masefield
Eliot
Gordon

Browning
Tennyson
Denham

Campbell
Wordsworth
Coleridge
Southey

Byron
Tennyson

Chaucer

Macaulay
Rudyard Kipling
Hardy
Handel Dickens Sheridan
Cumberland Henderson
Johnson Pritchard
Tudor Garrick Austen
Litlyngton Irving Keats
Shakespeare
Stapylton Benson Shelley

Phillips

St. Denis
Sharp
Prior
Shadwell
Mason

Booth
Arnold
Drayton

Caedmon

Scott
Ruskin
Goldsmith

Burns
Thomson
Brontë

Milton
Gray Spenser Butler

Ben Jonson

THE CLOISTERS

SAINT FAITH'S CHAPEL

PLANS COURTESY WALTER
ANNENBERG, FROM
*WESTMINSTER ABBEY*,
PUBLISHED BY THE
ANNENBERG SCHOOL OF
COMMUNICATIONS, 1972

**Browning,** whose ashes were being consigned to **Poet's Corner.** Afterward he wrote that Browning stood for "the thing that, as a race, we like best—the fascination of faith, the acceptance of life, the respect for its mysteries, the endurance of its charges, the vitality of will, the validity of character, the beauty of action, the seriousness, above all, of the great human passion." James' testimony to Browning seems a perfect testimony to Anglo-Saxon England, Westminster Abbey, and above all, to its corner of poets, where the recognition is the greatest a generous nation has to confer. All those honored here are not buried here, but among those honored are **Geoffrey Chaucer, Edmund Spenser, Ben Jonson** (who is buried upright!), **William Shakespeare, John Milton, John Dryden, Dr. Samuel Johnson, Thomas Gray, Richard Brinsley Sheridan, Oliver Goldsmith, William Blake, William Wordsworth, Samuel Taylor Coleridge, Percy Bysshe Shelley, John Keats, Thomas Babington-Lord Macaulay, Jane Austen,** the **Brontë** sisters, **Walter Scott, William Makepeace Thackeray, Charles Dickens, Henry Wadsworth Longfellow, John Ruskin, Rudyard Kipling, George Gordon-Lord Byron, George Eliot, Dylan Thomas, W.H. Auden, D.H. Lawrence, Lewis Carroll, Gerard Manley Hopkins,** and, since 1976, **Henry James.** One of the newest stones was unveiled on 11 November 1985. It is a memorial to the poets of World War I. Among those mentioned are **Rupert Brooke, Robert Graves, Herbert Read, Siegfried Sassoon,** and **William Owen.** Above the dates 1914-1918 is the statement from Owen: "My subject is War, and the pity of War. The poetry is in the pity." The ashes of **Sir Laurence Olivier,** Britain's finest actor this century, were buried in the abbey in 1990—a fitting tribute to this well-loved artist.

Ninety-minute **Supertours** of the nave, choir, Statesman's Aisle, Poet's Corner, Royal Chapels, and Coronation Chair are offered Monday through Saturday. (The **Jericho Parlour** and **Jerusalem Chambers** can only be seen on the tour.) Reservations should be made in the south aisle of the nave.
♦ Westminster Abbey: daily 9:30AM-4PM, unless attending a service. (Visitors may not walk around the abbey during services, but can sit and hear the excellent choir.) Services: M-F 8AM (communion), 12:30PM, 5PM (evensong); Sa 8AM (communion), 9:20AM (matins), 3PM (evensong); Su 8AM (communion), 10AM (matins), 11:15AM (sung Eucharist), 3PM (evensong). No visiting on Sunday. Royal Chapels: admission (including the Royal Chapels, Poet's Corner, etc.). M-Tu, Th-F 9AM-4:45PM (last admission 4PM); W 9AM-4:45PM, 6-7:45PM (free during the evening, and amateur

photography is only allowed then); Sa 9AM-2:45PM, 3:45-5:45PM. Supertours: M-F 10AM, 11AM, 2PM, 3PM; Sa 10AM, 11AM, 12:30PM. Off Parliament Sq. 071/222.7110

Within Westminster Abbey:

**Abbey Bookshop** Just inside the main entrance, to the right, is the official abbey shop, where you can buy books, postcards, drawings . . . even Westminster Abbey fudge. ♦ M-Sa 9AM-5PM. 20 Dean's Yd. 071/222.5565

**Chapter House** From 1257 until **Henry VIII's** reign, this exquisite octagon with a Purbeck marble roof (completed in 1250) served as the Parliament House for the Commons. ♦ Admission. Daily 10AM-4PM. 071/222.5897

**Pyx Chamber** Built circa 1090 and once the monastery treasury, the Pyx Chamber passed to the Crown during the Dissolution. Today, it contains the oldest altar in the abbey, dating from circa 1240. The word "pyx" referred to the large wooden chests that once held the standard gold and silver pieces against which coins were annually tested. ♦ Admission. Daily 10AM-4PM. 071/223.0019

**Great Cloister** The courtyard offers a breathtaking view of the buttresses and flying buttresses on the south side of the **Henry VIII Chapel.** The brass-rubbing center (071/222.2085) is open Monday through Saturday 9AM-5:30PM.

**Abbey Treasures Museum** This 11th-century holy **Madame Tussaud's** is the highlight of the day for children, who definitely prefer the macabre to the historical. The wax and wooden effigies were used for lyings-in-state and funerals, and the clothes are not costumes but the real thing, including **Nelson's** hat with its green eyepatch. The abbey represents the divine harmony of immortal man with God; the museum is an unnerving reminder of the mortal in everyone ♦ Admission. Daily 10:30AM-4PM. 071/223.0019

Near Westminster Abbey:

 **Dean's Yard** This is the point where Parliament confronts Public School. You can only gaze through the iron gate at the charming tree-shaded yard behind the abbey. The yard and the buildings of **Westminster School** arranged around it in **Little Dean's Yard,** which can be viewed through an arch o the square's east side, are not normally open to visitors; however, visits may be arranged during the school's Easter holiday by writing well in advance to The Bursar, Westminster School, Dean's Yard, London SW1.

---

**Restaurants/Clubs:** Red   **Hotels:** Blue
Shops/ 🌳 **Outdoors:** Green   **Sights/Culture:** Blac

**33 Broad Sanctuary** Opposite Dean's Yard is the end of **Victoria Street,** known as Broad Sanctuary. This takes its name from the area surrounding the west side of the abbey, which gave fugitives a safe haven from civil law in the Middle Ages. The most famous asylum-seeker was probably **Elizabeth Woodville,** wife of **Edward IV,** who came here with her sons, the sad and tragic Little Princes.

**34 Jewel Tower** In 1366, **Edward III** had the tower built, probably by **Henry Yevele,** to hold his jewels and silver. There are no jewels now in this surviving part of the royal Palace of Westminster. But you can see a permanent exhibition on the history of Parliament, including the drawings submitted in the competition for the Houses of Parliament. These fascinating architectural documents make you even more certain that **Charles Barry** and **Augustus Pugin** were the right men for the job. ♦ Admission. Tu-Su 10AM-1PM, 2-6PM Good Friday-30 Sept; Tu-Su 10AM-1PM, 2-4PM 1 Oct-Maundy Thursday. Abingdon St. 071/222.2219

**35 Victoria Tower Gardens** These gardens overlooking the Thames are ideal for a picnic lunch or an afternoon nap. Two varying principles of heroism can be found in the sculpture: **A.G. Walker's** statue of **Emmeline Pankhurst,** the leader of the women's suffrage movement, who lived from 1858 to 1928 and was often imprisoned for her beliefs; and a replica (1915) of **Rodin's** *Burghers of Calais* (1895), a monument to those who surrendered to **Edward III** in 1347 rather than see their town destroyed. ♦ Off Millbank

**36 Abbey Garden** The 900-year-old garden (it claims to be the oldest cultivated garden in England) is known for its lavender, which you can have shipped to the U.S. ♦ Th 10AM-6PM Apr-Sept; Th 10AM-4PM Oct-Mar. Band concerts: 12:30-2PM Aug to mid-Sept. Abingdon and Great College Sts

**37 Whippel & Co Ltd** The shop supplies garments, candles, sacramental wafers, and wine to priests, bishops, and other religious persons. A sign seen in the shop window read: "special offer on ready-to-wear, double-breasted cassocks." They will make beeswax candles in any size you want. ♦ M-F 9AM-5:30PM. 11 Tufton St. 071/222.4528

**38 Methodist Central Hall** This domed, listed building, which is an international headquarters for Methodism, was built by **E.A. Richards** and **H.V. Lancester** in 1912; the dome is the third largest in London, after St. Paul's and that of the Reading Room of the British Library. In addition to a place of worship, the Central Hall forms the venue for concerts and exhibitions; in the past, it has been used as an international press center. ♦ Chapel: daily for prayer. Services: Su 11AM, 6:30PM. Storey's Gate

Within Methodist Central Hall:

**The Cafe** $ Head downstairs for a cooked breakfast, and soup and sandwiches for lunch. It's a simple but welcome respite from the abbey crowds. ♦ Cafe ♦ Breakfast and lunch. Closed Sunday and Monday. 071/222.8010

**39 Westminster Arms** ★★$ Home-cooked steak, kidney pie, and real ale make this a popular pub with MPs, journalists, and young clerics in the neighborhood who are summoned to lunch by bells—in the past, by the Division Bell in the pub and nowadays by the church bells next door. A nice atmosphere. ♦ Pub ♦ Lunch and dinner. 9 Storey's Gate. 071/222.8520; fax 071/233.0162

**40 The Two Chairmen** ★$ This 18th-century pub takes its name from the chair carriers who brought customers to the **Royal Cockpit,** which stood on **Cockpit Steps** (adjacent) until 1810. Hence the name of the "Sedan Room" (the chairs were sedans), where you can lunch on fare such as lamb rosemary or mushroom stroganoff. ♦ Pub ♦ Lunch. Queen Anne's Gate and Dartmouth St. 071/222.8561

**41 Stakis St. Ermin's Hotel** $$$ Due to be refurbished in 1994, this ornate, marbled hotel is within shouting distance of Westminster Abbey, Buckingham Palace, and the Houses of Parliament. The exterior is unprepossessing, but inside, this Westminster Hotel recalls the elegance of Edwardian days, with a superb baroque staircase and wood-panelled bedrooms. It is so popular with lords and MPs, that the Parliament Division Bell sounds within the building, so that the politicians know when to get back to work. All rooms come with en suite facilities, color TV, radio, and refreshments (including fresh fruit and shortbread). Fourteen conference rooms cater to the business community, along with a grand ballroom for formal occasions.

Business types whisper to each other that St. Ermin's really does serve London's best breakfast. This is the place to try haggis, haddock, or porridge, items on the full English breakfast served in **The Carving Table** (★★$$), one of the hotel's two restaurants. ♦ Caxton St. 071/222.7888; fax 071/222.6914

Charles I, whose last word was "Remember," is remembered every year at 11AM on the Sunday nearest to 30 January, the date of his death. Hundreds of Cavaliers in full dress, members of the English Civil War Society, march to Banqueting House, where they lay a wreath at noon outside the window through which Charles climbed onto the scaffold.

**42 Wilkins** ★$ There aren't many of these around: a health-food cafe with delicious salads, thick homemade soups, and wholemeal bread, all served on scrubbed pine tables by the cheerful Italian staff. Counter service is available. Cheap, and fast. ♦ Vegetarian ♦ Breakfast and lunch. Closed Saturday and Sunday. 61 Marsham St. 071/233.3402

**43 St. John's, Smith Square** Itzak Perlman and **Yo-Yo Ma** have given lunchtime concerts in this church, along with the **Allegri, Endymion,** and **Amadeus** quartets and the **Academy of London Orchestra.** The musical reputation is high indeed, in part because each Monday the concerts are broadcast live on BBC Radio 3. You won't find this church unless you're looking for it, but it is a treasure: built in 1728 by **Thomas Archer,** it is original, idiosyncratic, and personal. After near destruction by bombs in 1941, St. John's was rebuilt but not reconsecrated. ♦ Smith Sq. General information: 071/222.2168. Box office: 071/222.1061

Within St. John's, Smith Square:

**Footstool** ★$$ Rather than dive into the nearest snack bar, walk a little farther along Millbank to the Footstool, which is hidden in the brick-built crypt of St. John's. Here you can see the lobbyists at rest and play, and the powers behind the Conservative Party lunching in the restaurant. Humbler office folk nibble quiche at the self-service wine bar. Open evenings when concerts are held. ♦ Continental ♦ Lunch. Closed alternate Thursdays, plus Saturday and Sunday. 071/222.2779; fax 071/233.1618

**44 Tate Gallery** If you like paintings but can only handle one major museum, the Tate is where you will find true happiness. It houses two great national collections comprised of more than 10,000 works, yet is accessible and welcoming. The collections are an interesting mix of mid-16th century British and modern international art, including the works of living artists that are, naturally, controversial. The Tate is now planning to separate the two collections. Until they do, it is a singular pleasure to be able to look at **Turners, Blake Whistlers, Sargents, Rothkos,** and **Giacomettis,** all hanging happily within minutes of each other.

The gallery began life through the generosity of **Sir Henry Tate** (of the sugar manufacturer Tate & Lyle), who donated his collection of "modern" British paintings and sculptures, and offered to pay for a building to house it. vacant lot on the River Thames at Millbank, previously occupied by **Jeremy Bentham's Model Prison** (from which less-than-model prisoners were sent down the Thames to the Colonies) was acquired, and the wedding-cake building with its majestic entrance, designed by **Sidney J.R. Smith,** opened in 1897. Its formative years were spent as a kind of annex of the National Gallery, but a formal albeit friendly, divorce took place in 1955, and the Tate was finally independent. In 1979, the northwest extension was created by **Michael Huskstepp.** You will recognize and revel in the lively good nature of this museum, a spirit that sets it apart in the world of cultural institutions and makes cultural fatigue wonderfully impossible.

The Tate Gallery issues free plans of the gallery at the entrance. Because the vast collection is changed regularly, this is an invaluable way to locate what you want to see

The **Turner Bequest** is among the great treasures London offers its citizens and visitors, and one of the truly remarkable collections of the work of a single artist. At his death in 1851, **J.M.W. Turner** left his personal collection of nearly 300 paintings and 19,000 watercolors and drawings to the nation, with the request that his finished paintings (some 100) be seen under one roof. In spite of his staggering generosity, his wish was ignored for more than 125 years. Finally, Turner's only hope has been realized with the **Clore Gallery**

Tate Gallery

extension, which was created in 1987 by **James Stirling** and **Michael Wilford & Associates** and makes up in concept and design for the long neglect of Turner's wish. The paintings are top-lit with daylight, the kind of light, with all its varied and changeable qualities, in which the artist expected his pictures to be exhibited. Works on paper (watercolors and drawings) hang in galleries where daylight is kept out in order to prevent the fading of the images. Not only has the architect taken great care to see that the art is sympathetically displayed and scientifically preserved, he has also made it possible for visitors to glimpse the River Thames as they stroll past the pictures. The Thames played a prominent part in Turner's life and art—he painted it, and he lived and died on its banks in Chelsea. Don't miss Turner's *Views of Petworth House, Sussex,* a painting of the home of his great patron and benefactor, **George Wyndham,** Third Earl of Egremont; *Peace: Burial at Sea,* a memorial to his friend, the painter **Wilkie,** who died at sea off Gibraltar; or the pictures of Venice.

Apart from the Clore Gallery, the collection of pre-Raphaelite paintings, and the major British works, the rest of the collection is rotated each year. If there is anything special you want to see, call to check that it is on display. Works to look out for are **Gainsborough's** *Sir Benjamin Truman, Suffolk Landscape,* and his portrait of the Italian dancer *Giovannae Baccelli;* **George Stubbs'** *Mares and Foals, The Haymakers,* and *The Reapers;* the polite paintings by **Sir Joshua Reynolds, Romney,** and **Lawrence,** which give you a glimpse into the serene world of the 18th century; the **William Blake** collection, the richest and most comprehensive in the world; the pre-Raphaelites, especially **Millais'** exquisite *Ophelia* and **Rossetti's** paintings of his wife, **Beata Beatrix;** the irresistible portraits of **John Singer Sargent,** especially *Carnation, Lily, Lily, Rose;* and **Whistler's** *Little White Girl: Symphony in White No. II.* Hanging nearby are the newly appreciated paintings of **Tissot.**

The **French Impressionist** collection marks the beginning of the Tate's modern collection, and includes **Manet's** *Woman with a Cat,* which once belonged to **Degas; Bonnard's** *La Table;* the brilliant Provence landscapes of **Cézanne;** and **Vuillard's** *Seated Woman.*

Cubism is represented with some outstanding pictures by **Braque, Picasso,** and **Juan Gris.** An exciting and remarkably comprehensible outline of 20th-century art includes works by **Kokoschka, Léger, Masson, Matisse, Edward Munch** (*The Sick Child*), **Kandinsky, Mondrian,** and **Malevich. Rodin's** large marble carving, *The Kiss,* made a few years after the version in the Musée Rodin, is one of the most popular pieces in the gallery.

The new display of the collection is the first comprehensive rearrangement in some 20 years. It gives greater prominence to 20th-century British art, including **Stanley Spencer's** two great Resurrection narratives set in Cookham and Port Glasgow. The story of British figure painting continues with the School of London paintings by **Francis Bacon, Lucian Freud, Frank Auerbach, Leon Kossoff,** and **R.B. Kitaj,** whose work has recently attracted increasing international attention. The grand central galleries have been restored to their original function as spaces for sculpture, and now show some of the masters of 20th-century British sculpture in the context of work by their European contemporaries. See especially work by **Richard Deacon** and **Tony Cragg,** who dominate the new generation of British sculptors. ♦ Free; admission for certain major exhibitions. M-Sa 10AM-5:50PM; Su 2-5:50PM. Between Millbank and John Islip St. 071/821.1313

Within the Tate Gallery:

**Tate Gallery Restaurant** ★★★$$ This restaurant is known for two things: the romantic and beautiful **Rex Whistler** mural *Expedition in Pursuit of Rare Meats,* painted in 1926–27, and the wine list, which is unquestionably the best in town due to the sheer number of superb bottles and the amazingly low prices. Refurnished by **Jeremy Dixon** in 1985, the restaurant is frightfully chic and comfortable. A lunch here is hard to beat, surrounded by the wit and elegance of the mural. Order a 1979 Château Beychevelle to go with your thoroughly English lunch of roast sirloin of beef or steak, kidney and mushroom pie. Your neighbors will be astute members of the wine trade, distinguished patrons of the arts, and sometimes couples who have come up from the country to compare their Joseph Wrights, Turners, and Stubbs with the Tate's. Enjoy the most charming lunchtime rendezvous in the whole of London. ♦ British ♦ Lunch. Closed Sunday. Reservations required far in advance. 071/887.8877

**Tate Gallery Shop** Superbly printed postcards, excellent books, T-shirts with masterpieces from the Tate, the ubiquitous Tate Gallery canvas bags, prints, posters, framing facilities, and a few special made-for-the-Tate items that change frequently. ♦ M-Sa 10AM-5:30PM; Su 2-5:30PM. 071/821.1313

**Coffee Shop** ★★$ Self-service and excellent food, with good game pies, pâtés, salads, and wine. The cakes, pastries, coffee, and tea make this a popular afternoon eating place. It seems like a great spot to meet people as well, as everyone sits at long crescent-shaped tables. ♦ Coffee shop ♦ M-Sa 10:30AM-5:30PM; Su 4-5:15PM. 071/821.1313

# St. James's

St. James's (pronounced by Londoners with two syllables as "Jameses") is all about mystery and history, royalty and aristocracy, pomp and civilized circumstance, and kings, queens, gentlemen, and ladies. In this elegant, anachronistic enclave, time seems to have stood still. Gentlemen still go to their clubs, an unchallenged English custom; shoes are still made with painstaking care for royal feet and hats sewn seamlessly for aristocratic heads; and when the Queen is home at **Buckingham Palace**, the royal standard flies. This neighborhood provides one of the most agreeable walks in London, where visitors can gaze around at a portrait of England and Englishness utterly unchanged by war, development, mass production, pollution, the weak pound, or the European Community. It's the England of history books and literature, heroes and heroines, **George Meredith** and **Oscar Wilde**, and fashionable **Edward VII**. Amid the champagne and syllabub, however,

egalitarians and feminists will perceive two ancient phenomena: the segregation of the classes and the segregation of the sexes.

You can begin the journey at a monument to the uppermost echelon of society, **Admiralty Arch**, designed as a tribute from Edward VII to his mother, **Queen Victoria**. Proceed to **Jermyn Street**, where window-shopping is like viewing museum exhibits and the prices can reach old master figures. In an area no larger than a football field, you can have a pair of shoes made to fit your feet, purchase the most handsome and most expensive pipe you'll ever own, and have a tailor take your measurements for custom-made shirts (with a minimum order of six and a minimum wait of six weeks). You can buy Cheddars, Stiltons, Wensleydales, and Caerphillys in **Paxton & Whitfield**, a shop that may convince you the French are only the second-best cheese producers in the world. You can choose wild hyacinth bath oil from a famous perfumery (**Floris**) or Ajaccio Violet cologne from a regal barbershop (**Trumper's**), drink excellent ale in a truly Victorian pub (the **Red Lion**) or dine in one of the best English restaurants in London (**Wilton's**). You'll see where kings and queens lived before they moved to Buckingham Palace and gaze at the windows of **Clarence House**, where **Prince Charles** resides. Afterward, have a look at some of the treasures from the royal collection, check out the royal horses and coaches, and end the day beside the shimmering lake in **St. James's Park**, London's oldest and perhaps most romantic greensward, where **Charles II** walked his spaniels.

St. James's on a Saturday feels like a Sunday. The streets are empty, despite the fact that most of the shops are open. If you want to watch the **Changing of the Guard** at Buckingham Palace, call for dates (083/912.3411) and then get there at least half an hour early. There are few places for visitors to wait out rainstorms near the royal palaces, so bring your umbrella if the sky looks threatening.

**1 Admiralty Arch** The inglorious car race around Trafalgar Square doesn't prepare you for this grand Corinthian structure in Portland stone, which is actually a screen with five arches: there is the center arch, whose iron gates open only for ceremonial processions, two side arches for traffic, and two smaller arches for pedestrians. Its very monumentality, created by **Sir Aston Webb** in 1911, is a surprise because it is so un-London. Admiralty Arch marks the first part of the royal processional route from **Buckingham Palace** to **St. Paul's Cathedral.** The structure was part of **Edward VII's** tribute to his mother, **Queen Victoria,** although the King himself died before the memorial was completed. ◆ Trafalgar Sq. Tube: Charing Cross, Piccadilly Circus

**2 The Mall** Two double rows of plane trees line this royal processional road (pronounced to rhyme with "pal"), which sweeps theatrically to a monumental climax. Laid out after the Restoration in 1660, the stretch from Trafalgar Square to Buckingham Palace was originally an enclosed alley for playing *paille maille* (a French game similar to croquet, called "pell mell" by the English). It was transformed to give a formal vista of Buckingham Palace by **Sir Aston Webb** in 1910 as part of a memorial to **Queen Victoria.** The present Mall runs just south of the original promenade, now used as a bridle path. On Sunday, the Mall is closed to traffic and becomes a place for strolling once more. ◆ Between Buckingham Palace and Trafalgar Sq. Tube: Charing Cross, Piccadilly Circus

**3 The Citadel** The enveloping ivy generates an air of mystery around what is actually a bomb shelter, built in 1940 for Naval officers and never demolished. Scrupulously maintained by the Parks Department, which mows the acre of grass on top, it serves as a reminder of the past era, before bomb technology made shelters like this obsolete. ◆ The Mall. Tube: Charing Cross, Piccadilly Circus

**4 Carlton House Terrace** These creamy white, glossy buildings facing the Mall are among the last contributions **John Nash** made to London before his death in 1835. The 1,000-foot-long terrace is a stately confection of Corinthian columns and human-scale arches; the former were evidently inspired by **Jacques Ange Gabriel's** buildings in the Place de la Concorde. The upkeep is considerable, but the clean outline, intercepted in the center by the **Duke of York Steps,** is a splendid contribution to the Mall: an impressive backdrop for royal processions by day, a royal wedding cake when floodlit at night.

Erected between 1827 and 1832, Carlton House Terrace replaced **Carlton House,** the palatial home purchased in 1732 by **Frederick,** Prince of Wales, who died before his father, **George II.** It was subsequently owned by **George III** (who went mad), and then by his son, the **Prince Regent,** who transformed it at staggering expense into what was considered the most beautiful mansion in England. But after he became **King George IV,** he and Nash agreed to demolish it and convinced Parliament to allocate funds for the conversion of **Buckingham House** into **Buckingham Palace.** The columns were saved and recycled into the portico of the **National Gallery,** and Nash was asked to build Carlton House Terrace. Originally, the terrace was to line both sides of the Mall in the style of **Regent's Park,** providing grand town houses for the aristocracy; unfortunately, only one side was built. ♦ Tube: Charing Cross, Piccadilly Circus

On Carlton House Terrace:

**Mall Galleries** These rooms exhibit traditional paintings by members of the **Royal Society of Portrait Painters** and the **Federation of British Artists,** as well as occasional shows by candidates for graduation from the various art schools. If you like **Turner** and **Constable,** come here to look for affordable English landscapes, watercolors, and oils reminiscent of their works. ♦ Nominal admission. Daily 10AM-5PM. 071/930.6844

**Institute of Contemporary Arts (ICA)** Founded in 1947, the ICA is a lively arts center with an industrious, avant-garde atmosphere. Its three galleries exhibit British and foreign photography, architectural drawings, paintings, and event-art, among other shows. In the evening, interesting foreign and cult movies are shown in the cinema, while experimental films, videos, and works by new filmmakers are screened in the cinémathèque. A children's cinema club offers screenings at 3PM every weekend. See films in the video library and experimental drama in the theater or visit the bookshop, which has all the latest art books as well as magazines, postcards, and **Virago** novels.

In order to see the exhibitions or even to have a cup of coffee, you must buy a day membership, which is a bargain if there's an appealing lunchtime event. Sometimes these events consist of well-known writers and artists interviewing other well-known writers and artists, and then taking questions from the public. ♦ Admission. Galleries: M, W-Su noon-7:30PM; Tu noon-9PM. Bookshop: noon-10PM. Cinema showings: M-F 5PM, 7PM, 9PM; Sa-Su 3PM, 5PM, 7PM, 9PM. Cinema: 071/930.3647. General information: 071/930.0493. Recorded box office information: 071/930.6393

Within the Institute of Contemporary Arts (ICA):

**ICAfe** $ Enjoy an Italian or vegetarian meal with a trendy beer (Rolling Rock, Becks, or Pils) at the bar upstairs while you gaze at the contemporary British art adorning the walls or listen to the arty talk from the nearest table. ♦ Italian/Vegetarian ♦ Bar: M-Sa noon-1AM; Su noon-3PM, 7-10:30PM. Cafe: lunch and dinner. 071/930.8535

**The Royal Society** Formed in the 1640s and formalized by **King Charles II** in 1660, the Royal Society at No. 6 is one of the most distinguished scientific bodies in the world. In the 17th century, the society was a hub of scientific discovery, where **Newton, Halley, Dryden,** and **Pepys** chatted about inventions, although Pepys, then president, never understood Newton's *Principia*. Past presidents include **Wren, Davy, Huxley, Thomson, Rutherford,** and **Fleming.** The society moved to Carlton House Terrace in 1966 after nearly 300 years in Burlington House on Piccadilly. ♦ Closed to the public

**5 Duke of York Steps and Duke of York Monument** **Benjamin Wyatt's** dramatic column, built in 1834, dominates Waterloo Place. The Duke of York, **Frederick,** was the second son of **George III.** His seven-ton bronze statue was financed by withholding one day's pay from all soldiers. Credited to **Sir Richard Westmacott,** the Duke stands 137 feet in the sky; since he died owing £2 million, some quipped that the pink-granite column was meant to keep him out of reach of his creditors. ♦ Tube: Charing Cross, Piccadilly Circus

**6 Waterloo Place** One of the few pieces of town planning in London is also one of the most impressive. **John Nash** built Waterloo Place in 1816 to commemorate **Wellington's** triumph over the French the previous year. It marks the beginning of Nash's triumphal route to Regent's Park. Carlton House Terrace frames Waterloo Place, which intersects Pall Mall on its way north into lower Regent Street and Piccadilly Circus. ♦ Tube: Charing Cross, Piccadilly Circus

"You ask, what was that song they sang at the opening—that's 'God Save The King.' You thought it was 'Sweet Land of Liberty'? So it is. You Yankees took it from us and put new words to it. As a matter of fact we took it from the Ancient Britons—they had it, England-may-go-to-hell—and the English liked it so much they took it over and made it 'God Save the King.'"

**Stephen Leacock,**
*Welcome to a Visiting American*

**Restaurants/Clubs:** Red    **Hotels:** Blue
**Shops/** ♣ **Outdoors:** Green    **Sights/Culture:** Blac

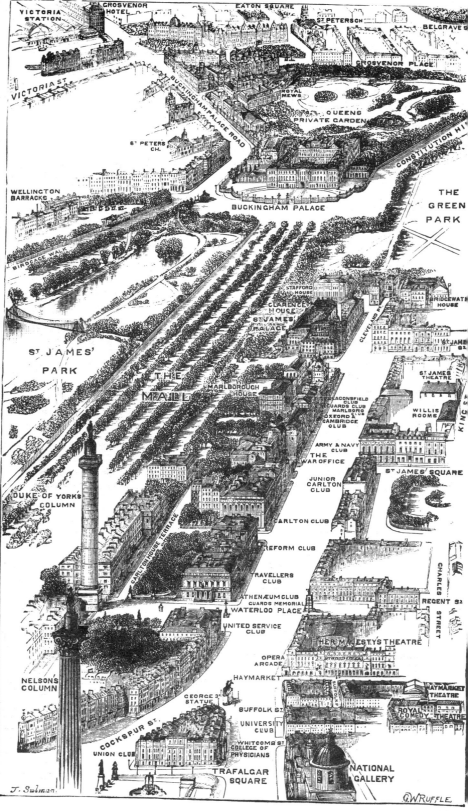

VICTORIA STATION

GROSVENOR HOTEL

EATON SQUARE

St PETERSCH

BELGRAVE S

VICTORIA ST.

BUCKINGHAM PALACE ROAD

ROYAL MEWS

GROSVENOR PLACE

QUEENS PRIVATE GARDEN

St PETERS CH.

CONSTITUTION HI

WELLINGTON BARRACKS

BUCKINGHAM PALACE

THE GREEN PARK

BIRDCAGE WALK

STAFFORD HOUSE

BRIDGEWATE HOUSE

CLARENCE HOUSE

CLEVELAND RA.

St JAMES' PALACE

St JAMES St

St JAMES' PARK

THE MALL

MARLBOROUGH HOUSE

St JAMES' THEATRE

WILLIS ROOMS

KING S

BEACONSFIELD CLUB
GUARDS CLUB
MARLBORO CLUB
OXFORD & CAMBRIDGE CLUB

ARMY & NAVY CLUB

DUKE OF YORKS COLUMN

THE WAR OFFICE

St JAMES' SQUARE

JUNIOR CARLTON CLUB

CARLTON HOUSE TERRACE

CARLTON CLUB

REFORM CLUB

CHARLES STREET

TRAVELLERS CLUB

ATHENÆUM CLUB

GUARDS MEMORIAL

WATERLOO PLACE

REGENT St

NELSON'S COLUMN

UNITED SERVICE CLUB

HER MAJESTY'S THEATRE

OPERA ARCADE

HAYMARKET

HAYMARKET THEATRE

ROYAL COMEDY THEATRE

SUFFOLK St

GEORGE 3rd STATUE

SUFFOLK St

COCKSPUR ST.

UNIVERSITY CLUB

UNION CLUB

WHITCOMB St

COLLEGE OF PHYSICIANS

TRAFALGAR SQUARE

NATIONAL GALLERY

J. Sulman

G.W.Ruffle.

**7 Statue of Edward VII** In front of the Duke of York Steps and facing Waterloo Place is **Edward VII,** looking hale and beefy, as **Sir Bertram MacKennal** immortalized him in 1921. The King inspired the Edwardian Age: a secure, elegant time for the rich and aristocratic, a world where to amuse and be amused were raisons d'être. Because of the long life of his mother, **Queen Victoria,** he reigned for only nine of his 69 years. He brought color and pageantry to the monarchy but also a sense of serious commitment to such issues as the quality of workers' lives and the treatment of Indians by English officials. Edward was aware that beyond Europe lay his empire, the largest the world had ever known. As King, he created the *entente cordiale* with France and used his considerable diplomatic skill and charm to ease the conflicts between Germany and England, conflicts that were tragically too deep for any monarch to resolve. However, it is his voracious appetite for which he is remembered: at his last formal dinner at **Buckingham Palace,** on 5 March 1910, he made his way through nine dishes, including salmon steak, grilled chicken, saddle of mutton, and several snipe stuffed with foie gras. He died two months later, yet souvenirs of the Edwardian Age are still tucked away in the small streets nearby. ♦ Tube: Charing Cross, Piccadilly Circus

**8 Carlton House Gardens** During World War II, the Free French occupied **No. 4,** where **de Gaulle's** message to his countrymen is inscribed on a plaque. ♦ Just behind Carlton House Terrace, the Mall. Tube: Charing Cross, Piccadilly Circus

**9 Athenaeum Club** This most august of the gentlemen's clubs occupies one of the most distinguished buildings in London, designed by **Decimus Burton,** the man who gave London Constitution Arch and the Screen at the entrance to Hyde Park, and completed in 1830. The cream stucco facade has pure architectural dignity. A Wedgwood-like frieze wraps around the building above the first-floor windows, while a large gilded figure of **Pallas Athene,** goddess of wisdom, practical skills, and prudent warfare, graces the porch and accurately sets the standards for those who enter—bishops, scientists, and the top brains of the Civil Service and Foreign Office.

Inside, the atmosphere is one of intimidating sagacity. A portrait of member **Charles Darwin** broods over the living. The **Royal Society's Dining Society,** an elite group within the formidably elite **Royal Society,** meets here, and those within that clever and select circle are de facto members of the Athenaeum, which was named after the **Emperor Hadrian's** university in Rome. If you meet an Englishman who is a member, be

impressed. ♦ Not open to the public. 107 Pall Mall. Tube: Charing Cross, Piccadilly Circus

**10 Institute of Directors** The **United Service Club,** known as the **Senior,** was founded in 1815 for the triumphant officers of the Napoleonic wars and inhabited this structure for 150 years. The first building commissioned by a club, it was originally designed by **John Nash** in 1828, but most noticeable are the alterations carried out by **Decimus Burton:** the Doric columns and the Corinthian portico. It's a handsome building, though not as unforgettably beautiful as the **Athenaeum** opposite. The granite mounting block outside on Waterloo Place was put there by **Wellington** to help short men get on their horses.

Modern lifestyles, incomes, and Labor governments do not lend themselves to a world of expensive exclusivity, and in 1974, when most clubs were enjoying a comeback, the Senior collapsed. Now it is a business center for the Institute of Directors. Ask at the reception area, and you can go inside to see the original 19th-century furniture designed for the club, including a 15-foot chandelier presented by **George IV** to commemorate the Battle of Waterloo. This inimitable masculine tonality of mahogany and leather is a gentlemen's club. ♦ 116 Pall Mall. Tube: Charing Cross, Piccadilly Circus. 071/839.1233

**11 Haymarket** A 17th-century market that supplied the horses of the Royal Mews, when the mews were on Trafalgar Square, gave this street its name. The market was placed here after **Lord St. Albans** was ordered to move it from Mayfair because of the filth that resulted from the cattle and sheep for sale. A market of some kind remained at Haymarket until the early 1800s. ♦ Tube: Piccadilly Circus, Charing Cross

**12 Haymarket Theatre Royal** Officially named the Theatre Royal, Haymarket, the **Society of West End Theaters** (and everybody else) lists this as the Haymarket. Whatever it's called today, it was the **Little Theatre** when it opened in 1720. **Henry Fielding,** whose first satire, *Tom Thumb,* ran here in 1730, was one of its managers—and the principal reason **Lord Chamberlain** instituted powers of censorship that were not lifted until 1968. After **John Nash** rebuilt the theater in 1820, the Haymarket hosted performers such as **Ellen Terry** and **Samuel Phelps.** Nash's exterior remains fairly intact, but the interior, redesigned first in 1905 by **C. Stanley Peach,** has been altered several times since, much to the discomfort of the audience. It seats 906 people. While the shows are independent and excellent, the wine at the bar is undrinkable. Tuck a bottle and some small glasses into your bag for a sidewalk intermission; you'll toast your own foresight. ♦ Haymarket. Box office: 071/930.8800

**13 Comedy Theatre** **Thomas Verity** built the Comedy in 1881; it was restored in 1955. More recently home to the American import, *Little Shop of Horrors,* this intimate 780-seat theater is well-suited to the modern productions it usually mounts. ♦ Panton St. Tube: Piccadilly Circus, Charing Cross. Box office: 071/867.1045. Credit card bookings: 071/867.1111

# Café Fish

**14 Café Fish** ★★$$ If you dream of oysters in tomato and coriander sauce and can dwell lovingly on the rich aromas of steamed bream, come devour your fishy fantasy. This bright, spacious restaurant has most every kind of edible sea creature you could possibly desire. The daily specials are usually the best form of fresh fish available in London. Café Fish is popular with businesspeople during the week, thanks to efficient, friendly service in both the restaurant and wine bar. ♦ Seafood ♦ Lunch and dinner. Closed Saturday and Sunday. 39 Panton St. Reservations recommended. Tube: Piccadilly Circus, Charing Cross. 071/930.3999

# THE STOCKPOT

**15 The Stockpot** ★$ Some call its setting animated, others just plain loud, but for years The Stockpot has been the salvation of hungry students and penurious travelers looking for agreeable, generous meals at cheap prices. Consequently, the lunchtime rush attracts office workers from all sides and is not for the fainthearted. Service, however, tends to be genial, if frantic; typical filling meals are spaghetti, chicken casserole, and Spanish omelets. Vegetarian dishes are always offered, and those partial to dessert will not be disappointed. ♦ International ♦ Breakfast, lunch, and dinner; lunch and dinner only on Sunday. No credit cards; minimum charge. 40 Panton St. Tube: Piccadilly Circus, Charing Cross. 071/839.5142. Also at: 18 Old Compton St. 071/287.1066; 273 King's Rd. 071/823.3175

**16 Burberrys** This raincoat manufacturer, famous for quality and its signature plaid, has been protecting the British from the elements for more than 150 years. Aviator **Sir John Alcock** kept himself warm and dry in Burberrys' gabardine on his first flight across the Atlantic, and soldiers in World War I wore Burberrys' trench coats. When the liveried attendant opens the door today, you enter a world of old-fashioned charm and grace. Either climb the wooden staircase in this glorious shop, or risk the ancient lift. ♦ M-W, F 9:30AM-6PM; Th 9:30AM-7PM. 18-22 Haymarket. Tube: Piccadilly Circus, Charing Cross. 071/930.3343. Also at: 165 Regent St. 071/734.4060

**17 Design Center** The best of British design, from toys to tackle, cars to cards, and woollies to Wellies, is displayed here. The government-sponsored **Design Council,** originally the **Council for Industrial Design,** has been providing exhibitions on the latest innovations in British domestic design since 1956. If you have questions about where to find something, the experts in the center offer free advice, and the selective Design Index lists approximately 7,000 manufacturers of well-designed goods. After looking at the exhibit, browse in the bookstore or refresh yourself at the coffee bar. ♦ M-Sa 10AM-6PM; Su 1-6PM. 28 Haymarket. Tube: Piccadilly Circus, Charing Cross. 071/839.8000

**18 Her Majesty's Theatre** This 1,209-seat theater changes its name to fit the sex of the sovereign—hence it's *Her* Majesty's, for now. The current building was erected in 1897 for **Sir Herbert Beerbohm Tree** by **C.J. Phipps** (who also built the **Savoy**), but a theater has stood upon this site since 1705. The first opera by **Handel** to be produced in England was performed here, as was the first Handel oratorio. Operatic connections continued in 1791, when **The Opera House** was built on the site, replacing the structure destroyed by fire the previous year. During the next century, **Jenny Lind** made her English debut here, as did **Beethoven's** *Fidelio.* Furthermore, the **Royal Academy of Dramatic Art (RADA)** had its beginnings here. These days, Her Majesty's is best known as the place to see **Andrew Lloyd Webber's** *Phantom of the Opera,* which has been playing here since 1986 (check the box office daily for returns). ♦ Haymarket. Tube: Piccadilly Circus, Charing Cross. Box office: 071/494.5400

**19 Crimean War Memorial** **Florence Nightingale** is one of the few women represented in this masculine part of London; in this statue, she holds her famous lamp. Standing next to her is **Sidney Herbert,** secretary of war during the Crimean campaign. "Honor," on the other side, cast from captured Russian cannons, seems to have her eye on the bearskin-attired guardsmen below. The memorial itself was designed by **John Bell** in the 1850s. ♦ Lower Regent St and Pall Mall. Tube: Charing Cross, Piccadilly Circus

**20 Pall Mall** Americans pronounce it like the brand of cigarettes, but the upper-class English who have their clubs here say "Pell Mell." Named after the ball game that was played in the Mall, which runs parallel, this is the ancient road from the City to St. James's. Pall Mall is lined with gentlemen's clubs and a few appropriately exclusive shops, but its residential character has given way almost entirely to offices. It is a stately boulevard by day, a windy, monumental wasteland by night. A word of warning: traffic tears down this broad one-way avenue with terrifying speed, so cross carefully. ♦ Tube: Green Park, Piccadilly Circus, Charing Cross

**21 Travellers' Club** The Travellers' was founded in 1819 by the **Duke of Wellington,** whose portraits loom from the club's walls, though the present building, designed by **Charles Barry,** dates from 1832. One of the requirements for membership is to have traveled at least 500 miles from London. As one might expect in the late 20th century, the candidates' book reveals that the present membership has gone somewhat farther afield. The special handrail on the staircase was put there to assist **Napoleon's** disabled foreign minister, **Talleyrand,** up the stairs. The plain stucco neoclassical facade shows Barry (who also designed Trafalgar Square and the Houses of Parliament) doing what he loved best. ♦ 106 Pall Mall. Tube: Charing Cross, Piccadilly Circus. 071/930.8688

**21 Reform Club** Members must subscribe to the **Reform Bill of 1832** (which gave the vote to middle-class men) in order to be accepted into this absolutely stunning club, another **Charles Barry** creation, completed in 1841. It looks like a film set, and a few films have been made here, but so great is the discretion or indifference that no one who belongs knows just which films. The design is Italian Classicism Without Bound, inspired by Rome's Palazzo Farnese. The silent interior includes a huge indoor courtyard with marble pillars and balconies, a vast library with leather chairs, library tables, and real fires in the enormous fireplaces. The kitchen is the size of a ballroom and has a good reputation. This is the club of economists, members of the Treasury, and increasingly, writers and television executives. Reform is enough of a concern at this club that it allows women to be members, but, as with most London clubs, it is not open to the public. ♦ 104-5 Pall Mall. Tube: Charing Cross, Piccadilly Circus

**22 Royal Automobile Club** Here is a club that takes members more readily than most. The opulent Edwardian building, built in 1911 by **Mewes and Davis,** with **E. Keynes,** contains rooms designed in grand Louis XVI style. More enticing, however, are the squash courts, Turkish baths, solarium, and the marble swimming pool, which is the most beautiful in London, its Doric columns covered in fish-scale mosaics. **George Bernard Shaw** swam in this pool and **J.P. Donleavy** swims in it when he's in London.

Many of the 12,000 members live abroad and use this as their London address. Unlike other clubs, no one seems to know anyone else, which probably explains why upper-crust spies **Guy Burgess** and **Donald MacLean** met here just before defecting to Russia in the '50s. There are three dining rooms, a bar, a post office, and bedrooms, which are modest, comfortable, and considerably cheaper than a hotel. Despite its democratic outlook, the only women you see here are wives and daughters of members. ♦ 89 Pall Mall. Tube: Green Park, Piccadilly Circus. 071/930.2345

**23 St. James's Square** This fine square was begun in 1665 by **Henry Jermyn,** first Earl of St. Albans and allegedly the secret husband of **Henrietta Maria,** widow of **Charles I** and mother of **Charles II.** While the King was in exile in France, he gave the land to the Earl in gratitude for his "faithful devotion." The square was designed with mansions on all sides for the nobility who wanted or needed to be near the palace. **Sir Christopher Wren** who created the church for this noble suburb (St. James's, Piccadilly), probably had a say in the dignified shaping of the square.

The gardens in the square's center are open to the public (which is unusual in London, where only residents hold keys to the carefully locked gates of most neighborhood squares). The handsome bronze statue by **John Bacon the Younger** of **William III** on horseback includes the molehill on which the horse stumbled, throwing the King and causing his death. During World War I, a rustic building resembling a country inn was erected at the square's center to quarter American officers. Called the **Washington Inn,** it stood until 1921. At **No. 32,** in the southeast corner, the allied commanders under **General Eisenhower** launched the invasions of North Africa in 1942 and of northwest Europe in 1944. On the north side of the square at **No.10** is **Chatham House,** the residence of three prime ministers: the **Earl of Chatham,** otherwise known as **Pitt the Elder;** the **Earl of Derby;** and **W.E. Gladstone. Wellington's** dispatch announcing his victory at Waterloo was delivered to **No. 16** by the bloodstained **Major Percy** to the **Prince Regent,** who was dining with his foreign secretary, **Lord Castlereagh.** Included with the dispatch were the captured French eagle standards, which are now in the **Wellington Museum** at Hyde Park Corner.

St. James's Square became famous overnight when the **Libyan People's Bureau** at **No. 5** was besieged on 17 April 1984. Gunmen within the building fired on demonstrators outside, killing young police officer **Yvonne Fletcher.** Because diplomatic immunity made it impossible for police to enter the building, the siege went on for 10 days, and the suspects were deported instead of arrested. Fresh flowers are placed on a memorial opposite No. 5 year-round in honor of Fletcher. ♦ Tube: Green Park, Piccadilly Circus

**24 London Library** "It is not typically English. It is typically civilized," wrote **E.M. Forster** in an essay on this private subscription library, founded in 1841 by **Thomas Carlyle** but built in the 1760s by **James Stuart.** The interior looks like a down-at-heel club, with worn leather chairs in the reading room, Victorian portraits on the walls, and high windows overlooking the square. Past members include **Lord Tennyson, W. E. Gladstone, Henry James, Thomas Hardy, H.G. Wells, Aldous Huxley, Virginia Woolf,** and **Edith Sitwell.** Current members are historians, biographers, critics, novelists, philosophers, playwrights, and scriptwriters, who all come to use some of the library's one million-plus books.

Unlike clubs in neighboring precincts, the London Library doesn't suffer from blatant misogyny, although the equal numbers of men and women you're likely to see in the reading room are a fairly recent occurrence, and the carpet on the stairs stops one flight before the ladies' loo. Annual membership is inexpensive, life membership isn't. There are special, shorter memberships available for visiting academics, writers, and literary Anglophiles. ♦ M-W, F-Sa 9:30AM-5:30PM; Th 9:30AM-7:30PM. 14 St. James's Sq. Tube: Green Park, Piccadilly Circus. 071/930.7705

**25 Colombina** ★★$$ The Neapolitan chef at this refreshingly simple and inexpensive trattoria prepares delicious deep-fried mozzarella in bread crumbs, along with excellent fish dishes and grills. Writers doing all-day stints in the London Library often break for nourishment here. ♦ Italian ♦ Lunch and dinner. Closed Sunday. 4-6 Duke of York St. Tube: Piccadilly Circus. 071/930.8279

**26 Wheelers in Appletree Yard** ★★$$ It's easy to miss this tiny restaurant tucked between St. James's Square and Duke of York Street. The smallest member of a 125-year-old chain of seafood restaurants, its menu is known for oysters and the Colchester specials, available around November. Try the grilled Dover sole or poached Scottish salmon, washed down with the house white wine. The chefs here have never figured out vegetables. ♦ Seafood ♦ Lunch and dinner. Closed Sunday. Duke of York St. Tube: Piccadilly Circus. 071/930.2460

"The English winter—ending in July to recommence in August."

**Lord Byron**

staurants/Clubs: Red    **Hotels:** Blue
ops/ 🌴 Outdoors: Green    **Sights/Culture:** Black

**27 Red Lion Pub** ★★★$ Dating from around 1880, this Victorian jewel has mahogany paneling and beautiful old mirrors, each engraved with a different British flower. Come early and have a delicious sandwich with your pint of bitter, or visit the excellent restaurant; later it becomes crowded and smoky. ♦ Pub ♦ M-Sa 11AM-11PM. 2 Duke of York St. Tube: Piccadilly Circus. 071/930.2030

**28 Jermyn Street** Named after the Earl of St. Albans, **Henry Jermyn,** this narrow street is only a few blocks long and the architecture isn't remarkable (Jermyn's west end was badly damaged during the 1940s raids, when all but one of the buildings between Duke and Bury streets were destroyed). But Jermyn is the essence of St. James's, an exclusive shopping club for well-to-do Englishmen who dress as the Duke of Edinburgh and Prince Charles do. Browsing and buying here is educational, sensual, and, so patrons maintain, worth the expense. ♦ Between the Haymarket and St. James's St. Tube: Piccadilly Circus, Green Park

**29 Rowley's** ★★$$ This small steak house serves nothing but charcoal-grilled steaks with butter. The set menu is reasonably priced and very good. ♦ British ♦ Lunch and dinner. 113 Jermyn St. Tube: Piccadilly Circus. 071/930.2707

**30 Trumper's** Ivan's, barbers to very distinguished heads (with royal warrants from **Edward VII, George V,** and **George VI**), was taken over by Trumper's, which has another shop in Mayfair. Trumper's hairbrushes, shaving brushes, soaps, hair tonics, and after-shaves are irresistible and legendary. The Ajaccio Violet men's cologne smells like violets, comes in old-fashioned bottles, and is pleasing to both sexes. ♦ M-F 9AM-6PM; Sa 9AM-5PM. 20 Jermyn St. Tube: Piccadilly Circus. 071/734.1370

**BATES**
*the*
**HATTER**

**30 Bates the Hatter** This tiny gentlemen's hat shop is undaunted by the bareheaded 20th century, and time seems to be on its side. Hats are reappearing, with low-crown felt fedoras selling more briskly than in the 1940s. You will pay less here than at the famous **Lock's** on St. James's Street. Be sure to admire **Binks,** the huge tabby cat who lived here from 1921 to 1926; he was so beloved that a taxidermist was enlisted after his death. ♦ M-F 9AM-5:30PM; Sa 9:30AM-4PM. 21A Jermyn St. Tube: Piccadilly Circus. 071/734.2722

## Jermyn Street Shopping Map

**HAYMARKET**

| | |
|---|---|
| Café Sogo | Royal Bank of Scotland |
| mall **No. 1 Jermyn Street** | Figaro *cafe* |
| Mono Mail Shop | Ceylon Tea Centre |
| department store **Lillywhites** | |

**REGENT STREET**

| | |
|---|---|
| Barclays Bank | Plaza Cinema |
| Spaghetti House | |
| menswear **Herbie Frogg** | |
| hairdresser, perfumer **Trumper's** | |
| menswear **Herbie Frogg** | Rowley's *English restaurant* |
| Bates the Hatter | Van Heusen *men's shirts* |
| shirtmakers **Hawes & Curtis** | Church's *men's shoes* |

**EAGLE PLACE**    **BABMAES STREET**

| | |
|---|---|
| National Westminster Bank | Astleys Briar *pipes* |
| | Coles *shirtmakers* |
| | Rupert Wace *ancient art* |
| Simpson's | T.M. Lewin *shirtmakers* |
| | Baresi *menswear* |

**CHURCH PLACE**

| | |
|---|---|
| | Kensington Carpets |

**DUKE OF YORK STREET**

JERMYN STREET

| | |
|---|---|
| | Harvie & Hudson *shirtmakers* |
| St. James's Church | Russell & Bromley *men's shoes* |
| The Wren Wholefood Café | Robin Symes *antiquities* |
| | Paxton & Whitfield *cheesemongers* |
| | Ormond's Restaurant |
| shirtmakers **Hilditch & Key** | Edward Green Shoes |
| | Floris *perfumers* |

**PRINCESS ARCADE**

| | |
|---|---|
| antiques, art **Mayorcas** | James Bodenhan *gifts* |
| fine gifts **Von Posch** | |
| toiletries **Czeck & Speake** | Pink *shirtmakers* |
| nightclub **Tramp** | Foster & Son *bootmakers* |
| | Cavendish Hotel |
| Fortnum & Mason | S. Franses *antique tapestries* |

**DUKE STREET**

| | |
|---|---|
| | John Bray *menswear* |
| | Harvie & Hudson *shirtmakers* |
| | Trevor Philip *scientific antiques* |
| clothing, tobacco **dunhill** | Eleganza Italiana *menswear* |

**PICCADILLY ARCADE**

| | |
|---|---|
| menswear **New & Lingwood** | Waterman *fine art* |
| antiques, fine furniture **Sarti Gallery Ltd.** | |
| | Taylor of Old Bond St. *hairdressers* |
| Victor Franses Gallery | Hilditch & Key *shirtmakers* |

**BURY STREET**

| | |
|---|---|
| menswear **Vincci** | Turnbull & Asser *menswear* |
| | Kurt Geiger *shoes* |
| Mokaris Espresso Bar | Vincci *menswear* |
| | R.E. Tricker *shoes* |
| Italian restaurant **Franco's** | Vincci *menswear* |
| National Westminster Bank | Davidoff *tobacco* |

**ST. JAMES'S STREET**

**30  Hawes & Curtis** Check out this shiny green-and-white shop if you're looking for a bargain on Jermyn Street (although that's almost a contradiction in terms). A selection of items is usually on sale, including shirts from **Turnbull & Asser,** which owns the shop. Be careful if you want to order anything special; Hawes and Curtis won't be hurried. ♦ M-F 9AM-6PM; Sa 9AM-5PM. 23 Jermyn St. Tube: Piccadilly Circus. 071/734.1020

**31  Simpson's** The department store's main entrance is on Piccadilly, but there are two entrances on Jermyn Street, and their steps offer a nice view of this once-and-now neo-Georgian street. (See page 74 for a complete description.) ♦ M-W, F-Sa 9AM-6PM; Tu 9:30AM-6PM; Th 9AM-7PM. Main entrance: 203 Piccadilly. Tube: Piccadilly Circus. 071/734.2002

**32  Harvie & Hudson** These third-generation shirtmakers use the finest cotton poplin, designed, colored, and woven just for them. The Windsor collars are slightly wide, and the prices for the tweed jackets and overcoats eminently reasonable. ♦ M-Sa 9AM-5:30PM. 96-97 Jermyn St. Tube: Piccadilly Circus, Green Park. 071/930.3949

**33  Hilditch & Key** The shop specializes in made-to-measure shirts for men and women, including royals and politicians—but of course these tailors are far too discreet to name names. All shirts are cut by hand: the bodies with shears, the collars with a knife. The collars, considered the most important part of a shirt, are turned by hand and have removable stiffeners that must be taken out before laundering. The buttons are made from real shells, never synthetic. Besides the fine English cotton poplins, there's a solid selection of Viyella, a soft, warm equal mix of cotton and wool. The women's shirts come in many of the same colors and fabrics as the men's but with additional choices of bright, clear colors created by H&K's own designers. The nightshirts (for men and women) and pajamas are wonderful. ♦ M-F 9:30AM-6PM; Sa 9:30AM-5PM. 37 Jermyn St. Tube: Piccadilly Circus. 071/734.4707

**34  Paxton & Whitfield** This shop occupies a house built in 1674, and at any one time you can find 300 cheeses from 11 countries inside. **Mr. Paxton** and **Mr. Whitfield** became partners 150 years ago, when the public predilection was for French cheeses. Now English cheeses are finally being acknowledged for their outstanding quality and for being ideal partners with wine. Taste the golden Cheddars, the peach- and ivory-colored Cheshires, the russet Leicester, the marbled green Sage Derby, the blue-veined Stilton, and England's first soft cheese, Lymeswold. The salespeople here are generous with samples. The shop also has fabulous game pies, hams, and pâtés, plus crackers and bread to accompany the cheese. This is a perfect place to assemble a picnic to take to St. James's Park. Stop at one of the wine merchants nearby to find a young claret to go with it. ♦ M-F 9AM-6PM; Sa 9AM-4PM. 93 Jermyn St. Tube: Piccadilly Circus. 071/930.0250

**34  Floris** Since 1730 the Floris family has been creating aromatic perfumes, bath oils, and soaps from the flowers of the English garden. Their jasmine, rose, gardenia, lily of the valley, and wild hyacinth all smell fresh and clean and as close to the real thing as you can imagine. **Jacqueline Onassis** favors the sandalwood fragrance, and **Nancy Reagan** started ordering the bath soaps after visiting **Buckingham Palace.** You will also find large natural sponges, fine English brushes, antique objects for *la toilette,* and a line of scents for men. The perfumer manufactures grooming preparations for **His Royal Highness the Prince of Wales,** who has given the shop the seal of excellence, a royal warrant. ♦ M-F 9:30AM-5:30PM; Sa 10AM-5PM Jan-Nov; M-W, F 9AM-6PM, Th 9AM-7PM, Sa 10AM-5PM Dec. 89 Jermyn St. Tube: Piccadilly Circus. 071/930.2885

**35  Fortnum & Mason** The rear entrance of the store known fondly as the "Queen's Grocer" is located on Jermyn Street. This is the best place in St. James's for breakfast and one of the best places in London for epicurean treats. The quickest route to the ice-cream concoctions at the **Fountain** is from this side of the store. (See page 72 for a complete description.) ♦ M-F 9:30AM-6PM. 181 Piccadilly. Tube: Green Park. 071/734.8040

**36  dunhill** It was on this very site in 1907 that **Alfred Dunhill** opened his small tobacconist shop. The philosophy that made his lighters, watches, fountain pens, and pipes famous throughout the wealthy world is: "It must be useful, it must work dependably, it must be beautiful, it must last, it must be the best of its kind"—also the motto of a new generation of ambitious consumers. Dunhill has expanded to meet their every desire, having dropped only the "It must be useful" as a strict requirement. ♦ M-F 9:30AM-6PM; Sa 10AM-5:30PM. 30 Duke St. Tube: Green Park. 071/499.9566

**37 Green's Champagne and Oyster Bar**
★★$$$ Green's is a gentlemen's club that is open to the public and filled with **Bertie Wooster** look-alikes, although the waiters aren't as deferential as **Jeeves.** It has a bar with booths for the secretive and an open restaurant for rubberneckers. The food, though very English, is better than you will find in any exclusive club. By all means, have champagne; then choose from a mountain of lobsters, crabs, oysters, and salmon, all fresh, simply prepared, and outstanding. During the season you can get grouse, pheasant, wild duck, and partridge, hung properly and roasted perfectly. The desserts are English favorites, such as treacle tart and gooseberry fool. Expect crowds at lunchtime. ♦ Modern British ♦ Lunch and dinner; lunch only on Sunday. 36 Duke St. Tube: Green Park. Reservations required. 071/930.4566

**38 Wilton's** ★★$$$ During **Johnny Apple's** long reign as the *New York Times* bureau chief in London, he wrote with care and affection about food and wine, nourishing the concept of good English cuisine as surely as the English scene nourished him. One of his favorite places was Wilton's, which celebrated its 250th anniversary in 1992. It changed locations but took its glass screens, Edwardian dining room alcoves, polished mahogany, and clubby atmosphere with it, so regulars would feel they were still on Bury Street. The smoked salmon, oysters, and game are excellent. The fish is innocently swimming in sea or stream only hours before it is placed in front of you. The ingredients are prime and English, and each meal is wisely prepared. In fact, the restaurant is considerably better than during its Bury Street days. ♦ Modern British ♦ Lunch and dinner; dinner only on Saturday. Closed Sunday. 55 Jermyn St. Jacket and tie required; reservations required. Tube: Green Park. 071/629.9955

# Crown Commodities: the Royal Family Talks Shop

Although it may be hard to picture them doing so, members of Britain's royal family have been known to, yes, go shopping. Whether the baskets and bags are filled by the sovereigns or their servants is a matter for speculation; however, finding out where the ruling class spends its cash is simple—look for a royal warrant, a coat of arms that represents one of four members of the royal family: the present **Queen,** the **Queen Mother,** the **Duke of Edinburgh,** and the **Prince of Wales.** When a supplier holds a royal warrant, it means that it provides goods to one of the "Big Four" by appointment. The privilege is worth having, since the supplier can then advertise to all and sundry that "royalty shops here"—not a bad way to drum up business. Like much of English heritage, the tradition began in the Middle Ages. **Henry VIII** gave his approval to a "King's Laundresse"; his daughter, **Elizabeth,** had her own "Operator for the Teeth." In order to qualify for the royal approval today, a business must have supplied goods or services to the royal household for three years running. At last count, there were around 800 or so royal warrant holders.

Some are easy to identify and fairly obvious. There is **Harrods,** of course, and **Hatchards,** the bookseller; both firms hold all four royal warrants, while **Lobb's,** the shoemaker, holds three. The **General Trading Company,** on Sloane Street, is a shop frequented by the **Prince** and **Princess of Wales,** who kept their wedding list there. **Twining and Co.,** on the Strand, has the honor of supplying all the royal tea, and **Hardy Brothers Ltd.** claims to have sold fishing rods to every Prince of Wales this century, including **Prince Charles,** while **Lock & Co.** serves as hatter to the Duke of Edinburgh. You can play "spot the warrant" throughout **St. James's** and **Piccadilly** (the insignia are usually displayed over or near the shop's door)—since these two areas are convenient to **Buckingham Palace,** they contain possibly the largest concentration of warrant holders in London.

The other way to find out what the royals use is simply to look at the goods. With this method, you can tell which marmalade the Queen prefers (it's probably sold at **Fortnum & Mason,** "the Queen's Grocer") and what cologne Prince Charles uses (from **Floris**). Touching on more delicate matters, every roll of **Andrex** brand toilet paper proudly displays the royal warrants of the Queen and the Queen Mother, an advertising coup for **Scott Limited,** the supplier that proclaims itself "by appointment . . . manufacturer of disposable tissues" to these two royal shoppers

**39 Turnbull & Asser** The name is familiar to Americans who wear English custom-made shirts, especially now that there's a Turnbull & Asser club in New York as well as department stores in the states that take appointments with their tailors. But those experiences aren't the same as coming into this solemn, dark, wood-paneled shop where you can't be certain if the person next to you is a duke or the salesman. The store's made-to-measure service takes six weeks, with a minimum order of six shirts after you approve the first. There are a lot of decisions to make: the shape of the collar; the length of the points, pockets, and monograms; the shape and color of buttons; a two- or three-button cuff. You also must be patient. First you are measured; then a sample shirt is made, which Turnbull will send to you. Next you must write a set of fastidious notes and return the shirt. This routine can go on for quite some time before you get a shirt that is perfect.

**Mr. Williams,** the managing director, cheerfully acknowledges that Turnbull & Asser shirts know their own way across the Atlantic, where **Ronald Reagan** has been a client. **David Bowie** bought his wedding shirt here. If you can't be bothered with the made-to-measure process, choose from the large selection of ready-mades. The store also sells blouses and shirts to women, including **Candice Bergen, Lauren Bacall,** and **Jacqueline Bisset.** Turnbull & Asser reflects Jermyn Street's **Beau Brummell** legacy rather more faithfully than the neighboring shirtmakers, for the Regency dandy could not resist fine craftsmanship, simple lines, and daring colors—in fact, Brummell emptied his pockets on many a stroll down the street and eventually died penniless in France. ◆ M-F 9AM-6PM; Sa 9AM-5PM. 71-72 Jermyn St. Tube: Green Park. 071/930.0502

**40 St. James's Street** The elegant street serves as compass for this royal and aristocratic quarter. At the bottom of the street is **Henry VIII's** gatehouse to **St. James's Palace,** with a sentry on duty. Pall Mall joins the street just in front of the palace, where the tradition of gentlemen's clubs continues, although the 18th-century clubs here are considered even more social and arrogant than the clubs farther along Pall Mall. There are no signs to indicate which club is which—if you're a member, you know, and if you aren't, you don't need to know. ◆ Between Pall Mall and Piccadilly. Tube: Green Park

**40 White's** London's oldest, most famous, and still most fashionable club was founded in the 1690s as **White's Chocolate House** (a meeting place where bitter hot chocolate was drunk). Built by **James Wyatt** in 1788, this is where **Evelyn Waugh** sought "refuge from the hounds of modernity" and where **Prince Charles** had his stag party the night before he married **Diana.** Known for its gambling as well as its nobility, the gaming room here was called "Hell" in the previous century. If you are sufficiently well-connected to be proposed and accepted for membership, there is a waiting list of eight years. ◆ 37-38 St. James's St. Tube: Green Park. 071/493.6671

**41 Davidoff** Using three recipes for flavor, **Zino Davidoff** has created a cigar and pipe smoker's heaven. He purveys the finest Havana cigars, which presumably are even more plentiful now that **Castro** has personally given them up. The shop has an ineffably masculine pull, with the handmade wooden humidors, the matchboxes, the cigar cases in leather, and the cigar holders. The sweet smell of unsmoked cigars evokes a sense of order, prosperity, and sedate virility, which vanishes with the first puff for the nonsmoker. ◆ M-F 9AM-6PM; Sa 9:30AM-6PM. 35 St. James's St. Tube: Green Park. 071/930.3079

**42 Boodle's John Crunden's** beautiful building, completed in 1765, is one of the best examples of club design in London, with a central arched Venetian window in the upper room. Two Rolls-Royces ferry members back and forth from their offices at lunch. Boodle's has been considered *the* club for fashionable men-about-town, with one of the best kitchens in clubland. ◆ 28 St. James's St. Tube: Green Park. 071/930.7166

**42 Economist Building Alison** and **Peter Smithson's** complex is considered one of the few examples of successful modern architecture in London. In 1964, the architects designed a group of buildings that are compatible with the 18th-century scale of St. James's Street yet maintain their 20th-century integrity. The complex provides a public open space, offices for *The Economist* magazine, a bank, and apartments. In the front court are **Henry Moore's** *Reclining Figure,* created in 1969, and **Michael Sandle's** *Der Trommler,* dating from 1985. ◆ 25 St. James's St. Tube: Green Park

"A family on the throne is an interesting idea also. It brings down the pride of sovereignty to the level of petty life. No feeling could seem more childish than the enthusiasm of the English at the marriage of the Prince of Wales. They treated as a great political event, what, looked at as a matter of pure business, was very small indeed. But no feeling could be more like common human nature as it is, and as it is likely to be."

**Walter Bagehot,** 1867
*The English Constitution*

**43 Longmire** This treasure trove is the only jewelry store in St. James's and is thus much patronized by royalty and the international upper crust. Alongside tempting displays of 19th- and 20th-century jewelry is representational and animal jewelry. **Mr. Longmire** keeps a book for clients searching for precious creatures to add to their collections. His regal displays shimmer with the stones of each month—September, for instance, is for sapphires. Heraldic work is engraved on signet rings and on one of the world's largest collections of cuff links, which can even be enameled to clients' original designs. ♦ M-F 9:30AM-5PM Jan-Oct; M-F 9:30AM-5PM, Sa 9:30AM-4PM Nov-Dec. 12 Bury St. Tube: Green Park. 071/930.8720

**44 Fox & Lewis** Since the United States' 1961 embargo on Cuban imports, about one-third of London's cigar business is with Americans, who come to this Dickensian shop in droves, following in the footsteps of **Robert Lewis'** most famous customer, **Sir Winston Churchill;** he opened an account on 9 August 1900 and placed his last order on 23 December 1964, a month before his death. There's a hoard of Churchill memorabilia here to prove it. ♦ M-F 9AM-5:30PM, Sa 9AM-4PM. 19 St. James's St. Tube: Green Park. 071/930.3787

**45 Brooks's** Inveterate gambler **Charles James Fox** was a famous member of this club, founded in 1762 but built 16 years later by **Henry Holland. Beau Brummell** won £20,000 in one night when this was a great gambling club for Whig aristocrats; now its members are far more cautious country gentlemen who wouldn't risk gambling away their land. ♦ 60 St. James's St. Tube: Green Park. 071/493.4411

**46 St. James's Club** $$$$ Current members must propose you for membership and second your nomination if you want to belong to this exclusive club. However, you can get a taste of its luxury before applying; you're allowed to stay once during the off-season (August and November through April). When Hollywood comes to London—**Steven Spielberg, Cher, Nastassja Kinski, Anjelica Huston, Chevy Chase, Liza Minnelli,** and **Dudley Moore**—it stays here. The interior features tented ceilings, Jacuzzis, mirrored walls (to augment the size of the rather small rooms), Art Deco furnishings, towels as thick as sable pelts, and a mirrored piano bar highly reminiscent of the one in *Casablanca*. **American Express Centurion Club** members have reciprocal privileges here, as do members of 100 affiliated clubs worldwide, including the St. James's Clubs in Los Angeles, Antigua, and Paris. ♦ 7 Park Pl. Tube: Green Park. 071/629.7688; fax 071/491.0987

**47 Stafford Hotel** $$$$ Located on a quiet cul-de-sac, this hotel is virtually a club for its loyal guests. Travelers who have stayed at too many anonymous, international luxury hotels will find this very English hotel a relief. The 73 rooms are large and comfortable. The Stafford dining room's wine list resembles that of a fine club—200 labels are housed in the cellars that once belonged to **St. James's Palace.** English businesspeople who lunch frequently know their palates won't be jaded by the delectable midday meal served here. Afternoon tea at the Stafford ranks high on the list of London's best; it's served in a room filled with antiques, silver teapots, Wedgwood china, and real logs burning in the fireplaces at each end of the room. If you're not staying in the hotel, do come for tea. ♦ 16-18 St. James's Pl. Tube: Green Park. 071/493.0111; fax 071/493.7121

**48 Spencer House** The entrance to this remarkable Palladian mansion (pictured above) faces St. James's Place, but its finest facade is turned toward Green Park. The house was begun in 1756 by **John Vardy,** who designed it for **John,** Earl of Spencer, an ancestor of **Princess Diana. James Stuart** took over its (mainly interior) construction in 1758; Stuart was nicknamed the "Athenian" for his love of classical architecture, and his anglicized Greek influence can be seen throughout the house. When completed in 1766, Spencer House was considered one of the finest residences London had ever seen. "I know not of a more beautiful piece of architecture," wrote **Arthur Young** after seeing it in 1772. The **J. Rothschild Administration** acquired Spencer House in 1985 and has restored its original splendor. On Sundays, visitors may admire Vardy's elaborate gilt-wood console tables in the dining room, enter Stuart's neoclassical painted room, and explore **Lady Spencer's** private drawing room. ♦ Admission. Su 11:30AM-4:45PM; tours every 15 minutes. Closed January and August. 27 St. James's Pl. Tube: Green Park. 071/499.8620

**48 Dukes Hotel** $$$$ In a gaslit courtyard behind St. James's Place is a kind of miniature palace, with 38 rooms, 28 suites, and an elevator that descends with the dignity of an elderly duchess. The hotel's clubby atmosphere suits the neighborhood, while its loyal clientele relishes the location (the heart of St. James's) and the staff's impeccable courtesy. Late at night, taxis turning around in the cul-de-sac are audible, so if noise is your pet peeve, ask for a room in the back. Excellent English food is served in the small dining room; try the bread-and-butter pudding. Tea is served until 5:30PM. ◆ 35 St. James's Pl. Tube: Green Park. 071/491.4840; fax 071/493.1264

**49 The Carlton** Built in 1827 by **Thomas Hopper,** this club for Conservative politicians is the domain of men, though **Margaret Thatcher,** of course, can enter, and her larger-than-life portrait hangs at the top of the double staircase inside. It was here that **W.E. Gladstone** was told by another member that he should be "pitched out of the window in the direction of the Reform Club." Today, the large drawing room overlooking St. James's Street is filled with ambitious young men dressed like **Sir Anthony Eden.** ◆ 69 St. James's St. Tube: Green Park. 071/493.1164

**49 Suntory** ★★$$$$ This is one of 10 restaurants in the world owned by the **Suntory Japanese Whiskey Company,** and the standards are nearly as high as the prices. Watch the chefs in the *teppanyaki* room dissect pieces of beef and seafood with mesmerizing skill. Everything gleams and sizzles with freshness. The Suntory's sushi has gotten a mixed reception; instead try its seasonal specialties, such as the beautiful fresh sardine and burdock tempura bound in *nori.* ◆ Japanese ◆ Lunch and dinner. Closed Sunday. 72-73 St. James's St. Tube: Green Park. 071/409.0201

**50 King Street** Completed in 1682, King Street's claim to fame was once the **St. James's Theatre,** which premiered **Oscar Wilde's** *Lady Windermere's Fan* and *The Importance of Being Earnest,* **Arthur Pinero's** *The Second Mrs. Tanqueray,* and, later, **Terence Rattigan's** *Separate Tables.* Unfortunately, the theater was demolished, even though **Vivien Leigh** interrupted a Parliamentary session in an attempt to save it. ◆ Between St. James's Sq and St. James's St. Tube: Green Park

**51 The Square** ★★$$$ In the middle of clubland and a stone's throw from the London Library, this restaurant gets too crowded—but that's a sign that delectable dishes are cooking in the kitchen. Try the grilled venison on broad and green beans followed by a caramelized banana tart. There's a commendable wine list, too. ◆ British ◆ Lunch and dinner; dinner only on Saturday and Sunday. 32 King St. Tube: Green Park. 071/839.8787

**52 Christie, Manson and Woods Ltd.** Better known simply as **Christie's,** this is one of the world's leading auction houses. In the art and antiques trade, **Sotheby's,** the largest auction house, is said to be run by businessmen

trying to be gentlemen, while Christie's is run by gentlemen trying to be businessmen. Founded in 1766, Christie's has occupied this address since 1823, except for a period during and after World War II when the building was under repair from damage suffered during the Blitz.

If you arrive in the morning (when sales are generally held), you may see millionaires battle over a **van Gogh** or **Picasso,** an emerald necklace, or a famous pop star's worldly goods. If very important paintings are being auctioned, representatives from the world's museums will be here, and the atmosphere will resemble a cross between a Broadway opening and an operating room, with the auctioneer both leading actor and surgeon. Items to be sold are on view in the rooms and galleries around the auction room; perusing them is like exploring an informal museum, with the bonus that if you lose your head over the 17th-century carpet or the sentimental Victorian watercolor of the girl and the rabbit, you can attend the sale and bid on it. Works of art and antiques aren't the only items to come under the hammer. From the start, Christie's has auctioned wine; it also sells vintage motorcars, tribal art, photographs, and stamps. For those whose haven't reached museum status, the auction houses now have premises that specialize in icons, non-masterpiece artwork, furniture, and carpets. ◆ M-F 9AM-5PM. 8 King St. Tube: Green Park. 071/839.9060; fax 071/839.1611. Also at: 85 Brompton Rd, South Kensington. 071/581.7611

**52 Spink & Son** These art dealers are reputed to be the largest in the world, specializing in coins, medals, Oriental and English art, fine gold, silver, and jewelry. The rooms have the atmosphere of a museum, but many of the treasures are affordable. The gallery exhibitions by living English artists deserve a look. ◆ Gold Bullion Department: M-F 9AM-4PM. Shop: M-F 9AM-5:30PM. 5-7 King St. Tube: Green Park. 071/930.7888

---

On rare days at home, the Queen is still surrounded at all times—by the famous corgis. Princess Diana describes the spectacle of her mother-in-law's canine guard as a "moving carpet," and servants invariably know the royal whereabouts by the noise of at least nine sets of paws pattering along the palace floors.

—*The Western Mail,* 9 August 1993

---

"London! It has the sound of distant thunder."

**James Bone,** London perambulator

---

**Restaurants/Clubs:** Red    **Hotels:** Blue
**Shops/** 🌳 **Outdoors:** Green    **Sights/Culture:** Black

**53 Lobb's** Four generations of Lobbs have shod the rich and famous since **John Lobb** walked from Cornwall to London to set himself up as a shoemaker. The list of distinguished feet served here is considerable: those of **Queen Victoria, Mountbatten, King George VI,** the current royals, **Cecil Beaton, Winston Churchill, Laurence Olivier, Groucho Marx, Frank Sinatra, Cole Porter,** and **Katharine Hepburn.**

In the basement of the shop, the wooden lasts of customers are kept until they die—and some for long after that. The construction method has changed little since Queen Victoria's day. The shoemakers draw an outline of your foot in their book, examine it from every angle in search of peculiarities, and then, on a long slip of paper, take a series of measurements, which are marked by snips in the paper. This is translated into wooden models of your feet, around which the leather is molded. After a few days of walking the streets of London, the hefty price may seem reasonable for shoes that fit perfectly. ♦ M-F 9AM-5:30PM; Sa 9AM-1PM. 9 St. James's St. Tube: Green Park. 071/930.3664

**53 St. James's Health Club** In keeping with the spirit of clubland, this is a men-only establishment. Male visitors who want to work off executive stress can pay a reasonable daily fee to use the sauna, steam room, and small gym, with towels and toiletries provided. Massages are also available. ♦ M-F 9:30AM-10PM; Sa 9:30AM-9PM; Su noon-9PM. 7 Byron House, 7-9 St. James's St. Tube: Green Park. 071/930.5568

**53 Lock & Co.** The house of Lock has been covering heads since 1679; it moved into this building in 1759. **Lord Nelson's** cocked hats were made here, and the **Duke of Wellington, Beau Brummell,** and all the American ambassadors to the Court of St. James's also purchased hats from Lock & Co. The first bowlers were produced here in 1850 for the gamekeepers of a **Mr. William Coke,** and the shop still refers to the style as a Coke. There are about 16,000 hats in stock, but you can have one custom-made with the French *conformateur* that has been used to determine head measurements for 150 years. The flat tweed caps are popular with English country-lovers such as **J.P. Donleavy** and **Prince Philip.** In fact, Lock holds Prince Philip's royal warrant and supplies older members of "The Firm," as the royals are affectionately known, with their tweed caps. **Paul McCartney** shops here, as does that Englishman personified, **Sir Alec Guinness,** but such Americans as **Elliott**

Gould and **Larry Hagman** have the good taste to shop here as well. ♦ M-F 9AM-5:30PM; Sa 9:30AM-12:30PM. 6 St. James's St. Tube: Green Park. 071/930.8874

**53 Overton's** ★★$$$ This old-fashioned, bow-windowed restaurant and oyster bar appeals to Anglophiles with a fondness for fish. Here are the English classics: smoked Scottish salmon, whitebait, and potted shrimps to begin, followed by Dover sole, turbot, halibut, salmon trout, and Scottish salmon. Stick to the grilled or poached dishes. The restaurant accommodates theatergoers by serving dinner from 6 to 11PM. ♦ British ♦ Lunch and dinner; dinner only on Saturday. 5 St. James's St. Tube: Green Park. 071/839.3774

**53 Berry Bros. and Rudd** A wonderful, Dickensian pile of a wine shop, with exquisite, strangely shaped black windows, Berry Bros. looks much as it did in the 18th century. The austere interior defies you to enter, but the brave souls who do step back in time. The long, dark room contains a large oval table, chairs, antique prints, a few bottles of wine, and a pair of enormous scales embossed with "The Coffee Mill," acquired from the grocer who originally occupied the site. Since the 1760s, clients have been weighing themselves on the scales, and their weights are recorded in the shop's ledgers. Weight-watching was serious business even in the days when corpulence signified prosperity. The **Duke of York,** who led his men up the hill and down again, weighed 14 1/2 stone (one stone is 14 pounds), but the weight of his brother, **King George IV,** famous for his large girth, is not recorded.

The wine, however, is what marks Berry Bros. and Rudd for posterity. The distinctive black-and-white labels have been appearing on bottles of claret for more than 200 years, and the cellars contain bottles that would fill many a Frenchman with awe. Consider a Julienas or a Moulin-à-Vent to take on a picnic in St. James's Park. Berry Bros. is also the developer and owner of **Cutty Sark** scotch whiskey. ♦ M-F 9:30AM-5:30PM. 3 St. James's St. Tube: Green Park. 071/839 9033

**54 Pickering Place** Timber wainscoting still lines this 18th-century alleyway. Halfway along Pickering Place is a plaque, "The Republic of Texas Legation 1842-45," commemorating the days when Texas was an independent republic and this was its embassy. It was rented to the Texans by **Berry Bros.** wine shop during a serious slump in the business of vintners. At the end of the alley is a court surrounded by houses that looks more like a cul-de-sac in a cathedral town than in the center of London. ♦ Between St. James's St and Pall Mall. Tube Green Park

**54 Crown Passage** Escape from elegance in a little haven of mediocrity. The sandwich bars serve ordinary sandwiches and awful coffee. A few antique and coin dealers are also on this lane. ♦ Between Pall Mall and King St. Tube: Green Park.

**55 Red Lion** ★★$ A popular spot, with the same name as the pub on the other side of St. James's Square, the Red Lion serves hearty home-cooked food. Tuck into fish-and-chips or a steak-and-ale pie in the restaurant upstairs. ♦ Pub ♦ Restaurant: lunch and dinner. Closed Saturday and Sunday. Pub: M-F 11AM-11PM; Sa 11AM-5PM. Crown Passage. Tube: Green Park. 071/930.4141

**56 Hardy Brothers Ltd.** This is considered London's finest shop for fishing tackle. **Queen Victoria** had a Hardy rod, as has every Prince of Wales this century, including **Prince Charles.** Hardy once developed a big-game reel for American novelist **Zane Grey,** which now goes for $7,000. You can buy a pair of hunter-green Wellingtons for considerably less. ♦ M-W, F 9AM-5PM; Th 9AM-6PM; Sa 9AM-4PM. 61 Pall Mall. 071/839.5515

**57 Oxford and Cambridge Club** This club is more democratic and less misogynistic than the others on Pall Mall, although true equality is yet to come. Out of a total membership of 4,000, women number only 500. They are called "women associate members" and cannot have lunch in the coffee room or read in the upstairs library or morning room bar. (It appears as though the club has no knowledge of the goings-on at Oxford and Cambridge, where distinctions of this kind have long been obliterated.) Nevertheless, it does offer reciprocal membership with numerous clubs in the United States, including the **University Club,** and lodging here costs a fraction of the rates at hotels. The dining rooms aren't fancy, but the wine lists are. The **Smirke** brothers built this headquarters in 1837. ♦ 71 Pall Mall. Tube: Green Park. 071/930.5151

**58 Schomberg House** The St. James's Street end of Pall Mall boasts a rare example of Queen Anne architecture. The warm brown-red brick, tall Dutch windows, and human scale of this house, built around 1698, come as a relief after the imposing Italianate stones and stucco that dominate this area. **Gainsborough** lived out his last years here, dying in 1788 after finally reconciling with his old friend and enemy **Joshua Reynolds.** His parting words were, "We are all going to Heaven and Van Dyck is of the company." After World War II, the house was gutted and filled with modern offices. Next door is the site of a house that belonged to the charming actress **Nell Gwyn,** mistress of **Charles II.** All the property on Pall Mall belongs to the Crown, with the exception of **No. 79,** because Gwyn refused to live in a house she didn't own. ♦ 82 Pall Mall. Tube: Green Park

COURTESY OF DAVID GENTLEMAN

**59 St. James's Palace** The whole St. James's area owes its development to the Palace of St. James's (whose name comes from the Augustinian hospital for leprous women that stood on this site in the 13th century). **Henry VIII** purchased the land in 1532 to build a small royal palace—initially a hunting lodge (he also enclosed some 300 acres to the south) and later his third royal residence. After the fall of **Cardinal Wolsey,** Henry switched his allegiance to **Whitehall Palace,** channeling his great energy and imagination into enlarging that royal abode even further. Even so, he regarded the rambling brick mansion called St. James's Palace (shown above) with affection. Feminine appreciation for the palace is suggested in its history of royal births— **Charles II, James II, Mary II,** and **Queen Anne** were all born at St. James's in the 1600s. Charles II never liked Whitehall, so he spent time, energy, and money building up St. James's. But it did not become the official residence of the sovereign until 1698, when Whitehall Palace burned down. It remained the monarch's London residence until **Queen Victoria** ascended to the throne in 1837 and moved the court, under strong pressure from her prime minister, to **Buckingham Palace.** Yet St. James's maintains a presence in modern British life. To this day, all foreign ambassadors present "their credentials" to the Court of St. James's before riding in the Glass Coach to Buckingham Palace.

The palace originally had four courts, but fire, rebuilding, and time have cut the number in half. The state rooms, which can be seen over the wall facing the Mall, were rebuilt by **Sir Christopher Wren** in 1703. The most charming surviving part of the Tudor palace is the gatehouse, with its octagonal clock tower, which faces St. James's Street. This four-story building of worn red brick sits astride a pair of vast old gates. The turrets crowned with battlements and the sentry box manned by a handsome soldier from the Guards seem too "Gilbert and Sullivan" to be true, but their anachronistic presence is a reminder of the pomp for which St. James's exists. ♦ Pall Mall. Tube: Green Park, St. James's Park

**60 Chapel Royal** This lovely chapel, west of the gatehouse at St. James's Palace, was built by **Henry VIII** in 1532. It is one of the great gems of Tudor London, with a coffered ceiling painted by **Hans Holbein.** Married beneath it were **William III** and **Mary II** (1677), **Queen Anne** (1683), **George IV** (1795), **Queen Victoria** (1840), and **George V** (1893). But what stirs the heart most is not the royal weddings, but **Charles I,** the sad, brave king who received communion in the chapel on the morning of his execution, 30 January 1649. This is one of five Chapels Royal in London, and as such, it is not subject to a bishop but owes its allegiance directly to the sovereign. Visitors can attend services in the chapel every Sunday from October until Easter. ♦ Su 8:30AM, 11:15AM Jan-Good Friday, Oct-Dec. Ambassadors' Court, St. James's Palace, Pall Mall. Tube: Green Park, St. James's Park

**61 Queen's Chapel** This 17th-century architectural gem by **Inigo Jones** was the first church built in the classical style; like Banqueting House in Whitehall, also by Jones, the interior is a perfect cube. The chapel was built for the **Spanish Infanta,** intended bride of **Charles I,** and then became the chapel of his wife, **Henrietta Maria,** also a Roman Catholic. Now it is one of five Chapels Royal. The gold-and-white coffered ceiling is original. On summer Sundays, the chapel is marvelously lit by the sun through the wide Venetian window, which occupies the entire east wall. ♦ Services Su 8:30AM, 11:15AM Easter-July. Marlborough Rd. Tube: Green Park, St. James's Park

**62 Friary Court** Every new sovereign is proclaimed from the balcony in this courtyard, and it was from here that the cheers of her subjects reached the ears of 18-year-old **Queen Victoria,** causing her to weep. The **State Apartments,** reached through the door in the northeast corner, are open only on special occasions, usually when royal gifts are on display, and the wait can be considerable. The **Armoury Room** is lined with ancient weapons, and the **Tapestry Room** with pictorial textiles woven for **Charles II.** The last person to have a hand at decorating these rooms was **William Morris** in the 1860s, an inspired choice by someone in the Queen's household, for the Morris genius was perfectly suited to the Tudor proportions. ♦ St. James's Palace, Pall Mall. Tube: Green Park, St. James's Park

"The English have an extraordinary ability for flying into a great calm."

**Alexander Woollcott**

**63 Marlborough House** Sir Christopher Wren built this residence (shown here) for **John Churchill,** first Duke of Marlborough, between 1709 and 1711—though it was more for the Duchess than for the Duke. Formidable, turbulent, brilliant, and beautiful, **Sarah Churchill,** first Duchess of Marlborough and lady-in-waiting as well as intimate friend of **Queen Anne,** laid the inscribed foundation stone that survives within the house. The Duchess had hated the monumental palace of **Blenheim** (which Queen Anne created for the Duke after his victory at the Battle of Blenheim), so she instructed Wren to make her London mansion strong, plain, and convenient. The Crown acquired the house in 1817. Unfortunately, the pure simplicity created by Wren has been disguised by the additions and enlargements made in the early 1860s by **James Pennethorne. Edward VII** lived here while he was Prince of Wales. **George V** was born in the house, and his consort, **Queen Mary,** lived here during her widowhood. In 1959, **Queen Elizabeth** presented the house to the nation so that it could become the **Commonwealth Conference Center** in London. ♦ Under restoration; currently closed to the public. Pall Mall (adjacent to St. James's Palace). Tube: Green Park, St. James's Park. 071/839.3411

**64 Clarence House** This house was built for the Duke of Clarence, later **King William IV.** Until **Queen Elizabeth's** accession to the throne in 1952, she and **Prince Philip** lived here. Now it is the dwelling of both the **Queen Mother,** who comes to the gate to greet the public on her birthday, 4 August, and her eldest grandson, **Prince Charles,** whose wife and sons live two miles away in **Kensington Palace.** When the Queen Mum is in residence, a lone bagpiper plays in the garden at 9AM, a gentle Scottish alarm clock for one of the best-loved members of the royal family. ♦ Pall Mall (west side of St. James's Palace). Tube: Green Park, St. James's Park

**65 Lancaster House** In 1825, **Benjamin Dean Wyatt** started construction of this house in light Bath stone for the **Duke of York,** who commissioned the extravagant home but died before paying for it, whereupon it was sold to the **Marquess of Stafford** (hence the structure was first called **York House** and then **Stafford House**). **Robert Smirke** completed it in 1840, and **Charles Barry** designed the interior. **Chopin** played for **Queen Victoria** in the **Music Room,** and the **Duke of Windsor** lived here when he was the Prince of Wales (from 1919 to 1930). Since being restored from war damage, the building has been a venue for state banquets and conferences. The Louis XV interiors are among the most sumptuous in London. ♦ Stable Yard Rd and Queen's Walk. Tube: Green Park, St. James's Park

**66 St. James's Park** In the 16th century, **Henry VIII** enclosed this, the oldest and most perfect of royal parks, which today comprises 93 acres and an enchantment of water, birds, views, gaslights, and Englishness. It is a royal park in the best sense of the word: monarchs have lavished their wealth and ingenuity on it, making it a graceful, contemplative place. Henry VIII drained the marshland between St. James's and Whitehall palaces to make a forest and deer-hunting park. **Charles I** created the ceremonious walks, and he strode bravely across the park to his execution. His son, **Charles II**, created what you see today; he hired French landscape gardener **André Le Nôtre** and, shortly after the Restoration, opened this exotic oasis of trees, flowers, ducks, geese, and pelicans to the public. In 1827, **George IV** enlisted **John Nash** to reshape the canal and create the meandering lake, spanned by a bridge that grants magical views of Whitehall and Buckingham palaces. Daily at 3PM the distinguished pelicans appear for an afternoon tea of whiting and other aquatic delicacies; they are direct descendants of the pair given to Charles II by a Russian ambassador. On the south side of the park runs **Birdcage Walk,** named for the aviaries Charles II established here for his amusement. ♦ Bounded by The Mall and Horse Guards Rd, and Birdcage Walk and Spur Rd. Tube: St. James's Park

**67 Buckingham Palace** The Royal Palace is the most looked-at building in London, not because of its magnificence (it is not very magnificent) and not because of its age (there are plenty of older buildings to see). The wistful gazes are inspired by the appealing mystique of the monarchy—and as **Maude** declared to her young lover in *Harold and Maude,* "We may not believe in monarchy, but we miss the kings and queens."

This is the oldest monarchy of all, and it resides in the last country in the world where monarchy exists on a grand and sanctified scale, with religious processions, a titled and healthy aristocracy—and, as the **Prince** and **Princess of Wales** prove, the adulation and reciprocal censure from the country's (if not the world's) people, which transcends nationality, social class, and party affiliation.

Her Most Excellent Majesty **Elizabeth the Second,** by the Grace of God, of the United Kingdom of Great Britain and Northern Ireland and of her Realms and Territories Queen, Head of the Commonwealth, Defender of the Faith, Sovereign of the British Orders of Knighthood, is the 40th monarch since the Norman Conquest, descended from **Charlemagne** and **King Canute.** Her accession in 1952 coincided with the beginning of the end of the British Empire, and she has presided over its dissolution with noble leadership. She is probably one of the best-informed diplomats alive today, having had continuous access to world leaders for 38 years. She has known **Churchill, Khrushchev,** and **Eisenhower,** and is acquainted with every major head of state around the globe. On Tuesday nights when she is in London, the prime minister goes to Buckingham Palace for a talk with her. The Queen's concern, excellent memory, and sharp insight have been appreciated by almost all the prime ministers of her reign.

Will she retire and turn the business over to her eldest son? The answer is no. The Queen is Queen for life, and the monarchy's continuity and survival depend on adherence to its spiritual laws: under the hereditary system, the last intake of breath by the dying sovereign coincides with the next intake by the living sovereign, hence the ancient cry, "The King is dead. Long live the King."

*Buckingham Palace*

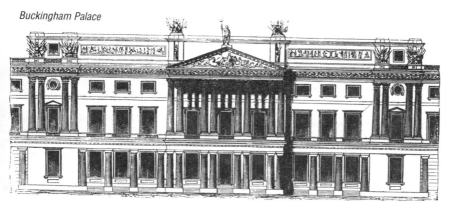

*Buckingham Palace*

When the Queen is in residence at Buckingham Palace, the royal standard flies overhead. The visitor's viewpoint is the rather dour eastern facade, completely rebuilt by **Sir Aston Webb** in 1913. The front western facade, visible only from a helicopter, is by **John Nash,** the palace's first architect (Nash began the building in 1820, and **Edmund Blore** finished it). The main building is flanked by two classical pavilions and overlooks an immense sweep of lawn, 45 acres of private gardens, woodlands, giant trees, more than 200 species of wild plants, a lake graced with pink flamingos, a leafy border, and tennis courts. This is where the Queen's garden parties are held each summer.

The original redbrick house, built for the Duke and Duchess of Buckingham in 1703, was bought by **George III** some 60 years later for his beloved **Queen Charlotte,** who filled it with children and made it into a family home, which became known as **Queen's House. George IV** commissioned Nash to make it into a residence worthy of a monarch, but the plans became grander and more difficult to execute with time. The transformation process had many of the elements of a Laurel and Hardy film, not the least being the scheme to surround the palace with scaffolding to disguise the fact that a new palace was being constructed, as Parliament had granted permission only for renovations and repairs. When the King died, an investigation into the palace's spiraling costs revealed financial irregularities. Nash, who had transformed London into a royal and elegant city, was dismissed by an outraged Parliament. Publicly disgraced, he died in 1835.

**William IV** was displeased with the work of Nash's successor, Blore, and offered the palace to Parliament as a permanent home following the fire that destroyed Westminster in 1834. When the government refused, William, claiming the air at **Kensington Palace** was better for his asthma, stayed there until his death.

Buckingham Palace became the official London residence of the sovereign in 1837, when **Queen Victoria** moved in. Those first days in her new home must have been a shock, because the drains did not work, the toilets weren't ventilated, and many of the 600 doors and 1,000 windows would not open and close. Yet the royal standard flew as repairs were made, and the Queen and her consort **Prince Albert** extended the palace, building the **State Supper Room** and the **Ball Room.** The Queen also had the marble arch removed from the front of the palace and placed at its present site on the north side of Hyde Park. By 1843, Victoria had written in her diary that she was very happy here.

Webb, architect for **George V** and his popular wife, **Mary of Teck,** transformed the facade of Buckingham Palace, replacing the flaking Caen stone with Portland stone and adding the French-inspired pilasters. George V also saw the 1911 unveiling of the **Victoria Memorial** in front of the palace: a sentimental wedding cake of a sculpture by **Sir Thomas Brock,** it features a seated Queen Victoria (13 feet high) facing the Mall, surrounded by the figures of Truth, Justice, and Motherhood— all dear to the Queen's heart. At the top, glistening in gold, Victory is attended by Constancy and Courage. It may suffer from Victorian sentimentality, but it is hard to imagine Buckingham Palace without it.

After much dithering and debate, word has finally come down that Buckingham Palace will be open to the public during the months of August and September in 1994. Seven thousand tickets will be sold each day on a first-come, first-served basis; visitors will be given a time at which they can enter. Eighteen major rooms, including the State Rooms, will be available for viewing. The **Changing of the Guard** now takes place at 11:30AM on alternate days throughout the year; the ceremony starts at 11:30AM inside the palace railings. ♦ Ticket office: daily 9AM until all tickets are sold. Palace: daily 9:30AM-5:30PM Aug-Sept. 071/930.5526. Information on Changing of the Guard: 0839/123411 (premium rate call). Tube: St. James's Park, Victoria, Green Park

**68 Queen's Gallery** This royal treasure chest, built by **John Nash** in 1830, was originally a conservatory and then a chapel. Her Majesty established it as an art gallery in 1962. There are continuous exhibitions, imaginative and scholarly, of the grand gifts to—and magnificent heirlooms of—the British monarchy, including paintings, drawings, sculptures, silver, cutlery, and furniture. The painting exhibitions change every 18 months, and there is also a shop inside for royalty fans. ♦ Admission; one admission ticket to both the Queen's Gallery and the Royal Mews is also available. Tu-Sa 10AM-5PM; Su 2-5PM. Shop: Tu-Sa 10AM-5PM. Buckingham Gate, Buckingham Palace Rd. 071/930.4832

**69 Royal Mews** All seven state carriages and coaches from all periods are on display in this circa-1826 building by **John Nash;** this is probably the finest and most valuable collection of state coaches in the world. Here is the **State Coach** acquired by **George II** in 1762 that is still in use today. It looks like the enchanted coach from *Cinderella,* with elaborate carvings representing eight palm trees, branching at the top and supporting the roof, and three cherubs, representing England, Scotland, and Ireland. It is 24 feet long, 8 feet wide, 12 feet high, and weighs 4 tons. The Royal Mews is also the home of the **Royal Horses,** which may be seen pulling carriages in Hyde Park around 10AM each morning. ♦ Admission. W noon-4PM Oct-Mar; W-Th noon-4PM Apr-July; W-F noon-4PM July to mid-Sept. Buckingham Palace Rd. 071/930.4832

**70 The Goring** $$$ Just behind the Queen's House is another family-run dwelling, albeit on a smaller scale. The **Goring** family has owned this old-fashioned hotel for nearly 80 years and regularly receives plaudits for its central location and high standards. There is a beautiful private garden, and the stylishly furnished rooms have solid marble bathrooms. The lobby areas are classically decorated and welcoming. ♦ 15 Beeston Pl, Grosvenor Gardens. 071/396.9000; fax 071/834.4393

Within The Goring:

**The Goring Restaurant** ★★$$ The meals live up to reasonable standards—not too expensive, and there's a tasty guinea fowl with stir-fried vegetables on the menu. Clarets and coffee are served. ♦ British ♦ Lunch and dinner. Closed Saturday. 071/396.9000

**71 Westminster Cathedral** Coming across this distinctive red-and-white structure is a sweet surprise, especially after the thundering traffic that surrounds nearby Victoria Station. The location is a shame, since the cathedral, the principal Roman Catholic church in England, is often overlooked. By London standards, it came on the scene relatively late, begun in 1894 by **John Bentley** at the behest of **Archbishop Herbert Vaughan,** who demanded something entirely different from Westminster Abbey. The Archbishop got what he wanted: Bentley mixed Romanesque and Byzantine influences, just as he mixed red brick with white Portland stone. The result is somewhat Venetian. Within, side chapels are decked with glowing mosaics, and there is a bronze by **Elizabeth Frink.** The view from **St. Edward's Tower,** a 273-foot campanile, is stunning. ♦ Admission for concerts; free for sightseeing. Daily 6:30AM-7PM winter; daily 6:30AM-8PM summer. Ambrosden Ave and Francis St. Tube: Victoria, St. James's Park. 071/834.7452

### Bests

**Robert Farago**
Hypnotherapist

Walking—anywhere.

Zapping sprightly children and lumbering adults with a laser gun at **Quasar** in Trocadero mall at Piccadilly Circus.

Watching any big, stupid, or violent 70mm American movie on Europe's largest cinema screen at **The Odeon,** Marble Arch.

Hypnotizing arachnophobics at the **London Zoo,** then watching them fall in love with the Mexican red-kneed, bird-eating spider.

Browsing at **Asprey's** on Bond Street for the world's most expensive and tasteless objets d'art.

Going for a death march through **Hampstead Heath,** then staggering back to **Louis Patisserie** in Hampstead for a life-saving peppermint tea.

Enjoying a **West End** play—anything as long as it's not a musical!

Cruising **King's Road/Chelsea** on my Harley-Davidson.

Eating organic steak or lamb from **Hampstead Butchers.**

Doing self-hypnosis lying in a deck chair, overlooking the lake at **Regent's Park,** on a sunny day.

# Mayfair/ Piccadilly

From its risqué beginning as the site of a ribald 17th-century festival, **Mayfair** has grown into one of the most desirable of London addresses. Bordered to the north and east by celebrated shopping thoroughfares **Oxford Street** and **Regent Street**, to the south by charismatic **Piccadilly**, and to the west by frenetic but fashionable **Park Lane**, this neighborhood is a playground for the wealthy. Such affluence grew from an initial half dozen estates. The owners, landed aristocrats, laid out the rectangular area in orderly patterns of generous avenues and stately squares, and lined them with their elegant mansions—which, of course, were equipped with mews in back for horses and carriages. After the rich and famous came the suppliers to the rich and famous; soon the district contained elite merchants as well as their prosperous patrons.

Today, diplomats from **Grosvenor Square** and financial magnates from **Brook Street** have replaced the dukes and duchesses, but the aristocratic ambience lingers. Mayfair and Park Lane are still the most expensive,

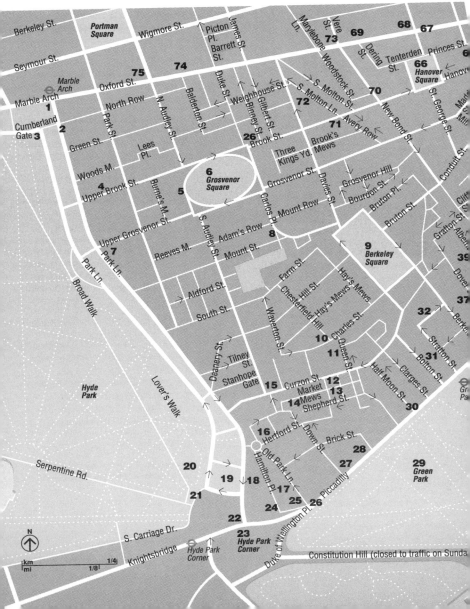

exclusive properties on Britain's Monopoly board, with the retail meccas of Oxford, **Bond**, and Regent streets close behind. Dotted in between are some of the most luxurious hotels and restaurants the pound can buy. To the south lies the "Magic Mile" of Piccadilly, named for a fashionable 17th-century collar called a "picadil." The street begins at **Hyde Park Corner** in an atmosphere of respectability, then coasts past the verdant **Green Park; The Ritz,** with its "romantic getaway" mystique; and tranquil **St. James's Church.** But as Piccadilly approaches the beloved statue of **Eros,** a popular meeting place in the center of **Piccadilly Circus,** the grandeur diminishes. Piccadilly Circus has consistently defied attempts to make it dignified. Confusion, traffic, and neon compose the scene (no wonder they call it a circus), yet Londoners and visitors fiercely defend this traffic circle cum meeting place and continue to flock here for conversation at the feet of the God of Love.

The best time to see Piccadilly is on a weekday, when the English gentry is on the prowl for cashmere sweaters and other such necessities. You can also observe a few of the blue bloods' haunts: the headquarters of London's cafe society (**Langans Brasserie** and **Café Royal**), one of the most beautiful dining rooms in the world (**Louis XVI Restaurant**), a Regency shopping center (the **Burlington Arcade**), what is probably the world's most opulent grocery store (**Fortnum & Mason**), and one of London's most intriguing galleries (the **Royal Academy of Arts**). Head back to Mayfair for afternoon tea at **Brown's Hotel,** and you will have indulged for a time in the upper-crust experience.

**1 Marble Arch** Built in 1827 by **John Nash,** this version of Rome's **Arch of Constantine** was originally meant to be a gateway to Buckingham Palace. Unfortunately, the royal coaches couldn't squeeze through, so the arch was built on the former location of the **Tyburn Gallows,** London's main site for public executions until the 18th century. Only the royal family and the King's Troop Royal Horse Artillery may pass through Marble Arch. However, the traffic incessantly whirling past tends to negate its dignity. ♦ Oxford and Park Lns. Tube: Marble Arch

**2 Park Lane** Once a narrow strip between a green oasis and prominent grand houses, Park Lane is now a hectic four-lane thoroughfare that runs past high-rise hotels and offices. From the 18th century onward, this street has been associated with wealth, though today's version is more the conglomerate than the private kind. Take a taxi ride here in the evening and you're likely to come across limos dropping off debutantes for a charity ball or powerful executives for a gala dinner; at any rate, you'll see a lot of slicked hair, tailcoats, and flowing gowns. ♦ Tube: Marble Arch, Hyde Park Corner

**3 Speakers' Corner** Oratory at the famous northeastern corner of Hyde Park dates back to 1872, when mass demonstrations at the site (against a proposed Sunday Trading Bill) led to the established right of assembly. The Corner is liveliest on Sunday mornings, and hecklers are part of the show. ◆ Tube: Marble Arch

**4 Le Gavroche** ★★★★$$$$ *The Good Food Guide* voted this one of London's top two restaurants in 1993. The justifiably renowned **Michel Roux** can be found in the kitchens producing divine recipes based on regional French cooking. Million-dollar deals are struck here as property developers bargain across the lunch table, while diplomats from the American Embassy speak softly in the green-and-copper basement rooms. Try the lobster salad, a wondrous concoction with gulls' eggs, followed by a white chocolate mousse with passion fruit sauce for dessert. Stick with the cheaper end of the fabulously expensive wine list. ◆ French ◆ Lunch and dinner. Closed Saturday and Sunday. 43 Upper Brook St. Jacket and tie required. Reservations required. Tube: Marble Arch. 071/408.0881

**5 American Embassy** The design of **Eero Saarinen's** bunkerlike embassy, completed in 1959, has few fans, especially since Georgian town houses were demolished for its construction. The **Duke of Westminster** still owns this land in the area known as "Little America," so even if it is the largest embassy in Britain (with 5.85 acres of floor space), it's also probably one of the only American embassies not to stand on "American" soil. Note the gigantic bald eagle on top; its wingspan is approximately 35 feet. ◆ 24 Grosvenor Sq (at S. Audley St). Tube: Bond St, Marble Arch. 071/499.9000

**6 Grosvenor Square** The largest square in London after Lincoln's Inn Fields, this was once the grandest address the capital could offer. In 1710, **Sir Richard Grosvenor** procured an act allowing him to build on his property, a group of fields in the area between Oxford Street and Park Lane. The entire estate was planned as a unit, with architecturally imposing Grosvenor Square at its heart. **Colen Campbell** designed the east side with uniform houses, but the rest grew up in a variety of Georgian styles, all overlooking a central formal garden said to have been laid out by **William Kent.** Today, fancy additions and rebuilding have erased the architectural consistency, and the garden is merely a swath of pleasant green, watched over by **William Reid Dick's** bronze of **Franklin Delano Roosevelt.** ◆ Tube: Bond St, Marble Arch

**7 Grosvenor House Hotel** $$$ The annual **Grosvenor House Antiques Fair** is held in this grand hotel, whose 454 luxurious bedrooms are desirable for the view over Hyde Park

alone. Nevertheless, it is the kitchens of the Grosvenor that have most elevated the hotel's reputation. ◆ 90 Park Ln. 071/499.6363; fax 071/493.3341

Within the Grosvenor House Hotel:

**The Pavilion Restaurant** ★★$$ Sorrel and ricotta soup, cod cooked with grain mustard, and pork rillettes with prune chutney are prepared by chef **Sean Davies** in an open kitchen and served in a colonial dining room. ◆ Continental ◆ Breakfast, lunch, and dinner; dinner only on Saturday. Closed Sunday. 071/499.6363

**Pasta Vino** ★★$$ Chef **Pino Longorso** concocts such Italian specialties as *penne al quattro formaggi,* veal scallopine with lemon and white wine, and tuna with onions, peppers and capers. The prix-fixe menu is "set to rise only by one penny a year." ◆ Italian ◆ Lunch and dinner. Closed Sunday. 071/499.6363

**Nico at 90** ★★★$$$ **Nico Ladenis** is the favorite chef of many London epicures. Some say his latest enterprise, named for its address, is London's finest restaurant. The Dover sole with wild mushroom sauce proves an excellent sample of the master's work. The wine list is likewise superb. ◆ French ◆ Lunch and dinner. Closed Saturday and Sunday. Reservations required. 071/409.1290; fax 071/355.4877

**8 Connaught** $$$$ Unless you know someone who has stayed at this hotel, it's almost impossible to get a room. The select guests—and the lucky ones—will feel like they're spending the night in a deliciously comfortable, English country mansion. All the bedrooms are different, with oil paintings, antiques, and flowers everywhere, and an open fire warms the sitting rooms. ◆ 16 Carlos Pl. Tube: Bond St. 071/499.7070; fax 071/495.3262

Within the Connaught:

**The Connaught Restaurant** ★★★★$$$ Allow plenty of time for dinner because some of the dishes take an hour to prepare. This restaurant is considered the most consistent town and the last bastion of traditional food, served on crisp linen tablecloths. Chef **Michel Bourdin's** French haute cuisine exemplifies what a master can do with roasted lamb, guinea fowl, calf's liver, and the ultimate dessert: bread-and-butter pudding. The *paillard de sauman Jean Trosgrois* (every word on the menu is in French) is recommended. The vintage ports here are truly vintage, and the wine is as expensive as it gets. ◆ French ◆ Lunch and dinner. Jacket and tie required. Reservations required. 071/499.7070

**9 Berkeley Square** Like Grosvenor Square, this Georgian square is associated with the rich and famous. In the late 1890s, **Waldorf Astor** lived at **No. 54,** followed by departmen

store tycoon **Gordon Selfridge,** whose legacy stands in Oxford Street. More recently, in the early 1970s, the elusive **Lord Lucan** played poker at **The Clermont Club. No. 44,** built by **William Kent,** is said to be the finest remaining example of a Georgian terraced house in central London. Centuries-old plane trees shade the west side of the square, where privileged young men and women sip champagne at the annual **Berkeley Square Ball.** You might want to find a spot here to sit and read **Michael Arlen's** 1923 short story, "A Nightingale Sang in Berkeley Square." ♦ Berkeley and Charles Sts. Tube: Green Park

**10 English-Speaking Union (ESU)** U.S. **Ambassador Charles Price II** called the ESU "without doubt the most effective and vigorous private group linking the United Kingdom, the United States, and many other nations in a worldwide effort to improve mutual understanding." Its headquarters—draped with both the Union Jack and the Stars and Stripes—has been located in **Dartmouth House** since 1927. The house dates to 1890, and a number of British aristocrats, including the **Earl of Dartmouth,** have resided here. Today, in addition to providing an assortment of educational opportunities and exchanges, the building hosts cultural activities—concerts, readings, lectures, and dramatic events, not to mention the annual **George Washington Ball.** ♦ M-F 8:30AM-8:30PM. 37 Charles St. Tube: Green Park. 071/493.3328

**11 Zen Central** ★★$$$ This chic noshing hole serves nouvelle Chinese food in designer surroundings. The customers are as fascinating to watch as the food is to eat. ♦ Chinese ♦ Lunch and dinner. 20 Queen St Mayfair. Tube: Green Park. 071/629.8089

**12 Shepherd's Market** The best way to reach this tiny square, filled with small white houses, boutiques, restaurants, and pubs, is from Curzon Street, through the covered passage at **No. 47.** This is the site of the infamous **May Fair,** begun by **Lord St. Albans** in 1686 and described on a local shop wall as "that most pestilent nursery of impiety and vice." In 1735, **Edward Shepherd** obtained a grant from **George II** for a marketplace to be located on the former grounds of the revelry. Although the market sent most of the bawdiness elsewhere, upscale ladies of ill repute are still occasionally seen flitting from doorway to doorway like beautiful ghosts. ♦ Queen St Mayfair and Curzon St. Tube: Green Park

**13 Al Hamra** ★★★$$ Many patrons think Al Hamra has the best Lebanese food this side of Beirut. The tabbouleh, *hummus,* and *f'ul medames* (broad beans sprinkled with parsley, olive oil, lemon juice, and garlic) are as well-presented as they are tasty, and the

*basturma* (lean smoked beef) is delicious. ♦ Lebanese ♦ Lunch and dinner. 31-33 Shepherd's Market. Reservations recommended. 071/439.1954

**14 L'Artiste Musclé** ★★$ Known as "The Muscley Artist" to the students and weary businesspeople who come here to regroup, this bistro feels like a Left Bank wine bar, complete with sullen French waitresses. Sit in the tiny upstairs dining room or at a bare wooden table in the wonderfully bohemian cellar; both areas fill quickly after 8PM. Beef bourguignonne and salmon steak are good choices, and there's *tiramisù* for dessert. Wine can be enjoyed at fair prices; pay a little more for the best. ♦ French ♦ Lunch and dinner; dinner only on Sunday. 1 Shepherds Market. 071/439.6150

**15 Les Saveurs** ★★★$$$ Don't let the stark dining room dissuade you from a truly exquisite experience. A young team prepares elegant dishes based on French cuisine but enhanced and individualized with Eastern spices. Consider the risotto of Dublin Bay prawns with truffle oil and the pigeon-breast ravioli with mushrooms. Then have a look at the selection of Rhône and Burgundy wines. Perhaps a trifle expensive in the evening, Les Saveurs' set lunch is one of the best bargains in town. ♦ French ♦ Lunch and dinner. Closed Saturday and Sunday. 37A Curzon St. Reservations recommended. Tube: Green Park, Hyde Park Corner. 071/491.8919

**16 London Hilton** $$$$ A range of options in the hotel's 486 rooms allow guests to select special treatment in the VIP club (with complimentary breakfast, drinks throughout the day, afternoon tea, and canapés), but club membership doesn't come cheap. The service is what you would expect from one of London's classier establishments, and the decor has been extensively refurbished. ♦ 22 Park Ln. Tube: Hyde Park Corner. 071/493.8000; fax 071/493.4957

Within the London Hilton:

**Windows on the World** ★★$$$$ The best part of the Hilton is this restaurant, which has a marvelous view across London, Hyde Park, and even into the Queen's backyard at Buckingham Palace. Go for the cold food at lunchtime, when fans of the royals can peek at the occasional garden party. Avoid stopping for a quick cup of coffee in the **Brasserie,** or it will be the most expensive one you'll drink in London. **Trader Vic's** cocktail bar and restaurant serves Polynesian food in the basement. ♦ French ♦ Lunch and dinner; dinner only on Saturday; lunch only on Sunday. Jacket and tie required for dinner. Reservations recommended. 071/493.8000

---

**Restaurants/Clubs:** Red    **Hotels:** Blue
Shops/ ♠ Outdoors: Green    **Sights/Culture:** Black

**17 Four Seasons Hotel** $$$$ Known until recently as the **Inn on the Park,** the Four Seasons is suffused with the elegance of past eras. A stay here is a bit like traveling first class on a 1930s ocean liner decorated with fabulous antiques. **Howard Hughes** was a guest in his declining and difficult years, so the service has a pretty solid track record. Starting at 3PM, afternoon tea is served in the ground-floor lounge, all sweetness and light, with harp or piano music in the background and views of the hotel's private gardens. You'll enjoy the largest choice of teas in London, as well as a filling sequence of sandwiches, scones, and pastries. ♦ Hamilton Pl. Tube: Hyde Park Corner. 071/499.0888; fax 071/493.1895

Within the Four Seasons Hotel:

**Four Seasons** ★★★$$$$ Unflappable gastronomes have been known to get excited about this restaurant. Former chef **Bruno Loubet** has been replaced by **Christopher Nouvelli,** who presides over a long, intricate, some might say extravagant, menu. The spit-roasted chicken with *boudin blanc* and morels is divine. On hot days, ask for one of the spectacular salads. There is a minute private garden to look at, and an extensive wine list. Customers are asked to leave their portable phones with the manager. ♦ French ♦ Lunch and dinner. Jacket and tie required for dinner. 071/499.0888 ext 3172

**Lanes** ★★$$$ Try the prix-fixe buffet for lunch. After dark the restaurant is transformed into a smart venue offering light post-theater suppers. The grilled monkfish is delicious. ♦ Modern British ♦ Breakfast, lunch, and dinner; dinner only on Sunday. 071/499.0888

**18 The Dorchester** $$$$ Opulence was the keynote of the hotel's multimillion dollar restoration, as befits the expectations of its owner, the **Sultan of Brunei,** who is the richest man in the world. The imposing foyer has a black-and-white marble floor, while the long, marble-pillared **Promenade** is one of the best places to have afternoon tea in London. Many of the 248 bedrooms and suites, which are listed with the historical society, have been returned to their original splendor (they were created by **Curtis Green** from 1928 to 1931), and some of the rooftop suites are spectacular. The luxurious bathrooms have white Italian marble and—incredible for England—powerful showers. ♦ 53 Park Ln. Tube: Hyde Park Corner. 071/629.8888; fax 071/409.0114

Within The Dorchester:

**The Grill Room** ★★★$$$ The emphasis is on British food—roast beef with Yorkshire pudding, saddle of lamb, shepherd's pie—stylishly served from beautiful carving trolleys. Follow a hearty entrée with some delights from the English cheese board. Health-conscious diners will be pleased to know there's a low-cholesterol menu. The breakfasts served here are as superior as the rest of the hotel: egg-and-bacon lovers should splurge on the traditional English, while heart-rate watchers can go for fruits and whole-grain cereals. ♦ British ♦ Breakfast, lunch, and dinner. Reservations recommended. 071/629.8888

**The Terrace** ★★★$$$$ When you book ask for a table in the central gazebo, where you can eat a private supper out of sight of other couples, serenaded by a dance band or a pianist until 1AM. The cooking is modern, international, and divine—but breathtakingly expensive. Start with the mousseline of Scottish salmon with caviar and follow with the roasted breast of Barbary duck. Desserts like *tiramisù* will tempt even the health nuts in your party. ♦ French ♦ Dinner. Closed Sunday and Monday. Jacket and tie required for dinner. Reservations recommended. 071/629.8888

**Oriental Room** ★★★$$ Under the watchful eye of *chef des cuisines* **Willi Elsener,** this exclusive and expensive Chinese restaurant has earned plaudits from the critics. Try the delicious dim sum at lunchtime, or, if you're feeling especially flush, have a luxurious nibble of abalone. ♦ Chinese ♦ Lunch and dinner; dinner only on Saturday. Closed Sunday. 071/629.8888

**19 Statue of Lord Byron and his Dog** **Richard Belt's** feeble and boring statue of the poet, created in 1880, is separated from the *Statue of Achilles* by Park Lane. It was chosen by sentimental Victorians who rejected the artist most suited to re-create Byron, **Rodin.** ♦ Bounded by Achilles Wy, Curzon Gate, and Park Ln. Tube: Hyde Park Corner

**20 Statue of Achilles** Behind Apsley House in Hyde Park is a memorial to the **Duke of Wellington** financed by the **Ladies of England.** The statue was cast from French cannons captured at Salamanca, Vitoria, and Waterloo by **Sir Richard Westmacott** in 1822. At one time *Achilles'* flagrant nudity was a shock (a fig leaf was even added to protect Victorian sensibilities). ♦ SE corner of Hyde Park. Tube: Hyde Park Corner

**21 Queen Elizabeth Gate** The name refers not to the present sovereign but to her mother, affectionately known as the "Queen Mum." The frilly wrought-iron gates, designed by **Giuseppe Lund,** were erected in 1993, along with sculpture by **David Wynne.** The installation has provoked controversy, but the Queen Mother herself seemed pleased. ♦ Behind Apsley House. Tube: Hyde Park Corner

**22 Apsley House (The Wellington Museum)** Although Apsley House never looks open and requires subterranean tenacity to reach, the effort is well worth it. Originally built in 1771 by **Robert Adam** for **Henry Bathurst, Baron Apsley,** the honey-colored stone house was enlarged and remodeled in 1828 by **Benjamin Dean Wyatt.** This was the home of the **Duke of Wellington, Arthur Wellesley,** sometimes known as the Iron Duke and forever remembered as the man who finally defeated **Napoléon.** The attic is still the home of the present-day duke.

The structure is a mix of flawless proportions and appended grandeur made possible by a gift of £200,000 from Parliament in gratitude for the victory over Napoléon in 1815. Inside the house, the French emperor looms considerably larger than he did in life: a statue by **Canova** expands Napoléon to an idealized 11 feet and covers him not in medals but with a fig leaf. Napoléon commissioned the statue, then rejected it for failing to express his calm dignity—and because it depicts the winged figure of Victory turning away from him. It stayed packed away in the basement of the Louvre until 1816, when it was bought by the British government and presented by **George IV** to the Duke of Wellington, for whom Victory had been perfectly placed.

The museum contains an idiosyncratic collection of victors' loot, along with glorious batons, swords, and daggers. Soldiers carried off loads of dinner plates so there are stupendous services of Sèvres, Meissen, and Berlin porcelain, plus silver and gold plate on display (including the ultimate extravagance: a gold-plated silver dinner service). The focal point of the china collection is the Egyptian Sèvres service commissioned by Napoléon as a divorce present for **Josephine.** Together in a museum as they would never have been in life are Wellington's sword and Napoléon's court sword (taken from his carriage after the Battle of Waterloo), along with flags, medals, and snuffboxes.

The **Piccadilly Drawing Room,** on the first floor, is a jewel, with wall hangings, butter-yellow curtains, windows that frame Hyde Park Corner, and excellent paintings, including *Chelsea Pensioners Reading the Waterloo Despatch* by **Sir David Wilkie.**

The **Waterloo Gallery,** designed by Benjamin Dean Wyatt in 1828, is the showpiece of Apsley House. Banquets were held in this vast 90-foot corridor each year on the anniversary of the great victory over the French at Waterloo. (These banquets are now held at Windsor and presided over by the Queen and the current Duke of Wellington.) The room was designed to showcase the Duke's magnificent art collection, particularly the Spanish pictures captured in 1813 at the Battle of Vitoria and subsequently presented to the Duke by **King Ferdinand.** The collection includes paintings by **Rubens, Murillo** (the beautiful *Isaac Blessing Jacob*), **Correggio** (*The Agony in the Garden*, which was

the Duke's favorite), and four outstanding pictures by **Velázquez,** including the early *Water Seller of Seville.* One of the two notable **Van Dycks** in the room is *St. Rosalie Crowned with Roses by Two Angels.* The windows, which are fitted with sliding mirrors that at night evoke Louis XIV's *Galerie des Glaces* at Versailles, are almost as fascinating as the pictures.

At the far end of the Waterloo Gallery is **Goya's** *Equestrian Portrait of Wellington.* But x-rays show the picture was originally of **Joseph Bonaparte,** Napoléon's brother. Last-minute political alterations called for the head to be replaced with Wellington's, who never liked the painting and kept it in storage in his country house at Stratfield Saye, Berkshire. But the painting that may cause the most excitement is that by **Sir Thomas Lawrence** of the Duke of Wellington; until June 1990, this likeness appeared on the back of every £5 note. Unfortunately, visitors cannot currently see any of these treasures, as the entire house is being refurbished. At the earliest, the gallery will reopen sometime in 1995. ♦ 149 Piccadilly. Tube: Hyde Park Corner. 071/499.5676

**23 Hyde Park Corner** "It is doubtless a signal proof of being a London-lover *quand même* that one should undertake an apology for so bungled an attempt at a great public place as Hyde Park Corner." That, at least, was **Henry James'** opinion, written at the turn of the century. Many decades, improvements, and embellishments later, Hyde Park Corner remains lost in confusion and now suffers the ultimate indignity: it has become a traffic island, albeit a grand one. In order to reach this triangular patch, you must go into a warren of underpasses, where you can probably make your way by following the forlorn sounds of an equally forlorn harmonica player.

On top of the arch is the beautiful and dramatic **Goddess of Peace,** depicted reining in the Horses of War. Placed on the corner in 1912 after the Boer War, the statue presents an almost identical profile from either side.

*Goddess of Peace*

Looking at her, you almost forget that 200 cars a minute are circling the corner. The sculptor was **Adrian Jones,** a captain who had spent 23 years as a cavalry officer. The chariot is a quadriga: it is pulled by four horses abreast. Sadly, World War I broke out two years after this monument to peace was placed at Hyde Park Corner, and the memorials that surround the statue today are for the many thousands who died in a worldwide stampede of the Horses of War.

Few arches have been pushed around as much as the one here, which was designed by **Decimus Barton.** It was originally built as a northern gate to the grounds of **Buckingham Palace** and crowned with a statue of the **Duke of Wellington;** then it was aligned along the same axis as the neighboring Ionic **Hyde Park Screen,** which Burton designed in 1825. The arch was placed here in 1828. In 1883, however, it was repositioned along the axis of **Constitution Hill,** and now it leads nowhere. It has been called **Wellington Arch** and **Green Park Arch** but is now usually referred to as **Constitution Arch.**

A statue of **David,** with his back to the motorized world, commemorates the **Machine Gun Corps.** Designed by sculptor **Francis Derwent Wood** in 1925, it proclaims that "Saul hath slain his thousands but David his tens of thousands." Facing the old Lanesborough Hotel is the massive, splendid **Royal Artillery Monument,** designed by **C.S. Jaeger** in 1920. It bears the simple, sad inscription: "Here was a royal fellowship of death." Four bronze figures, heavy with the knowledge of death, surround a huge gun aimed at the Somme, a battlefield in France where so many men of the Royal Artillery died during World War I. Finally, the statue facing Apsley House was created by **Sir J.E. Boehm** in 1888. It shows the **Duke of Wellington** on his beloved horse, **Copenhagen,** who bore his master nobly for 16 hours at the **Battle of Waterloo.** (When Copenhagen died in 1836, he was buried with full military honors.)
♦ Tube: Hyde Park Corner

**24 Inter-Continental** $$$$ The English like to stay here and pretend they're in America. They are dazzled by the telephones, efficient showers, and bathroom scales, as well as the oversize everything—rooms, beds, towels, closets. In true American style, you'll find them discussing business over breakfast in the **Coffee House.** The elegant women in the posh lobby are more likely to be company

presidents than the wives of company presidents. The Inter-Continental (depicted below, at left) may lack English charm, but you can be certain that nothing will go wrong. At the top of the building is the **Nightclub,** where you can gaze through vast glass windows at the twinkling lights of the evening traffic cutting through the deepening green of the parks. ♦ 1 Hamilton Pl. Tube: Hyde Park Corner. 071/409.3131; fax 071/409.7460

Within the Inter-Continental:

**Le Soufflé** ★★★$$$$ With caviar and cool yellow-and-turquoise pastels, Le Soufflé exudes luxury. Aware that they're at one of London's top restaurants, diners sip their champagne (choose from 15 on the wine list) with the nonchalance of film stars. Tuck into the asparagus and smoked salmon served with caviar and chive butter sauce to start; then feast on breast of duck with fresh oyster mushrooms. If those dishes sound too rich, ask for the *cuisine de vie* (healthy eating) menu. For the irresolute and hungry, there's a set dinner menu with seven courses. The menu changes completely every two weeks and varies seasonally. This is a trend-setting restaurant, named for the specialty of chef **Peter Kromberg,** so you'll eat it here first, then find it elsewhere. The wine list is a labor of love, even though these prices are usually associated with things that are forever. Have a look at the special sommelier's choice.
♦ French ♦ Lunch and dinner; dinner only on Saturday. Closed Monday and Sunday. Jacket and tie required for dinner. 071/409.3131

**Coffee House** ★★$ The *Times* rates breakfasts here as among the best in London. There's a choice of four: the basic Continental; the fruit-and-grain buffet; the classic English breakfast with kippers, kedgeree, kidneys, and so forth; and Japanese sushi or seafood. You can also order à la carte. Famous chefs congregate here from time to time.
♦ International ♦ Breakfast, lunch, and dinner 071/409.3131

**25 Hard Rock Cafe** ★★$$ People have been waiting in line to eat here for almost two decades, undeterred by rain, sleet, or snow. For Americans, a meal here is a nostalgic trip home to the 1960s: Budweiser beer, Chicago Bears, hamburgers the size of a catcher's mitt, waitresses with name tags (Dixie, Cookie), and hot fudge sundaes. The best time to go is late afternoon, after lunch and before dinner, when the music isn't brain-damagingly loud, and you don't have to wait. No reservations are taken. ♦ American ♦ Lunch and dinner. 150 Old Park Ln. Tube: Hyde Park Corner. 071/629.0382

**26 Piccadilly** Once the "Magic Mile" was simply a western route out of London, but when a 17th-century tailor named **Robert Baker** came on the scene, the street's name and image changed forever. Baker made his fortune selling the "picadil," a stiff, ruffled collar, to slaves of fashion at court. The mansion he built was called **Piccadilly Hall,** and the name stuck. Now Piccadilly street is lined with sights, some appealing, some overbearing.

**27 Athenaeum** $$$$ Smaller than its modern neighbors, the Athenaeum offers old-fashioned service and amenities that make you feel like you're staying in a private house: towels the size of tents, monogrammed linen sheets, and telephone and switchboard services. However, the hotel is being refurbished, which will bring a new decor and the addition of a gymnasium. If you like to begin the day with a jog, Green Park and Hyde Park are just off the doorstep. There is a breakfast buffet, and the excellent **Windsor Lounge** (★★$$$) is a popular restaurant for lunch. Those planning a longer stay should inquire about the adjoining apartment house. ◆ 116 Piccadilly. Tube: Hyde Park Corner, Green Park. 071/499.3464; fax 071/493.1860

**28 Park Lane Hotel** $$$$ Old, lovely, and full of character, the Park Lane Hotel isn't on Park Lane but rather on Piccadilly, overlooking Green Park. The rooms are personal, the suites have their original 1920s decor and dreamy Art Deco bathrooms, and the clientele is fiercely loyal. The hotel's ballroom—a monument to the Deco period—regularly hosts debutante and charity balls; the entrance was used for filming *Brideshead Revisited.* ◆ Piccadilly (between Brick and Down Sts). Tube: Hyde Park Corner, Green Park. 071/499.6321; fax 071/499.1965

Within the Park Lane Hotel:

**Brasserie on the Park** ★★$$ A 1980s Art Deco setting is teamed with brasserie classics—onion soup, steaks, fish cakes, English grills, French country dishes, and slimming salads. ◆ Continental ◆ Lunch and dinner. 071/499.6321

**Bracewells** ★★★$$ Louis XVI carved paneling (from the London home of American financier **John Pierpoint Morgan**) makes this restaurant feel like a gentlemen's club, and the wine list has the labels and prices that are usually found only in such privileged places. ◆ Continental ◆ Lunch and dinner; dinner only on Saturday. Closed Sunday. 071/499.6321

**29 Green Park** Greener than emeralds from Asprey, these 60 acres of sable-soft grass offer the kind of luxury money can't buy in a city. The land was first enclosed by **Henry VIII** as a hunting ground, then made royal by **Charles II,** who established the **Snow House** in the center (now marked only by a mound) for cooling the royal wines. There are no flower beds in the park. Instead, ancient beech, lime, and plane trees spread their limbs like maps of the world. In spring, a tapestry of daffodils and crocuses is woven. Renting one of the sloping canvas chairs costs a few pence; the chair collector will give you a little sticker as proof that you have paid. Sit down and read *English Hours* by **Henry James** or the morning newspaper. Or just observe the perfect Englishness all around you. The noble mansions circling Green Park that created the atmosphere of wealth and high society have nearly all disappeared, replaced by their 20th-century equivalent, deluxe hotels. Still, the feeling of grandeur continues, undefeated and immediately perceptible. ◆ Bounded by Piccadilly, Grosvenor Pl, Buckingham Palace, and Queen's Walk. Tube: Green Park

**30 Half Moon Street** Poke around for a few minutes—this street is haunted by some very distinguished ghosts. Author and reluctant lawyer **James Boswell** resided here, recording his walks with **Samuel Johnson** and trying endless remedies for his gonorrhea, which he described graphically in his London journal. Novelist **Fanny Burney** also called the street home for a time, as did the essayist **Hazlitt** and the poet **Shelley.** Inside the world of fiction, Half Moon Street was the address of **P.G. Wodehouse's** Bertie Wooster and his faithful Jeeves. ◆ Off Piccadilly. Tube: Green Park

**31 Langan's Brasserie** ★★★$$$ Like the Café Royal and the Closerie des Lilas, Langan's Brasserie will eventually be immortalized in the literature of the age, even though the brilliant society recalled will be of the deal-making Hollywood genre, and not that of *The Sun Also Rises.* The beautiful, clever, rich, and promising come here to see and be seen, and it is good luck for everybody that the food is as tasty as it is, thanks to chef and part owner **Richard Shepherd** (**Michael Caine** also owns a part). Dress glamorously and take a look at the pictures (Langan's eye for 20th-century British is still represented on the walls). The bourgeois classics like bangers 'n' mash (sausage links and mashed potatoes) and bubble 'n' squeak (fried pureed potatoes and cabbage) are cooked to perfection. Rumor has it that famous people get better seats and the lesser known get what they're given; of course, this is rigorously denied by the restaurant, so don't let them put you upstairs. Jazz bands play every evening. Avoid Langan's on Saturday night, when *le tout Londres* is nowhere near London and the restaurant fills with couples from the suburbs. ◆ British ◆ Lunch and dinner; dinner only on Saturday. Closed Sunday. Stratton House, Stratton St. Reservations recommended. Tube: Green Park. 071/493.6437

---

Restaurants/Clubs: Red      Hotels: Blue
Shops/ 🌳 Outdoors: Green      Sights/Culture: Black

**32 Mayfair Inter-Continental** $$$$ This unassuming sister to the **Inter-Continental** down the street is an appropriate neighbor for Langan's. **Michael Jackson** has stayed here while on tour, barricaded from the press and inevitable groupies; **Neil Diamond** and **Billy Joel** have been guests, too. The caliber of clients seems odd because at first glance there's not much special about the hotel. Its staff manages to look as if nothing unusual is up, while the bar appears to be filled with secret service agents from various countries ignoring the piano player serenading them until 2AM. Upstairs, guests can choose the look of their bedrooms: English dark wood and leather, or French velvet and ornate. ◆ Stratton St. Tube: Green Park. 071/629.7777; fax 071/629.1459

Within the Mayfair Inter-Continental:

**Le Château Restaurant** ★★$$$ To complement the hotel's ambience; chef **Michael Coaker** serves contemporary international cuisine. Try his delicious sautéed loin of lamb or the smoked duck salad with lobster vinaigrette. ◆ French ◆ Lunch and dinner; dinner only on Saturday. Reservations recommended. 071/629.7777

**33 The Ritz** $$$$ Two more evocative words are hard to imagine. Such is their power that the name can be spelled in light bulbs and still look glamorous. The hotel (shown here) named for **César Ritz,** the Swiss hotelier who founded the **Savoy,** was built in the style of a Beaux Arts château with a Parisian arcade from the designs of **Mewès and Davis** in 1906. For ordinary, aspiring folk, this is an aristocratic world of elegance, beauty, and perfection that is rooted in the past, even if the champagne era has little in common with the Perrier age. Applying gallantry to modern hotel service, the Ritz is dedicated to the memory of that bygone age when men and women once danced cheek to cheek while orchestras played; waiters were anonymous and moved like members of a corps de ballet; and hotels were an art, one of the civilizing forces in any capital city. To prove it, tea dancing has become a regular event again.

Tea at the Ritz is undeservedly popular—you must book ages in advance and it is about as special as tea at Paddington Station. Most Londoners forgo this mediocre pleasure and have a better tea at **Brown's Hotel,** returning here for a glass of champagne after the afternoon hordes have gone. The Ritz still puts on the Ritz, so jackets, ties, and all such formality are required. ◆ Piccadilly. Tube: Green Park. 071/493.8181; fax 071/493.2687

Within The Ritz:

**Louis XVI Restaurant** ★★★★$$$$ A wonderful way to begin any day is with a stroll in Green Park followed by breakfast at the Ritz. The menu offers such English treats as Cumberland sausage, Lancashire black pudding, Finnan haddock kedgeree, and Scotch kippers. In addition, there's an appealing fruit and grain buffet or the traditional eggs Benedict. Yet dinner at Louis XVI Restaurant is the Ritz's finest hour. The delicate murals of the world's grandest dining rooms, subtly illumined at breakfast and lunchtime by dreamy London daylight, are transformed at night by resplendent chandeliers and gilt ornamentation. Take a table by the windows overlooking Green Park and indulge in grilled Dover sole and Krug Grande Cuvée. ◆ British ◆ Breakfast, lunch, and dinner. 071/493.8181

**34 Le Caprice** ★★★$$$ London's chic set nibbles and chatters the night away while glancing around to see who else is here. Le Caprice has an extensive and deceptively simple brasserie-style menu and wine list. *The* place to go, it is located just behind the Ritz. ◆ British ◆ Lunch; dinner also on Saturday. Closed Sunday. Arlington House, Arlington St. Reservations recommended. Tube: Green Park. 071/629.2239

**35 Barclays Bank** Influenced by a bank in Boston, this opulent institution, designed by **William Curtis Green** in 1922, has marble floors and a Renaissance interior with rich Venetian-red pillars. It is worth coming here to cash your checks just to experience the furniture and the rest of the surroundings. ◆ 160 Piccadilly St. Tube: Green Park

**36 John Murray** The publisher opened his office on Albemarle Street in 1812 and went on to publish the works of **Lord Byron, Jane Austen, George Crabbe,** and other literary greats. This is where Byron's autobiography was burned after his death because the poet's friends thought it was too shocking. His mistress, **Lady Caroline Lamb,** haunts the building. The seventh **John Murray** runs the firm today. ◆ 50 Albemarle St. Tube: Green Park

## CHEZ GÉRARD

**37 Chez Gérard** ★★$$ If the waiters seem a trifle impatient or ignore you altogether, the food will make up for it. Ensconced in Chez Gérard's warm dining room with wood floors select crudités as a light starter or *moules marinières* as a more ambitious beginning;

follow these with the excellent grilled salmon served with lemon and watercress or steak tartare. A bottle of Chablis or Côtes du Rhône will enhance the meal, and either the excellent cheese board or a chocolate concoction from the dessert menu will bring it to a satisfying conclusion. ♦ French ♦ Lunch and dinner; dinner only on Saturday. 31 Dover St. Reservations recommended. 071/499.8171

**38 Granary** ★★$ Come for simple dishes such as avocado stuffed with prawns, spinach, and cheese or lamb casserole with lemon and mint. Try one of the delicious English puddings. ♦ British ♦ Lunch and afternoon tea. 39 Albemarle St. Tube: Green Park. 071/493.2978

**39 Brown's Hotel** $$$$ There is no discreet plaque saying that **Henry James** stayed here, and he probably didn't, but there is something perfectly Jamesian about this hotel just off Piccadilly. It is favored by the kind of Anglophile Americans who come to England once a year to look at pictures, visit their tailor, see a few plays, and socialize with friends they have known since the War. **Theodore Roosevelt** and **Edith Carow** honeymooned here in 1886 (they got married a few blocks away, at **St. George's, Hanover Square**), and **Franklin D. Roosevelt** spent his wedding night with **Eleanor** here in 1905. Today, Brown's retains that intimate and democratic feel of an English country house. The restaurant is worthy and traditional, and this is one of the most quintessentially English places for tea in London. The rooms are intimate and lamp-lit, the sofas and chairs solid and comfy, and the sandwiches, scones, and cakes plentiful and superb. Naturally, it gets crowded, so book ahead if possible. ♦ Afternoon tea: daily 3-6PM. 30-34 Albemarle St. Tube: Green Park. 071/493.6020; fax 071/493.9381

**40 Museum of Mankind** If you leave the Burlington Arcade on the northern end at Burlington Gardens and turn right, you may find yourself in a Bengalese village or with a primitive mountain tribe in Peru. Take your chances and go to the Museum of Mankind, one of London's least known and most imaginative museums. It was built in 1866 by **Sir James Pennethorne** as the headquarters of **London University.** Today, it is the ethnographic department of the **British Museum.** Children love the tribal skulls, sculpture, masks, weapons, pottery, textiles, and puppets from all over the world, especially the Native American warbonnets, bows and arrows, and peace pipes. The permanent collection (in Room 8) includes a life-size skull carved from a piece of solid Mexican crystal and stunning Beninese bronzes from Africa. A very realistic exhibition is staged once a year; it might be, for example, a visit to the Day of the Dead in Mexico, with

spectacular memorials made of papier-mâché sculptures, sugar figures, fruit and vegetables perfumed with incense, and marigolds created for the day the dead return to greet the living. All this is in the heart of (but light-years away from) Piccadilly. The exterior of the museum is an example of High Victorian architecture, with statues of leaders in science and philosophy punctuating the sky; it is also a confusion of styles: classic versus Italian Gothic. The bookshop carries replicas of artworks and artifacts. ♦ Free. M-Sa 10AM-5PM; Su 2:30-6PM. 6 Burlington Gardens. Tube: Green Park, Piccadilly Circus. 071/437.2224

Within the Museum of Mankind:

**Cafe de Colombia** ★$ Tuck into a light lunch or nibble on an excellent cake at teatime. As the cafe's name suggests, they know how to make good cappuccino—a rare talent in London. ♦ Continental ♦ Lunch and afternoon tea; afternoon tea only on Sunday. 071/287.8148

**41 Royal Academy of Arts, Burlington House** **Colen Campbell** built the last surviving palace of 18th-century Piccadilly with a pure Palladian facade around 1717 for **Richard Boyle,** third Earl of Burlington. As the drawings below illustrate, the second story was added, and the Piccadilly frontage was replaced with the neo-Renaissance front by

*From an engraving by Jan Kip after Leonard Knyff, 1707*

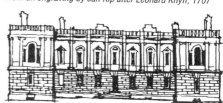

*After the changes made circa 1717*

*The present front, developed by Sydney Smirke, 1872-74*

COURTESY ROYAL ACADEMY OF ARTS

**Banks and Barry** in 1873. Its imposing grandeur is lightened by colorful banners heralding the exhibitions inside. These—as well as the Royal Academy itself—are always worth seeing.

In the courtyard stands *Sir Joshua Reynolds,* a statue of the first president of the Royal Academy. In the rooms along the quadrangle, learned societies have their headquarters: the **Geological Society,** the **Royal Society of Chemistry,** the **Society of Antiquaries,** the **Royal Astronomical Society,** and, until recently, the most prestigious society of all, the **Royal Society,** whose members are Britain's most outstanding scientists (this headquarters is now in Carlton House Gardens).

Founded in 1768, the Royal Academy marked the recognition of the importance of art and artists in this country and, for better or worse, made artists members of the Establishment. Artistic temperament being what it is, many painters refused to exhibit at this Official Marketplace for Art: **George Romney, William Blake, Dante Gabriel Rossetti,** and **James Abbott McNeill Whistler** declined, while **Thomas Gainsborough** initially exhibited. The division hasn't really healed with time—you can be certain that **Francis Bacon** was not part of the academy, yet **David Hockney** is. The initials "RA" after an artist's name (meaning he or she has been one of the honored 80 Academicians) may add to the price of an artist's work in the salesrooms but do not significantly affect his or her reputation in the art world.

In the center of the entrance hall are ceiling paintings by **Benjamin West:** *The Graces Unveiling Nature* and *The Four Elements.* There are two paintings by **Angelica Kaufmann** at each end: *Genius and Painting,* near the door to the **Friends Room** on the east, and *Composition and Design,* on the west. Above the central staircase is a circular painting by **William Kent:** *The Glorification of Inigo Jones.* The first floor includes the **Saloon,** the only surviving part of Burlington House by Colen Campbell, with a ceiling by **William Kent.**

In the last 10 years, the Royal Academy has entered a livelier, more innovative phase. Exhibitions take place in the rooms on the first and second floors. The **Summer Exhibition** is the big event of the year at the academy and one of London's more important social occasions. Some 14,000 works by 4,000 artists are submitted, with 1,300 finally selected. The gala opening in June looks like a royal garden party with pictures. The academy's reputation now rests on its international art exhibitions (this is where the enormous 1990 **Monet** show originated), which last for three months at a stretch. Parts

of the permanent collection are on view in the Private Rooms on the first floor. Splendid pictures by **Gainsborough, Sir Joshua Reynolds, John Constable, Sir Henry Raeburn, Sir Alfred Munnings,** and **Walter Sickert** are currently on show, while sculptures by **Sir Eduardo Paolozzi** and **Sir Sidney Nolan** are displayed around the building.

The second floor houses the award-winning **Sackler Galleries,** designed by **Sir Norman Foster** and opened by Her Majesty The Queen in 1991. These galleries are reached by a glass elevator that opens onto the spacious sculpture gallery where the academy's most prized possession, **Michelangelo's** *Madonna and Child with the Infant St. John,* carved in 1505, is on permanent display. It is one of only four major sculptures by the artist outside of Italy. ◆ Admission. Daily 10AM–6PM. Piccadilly. Tube: Green Park, Piccadilly Circus. 071/439.7438

Within the Royal Academy of Arts, Burlington House:

**Royal Academy Shop** Jam-packed with wonderful items, this shop contains easels, brushes, and paints, a framing service, jigsaw puzzles of popular paintings, a large collection of art books, catalogs from exhibitions abroad, original items by academy artists and silk scarves designed by them, plus the obligatory canvas museum bags. ◆ Daily 10AM–5:45PM. 071/439.7438

**Royal Academy Restaurant** ★★$ Big and cafeterialike, the Royal Academy Restaurant provides a welcome refuge from the nonstop glamour of Piccadilly. Women in tweed suits and sensible shoes, in town for the day, sit in the attractive paneled room, tranquilly sipping tea and indulging in cakes. Hot and cold meals are served at lunchtime, along with a decent salad bar. ◆ International ◆ Lunch and afternoon tea. 071/439.7438

**42 Burlington Arcade** This Regency promenade of exclusive shops, designed and completed in 1819 by **Samuel Ware,** might be considered a forerunner to the modern shopping malls that bear little resemblance to it. Inspired by Continental models and built in the years after Waterloo for **Lord George Cavendish,** the arcade provided the gentry with a shopping precinct free of the mud splashed by carriages and carts on Piccadilly and it prevented the locals from flinging their garbage into his back garden. The three cheerful top-hatted beadles who patrol the arcade today are the smallest police force in the world. Originally they were installed to protect prosperous shoppers from pickpockets and beggars. Now they will ask you not to whistle or run, and they lock the gates at 6PM Monday through Saturday and at 7PM on Thursday. Though Burlington

## Burlington Arcade Shopping Map

Arcade was badly damaged in the Blitz, it was rebuilt and today exudes an atmosphere of intimate but conceivable luxury, with 35 shops full of lasting treasures. Admire the glass roof and the iridescent green paintwork complemented by gold lettering on the delicately detailed shop fronts. The ostentatious facades were added in 1911.
♦ Tube: Green Park, Piccadilly Circus

Within Burlington Arcade:

**Irish Linen Company** Linen napkins that could sail a small ship, sheets that assume you use a professional laundry service, and special cloths for drying the Waterford crystal wineglasses that grace fine linen tablecloths can be found in this shop. ♦ M-F 9:15AM-5:45PM; Sa 9AM-4:30PM. Nos. 35-36. 071/493.8949

**N. Peal** Wise Englishwomen would rather be draped in cashmere than diamonds, and they stroll through the arcade on weekdays wearing the clothes to prove it. The three N. Peal shops in the arcade have the best cashmere in London—from the addictive kneesocks for women to the handsome capes. Remember when you enter these shops: the best is never cheap. ♦ M-Sa 9:30AM-6PM. Men's shop: No. 54. 071/493.5378. Men's and women's shops: Nos. 37-40, 71. 071/493.0714

**S. Fisher** A 10-ply cable-knit cashmere sweater will set you back a bit but should keep you warm for life. There's a beautiful choice of cashmere and Irish sweaters here, as well as Barbours and Burberrys. ♦ M-W, F-Sa 9AM-6PM; Th 9AM-6:30PM. Nos. 22-23, 32-33. 071/493.4180

**St. Petersburg Collection** Carl Fabergé's grandson, **Theo,** continues the family tradition of creating exquisite one-offs and such limited-edition miniature objets d'art as his Phoenix egg. He'll also create a dinner service for you or re-create irreplaceable pieces lost from antique services. Browse in the new upstairs art gallery while you wait. ♦ M-Sa 9AM-6PM. No. 42. 071/495.2883

**Richard Ogden** Antique jewelry, with museum-quality pieces of Art Nouveau, is for sale here. ♦ M-F 9:15AM-5:15PM; Sa 9:15AM-5PM. Nos. 28-29. 071/493.9136

**Map World** At the most recent addition to the arcade, all sorts of antique maps are available for all sorts of prices. Consider such geographical oddities as "A New Mappe of the Romane Empire" by **John Speede,** created around 1626. ♦ M-Sa 10AM-5:30PM. No. 25. No phone

**Michael Rose** Mr. Rose calls his shop "the source of the unusual." It specializes in handmade period and modern engagement and wedding rings ("the largest collection in Europe"), as well as all types of antique jewelry, including **Fabergé.** ♦ M-Sa 9:30AM-6PM. No. 3. 071/493.0714

**W&H Gidden** The smells in this shop are reminiscent of leather shops in Florence: rich, pungent, and costly. Gidden has been the saddler to the sovereign since 1806; these premises, however, contain purses, wallets, portfolios, and various accessories. Gidden has an older, larger shop, specializing in equestrian gear, about a block away in Mayfair. ♦ M-Sa 9:30AM-6PM. Nos. 1-2. 071/495.3670. Also at: 15D Clifford St. 071/734.2788

**Sutty** Since 1962, **Michael Sutty** has been creating and decorating bone china sculptures and figurines for presentations to most members of the royal household as well as the likes of **Margaret Thatcher.** He works in Stoke-on-Trent, but his wares—and those of other figurine artists—are sold here. Stop by if you're interested in "strictly limited" editions of the Buckingham Palace Guards or in a handmade pewter chess set from the American Civil War. ♦ M-W, F-Sa 9AM-6PM; Th 9AM-7PM. No. 62. 071/495.3099

**Goldsmiths & Silversmiths Association** A golden grasshopper with a ruby eye sits next to glowing pink pearl earrings. This delightful shop has the most unusual jewelry in the arcade. ♦ M-F 9AM-6PM; Sa 9AM-5PM. 071/499.1396

**Penhaligon** These very British and very special perfumes all carry the scent of an English country garden. Try "Bluebell" (people will whisper, "Where did you get it?"). The labels are enchanting, while the antique silver bottles are truly tokens of love. ♦ M-Sa 9:30AM-5:30PM. Nos. 16-17. 071/629.1416

**Charles Clements** This is one of the most reputable shops for English gifts that will fit inside your suitcase: silver wine coasters (handsome Georgian reproductions), silver pepper mills (a nice wedding present with engraved initials and date), and a large selection of corkscrews and fine knives. ♦ M-Sa 9AM-5:30PM. Nos. 4-5. 071/493.3923

**43 Piccadilly Arcade** Thrale Jell built this extension of the Burlington Arcade a century later, in 1910. Today, its charming, casual row of shops connects Piccadilly to Jermyn Street. ♦ Tube: Piccadilly Circus

Within Piccadilly Arcade:

**Waterford Wedgwood** These China specialists have a complete and tempting collection of **Wedgwood** and **Spode.** All the price lists include the import cost and the amount in dollars. ♦ M-F 9AM-6PM; Sa 9:30AM-5PM. Nos. 173-174. 071/629.2614

**Armory of St. James's** Decorations and medals for the otherwise unrewarded may be purchased here. ♦ M-F 9:30AM-5:30PM; Sa 11AM-4PM. No. 17. 071/493.5082

**Benson & Clegg** The tailors to **George VI** will make you a suit or provide a set of dazzling buttons and hand-embroidered crests for your own blazer. ♦ M-F 9AM-5PM; Sa 9AM-noon. No. 9. 071/491.1454

**New and Lingwood, Ltd.** On the Jermyn Street side is one of the best and least-known shops in the arcade. It started as the London branch of the **Eton** shop, which has been outfitting Etonians for decades. The branch here has splendid, ready-made shirts and a small but choice selection of sweaters. A forest-green, cable-knit cashmere sweater from New and Lingwood is a commitment that's worth every pound and pence. Shirts are also made to order. Upstairs is **Poulsen and Skone,** makers of fine footwear; a custom-made pair requires another serious investment, but the shoemakers share the burden, providing lifelong care and service. The ready-made shoes are quite wonderful, too. ♦ M-F 9AM-5:30PM; Sa 10AM-5PM. No. 53. 071/493.9621

## Fortnum & Mason

**44 Fortnum & Mason** Inside one of the world's most magnificent groceries and oldest carryout stores, crystal chandeliers reflect off polished mahogany, highlighting temptations of caviar, truffles, marrons glacés, hand-dipped chocolates, Stilton cheeses, teas, honeys, champagnes, and foie gras. On the hour, two mechanical figures emerge from the store clock's miniature doors: dressed in the livery of 18th-century servants, Mr. Fortnum and Mr. Mason turn and nod to each other while the bells chime sweetly. The clock was placed here in 1964, making it a relatively recent addition to this treasure house, which has been serving the privileged since 1707.

Those luxurious hampers filled with gourmet foods, always seen at **Ascot and Glyndebourne,** began in 1788 as packed lunches (known as "concentrated lunches") for hunting and shooting parties as well as members of Parliament who might have been detained. The fortunate recipients would dine on game pies and boned chickens, lobster and prawns. During the Napoléonic Wars, officers in the **Duke of Wellington's** army ordered hams and cheeses. Baskets were sent to **Florence Nightingale** in the Crimea, to **Mr. Stanley** while he was looking for **Mr. Livingstone,** and to suffragettes confined in London's **Holloway Prison,** who shared their hampers with fellow prisoners. If you're lucky enough to have tickets for Ascot or Wimbledon, or if you just feel like having a lavish picnic in one of London's parks, indulge in a hamper worthy of the occasion. Make sure you ask for the Picnic Hamper the day before you want it, and choose among the cold delicacies, which include Parma ham and melon, smoked salmon cornets, fresh-roasted *poussin,* ox tongue, salad, profiteroles, cheeses, champagne, and chocolate truffles. Add a thermos of coffee, and you'll have a lordly repast under an English sky for less than you would pay in most terrace restaurants.

While shopping here you may choose to be assisted by gentlemen in morning coats, who will accompany you from department to department, write down your choices and requests, and offer advice with knowledge, patience, and charm. Fortnum's blue-green tins of tea are as much a sign as a guarantee of good taste. Try the Finest Broken Orange Pekoe, a delicious everyday tea (you will be encouraged to put less tea in the pot and to drink it without milk in order to appreciate the true flavor). If you provide a sample of your local water, the store will carefully match it with one of its 68 varieties of tea; there is even a New York blend. The cakes and Christmas puddings are bought by those in the know (**Mrs. Thatcher** bought her son's wedding cake here). Not only are the deluxe fruitcakes in a class of their own, they are (oddly) cheaper than those found in similar stores in London. Tastes are available in the cake shop's cafe at the back of the store. Fortnum's is also one of the few stores in England where some American produce is available. After you have wisely invested a fortune in English honeys, Fortnum's own marmalades, teas, a game pie or two, a tin of English biscuits, a couple of crocks of Stilton, and a jar of Gentlemen's Relish (a very special anchovy paste) decorated with pheasants, consider lunch at **Fortnum's Fountain Restaurant.** ♦ M-Sa 9:30AM-6PM. 181 Piccadilly. Tube: Green Park. 071/734.8040

Within Fortnum & Mason:

**Fountain Restaurant** ★★★$$ The Fountain Restaurant's much-loved murals have been returned to the walls, and there's a counter for those who pop in alone and want a simple, pleasing meal. The restaurant is also open in the evening, so you can come here for dinner, before or after the theater. The grills are first-class, the game, steak, and kidney pies excellent, and if you just want something light, the sandwiches are fit for Ascot. To accompany one of the famous ice cream sundaes, fabulous coffee, espresso, and cappuccino are served at the counter. The Fountain is a favorite place for tea, and a number of writers, artists, faded rock stars, and other local figures use this as their club. It is without a doubt the best place in the area for breakfast, but if you have already eaten, come for what the English call "elevenses" (typically coffee and a Danish). This restaurant is located underneath Fortnum's with a separate entrance on Jermyn Street. ♦ British ♦ Breakfast, lunch, afternoon tea, and dinner. Closed Sunday. 071/734.8040

**St. James's Restaurant** ★★★$$ The fourth-floor restaurant is far less known than the Fountain; hence, it is quieter and ideal for exchanging confidences over roast beef and Yorkshire pudding. Your neighbors will look like they have come to London to bid on a little something at Christie's or Sotheby's—very tweedy and proper. ♦ British ♦ Breakfast, lunch, and afternoon tea. Closed Sunday. 071/734.8040

**The Patio** ★★$ A light snack here will keep you going after shopping around the store has roused your appetite. ♦ British ♦ Breakfast, lunch, and snacks. Closed Sunday. 071/734.8040

**45 Albany** **Sir William Chambers** built this residence for **Viscount Melbourne** in 1774. It looks like an English Palladian version of a Parisian *hôtel particulier.* **Henry Holland** converted its garden to chambers for bachelor gentlemen in 1803. This building has been the home of **Lord Byron, Thomas B. Macaulay, Lord Gladstone,** and, more recently, **J.B. Priestley, Graham Greene,** and 1960s British film star **Terence Stamp.** ♦ Albany Courtyard. Tube: Piccadilly Circus

**46 Swaine & Adeney** As one of London's oldest and most traditional family-run businesses, Swaine & Adeney is graced with two Royal Warrants: Whip and Glove Makers to the Queen and Umbrella Makers to the Queen Mother. In a country where rain is a national preoccupation, brollies are serious business, and Swaine & Adeney makes the Rolls-Royce of collapsible shades. Ask one of the salespeople to explain the difference between the traditional and the classic umbrella; then examine the runners, and open the caps and ferrules, and the hand and top springs. There's a wide selection of handles: crooks steamed and bent by hand; woods, including malacca, whangee, chestnut, cherry, hickory, ash, and maple; and leathers, such as hand-sewn calf, morocco, pigskin, ostrich, lizard, or crocodile. The choice of fabrics includes a variety of nylons or the best English silk. If, in the end, you choose the classic Brigg umbrella with the best English black-silk cover, malacca crook, and gold collar engraved with your name and address, be assured that waiters will understand when you say you wish to keep your umbrella. There are also walking sticks—some sinister, but all remarkable. In the basement **Gun Room,** you will find the finest in country clothing, including the whole range of **Barbours** (dark-green, waxy raincoats) worn by the landed gentry, and everything to do with the sartorial side of riding and hunting. ♦ M-W, F-Sa 9:30AM-6PM. Th 9:30AM-7PM. 185 Piccadilly. Tube: Green Park. 071/734.4277

**Restaurants/Clubs:** Red    **Hotels:** Blue
**Shops/ 🌳 Outdoors:** Green    **Sights/Culture:** Black

**46 Hatchards** Booksellers since the 18th century, this shop still has the rambling charm of that age, but it has displayed considerable smarts about moving into the paperback era. Now it is a veritable book emporium, with an excellent selection of children's books (third floor), art books (second floor), and reference books (first floor), including dictionaries, Bibles, and the Oxford companions to music and literature. In the literature department (second floor), you can buy all 12 volumes of **Byron's** *Letters and Journals*, edited by **Leslie Marchand,** or you can settle for the single volume of Byron's biography (all published by **John Murray,** a few yards down the street). You'll find the complete works of just about all your favorite English writers, as well as secondhand and rare books. As you enter from Piccadilly, have a look at the recent hardcover fiction. In the modern annex, a travel section with all sorts of guides will keep you going for years. The charming shop assistants can trace any book you care to name if it's still in print. If books are your passion, this is paradise. ♦ M-F 9AM-6PM; Sa 9:30AM-6PM. 187 Piccadilly. Tube: Green Park. 071/439.9921

**47 Sackville Street** Take a quick look at this almost purely Georgian street, which radiates a confident modesty. ♦ Between Piccadilly and Vigo St. Tube: Piccadilly Circus

**48 Midland Bank** Built by **Sir Edwin Lutyens** in 1922, this charming neighbor of St. James's Church is worth a glance. The architect kindly deferred to St. James's by creating a bank on a domestic scale in brick and Portland stone. ♦ 196A Piccadilly. Tube: Piccadilly Circus

**49 St. James's, Piccadilly Sir Christopher Wren,** the man who gave London **St. Paul's Cathedral** and some 50 other churches, completed this place of worship (shown below) in 1864. From the outside, the newly pointed brick, the replaced and restored spire, and the crafts market in the courtyard give no clue of the miracle within. But when visitors walk inside they are typically awestruck by the wide-open space, the barrel-vaulted roof, the rows of two-tiered windows, the Corinthian columns, the brass, the gilt, the paint. . . . This has always been a fashionable church, especially designed for large weddings. The organ was built for **James II.** In 1757, **William Blake** was christened at the wonderful white-marble font, whose figures of Adam and Eve and the Tree of Life were

carved by **Grinling Gibbons.** Of St. James's, his favorite church, Wren said, "There are no walls of a second order, nor lanterns, nor buttresses, but the whole rests upon pillars, as do also the galleries, and I think it may be found beautiful and convenient; it is the cheapest form of any I could invent." The church is also a moving tribute to its congregation. Almost completely destroyed in the bombing of 1940, it was restored through determination and dedication. The spire was completed in 1968 by **Sir Albert Richardson.** This is an active church today, running lectures on various aspects of faith most evenings. ♦ Daily 10AM-6PM. Services: Su 8:30AM, 11AM, 5:45PM. Lunchtime concerts: Th-F 1:10PM. 197 Piccadilly. Tube: Piccadilly Circus

Within St. James's Yard:

**The Wren at St. James's** ★★$ Come to this cheerful place for homemade vegetable soups (served with thick slices of whole-grain bread), herbal teas, and fresh salads, as well as cakes, fruit tarts, and coffee. ♦ Vegetarian ♦ Breakfast, lunch, and dinner; breakfast, lunch, and afternoon tea only on Sunday. Entrance on Jermyn St. 071/437.9419

**49 Simpson's** Most people have gotten used to this ultramodern building. It was one of the great pioneering store designs, built in 1935 by **Joseph Emberton** with lavish use of materials including glass elevators, travertine floors, space, and light. But does it belong to Piccadilly? Fifty years later, Londoners accept the store (and its superb clothing under the **Daks** label), while visitors complain that it is an eyesore. But architects admire what they see (especially when lit at night) and what they don't see: the welded-steel structure (the second in England) with massive girders on the first floor. Simpson's has developed an impressive women's department, with three floors of French, English, and American designer fashion rubbing shoulders with tweedy country suits; but it is known mainly for its men's clothes, including the highest-quality suits, tweed jackets, overcoats, and raincoats. The service is slow but courteous, and intelligent. Within Simpson's are a barbershop and **Jeeves,** a specialist dry cleaners. ♦ M, W, F-Sa 9AM-6PM; Tu 9:30AM-6PM; Th 9AM-7PM. 203 Piccadilly. Tube: Piccadilly Circus. 071/734.2002

Within Simpson's:

**Simpson's Restaurant** ★★$$$ Oddly enough, this restaurant combines an English restaurant with a Japanese sushi bar. Diners wear the kind of clothes sold in the store (smart, traditional, English) and eat the kind of food they probably could have in their own country houses. The restaurant serves proper English breakfasts (eggs, bacon, sausage, kidneys, and kippers). At lunch, choose between sushi and roast joints—beef and lamb—carved from the trolley. There are English cheeses, trifle, and syllabub for dessert. If you sit at the sushi bar, you will be entertained by the chef in action. ◆ British/Japanese ◆ Breakfast and lunch. Closed Sunday. 071/734.2002

**Simpson's Wine Bar** ★★$ This light, airy slip of a wine bar overlooks Jermyn Street. The food is basic—coffee, croissants, and Danish pastries in the morning and quiche and salad at lunch, when it fills with well-dressed people who want to eat simply and quickly. ◆ Wine bar ◆ Breakfast, lunch, and afternoon tea. Closed Sunday. 071/734.2002

**49 Piccadilly Market** This lively crafts market always attracts large crowds with its good and modestly priced assortment of pottery, hand-knit sweaters, carved wooden toys, and enameled jewelry. ◆ F-Sa 9AM-6PM. St James's Courtyard. Tube: Piccadilly Circus

**50 Le Meridien Hotel** $$$$ Formerly called the **New Piccadilly Hotel,** Le Meridien was London's newest and most elegant hotel in 1908. One of the leading Edwardian architects, **Norman Shaw,** combined dazzling opulence with architectural perfection for its design. Throughout the 1920s and 1930s, the hotel's reputation held fast, but it declined rapidly after World War II. Now **Air France's** company, **Le Meridien,** is the proud owner, and after a generous physical and psychological face-lift, the hotel is once again a Piccadilly showpiece. The ubiquitous harpist (a must on London's current hotel scene) welcomes you to late 20th-century notions of essential luxury: a golf-practice area, health club with squash courts, solarium, swimming pool, Nautilus gym, Turkish baths, sauna, Jacuzzi, beauty salon, and fitness-cuisine brasserie. The glamour is in the facilities; the rooms are comfortable, tasteful, and elegant. ◆ Piccadilly. Tube: Piccadilly Circus. 071/734.8000; fax 071/437.3574

Within Le Meridien Hotel:

**Oak Room Restaurant** ★★★$$$$ The original, pale, oak-paneled elegance illumined with magnificent chandeliers looks like a set from "Edward and Mrs. Simpson." Executive chef **David Chambers** prepares splendors to equal the setting, with entrées such as steamed sea bass on snow peas and celeriac. The street of Piccadilly has become a battleground for excellent chefs determined to turn a bit of London into a gourmet delight. This little part is a success. ◆ French ◆ Lunch and dinner; dinner only on Saturday. Closed Sunday. 071/734.8000

**Terrace Garden Restaurant** ★★$$$ This stunning brasserie in a conservatory retains an undiscovered feel; it's a nice place to begin the day or end a theater evening. The crab soup, served with Gruyère and croutons, is savory. There is a daily three-course table d'hôte, and

afternoon tea is served from 3 to 5:30PM. Business London eats its power breakfasts here. ◆ French ◆ Breakfast, lunch, afternoon tea, and dinner; afternoon tea and dinner only on Sunday. 071/734.8000

**51 Cording's** If London weren't a Dickensian tangle of ground leases, this shop would have been abolished and the grandeur of the Piccadilly Hotel extended. Only the web of property laws enabled the ceremonial designs of **John Nash** to be destroyed and this little store to remain. Cording's has been here since 1839 and has kept its character in an ever-changing world. You can get terrific raincoats, waterproof boots, country woolens, and tweeds, all high quality and somewhat lower-priced than at neighboring Burberrys and Simpson's. ◆ M-F 9AM-6PM; Sa 10AM-5PM. 19 Piccadilly. Tube: Piccadilly Circus. 071/734.0830

**51 Criterion Brasserie** ★★$$ Located on Piccadilly Circus, the restaurant was designed by **Thomas Verity** in 1870, along with the Criterion Theatre, when Piccadilly was the hub of the Empire. As the area declined and became populated by junkies, derelicts, boarded-up buildings, sex cinemas, and kebab houses, the Criterion sank to a new low as the fastest cafeteria in London, serving 20 meals a minute. In 1983, **Trusthouse Forte** decided to rehabilitate it. Behind decades of plywood and Formica, grease and smoke, they struck gold, or the closest thing: shimmering, dazzling, gold-mosaic, Byzantine vaulted ceilings and marble walls. Restored to its Victorian splendor, this is one of the prettiest restaurants in London. ◆ Italian/American ◆ Lunch, afternoon tea, and dinner; lunch and afternoon tea only on Sunday. 222 Piccadilly. Tube: Piccadilly Circus. 071/925.0909

The grand baroque facade of Le Meridien Hotel is without a doubt the most handsome part of the present quadrant surrounding Piccadilly Circus. The tragedy is that it was built at the terrible expense of John Nash's original quadrant, which was destroyed to make way for the hotel. Nash's elegant and ceremonial conception was shattered, for once not out of the greed of business and the indifference of the public but due to the architectural citadel itself, which purposely ignored Nash's remarkably fine plan. The guilt does not rest on Sir Norman Shaw, who attempted to restore the graciousness of this area and produced magnificent plans that respected the genuis of Nash. Shaw was defeated and withdrew his name from the Piccadilly Development of 1912, dying soon after. The ghost of Nash has haunted this site ever since, making it almost impossible to successfully resurrect the dignity that would have made Piccadilly Circus worthy of a great city.

**52 SOGO** Inside this Japanese designer emporium, the latest British names (**Paul Smith, Jasper Conran, Katherine Hamnett,** and **Vivienne Westwood**) rub shoulders with **Hanae Mori** and **Etienne Aigner.** This is the only store in London to have come up with a tourist-friendly approach to VAT refunds: salesclerks sort it out while you pay the bill. When you're through shopping, sit down for some sushi at **Cafe SOGO.** ◆ M-Sa 10AM-6PM. 225-229 Piccadilly. Tube: Piccadilly Circus. 071/333.9000

**52 Tower Records** A whole block and several floors of records (they still sell vinyl here), tapes, CDs, and videos draws countless customers through the glass doors of one of London's largest music stores. You'll find tunes with every kind of beat and from almost any country. The desk in the ground-floor foyer handles bookings for certain concerts. ◆ M-Sa 9AM-midnight; Su 11AM-10PM. Piccadilly Circus. Tube: Piccadilly Circus

**53 Eros** After a hiatus of almost two years, during which he was treated for nearly a century of exposure to the elements, the God of Love has returned and once more reigns over Piccadilly Circus. The city's best-loved statue symbolizes London itself to people all over the world. It is a memorial to the virtuous **Lord Shaftesbury,** a tireless reformer and educator who lived from 1801-85. The sculptor, **Alfred Gilbert,** was no less idealistic; he believed Shaftesbury deserved a monument that would represent both generosity of spirit and love of mankind, and would symbolize, according to the sculptor, "the work of Lord Shaftesbury, the blindfolded Love sending forth indiscriminately, yet with purpose, his missile of kindness, always with the swiftness the bird has from its wings, never ceasing to breathe or reflect critically, but ever soaring onwards, regardless of its own perils and dangers."

Gilbert created his statue in aluminum, marking the first time the material had been used for such a structure. As a result, the eight-foot figure is so light that it sways in the wind. Gilbert

*Eros*

was paid £3,000 for his work, even though it had cost him £7,000 to build it. His eventual and inevitable bankruptcy left him with little alternative but to leave the country, living first in Belgium and then in Italy. Lord Shaftesbury himself died lamenting, "I cannot bear to leave this world with all the misery in it." He would presumably have been sadder still to know what misery had afflicted the artist who tried to honor him. Although the creator of Eros was rejected, the statue has an enduring place in the hearts of Londoners. ◆ Tube: Piccadilly Circus

**54 Criterion Theatre** Tawdry signs have long buried the French-château facade of this theater, designed in 1870 by **Thomas Verity.** It is London's only underground theater in the physical sense of the word: patrons go down series of steps, even for the upper circle. The lobby is decorated with Victorian tiles. The theater, which seats 603, was completely refurbished in 1992. ◆ Piccadilly Circus. Tube: Piccadilly Circus. 071/839.4488

**55 Trocadero** The history of the "Troc" on this site goes back to the 1740s, when it was a tennis court. In the 19th century, it went from circus to theater to music hall to restaurant. In the 1920s and '30s, the Trocadero flourished with **Charles Cochran's** "Supper Time Revues." Now it is an entertainment complex made for tourists and enjoyed by English visitors from the provinces, families, and young people. Its 200,000 square feet contain the first **Guinness World of Records Exhibition; Star Tracks,** where future celebs can make their own pop videos with backing tracks and instruments; a terrific record shop (**HMV**); a large bookstore (**Athena Books**); **Funland/Laser Bowl,** with bumper cars and electronic games at the former and "Flying Aces," a dogfight simulator, at the latter; a nightclub (**Shaftesbury on the Avenue**); and the **Golden Nugget Casino,** with 14 roulette wheels and 10 blackjack tables (casinos in England require membership: apply in person, produce your passport, then wait 48 hours). Comestibles from around the world are available on **Food Street.** Restaurants and shops stay open late every day. ◆ Funland/Laser Bowl daily 10AM-1AM; 071/287.8913. Golden Nugget Casino: daily 2PM-4AM; 071/439.0099. Guinness World of Records Exhibition and Star Tracks: daily 10AM-10PM; 071/439.7331. Shaftesbury on the Avenue: daily 9:30PM-3AM; 071/736.8630. 13 Coventry St. Tube: Piccadilly Circus. 071/736.8630

Within the Trocadero:

**Planet Hollywood** ★★$ Movie razzmatazz has come to London in the beefy shapes of **Arnold Schwarzenegger, Bruce Willis,** and **Sylvester Stallone,** who own this restaurant just as they do the one in the U.S. If you want a taste of California—gourmet pizzas, Beverly

Hills salad, lots of pasta—it's here. You may even spot a star or two, but be prepared to wait for the privilege. ◆ American ◆ Lunch and dinner. 071/287.1000

**56 Regent Street** Signs of the grand designs of **John Nash** are apparent here, with Regent Street running southward to Waterloo Place and the Mall, and northward to Oxford Street and Regent's Park. Unfortunately, what you see and what Nash actually created are different things. Nash planned Piccadilly Circus as an elegant square with a long arcade, very much like the Rue de Rivoli running alongside the Tuileries in Paris. The **Quadrant,** an even larger version of the crescent at Regent's Park, was the essence of the scheme—so crucial that Nash financed its construction out of his own pocket, persuading his builders to accept leases instead of payment when his money ran out.

Completed in 1819, the Quadrant must have been very handsome indeed. Its destruction began in 1848, with serious obliteration in 1905. Since then planners have tried with monotonous regularity to restore and re-create Piccadilly Circus. The latest attempt is the 1986 effort visible today: a precinct that one hopes won't succumb to the shabbiness to which the area is prone.

Sightseers should go to Regent Street when the shops are closed; it is then quite prepossessing and deserted. Remember to look up: a lot of fine detail can be found at the tops of the buildings. For shopping, the street is somewhat deficient; considering its central location and length, it has more than its share of airline offices and ordinary chain stores. However, there are some notable exceptions. Start with **Acquascutum** (reputed to be **Margaret Thatcher's** outfitter) at the Piccadilly Circus end, followed by **Garrard** (the **Queen's** jewelers), and then walk purposefully up to **Mappin & Webb,** another high-class jewelry store. If you feel the urge to buy china, wait until you've seen **Liberty,** an extraordinary department store, much loved by the English gentry. It has an eccentric collection of china from all over the world in the basement, though it is better known for its sensational designer fabrics. (Although Liberty looks Elizabethan, it was built out of timbers from two men-of-war ships in 1925.) Don't forget to look in **Hamleys** toy shop, but be prepared for a long visit if you have children because they'll never want to leave.

To the right of Regent Street is **Waterloo Place,** presided over by the **Duke of York Column,** created in 1834 by **Benjamin Wyatt.** This street was meant to mark the southern end of Nash's triumphal way from Carlton House Terrace to Regent's Park. In the distance you can see the Victoria Tower. ◆ Between Piccadilly Circus and Oxford Circus. Tube: Piccadilly Circus

**57 Piccadilly Theatre** This large, comfortable theater has air-conditioning, which is fortunate given that it seats 1,128. It's a good venue for the less-hyped musicals. ◆ Denman St. Tube: Piccadilly Circus. General information: 071/867.1118. Credit card bookings: 071/867.1111

**58 Café Royal** ★★★$$$ **Wilde** and **Whistler** met here, as did **Dylan Thomas** and warlock **Aleister Crowley**—the latter wearing only a cape. Established in 1865, Café Royal merits a visit just to check out the extravagant rococo **Grill Room. Herbert Berger's** fine menu, however, is worthy of the surroundings; it includes a fillet of sea bass as well as veal medaillons with foie gras, savoy cabbage, and a sauternes sauce. Come for the ambience and stay for the food. ◆ Continental ◆ Lunch and dinner; dinner only on Saturday. Closed Sunday. 68 Regent St. Reservations recommended. Tube: Piccadilly Circus. 071/439.6320

**59 British Designer Knitwear Group** This shop claims to be the only establishment in the West End to sell handmade woolens from all over the British Isles. Designers include **Ann Arundel, Maggie White,** and **Judith Harrison,** and while some of the items are, as a Brit would say, decidedly "twee," others—such as the Irish pullovers from the Aran Islands—are definitely worth a look. ◆ M-W, F 10AM-6PM; Th, Sa 10AM-7PM. 2-6 Quadrant Arcade, 80 Regent St. Tube: Piccadilly Circus. 071/439.4659

**60 Henry Sotheran** Row upon row of glorious antique leather-bound books greet you here, glistening like chestnuts. ◆ M-F 9:30AM-6PM; Sa 10AM-4PM. 2 Sackville St. Tube: Piccadilly Circus. 071/439.6151

**60 Folio Books** This bookshop makes handsome editions of all the favorite English works. A beautifully bound and printed set of **Jane Austen** novels is a timeless treasure. ◆ M-F 10AM-6PM; Sa 10AM-1PM. 2 Sackville St. Tube: Piccadilly Circus. 071/629.6517

**61 Legends** Tucked away on staid and sensible Old Burlington Street is a place where you can dance till you drop. This club has a typical glossy modern look and reasonable prices. Some nights feature house music, attracting a young crowd. Unless you're into techno-trance, call ahead to find out what kind of music is spinning. ◆ Hours vary (usually daily early evening-3AM). 29 Old Burlington St. Tube: Piccadilly Circus. 071/437.9933; fax 071/734.3224

**Restaurants/Clubs:** Red
**Shops/ ⏚ Outdoors:** Green

**Hotels:** Blue
**Sights/Culture:** Black

## Regent Street Shopping Map

OXFORD STREET

| Left side | Right side |
|---|---|
| casualwear **Benetton** | **Shelly's** shoes |
| **PRINCES STREET** | **Ratners** jewelry |
| fine chocolates **Godiva** | **Bally of Switzerland** watches |
| woolens **House of Scotland** | **Laura Ashley** womenswear |
| soaps, perfumes **Crabtree & Evelyn** | **Thorntons** chocolates |
| film processing **City Photo** | **Off the Cuff** shirts, ties |
| menswear **Damart** | **National Westminster Bank** |
| woolens **London House** | **LITTLE ARGYLL STREET** |
| opticians **Dolland & Aitchin** | |
| **HANOVER STREET** | **Dickens and Jones** department store |
| building society **The Woolwich** | |
| Irish Airlines **Aer Lingus** | |
| **MADDOX STREET** | **GREAT MARLBOROUGH STREET** |
| TVs, stereos **Panasonic** | |
| fabrics **Tops** | **Liberty** designer department store |
| **Hair & Beauty Salon** | |
| **Cyprus Airlines** | **Barclays Bank** |
| woolens **Scottish Wear** | |
| Moroccan Airlines **Royal Air Maroc** | **The Gap** upmarket casualwear |
| fine china **Villeroy & Boch** | |
| **CONDUIT STREET** | **FOUBERT'S PLACE** |
| bags, handbags **Henry's** | **Jaeger Man** menswear |
| **The Pen Shop** | **House of Chinacraft** |
| casualwear **Racing Green** | |
| woolens **The Scotch House** | |
| jewelry **Peter Trevor & Co. Ltd.** | **Hamleys** toys |
| fabrics, fine woolens **Court Textiles** | |
| Israeli Airlines **El Al** | **London House** woolens |
| **NEW BURLINGTON PLACE** | |
| **Noble Furs** | |
| Australian clothing **R.M. Williams** | |
| **Royal Jordanian Airlines** | |
| **House of Cashmere** | |
| Saudi Airlines **Saudia** | |
| menswear **Regents** | |
| **NEW BURLINGTON STREET** | **Mappin & Webb** jewelry |
| **Japan National Tourist Organization** | **Next** clothing |
| coats **Burberrys** | **Waterford Wedgwood** fine china |
| fine china **Villeroy & Boch** | **British Airways** |
| **The English Teddy Bear Company** | **BEAK STREET** |
| menswear **Cougar** | **Lawleys** china, glass |
| **The Woollen Centre** | **Bally of Switzerland** shoes |
| **Singapore Airlines** | **Viyella** womenswear |
| | **Gap Kids** children's clothing |
| **Oxfords** | **The Disney Store** |
| **Scottish Woollens** | **The Cashmere Gallery** |
| porcelain, glass **Wilson & Gill** | **Reject China Shop** |
| gifts, glass, china **Thomas** | **Lloyds Bank** |
| **Midland Bank** | |
| **HEDDON STREET** | **REGENT PLACE** |
| woolens **The Highlands** | **Boodle & Dunthorne** jewelry |
| coats, leather goods **Cyril** | **Rymans** stationery, office supplies |
| menswear **Hunters** | **Watches of Switzerland** |
| fabric **Fine Textiles** | **Tie Rack** ties, shirts, underwear |
| pen specialists **Pencraft Ltd.** | **Burton/Dorothy Perkins** clothing |
| **TSB Bank** | **Garrard** jewelry |
| **VIGO STREET** | **GLASSHOUSE STREET** |
| menswear **Austin Reed** | |
| shoes **Clarks** | **Acquascutum** clothing |
| **The London Textile Company** | **Dunn & Co.** menswear |
| **SWALLOW STREET** | |
| bank **Bristol & West Building Society** | **Brothers** menswear |
| shirts, ties **Off the Cuff** | |

REGENT STREET

Map continues on next page

**Regent Street Shopping Map, cont.**

womenswear **Buzzz**
handbags, gifts **Saisburys**
theater tickets **Foreign Exchange**

**Chinacraft**
designer eyewear **Paris-Miki**

REGENT STREET

**Scotch House** woolens, tartans
**Metro Goldwyn Mayer Cinema**

QUADRANT ARCADE
**British Designer Knitwear Group**
handmade sweaters
**Alexandra** sportswear
**Angus Steak House**

**AIR STREET**

socks, underwear **Sock Shop**
menswear **Brampton**
womenswear **Jigsaw**
ties, underwear **Tie Rack**
CDs, tapes, videos **Tower Records**

**Café Royal** cafe, bar
**House of Cashmere**
**Estridge** cashmere
**Stereo Regent Street**
**Barclays Bank**

**PICCADILLY CIRCUS**

**62 Savile Row** The tailors on this street, rightly famed the world over for their expertise, may have to move their shops, some after nearly 200 years at this location. Formerly, the government classified their businesses as light industrial and allowed them to occupy space in this desirable section of town, but times have changed: the government has altered their status, and developers are hungry for this prime real estate. Over the 1990s, big business and banks will take over the tailors' premises. It is strange that the Savile Row tailors should be so poorly regarded in their own country, as they bring about £20 million annually to the British Exchequer. Forty percent of this comes from the U.S. while less than 30 percent is from the Brits themselves. ◆ Tube: Piccadilly Circus

On Savile Row:

**Gieves & Hawkes** Founded in 1785, this is the oldest tailor on the street. Its representatives once followed the British Fleet around the world, dressing such illustrious figures as **Nelson, Wellington, Livingstone,** and **Stanley,** not to mention the infamous **Captain Bligh** of the Bounty. ◆ M-Sa 9AM-6PM. No. 1. 071/434.2001

**Dege** Four of the street's top tailors work under one roof at Dege (pronounced deejzh). Customers include men from the military and **Lord King** from British Airways. There is a ladies' tailor as well. ◆ M-F 9:15AM-5:15PM; Sa 9:30AM-12:30PM. No. 10. 071/287.2941

**Henry Poole & Co.** This establishment has tailored gentlemen's clothes for 160 years; in Victoria's day, it dressed the French aristocracy (or what was left of it), including **Baron de Rothschild** and **Prince Louis-Napoléon.** Cutters from this company visit the U.S. to attend to the wealthiest of American society. ◆ M-F 9AM-5PM. No. 15. 071/734.5985

**Anderson & Sheppard** The tailor here, **Arthur Mortenson,** is renowned for his ability to sew a Sholte shoulder, which is softer and

deeper than the traditional English cut. This explains why American ambassadors have been dressed here but not why **Prince Charles,** the quintessential Englishman, is a client. ◆ M-F 8:30AM-5PM. No. 30. 071/734.1420

**63 Hamleys** First established as the 18th-century "Noah's Ark" on High Holborn, the shop with the "infinite variety of toys, games, magical apparatus and sports goods" moved to Regent Street in 1881; shortly afterward, it introduced table tennis to London. Today, the variety of toys and games still seems limitless, spread out as it is over six levels. Unless you have a strong constitution, avoid Hamleys like the plague near Christmastime, when a one-way system is in operation to keep the aisles from getting jammed. Any other time of year, indulge the child in yourself. ◆ M-W 10AM-6PM; Th 10AM-8PM; F-Sa 10AM-7PM; Su noon-6PM. 188 Regent St. Tube: Oxford Circus. 071/734.3161

**64 Liberty** Since the shop opened in 1875, the name Liberty has remained synonymous with the best in high-quality printed fabrics. Founder **Arthur Lasenby Liberty** was a fan of the Orient, and his skill at importing and selling exotica actually helped foment the pre-Raphaelite movement (**Ruskin, Rossetti,** and **Whistler** were all regular customers). The remarkable Tudor-style building is worth experiencing for its architecture alone. Built in the 1920s, it is not authentic, but the beams and timbers came from two 19th-century ships, while the interior features linen-fold paneling, balustrades, oak staircases, stained glass, and Italian carving. A frieze on the Regent Street frontage, completed in 1925, shows goods being transported from Asia to Britain. Of course, the merchandise housed here also merits admiration. Rummage in the remnants section of the fabrics department for designer prints at bargain prices. ◆ M-Tu, F-Sa 9:30AM-6PM; W 10AM-6PM; Th 9:30AM-7:30PM. 210-220 Regent St. Tube: Oxford Circus. 071/734.1234

# Oxford Street Shopping Map

**PARK LANE**

**Virgin Megastore**

**Cumberland Hotel**

**Kentucky Fried Chicken**

**OLD QUEBEC STREET**

**Evans** *womenswear*
**Salisbury's** *bags, leather goods*
**Next** *womenswear*
**Cascade Shops** *clothing, gifts*
**Benetton** *woolens*

**Pizza Hut**

*department store* **C&A**

**Littlewoods** *department store*

**PARK STREET** / **PORTMAN STREET**

*electrical goods* **Dixons**

**Saxone** *shoes*
**Baggage Co.**
*stationers* **Rymans**
**Russell & Bromley** *shoes*
*ties, shirts* **Tie Rack**
**Boots** *chemist*
*menswear* **Oakland**
**Etam** *womenswear*
*womenswear* **Hennes**
**Clarks** *shoes*
**Aberdeen Steak House**
**H. Samuel** *jewelry*
*children's clothing* **Adams**
**Bally** *shoes*
*children's clothing* **Jacadi**
**House of Cashmere**
*underwear* **Knickerbox**
*woolens* **House of Scotland**
*maternity and children's clothing* **Mothercare**
*restaurant* **American Burger**

**Marks & Spencer** *department store*

**NORTH AUDLEY STREET** / **ORCHARD STREET**

**OXFORD STREET**

*womenswear* **Laura Ashley**
*denims* **Jean Jeanie**
*menswear* **Grip**
*cashmere, woolens* **London House**
**Churchill Gifts**
*chemist* **Boots**
*socks, stockings* **Sock Shop**
**Midland Bank**

**Selfridges** *department store*

**BALDERTON STREET**

**Burger King**
*fine china, gifts* **Samuel Maynard**

**LUMLEY STREET**

*clothing* **Principles**
*menswear* **Ciro Citterio**

**DUKE STREET**

**Barratts** *shoes*
**Jane Norman** *womenswear*
**Stylo** *sports gear*

*shoes* **Bertie**
*cards, stationery* **Scribbler**

**BINNEY STREET** / **BIRD STREET**

**Lloyds Bank**
**Pizzaland**

**C&A**

**GILBERT STREET** / **JAMES STREET**

*womenswear* **Gap**
*clothing* **Jeans West**
*chemist* **Boots**
*shoes* **Faith**
**Bond Street Tube**
*clothing* **Burtons/Dorothy Perkins**

**Body Shop** *lotions, perfumes, toiletries*
**Suits You** *menswear*
**Bally** *shoes*
**Woodhouse** *menswear*
**Kookai** *womenswear*
**Lilley & Skinner** *department store*

*Map continues on next page*

## Oxford Street Shopping Map, cont.

| | |
|---|---|
| **DAVIES STREET** | **STRATFORD PLACE** |
| **SOUTH MOLTON STREET** | **Sunglass Hut** *sunglasses* |
| **Bond Street Tube** | **Art of Silk** *ties, waistcoats* |
| *menswear* **Oakland** | **MARYLEBONE LANE** |
| **House of Cashmere** | **Trustee Savings Bank** |
| *chocolates* **Thorntons** | **British Telecom** |
| *cafe* **Le Croissant** | **Off the Cuff** *ties, boxers* |
| **WOODSTOCK STREET** | **MARYLEBONE LANE** |
| **Wendy's** | |
| *cafe* **Bonjour Paris** | **Debenhams** *department store* |
| *shoes* **Dolcis** | |
| **NEW BOND STREET** | **VERE STREET** |
| *womenswear* **Next** | **E. Joseph Booksellers** |
| | *antiquarian and rare books* |
| | **Bank of Scotland** |
| *womenswear* **Stefanel** | **Smokers** *pipes, tobacco* |
| **DERING STREET** | **Sock Shop** |
| *womenswear* **The Gap** | **K Shoes** |
| *watches* **Swatch** | **D.H. Evans** *department store* |
| | **OLD CAVENDISH STREET** |
| *sports gear* **Olympus** | |
| *shoes* **Babers/Church** | **John Lewis** *department store* |
| *shoes* **Saxone** | |
| *ties, shirts* **Tie Rack** | |
| *accessories* **Accessorize** | |
| **HAREWOOD PLACE** | **HOLLES STREET** |
| **McDonald's** | **Wallis** *womenswear* |
| *clothing* **Genel** | **Clinton** *cards* |
| *menswear* **Mr Havard** | **Body Shop** *lotions, perfumes* |
| **Bureau de Change** | **Dash** *womenswear* |
| **Deep Pan Pizza** | **Monsoon** *womenswear* |
| *menswear* **Cecil Gee** | **Jane Norman** *womenswear* |
| *womenswear* **River Island** | **Clarks** *shoes* |
| *jewelry* **Ernest Jones** | **BHS** *department store* |
| **Scottish Woolens** | |
| *cafe* **Le Croissant Français** | **H. Samuel** *jewelry* |
| | **Ravel** *shoes* |
| **JD Sports** | **Bally** *shoes* |
| *womenswear* **Richards** | **Mister Byrite** *menswear* |
| *opticians* **For Eyes** | **JOHN PRINCE'S STREET** |
| *socks, stockings* **Sock Shop** | |
| **South African Airways** | **Hennes** *womenswear* |

**OXFORD STREET**

**REGENT STREET**

**65 Godiva** Taste some of the best truffles in Europe, or simply rest your shopping-weary feet over a cappuccino. ♦ M-W, F-Sa 9:30AM-6PM; Th 9:30AM-7PM. Princes and Regent Sts. Tube: Oxford Circus. 071/495.2845

**66 Hanover Square** This formal square was built in 1717 to reflect the baroque style of **King George I's** German House of Hanover. Early residents included two of the King's mistresses. While the square's architect is unknown, **John James** designed the **St. George Hanover Square Church,** just south on St. George Street. Completed in 1724, it was the site of several famous weddings, including those of **Percy Bysshe Shelley, Benjamin Disraeli,** and **George Eliot.** ♦ Tube: Oxford Circus

**67 Oxford Street** What was once a Roman road from Hampshire to the Suffolk coast was already a renowned commercial strip by the 19th century. It is said that some of the modern-day fruit and flower sellers are descended from the original traders who once pushed their barrows along this street, now home to two giant department stores. An estimated 464,500 square miles of selling space lines the street, and not all of it is worth looking at. However, those who can tolerate crowds will want to give the bigger firms a try. **Oxford Circus,** at the junction of Oxford and Regent streets, was part of **John Nash's** grand plan, though it was rebuilt by **Sir Henry Tanner** in the early 1920s.

## Bond Street Shopping Map

**OXFORD STREET**

shoes **Dolcis**
womenswear **Warehouse**
womenswear **Blazer**
menswear **Cecil Gee**
Japanese/Korean restaurant **Mirinae**
shoes **Grant**

**Next** clothing

**Berkertex** bridalwear

**Bambino** children's clothing
**Cerruti 1881** clothing

**BLENHEIM STREET**

shoes **Kurt Geiger**
shoes **Carvela**
**Royal Bank of Scotland**
linen, lingerie **Frette**
womenswear **Betty Barclay**
shoes **Lanzoni**
**Phillips Auctioneers**
womenswear **The Discount Designer**
shoes **Ivory**
womenswear **Laurel**
womenswear **Alexan**
designer menswear **Lanvin**
shoes **Russell & Bromley**

*NEW BOND STREET*

**DERING STREET**

**Louis Féraud** womenswear
**Timberland**

**Etienne Aigner** clothing, bags

**Please Mum** children's clothing
**Robina** womenswear
**Escada** womenswear

**Guy Laroche** womenswear

**Dixon's** electrical goods

**BROOK STREET**

shoes **Bally**

silk clothing **Cecil Gee**

**Fenwick's** department store

**Cornelia James** gloves by royal appointment

**Jason** fabrics

**LANCASHIRE COURT**

**Lane Fine Art**
44 shops **Bond St. Antique Centre**
menswear **Herbie Frogg**
cameras, TVs, radios **Wallace Heaton**
**Midland Bank**

**White House** linen, clothing
**Chappell** pianos
**Magli** shoes
**F. Pinet** women's shoes

**GROSVENOR STREET**

leather accessories **Loewe**
clothing **Beale & Inman**
shoes **Church's**
fabrics **Simmonds**
menswear **Yves Saint Laurent**
womenswear **Marie Claire**

**MADDOX STREET**

**Rossini** menswear, furs
**Massada** antique jewelry
**Smythson** stationers
**Herbie** menswear
**Arzani** menswear
**Pal Zileri** menswear
**Ermeneglido Zelga** menswear
**Fogal** hosiery

**BLOOMFIELD PLACE**

antique jewelry **S.J. Phillips**
menswear **Zilli**
fine furniture **Mallett**
clothing **Polo/Ralph Lauren**
antiques **Partridge**
fine art **Wildensein & Co.**
**The Fine Art Society**
leather travel goods **Louis Vuitton**
luxury goods **Iseton**

**Sotheby's** auctioneer
**Richard Green** paintings
**Fior** jewelry
**Herbert Johnson** hatters
**Gordon Scott** shoes
**Celine** accessories
**Wana** womenswear
**Tesslers** antique jewelry
**Russell & Bromley** shoes

*NEW BOND STREET*

**BRUTON STREET**

clothing **Hermès**

cashmere **Ballantyne**
womenswear **Valentino**
fine art **John Mitchell & Son**
ornaments **Lalique**
**Church's Shoes**
**London Savoy Tailors Guild**

**CONDUIT STREET**

**Philip Landon** menswear
**Moira** '30s antique jewelry
**European** menswear
**Air India**

**CLIFFORD STREET**

**Watches of Switzerland**
**Patek Phillippe** watches
**Georg Jensen** silver, porcelain
**Chopard** jewelry
**Adler** jewelry
**Hennel** jewelry

**GRAFTON STREET**

*Map continues on next page*

## Bond Street Shopping Map, cont.

**BROMPTON ROAD**

jewelry, gifts **Asprey Bond St Ltd.**
jewelry **Collingwood**
jewelry **Bulgari**
womenswear **Karl Lagerfeld**
jewelry **Ilias Lala Unis**
watches, jewelry **Cartier**
shoes **Rossetti**
clothing **Henry Cotton's**
jewelry **Boucheron**
jewelry **Tiffany**
womenswear **Chanel**
woolens **William Bill**

**THE ROYAL ARCADE**

chocolates **Charbonnel et Walker**
silversmith **Holmes**
shoes **Bally**
**Gucci**

**STAFFORD STREET**

clothing **Gianni Versace**
art gallery **Entwistle**
art gallery **Deborah Gage**
**Marlborough Fine Arts**
**Lloyds Bank**
art gallery **Noortman**
fine art **Thomas Agnew & Son**
art gallery **Thomas Gibson**

**Philip Antrobus** jewelry
**Adele Davis** womenswear

**Anne Bloom** jewelry
**Ciro** jewelry
**Bentley & Co.** jewelry
**GRAFF** jewelry
**Rolex** watches
**Richard Green** art gallery
**National Westminster Bank**

**BURLINGTON GARDENS**

**Salvatore Ferragamo** womenswear
**Chatila** jewelry
**Pierre Cardin** clothing
**Sulka** menswear
**Clough** jewelry, pawnbroking
**Frost & Reed** art gallery
**Ricci Burns** womenswear
**Colnaghi Art Gallery**
**The Leger Art Galleries**
**Benson and Hedges**
**Ginza Gamagataya & Taylor**
**Ana House**
**Takashimaya** luxury goods
**WR Harvey & Co.** antiques
**Fenzi** womenswear
**Kings of Sheffield** silver, antiques
**Watches of Switzerland**

**OLD BOND STREET**

**PICCADILLY**

**68 John Lewis** Known for the quality of its merchandise, this department store is particularly good for fabrics and drapes. Its motto is: "Never knowingly undersold." ♦ M-W 9AM-5:30PM; Th 9:30AM-8PM; F-Sa 9:30AM-5:30PM. 278 Oxford St. Tube: Oxford Circus. 071/629.7711

**69 D.H. Evans** Women's fashions are this store's strength, and there is also an able hairdresser on the top floor. If you can fight your way past the ground-floor armies of salespeople eager to spray you with the latest fragrance, you'll have ample opportunity to browse for accessories. ♦ M-Tu 10AM-6:30PM; W, F 10AM-8PM; Th 10AM-9PM; Sa 9AM-8PM; Su 11AM-6PM. 318 Oxford St. Tube: Bond St. 071/629.8800

**70 Bond Street** This is Fifth Avenue, Rodeo Drive, and the Faubourg-St.-Honoré rolled into one. Imperturbably chic, Bond Street leads from Piccadilly to Oxford Street and is paved all the way with Gold American Express cards. A few years ago, the legendary shopping street celebrated its 300th birthday, cheating only a little bit: **Old Bond Street** was built in 1686, but **New Bond Street**, which begins at Clifford Street, only dates back to 1721. You can blame the confusing street numbering system on Parliament, which, in 1762, forbade the use of hanging signs to identify shops (too many customers were being clobbered in high

winds) and numbered the streets separately, first up the east side toward Oxford Street and then down again on the west.

Art galleries flourish on and around Bond Street: buy a **Turner** at **Thomas Agnew & Son,** a **Francis Bacon** at **Marlborough Fine Arts,** a **Vanessa Bell** at **Anthony d'Offay,** or an unknown at **Sotheby's,** the world's largest auction house. If art is your interest, do look along Albemarle, Dover, and Grafton streets. Antique lovers should turn left into Burlington Gardens, then left again into a maze of back streets crammed with the old, the opulent, and the unusual.

You can shop at an almost endless number of international fashion boutiques—**Gucci, Hermès, Cartier, Louis Vuitton, Karl Lagerfeld, Ralph Lauren, Chanel, Kurt Geiger.** The challenge is to find something uniquely English: turn left onto Brook Street (it cuts across Bond) and look at **Courtenay** with its British outdoor clothing, silky underwear, and nighties (no, the British don't wear thermals under those tweeds) or **Shirley Parker** for classic womenswear; then stroll along South Molton Street to find **Browns,** the stylish boutique patronized by stars such as **Elton John** and **Joan Collins.** If, instead, you turn right onto Brook Street you will find **Halcyon Days**—a darling little gift emporium filled with knickknacks by Royal Appointment.

**Along Bond Street:**

**Gianni Versace** The staff simply wouldn't dream of telling you the cost of all the marble in this lavish store, and you might prefer not to know. After you've looked over the Versace ready-to-wear and couture collections for men and women with the designer's matching accessories, you may never want to shop anywhere else. ♦ M-Sa 10AM-6PM. 34-36 Old Bond St. Tube: Green Park. 071/499.1862

**Smythson** Very Bond Street and very English, Smythson's invitations feel like diplomas and are the most desired in town. The leather address books and diaries are equally coveted, and even though it's *un peu* pretentious, the address book divided into three sections and inscribed simply "London/ New York/Paris" is truly useful for fortunate vagabonds. ♦ M-Tu, Th-F 9:15AM-5:30PM; W 9:30AM-5:30PM; Sa 10AM-1:30PM. 44 New Bond St. Tube: Bond St. 071/629.8558

**Asprey Bond St Ltd.** Allow the doorman to welcome you to England's most luxurious jewelry and gift shop, which specializes in the finest and the rarest, from crocodile suitcases to **Fabergé** frames. ♦ M-F 9AM-5:30PM; Sa 10AM-5PM. 165-169 New Bond St. Tube: Green Park, Piccadilly Circus. 071/493.6767

**Charbonnel et Walker** The fabulous chocolates come in boxes that are equally treasured. ♦ M-F 9AM-5:30PM; Sa 10AM-4PM. 28 Old Bond St. Tube: Green Park, Piccadilly Circus. 071/491.0939

**71 Claridge's** $$$$ If the royal family favors one hotel above all others for functions, it is Claridge's. The service at this reassuringly old-fashioned and unassuming establishment is always respectful (you'd be respectful, too, if you dealt with as many governmental higher-ups and diplomats as it does). Drinks are brought to your seat by a liveried footman; there is nothing so vulgar as a bar. Evocative of the '30s, a Hungarian quartet entertains daily in the foyer floored with glossy black-and-white marble tiles. Even though it's owned by the **Savoy Group,** the restaurant here is not particularly famous, but it is an aesthetic delight, with floor-to-ceiling Art Deco mirrors along the walls. If you can afford to stay in one of Claridge's huge bedrooms, where you'll be warmed by a real log fire and pampered by a separate dressing room, you'll learn why the Queen is so fond of the place. ♦ Brook St. Tube: Bond St. 071/629.8860; fax 071/499.2210

Within Claridge's:

**The Causerie** ★★★$$$ This green and cream room is one of the few places in London where it is possible to enjoy a first-class *smörgåsbord.* Sample the five types of herring, as well as the wonderful smoked beef, but save room for dessert, in particular the three-chocolate mousse. The appropriate beverage is a glass of champagne. ♦ Scandinavian ♦ Lunch. Closed Saturday and Sunday. Reservations recommended. Jacket and tie required. 071/629.8860

**72 Gray's Antique Market/Gray's Mews** If prices for the collectibles, fashion jewelry, and curios jumbled up in these stalls are not the lowest, they are at least reasonable, and all items are backed up by a guarantee of authenticity; 160 antiques dealers display their wares here. ♦ M-F 10AM-6PM. 58 Davies St and 1-7 Davies Mews. 071/629.7034

**73 E. Joseph Booksellers** Just off Oxford Street is a third-floor shop you might expect to find on Charing Cross Road. This business has been selling books since 1876, and it is one of the few antiquarian and rare-book establishments that doesn't specialize in intimidating potential customers. First-time collectors are as welcome as experienced buyers, and anyone may come inside to gaze at the beautifully bound volumes of **Jane Austen's** and **Ben Jonson's** works, as well as the first editions of **Agatha Christie's** mysteries and *Winnie the Pooh.* ♦ M-F 9:30AM-5:30PM. One Vere St. 071/493.8353 fax 071/629.2759

**74 Selfridges** Although this department store, which opened in 1909, has become a British institution, it is actually an American import, developed by a retail magnate from Wisconsin **Gordon Selfridge.** Its display windows, situated between 22 Ionic columns, create sidewalk crowds at Christmas, and its perfume counter is said to be the largest in Europe. The is the second-largest department store in London (next to **Harrods**). The food hall and the stationery section are both great fun. ♦ M-W, F-Sa 9:30AM-7PM; Th 9:30AM-8PM. 400 Oxford St. Tube: Marble Arch, Bond St. 071/629.1234; fax 071/495.8321

**75 Marks & Spencer** It is claimed that at any given time 8 out of 10 people in London will be sporting underwear from this decidedly British institution, often called "Marks & Sparks" or simply "M&S." While its undergarments are indeed good, so are its woolens, clothing for both sexes, coats, housewares, and famous food department, where the items under its own label match up to those of **Harrods**—and are better priced. ♦ M-W, F-Sa 9AM-7PM; Th 9AM-8PM. 458 Oxford St. Tube: Marble Arch. 071/935.7954

## Bests

### Debora Weston
Actress

Visit the fabulous **Berwick Street Market,** especially on a late Saturday afternoon when all the fruit and vegetables sell for giveaway prices. If the fresh figs and nutty brown Russet apples don't make you go weak at the knees, the big burly men calling you "Luv" and "Duck" certainly will.

A few minutes away by foot is **Old Compton Street.** Make the effort to squeeze your way into **Patisserie Valerie,** where you'll find some of the best French pastry in town. Then push yourself away from your crème brûlée and wander toward **Covent Garden** and eventually you will stumble upon **Neal's Yard,** a cornucopia of health-related shops offering everything from essential oils to information on where to find the nearest yoga class.

After your New Age cup of tea, you'll be ready for an exotic dinner at **Melati,** a hole-in-the-wall Malaysian restaurant on Great Windmill Street. The Melati waiters will correct your order if they don't think you've chosen well.

Theater is London—by all means, see a **West End** musical, but save some time for the smaller venues that keep the magic of theater collaboration alive. The **Royal Court Theatre** (Sloane Square), the **Gate Theatre** (Notting Hill), the **Almeida Theatre** (Islington), and the **Cockpit Theatre** (Marylebone) top my list.

My favorite Sunday includes a shopping spree at **Camden Town Market** to stock up on trendy clothes (especially anything black and tight) and antique jewelry. A quick walk up to **Hampstead** via the heath will get you in shape for a wonderful traditional Sunday lunch at **Jack Straw's,** an old pub at the top of Hampstead Hill. Book a table at the rooftop restaurant and enjoy a view of London that's only marginally more wonderful than the roast potatoes and Yorkshire pudding. Assuming you haven't drunk so much beer that the only choice is to stagger back to your bed and watch the Sunday afternoon soccer match, roll your way 10 minutes down the road and pay a visit to **Dr. Freud's House,** a gem of a museum where your id, ego, and super-ego will all feel equally at home.

### Jane Annakin
Agent, William Morris Agency

**Victoria and Albert Museum**—stroll through the eclectic collections of objets d'art from around the world or just sit in the Italian-style gardens.

**Neal's Yard** and **Neal Street** in Covent Garden—visit ethnic, esoteric shops, get your personal horoscope read, or choose a crystal.

Walk through **Belgravia** on an early summer evening and admire the elegance of bygone days.

**St. James's Park**—feed the water fowl at London's smallest park.

Visit **Greenwich** (home to the *Cutty Sark,* the Royal Observatory, and Queen Charlotte's Palace) by riverboat and see London from a different perspective.

A concert box at **The Albert Hall.**

### Tom Cook
Artist/Former Television Executive

Christmas in **Covent Garden** when the only sounds to be heard are the cooing of pigeons and the flapping of canvas against the metal frames of the empty market stalls—in sharp contrast to the din of 12 million people who visit the area the rest of the year.

Bumping into **Kurt Vonnegut** at the **Whitechapel Art Gallery**—he's much taller than I expected.

Listening to **Syed** play the sitar while munching on a "Nervous Actor" (chicken and ham sandwich) at his **Designer Sandwiches** shop on Endell Street.

Shopping for cheese, sausages, and vegetables at the **Berwick Street Market** in Soho, one of the few places in Britain where "Englishness" merges seamlessly with Continental sensibilities.

The orange and yellow neon glow of **Cambridge Circus** on a rainy evening.

Getting free lessons from **Gauguin, van Gogh, Rembrandt, O'Keeffe,** and the **Lascaux Cave** painters by browsing in **Dillon's Art Bookshop** in Covent Garden and then going next door to **Edward Stanford** to appease my travel fantasies.

Walking through **Chinatown.**

Taking in the relatively unspoiled view of 18th- and 19th-century London, including the best of **St. Paul's Cathedral,** from the upstairs dining room of the **East of the Sun, West of the Moon** restaurant/brasserie at Gabriel's Wharf on the south bank of the Thames.

### Reverend Dr. Judith A. Walker-Riggs
Minister, Rosslyn Hill Unitarian Chapel

Walking in **Hampstead Heath** off Well Walk—Take the right fork of the path, which leads to an open field with a view of all London stretched out before you.

Walking over **Waterloo Bridge** at dusk, from Waterloo Station toward the Houses of Parliament. Everything is lit up and glorious—a cityscape at its romantic best.

Eating at **Byron's** on Downshire Hill, Hampstead—great food without outrageous combinations and prices.

Attending New Age events, lectures, and performances at **St. James's,** Piccadilly.

Reading the "quality" press, especially **Mathew Paris** in the *Times.*

Any canal boat ride—like the one from **Camden Lock**—for an unusual view of the city.

# King's Road/Chelsea

Avant-garde **King's Road**, once synonymous with the swinging London of the 1960s, runs the entire length of the affluent riverside village known as **Chelsea**. A highway created by **Charles II** as his royal route to **Hampton Court**, another royal palace, the street is now a stage set for an assortment of marginal, hip Londoners (from rockers to punks to the hip-hop crowd), in sharp contrast to the surrounding cosmopolitan village of upscale town houses (there are relatively few apartments in this area) inhabited by privileged professionals. Chelsea dwellers live on tree-lined streets in domestic tranquility and endure the anarchy and decadence of King's Road with humor. In fact, they're more preoccupied with changes in their lifestyle (boutiques and antique markets have replaced the local fishmonger, greengrocer, and baker) than they are with the eclectic parade of denizens along the borough's main route.

Cozying up to the River Thames southwest of **Westminster** and south of **Hyde Park**, this section of London is one of the most intimate in the city. The

uman-scale streets and architecture provide a counterpoint for the imposing ublic buildings and monuments of other areas that dwarf pedestrians. Some ondoners consider **Christopher Wren's** magnificent **Royal Hospital** here ne of the most beautiful buildings in the city. Aesthetics aside, the building till functions as a hospital and residence for war veterans (mostly alumni of World War II), whose distinguished scarlet and blue uniforms are part of the conography of Chelsea life.

t is here, in Chelsea, in houses that appear grand according to today's tandards, that authors **Oscar Wilde**, **Thomas Carlyle**, and **George Eliot**, and ainters **James Whistler**, **John Singer Sargent**, and **J.M. Turner** lived. Novelist **Henry James** and painters **Augustus John** and **Dante Gabriel Rossetti** were among the illustrious intellectuals, artists, and bohemians who esided in the neighborhood at one time or another. It doesn't take a articularly vivid imagination to picture them walking these streets, which ave changed so little since their tenure here.

Chelsea is known for its vitality, but also for trendsetting and juxtaposing styles. Until 1985, **Margaret Thatcher's** private London address was here; but this is also where **Mary Quant** launched miniskirts, where the **Rolling Stones** lived once they'd gotten some satisfaction, and where punk began. The village is also home to the **Designer's Guild**, a fabric, furniture, and interior design shop where trends are being set today; and to **Sloane Square**, a small plaza that has become synonymous with a type of upper-class, inbred Londoners known familiarly as **Sloane Rangers.** Sloanes are preppy to the extreme: the women have a marked preference for pearls (even with sweatshirts), ruffles, and floral prints, especially in the country-style interiors of their homes. They often favor pet phrases that brand them as "Sloanes" and they have a distinctive accent. Pundits often point to **Princess Diana**, before **Charles**, as a prime example of the species.

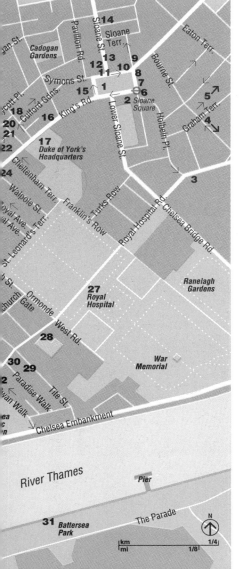

The ideal day to visit Chelsea is on a Saturday, when King's Road is in full bloom, complete with archetypes, poseurs, newlyweds on their way to **Chelsea Town Hall** for the final formalities, Sloane Rangers, and tourists. To get a feel for the yin and the yang of the quarter, make sure you spend some time exploring side streets as well as King's Road.

**1 Sloane Square** Chelsea begins here, under a tent of young plane trees. A running soundtrack of cars and taxis in the background drowns out the watery music of **Gilbert Ledward's** Venus fountain, presented to Chelsea by the **Royal Academy** in 1953. Nothing grows in the square save trees, but color is provided by the flower sellers who purvey fluorescent blooms here, day in and day out, year-round. The square was named after one of Chelsea's most distinguished residents, **Sir Hans Sloane,** a wealthy physician at the beginning of the 18th century who was also president of the **Royal Society,** an organization founded more than 300 years ago to further scientific knowledge. Sloane, who at one time owned practically all of the village of Chelsea, lived in **Henry VIII's** former manor house. His vast collection of plant specimens, fossils, rocks, minerals, and books, amassed over a lifetime, formed the foundation of the **British Museum.** ◆ Bounded by Sloane St and King's Rd, and Lower Sloane St and Cliveden Pl

**2 W.H. Smith** This ubiquitous bookseller (there are 70 branches within London), located on the south side of Sloane Square, is a good place to acquire maps, guidebooks, writing paper, pens, magazines, newspapers, and paperbacks. There is also a large selection of international periodicals. ◆ Newsstand: M-F 8AM-6:15PM. Main shop: M-F 8:45AM-6:15PM; Sa 9AM-6:15PM. Sloane Sq. 071/730.0351

*L'incontro*

**3 L'incontro** ★★$$$ A bit off the beaten track, L'incontro does not look like a restaurant that would attract much evening business. Yet even on a Sunday it can be crowded with customers, among them celebrities such as **Jason Robards,** seated at the exquisitely laid tables. An abundance of Italian waiters ease dishes on and off your table with polished grace. Pasta made on the premises provides the base for wild mushroom or fresh crab sauce, and each bite of the baked monkfish in garlic and butter sauce dissolves delectably in your mouth. Vegetables, however, can be disappointing, although the restaurant claims they're supplied fresh daily. Still, the entrées, the delicious breads and, above all, the truly "orgasmic" *tiramisù* more than compensate for a few soggy beans. Be prepared to pay handsomely for your meal. Nor do wines come cheap here; however, the Italian selection provides refreshing diversity and quality compared to that of many other London restaurants. ◆ Italian ◆ Lunch and dinner; dinner only on Saturday and Sunday. 87 Pimlico Rd. Tube: Sloane Sq. Reservations recommended. 071/730.3663

**4 Mijanou** ★★★$$ If you have never had the experience of dining in a British "front room" (living room), then this is probably the closest you'll come in London. In the cozy atmosphere of this 32-seat bistro, husband and wife team **Sonia** and **Neville Blech** serve French cooking with Mediterranean flourishes. Try the terrine of quail with foie gras for starters and opt for one of the recommended entrées such as housemade ravioli—each stuffed with a different vegetable purée—or *carré d'agneau* (rack of lamb) cooked in saffron and yogurt. Unless you're an oenophile with an encyclopedic memory, you'll appreciate the wine list, which is coded to match the dishes on the menu. Mijanou (which is the nickname of one of the Blechs' daughters) has a solid clientele of regulars, which in and of itself is a good recommendation. ◆ French ◆ Lunch and dinner. Closed Saturday, Sunday, and bank holidays, plus three weeks in August, two weeks at Christmas/New Year, and one week at Easter. 143 Ebury St. Reservations recommended. 071/730.4099

**5 Alison House Hotel** $ In the posh Belgravia district, within walking distance of Victoria Station, this small B&B, run by friendly, helpful proprietor **Gareth Owen,** is justly proud of itself. All 11 rooms (singles, twins, doubles, and triples) come with color TV, hair dryers, and a sink. The price includes a full English breakfast (eggs, bacon, sausage, and toast, with baked beans or tomatoes as an extra). If you share bathroom facilities, a standard twin, double, or triple works out to only a couple of pounds more than staying at many youth hostels. But you can pay a bit more for a room with bath. This well-located hotel, in its price range, is hard to beat. ◆ Deposit required. 82 Ebury St, Belgravia. 071/730.9529

**6 Sloane Square Tube Station** The aboveground station was built over the **River Westbourne,** which flows through an underground cast-iron conduit above the train tracks. In 1940, a German bomb hit the station. It fractured a gas main, injuring and killing scores of employees and passengers. This is the only tube station that serves Chelsea; it does so via the District and Circle lines. ◆ Sloane Sq

**7 Royal Court Theatre** *Look Back in Anger* by **John Osborne,** an explosive 1950s drama whose kitchen-sink realism was unlike anything the class-conscious English theater had ever seen before, put the Royal Court Theatre on the map. But it wasn't surprising that this theater, which produced the early plays of **George Bernard Shaw** from 1904 to 1907, would risk provoking audiences unaccustomed to bitter sarcasm and realism on stage. The Royal Court is now the resident theater for the **English Stage Company,** which carries the torch with its original and controversial productions. The Royal Court was built by **Walter Emden** and **W.R. Crewe** in 1887 and 1888; the version you see today has been rebuilt once and remodeled twice. ♦ Sloane Sq. Box office: 071/730.1745. Credit card orders: 071/730.2554

**8 Oriel Grande Brasserie de la Place** ★$$ A relative newcomer to Sloane Square, this French cafe has most of the advantages of the genre: hot coffee and croissants served early in the morning, *croques monsieur* served all day, good wine by the glass, newspapers on sticks, and attractive cane chairs pulled up to marble-top tables. The only thing lacking is the speed and professionalism of French waiters, sadly absent in their English counterparts. This is the best place in the area for observing Sloanes and Chelsea poseurs, but eat elsewhere if you're famished, since the food takes forever to arrive. The Oriel gets crowded at lunch and late in the afternoon, so watch your belongings. ♦ French ♦ Breakfast, lunch, and dinner. 50-51 Sloane Sq. 071/730.2804

**9 David Mellor** Outstanding contemporary designs for the kitchen and dining room are the hallmark of this inimitable store, whose offerings include handmade wooden salad bowls, pottery bowls, and glassware—the best from British craftspeople, along with a superb selection from France. Since staff are both friendly and helpful, you may have to wait your turn. The specialty is cutlery designed by the great man himself, who, incidentally, is no relation to the Tory MP of the same name. ♦ M-Sa 9:30AM-5:30PM. 4 Sloane Sq. 071/730.4259

**10 Royal Court Hotel** $$$ No matter how much they alter this place, it still has the relaxed atmosphere of a provincial English country hotel. The 101 rooms have all the modern comforts, including 24-hour room service. The doorman, with his gold-and-black braided uniform, despite having dispensed with his original top hat, has become a fixture in the square. ♦ Sloane Sq. 071/730.9191; fax 071/824.8381

Within the Royal Court Hotel:

**No. 12** ★$$ Once known as the **Old Poodle Dog,** this restaurant has since received a name change as well as a refurbishing. Surrounded by French tapestries and contemporary prints, diners can select good, reliable entrées such as corn-fed chicken, duck with honey sauce, or salmon. Frequented by quiet, well-to-do, older Chelsea residents who still remember the neighborhood when it was a village, the 60-seat restaurant is especially good for an early English breakfast. ♦ Continental ♦ Breakfast, lunch, and dinner. 071/730.1499

**11 Sloane Street** Some say this is what Bond Street was like 30 years ago. Sloane Street has quietly become one of the smartest streets in London, taking its lead from **Harvey Nichols**—by far the most stylish department store in London. Designers **Valentino, Ungaro, Bruno Magli,** and **Chanel** have been joined by such fashion innovators as **MaxMara** and **Katherine Hamnett.** The fashion world can be found sipping cappuccino at **L'Express** in the basement of Harvey Nichols. ♦ Between Knightsbridge and Sloane Sq

**12 General Trading Company (GTC)** The GTC, just off Sloane Square, epitomizes everything Sloane—and if you still aren't sure what that means, go in and look around. It is a Sloane-size country house of a store, with irresistible objects that fit into English country life, London-style, from Chatsworth to Battersea. Check out the china department, the antiques (upstairs), the garden department, and the children's toy department, which is open only between September and December. Once nice young girls (pronounced *gels*) worked in florist shops in the hope that they might meet their prince. Now that the royal life has been found lacking by those Sloane fairy-tale seekers, **Princess Diana** and the **Duchess of York,** the *gels* now work in estate agencies or the GTC, waiting for lords rather than princes to whisk them off their feet. The cafe downstairs serves Sloanish foods like lasagna and salad, lemon syllabub, and chocolate cake. Although you can expect long lines at lunchtime, this is an excellent place to observe Sloane accents, sartorial habits, and Sloanedom in general. ♦ M-Tu, Th-Sa 9AM-5:30PM; W 9AM-7PM. 144 Sloane St. 071/730.0411; fax 071/823.4624

**13 Holy Trinity** In spite of the destruction of the vault over the nave by German bombs in World War II, this church, built between 1888 and 1890 by **J.S. Sedding,** is a Gothic Revival homage to the 19th-century Arts and Crafts Movement. Among the pre-Raphaelite treasures are the stunning east window, designed by **Sir Edward Coley Burne-Jones** and made by **William Morris,** and the grill behind the altar by **Henry Wilson.** The church also has an excellent Walker organ. From autumn to June, lunchtime concerts are held on Tuesday by students from the Royal College of Music; phone for details. ♦ Services Su 8:45AM, 11AM. Sloane St. 071/235.3383

When George Bernard Shaw offered Winston Churchill tickets for the first night of *St. Joan* for himself and "a friend, if you have one," Churchill replied that he was sorry he would not be able to attend and asked for tickets for the second night, "if there is one."

## Sloane Street Shopping Map

**SLOANE SQUARE**

Left side:

National Westminster Bank
Holy Trinity
womenswear **Emanuel Kenel**
jewelry **Cobra & Bellamy**
pharmacy **Andrews**

**SLOANE TERRACE**
dry cleaning **Sketchley**
interior design **Jane Churchill**
real estate **Knight Frank & Rutley**

**WILBRAHAM PLACE**
florist **Moyses Stevens**
**Cadogan Travel**
grocery store **Europa**

**ELLIS STREET**

**CADOGAN PLACE**

*(SLOANE STREET)*

**CADOGAN PLACE**
bank **Coutts & Co.**
restaurant **Rib Room**
womenswear **Jaeger**

**COTTAGE WALK**
menswear **Daniel James**
womenswear **169 Sloane Street**
dry cleaner **Sketchley**
grocery store **Sloane Street Superstore**
womenswear **Valentino**
clothing **Henry Cottons**
clothing **Giorgio Armani**
fashion store **Hermès**
womenswear **Georges Rech**
clothing **Daks**
**National Westminster Bank**
pub **The Gloucester**
jewelry **Cartier**
silversmith **Dibdin**

Right side:

**Midland Bank**
**General Trading Company** *department store*
**Cafe de Blank**
**India Jane** *fine gifts*
**Savills** *real estate*
**Hackett** *menswear*
**Jane Churchill** *lighting, linen, accessories*
**Partridges** *deli*
**Coles** *shirtmaker*
**Vidal Sassoon** *hairdresser*
**Presents** *gift shop*
**Dollond & Atchison** *optician*

**CADOGAN GARDENS**

**CADOGAN GATE**

**PAVILION GARDENS**
**Cadogan Hotel**

**PONT STREET**
**Danish Embassy**
**Ivor Gordon** *fine jewelry*
**Stephanie Kellan** *shoes*
**Gina** *women's shoes*
**New Art Centre**
**Lady Daphne** *frames, lamps, clocks*
**Designer's Annexe** *womenswear*
**Mario Saba** *jewelry*
**Walter Moda** *menswear*
**Walter Steiger** *shoes*
**Hilditch & Key** *shirtmakers*
**Emmanuel Ungaro** *womenswear*
**Walter Steiger** *shoes*

**HANS CRESCENT**
**Yves Saint Laurent** *womenswear*
**MaxMara** *womenswear*
**Chanel** *womenswear*
**National Bank of Pakistan**
**National Bank of Abu Dhabi**
**Joseph** *womenswear*
**Christian Dior** *womenswear*
**Equipment** *womenswear*
**Katherine Hamnett** *womenswear*
**The Chelsea Hotel**

*Map continues on next page*

**14 Hotel Wilbraham** $ One of the rare hotels to offer the shabby-genteel atmosphere of country England in the heart of London, this one does so at refreshingly low prices. The hotel is privately owned and unashamedly old-fashioned, with floral wallpaper and formal politeness among the staff that is on the wane in other establishments. Ask for a largish room with your own bath and you will be pleased; otherwise beware—the single room are tiny. All 50 rooms have telephones and room service, and the hotel runs a small restaurant on the premises. Since the Wilbraham is nearly always full, book at least two months in advance. ♦ 1 Wilbraham Pl (at Sloane St). 071/730.8296; fax 071/730.6815

### Sloane Street Shopping Map, cont.

**HARRIET STREET**

menswear **Cecil Gee**
womenswear **Nicole Farhi**
womenswear **Monsoon**
shoes **Fratelli Rossetti**
linens **Descamps**
luggage **Louis Vuitton**

clothing **Hilton**
womenswear **Designer Club**
**Midland Bank**
**Diagnostic & Advisory Hair Centre**
hairdresser
shoes **Bruno Magli**

**National Bank of Dubai**

department store/restaurant **Harvey Nichols**

**SLOANE STREET**

**Gucci**
**Joseph** womenswear
**Kenzo** womenswear
**Sloane's Café Bistro** restaurant
**Cashmeres** women's knitwear
**Oilily** children's clothing
**The Coach Store** luggage
**Christian Lacroix** womenswear
**Celine** womenswear
**Brown's** womenswear
**La Cicogna** maternity and children's clothing
**Esprit** womenswear

**BASIL STREET**

**Alfred Dunhill** luxury goods
**Cashmere Stop** women's knitted clothing
**Bureau de Change**
**Design Label** womenswear
**Knightsbridge Tube Station**

**KNIGHTSBRIDGE**

**15 Peter Jones Department Store** Sloane Square's emporium is a much acclaimed piece of modern design that still succeeds 50 years after it was built. The main architects—**Crabtree, Slater,** and **Moberly**—followed the curve of King's Road, and by 1938 had created a building that possessed the grace and shapeliness of an ocean liner. Duchesses and secretaries shop here, and this is where Sloanedom buys school uniforms. You may even see ladies in tiaras leaving with a small gift for their dinner-party hostess. The store carries great kids' stuff: well-made, classic English children's clothes at very reasonable prices. The china and glass department has a superb selection of English patterns, and the linen department offers beautiful Egyptian cotton sheets, Scottish woolen blankets, and Irish linen tablecloths and napkins. Fascinating vases and ornaments from all over the world are displayed on the ground floor. On the first floor, you'll find ladies' leather gloves lined in cashmere and sensible country shoes for a lot less than you would pay elsewhere. For antiques and rugs, take the lift to the fifth floor. Members of the helpful sales staff are all called partners (at the end of the year they get a share of the profits). The cafe on the fifth floor serves excellent food all day to famished shoppers. ♦ M-Tu, Th-Sa 9AM-5:30PM; W 9:30AM-7PM. Sloane Sq. 071/730.3434; fax 071/730.9645

**16 Body Shop** It's easy to get hooked on these beauty products made from appetizing natural ingredients: rosemary, jojoba, cocoa butter, honey, and orange blossom. They are sold in refillable plastic bottles at reasonable prices,

and are not tested on animals. The shop now offers a range of perfumes that resemble big-name fragrances, but these sell at everywoman prices. New lines include the **Endangered Species** and **Trade Not Aid** products. ♦ M-Sa 9:30AM-6:15PM. 54 King's Rd. 071/584.0163

**17 Duke of York's Headquarters** Behind the iron railings lie the barracks of several London regiments of the **Territorial Army.** The handsome Georgian brick building with its central Tuscan portico (best viewed from Cheltenham Terrace) was originally built in 1801 by **John Sanders,** a pupil of **Sir John Soane,** as a school for the orphans of soldiers. Called the **Royal Military Asylum,** the school that dressed the children in bright red-and-blue uniforms left Chelsea in 1909 when it moved to Dover and Southampton. ♦ King's Rd

**18 Bellville Sassoon** When **Princess Diana** was England's fashion ambassador, before she separated from **Charles,** this was one of her favorite high-fashion shops. Tucked away down a side street, it sells beautiful, superior-quality dresses and suits. ♦ M-Tu, F 9:30AM-5:30PM; W 9:30AM-7PM by appointment. 18 Culford Gdns. 071/581.3500

---

"London—the smokey nest fated to be my favourite residence."

**Mendelssohn**

---

**Restaurants/Clubs:** Red    **Hotels:** Blue
**Shops/ ♣ Outdoors:** Green    **Sights/Culture:** Black

**19 Admiral Codrington** $ A haunt for both yuppies and Sloanes, the **Admiral Cod,** as it's affectionately known, welcomes children both in the conservatory and restaurant, but not in the pub. Even if it's raining, the Plexiglas roof allows you to sit in a bright, cheery room, surrounded by hanging plants. ◆ Pub ◆ M-Sa 11AM-11PM; Su noon-3PM, 7-10:30PM. 17 Mossop St. 071/581.0005

**20 John Sandoe Books** Just off King's Road, John Sandoe is one of the best literary bookshops in London, beloved by readers and writers alike. Although the owner has now retired, his staff has a knowledge of books that would put many an Oxford don to shame. The shop, which allows writers to buy books on credit, has a devoted clientele of literate aristocrats, and will send your books to you anywhere in the world. ◆ M-Tu, Th-Sa 9:30AM-5:30PM; W 9:30AM-7:30PM. 10 Blackland's Terr. 071/589.9473

**21 English Garden** ★★$$$ A lovely plant-filled conservatory at the back of a dark, heavily draped front room provides the setting for a scrumptious and sometimes innovative menu. Try the brie in filo pastry to start, then move on to grilled lobster and scallops in herb-hollandaise sauce, or the watercress-mango salad. The wine list is jolly good, too. If you're watching your wallet, note that lunch is a lot cheaper than supper here. ◆ British ◆ Lunch and dinner. 10 Lincoln St. 071/584.7272

**22 G&D Boulangerie** ★★$ It's worth knowing about this place when you need a quick coffee and croissant, despite the fact that you'll have to enjoy it either standing or perched on a stool. ◆ Cafe ◆ Breakfast, lunch, and early dinner. Closed Sunday. 74 King's Rd. 071/584.1873

**23 Hobbs** Comfortable shoes with great style and a look definitely their own are the stock in trade at Hobbs. Designed by **Marilyn Anselm,** this wonderfully affordable footwear is made in Italy. The clothes, while interesting, aren't as unique as the shoes. ◆ M, Th-Sa 10AM-6PM; Tu 10:30AM-6PM; W 10AM-7PM. 84 King's Rd. 071/581.2914

**23 Chelsea Kitchen** ★$ Cheap and honest, the Chelsea Kitchen is related to the **Stockpot** chain of restaurants, and after three decades,

it has become a King's Road institution. Everything is fresh and homemade, including the breads, scones, and pastries. The menu changes twice daily and regulars play "name that cuisine," trying to identify whether the dish they order is Italian, Spanish, French, or English. This place is also popular for English and Continental breakfasts. ◆ International ◆ Breakfast, lunch, and dinner. 98 King's Rd. 071/589.1330

**24 Pied à Terre** Look here for high-fashion French and Italian shoes in great colors and first-rate designs. In winter, the boots are handsome, indeed. This is just one of several outlets in London. ◆ M-Tu, Sa 10AM-6:30PM; W 10AM-7:30PM; Th-F 10AM-7PM. 33G King's Rd. 071/259.9821

**25 Monkeys** ★★$$ Hidden away in a back street, this restaurant is a real find. Amid cartoons, paintings of monkeys, and pine paneling, London's chic set nibbles on the quail's egg salad or beef stroganoff. There's a treacle tart and real custard for dessert. ◆ British ◆ Lunch and dinner. Closed Saturday, Sunday, and three weeks in August. 1 Cale St, Chelsea Green. 071/352.4711

**26 Royal Avenue** All that materialized of the triumphal route intended to connect the **Royal Hospital** with **Kensington Palace,** this ambitious avenue, conceived by **Sir Christopher Wren** for **William III,** never got beyond King's Road. But the four rows of majestic plane trees, with 19th-century houses as a backdrop, make a magnificent impression. The avenue is also **James Bond's** London address. **Bram Stoker,** creator of *Dracula,* lived at **No. 18** between 1896 and 1906. To the south lies **Burton's Court,** a large playing field with an 18th-century gate that was the original entrance to the Royal Hospital. Open-air art exhibitions are held here on Saturday in the summer. ◆ Between King's Rd and St. Leonard's Terr

**27 Royal Hospital** Guidebooks perpetuate the myth that **Nell Gwyn,** mistress of **Charles II,** was so moved when a wounded soldier begged for alms that she persuaded the King to build the Royal Hospital. It's more likely, however, that Charles, impressed and inspired by reports of **Louis XIV's** Hôtel des Invalides, decided to emulate him. In 1682, diarist **Sir**

*Royal Hospital*

John Evelyn and Army Paymaster General **Sir Stephen Fox** drew up plans for a hospital and residence for army pensioners, and Charles II commissioned **Sir Christopher Wren,** who chose the magnificent river site, to build it. After St. Paul's, this building, finished in 1686, is considered Wren's masterpiece. The glorious elders' home still provides shelter to 400 war veterans known as the **Chelsea Pensioners,** and there's a waiting list to get in.

On 29 May each year, the pensioners celebrate **Oak Apple Day,** commemorating Charles II's escape from Cromwell's troops (he hid in an oak tree after the Battle of Worcester) by placing a wreath of oak leaves around the neck of the bronze statue of Charles II in the **Figure Court.** The statue was cast in 1676 by **Grinling Gibbons.** On Oak Apple Day, the pensioners change from their blue winter uniforms, designed in the time of the Duke of Marlborough, to their scarlet summer tunics and receive double rations. This colorful ceremony is not open to the public, but civilians who ask for permission to attend, in writing and well in advance, are sometimes admitted. You can see the pensioners, at all times of the year, proudly walking the streets of Chelsea resplendent in their uniforms. Even the King's Road trendies make way for them to pass.

The hospital consists of a central block, which houses the chapel and the main mall, connected by an octagonal vestibule. The pensioners live in the twin galleries, or wings, which run at right angles to the river. The small museum in the **Secretary's Office Block** on the east side of the hospital, designed in 1816 by **Sir John Soane,** contains prints, uniforms, medals, and photographs associated with the hospital and its history, including two large paintings in **Wellington Hall**: the *Battle of Waterloo* by **George Jones,** and **Haydon's** *Wellington Describing the Field of Waterloo to George IV.*

The pensioners have their meals in the **Great Hall** under the *Triumph of Charles II,* a huge painting by **Antonio Verrio** of the King on horseback crushing serpents, with the Royal Hospital in the background. Around the hall are portraits of British kings and queens from Charles II to Victoria. When Wellington was laid in state here in 1852, two mourners were trampled to death by the crowds.

The chapel is pure Wren, with his signature black-and-white marble floor, fine carved paneling by Gibbons, and **Sebastiano Ricci's** *Resurrection* over the altar. The glass case beside the altar contains a prayer book, placed there in 1690, opened to a prayer of thanksgiving for the Restoration (the reestablishment of the monarchy under Charles II in 1660), without which there would be no Royal Hospital. Visitors are welcome to

attend services on Sunday. The best way to see the Royal Hospital is with a Chelsea Pensioner as your guide, and there is almost always one around willing to provide this service. (A gratuity is usually welcome.)

In the 18th century, the vast **Ranelagh Gardens** of the Royal Hospital were open to the public, complete with a gilt amphitheater and a site for eating, drinking, music, masquerades, fireworks, and balloon flights. **Canaletto** painted them, **Mozart** played in them, the royal family enjoyed them, and all levels of London society took pleasure in them—until 1803, when they closed their doors. Now this part of the Royal Hospital grounds is the site of the **Chelsea Flower Show,** and for four days in May some of the exuberance and pleasure of those early times is rekindled. The grounds, chapel, and **Great Hall** are open to the public, as are the **State Apartments,** at certain times (call to find out schedules). ♦ Free. M-F 10AM-noon, 2-4PM. Chapel services Su 8:30AM, 11AM, noon. Royal Hospital Rd. 071/730.0161

**28 National Army Museum** The Royal Hospital doesn't feel like a hospital, nor does it exude military history, though many of the pensioners are war heroes. Just next door, however, the National Army Museum covers British Army history from the 15th century to the present, including the Falklands War of 1982. The museum houses five galleries: one for weapons, another for uniforms, an art gallery, and two that cover army history, beginning with the *Yeoman of the Guard* in 1485. There are lots of models and dioramas of battles, and the skeleton of **Napoleon's** horse, **Marengo.** Originally founded at Sandhurst in 1960 and opened here in 1971, the museum is a must for students of military history. The museum owns **Hitler's** telephone switchboard, which was captured in Berlin in 1945. On the board are direct lines to infamous people like **Goebbels** and **Himmler.** There is also a permanent exhibit of the **Battle of Waterloo,** which includes a 400-square-foot model of the battle itself. Artists represented in the art gallery include **Sir Joshua Reynolds, George Romney, Sir Thomas Lawrence,** and **Thomas Gainsborough.** ♦ Free. Daily 10AM-5:30PM. Royal Hospital Rd. 071/730.0717

**29 Tite Street** The favored haunt of artists and writers in the late 19th century, Tite Street sheltered a number whose names are familiar. The brilliant and eccentric **Oscar Wilde** lived at **No. 34** with his wife from 1884 until 1895. The study where he wrote *Lady Windemere's Fan, An Ideal Husband,* and *The Importance of Being Earnest* was painted buttercup-yellow with red lacquer accents. The dining room, in shades of ivory and pearl, exuded tranquility, the one quality that permanently and fatally eluded Wilde. The author was arrested and imprisoned for homosexual offenses; while he was in **Reading Jail,** he was declared bankrupt and his house was sold. When he was released, he moved to France, where he died in 1900. A plaque was placed on Wilde's house in 1954, on the centenary of his birth, by **Sir Compton MacKenzie,** before an audience of Chelsea artists and writers.

The American artist **John Singer Sargent** lived at **No. 31** in a studio house that is pure Chelsea. Here he painted his portraits of the rich, famous, and often beautiful, including actress **Ellen Terry,** who lived nearby on King's Road, and the American writer who

lived around the corner on Cheyne Walk, **Henry James.** Sargent died here in 1925.

The bohemian portrait painter **Augustus John** had his studio at **No. 33. No. 13** is the former home of one of America's greatest painters, **James Whistler.** A libel suit he brought against critic **John Ruskin** left Whistler with huge and unpayable legal costs, and he was declared bankrupt in 1879. No. 13 was his first permanent address after the lawsuit, but the disgruntle artist lived at a total of nine Chelsea addresses before he died in Cheyne Walk in 1903. ♦ Between Tedworth Sq and Chelsea Embankment

# The Not-So-Secret Garden

The English, while not considered a passionate race, can be fanatically emotional and committed when it comes to their pets and their gardens. One of the great yearly events in London, guaranteed to cause hearts to quicken, is the **Chelsea Flower Show,** the largest, most popular, and most prestigious flower show in the world. For four days during the third week in May (Tuesday through Friday), a flower-lover's paradise covers 22 acres of the **Royal Hospital** grounds in Chelsea. Inevitably, rain falls and flowers and guests crowd under the great marquee, an enormous tent in which rare and ornamental flowers and plants are displayed, for protection (be forewarned: temperatures inside soar on hot days!). But in 1989, the sun surprised exhibitors and visitors alike by shining gloriously—a bit too gloriously, in fact. Both blooms and bloom lovers wilted badly in the heat.

For 40 days and 40 nights—21 days to put up the show, 4 days for the show itself, and 15 to take it down—the **Royal Horticultural Society** choreographs this immense and increasingly international event. Amateurs and professionals as well as the nonhorticultural come to look at, learn about, judge, worship, and buy everything from Georgian roses to gardener's knee-pads and Gothic garden benches.

The British class structure is evident at this most English event, beginning with a special preview for the flower-loving royal family. On the first two and a half days, only members of the Royal Horticultural Society are admitted. On Thursday and Friday, doors open to the public. In recent years, up to 70,000 people a day came to see the show, but since 1987, numbers have been restricted to an average of 48,000 daily.

After 5:30PM on Thursday, the cost of admission is reduced (the show goes on until 8PM). On Friday at 5PM, many of the plants are sold off at closing, and six-foot delphiniums and fuchsias can be seen wobbling through **Sloane Square Station's** ticket barriers and standing at bus queues as proud owne totter home with their trophies.

You can sup on anything from champagne and strawberries, beer and sausages, or tea and scones at the show. There is wonderful shopping, too, with stands selling everything from handmade wicker baskets and English *wellies* to priceless botanical prints, floral tea towels, bowls of potpourri, and rar gardening books. The great attraction, of course, is the gardens planted for the occasion—magnificent combinations of flowers, shrubs, garden seats, sto paths, arbors, sunken ponds, gazebos, and statuary Every inch of soil is densely packed with parterres o pink and white lupins, blue phlox, pale-green bells o Ireland, white and pink poppies, light-green tobacc plants, pink foxgloves, white snapdragons, creamy-green mignonettes, pale-blue Canterbury bells, lavender, an honor-guard of delphiniums—and eac species is labeled with its Latin name. The genius o these gardens is that, in spite of the unreliable and unpredictable nature of plants, they all look perfect, even those that didn't win one of the Gold Medals (59 were awarded in 1993).

To attend the flower show during the opening days, you must become a member of the Royal Horticultural Society. Otherwise, call the **Flower Show Information Line** at 071/828.1744 in September when advance tickets go on sale. To purchase tickets with a credit card, call 071/396.47 (there's no booking fee). Children under five and babies are not admitted.

**30 Foxtrot Oscar** ★★★$$ Despite its name, which is military jargon for a two-word expletive that starts with the same initials, this restaurant, owned by an old Etonian, is very popular because of its grilled steaks, terrific salads (seafood, smoked goose), imaginative and tasty versions of English classics like kedgeree and steak-and-kidney pie, and a creative wine list. No wonder it's full of Sloanes and London's glitterati, wearing bright colors and suntans, and talking loudly. When they get very noisy, the English nickname them "Hooray Henrys." But ignore them: this place is so reasonably priced, clever, and relaxed that it is well worth putting up with the diners at the next table. ♦ British ♦ Lunch and dinner. 79 Royal Hospital Rd. Reservations required. 071/352.7179

**31 Japanese Peace Pagoda** If you walk to the end of Tite Street on the Embankment and look across the River Thames, you can see the newest addition to the London riverside—the Japanese Peace Pagoda. The 100-foot bronze and gold-leaf Buddha, staring out over the river, was inaugurated in May 1985. This temple of peace was built in 11 months by 50 monks and nuns, mainly from Japan. Some Buddhist monks actually live in a small wooded area in Battersea park where the pagoda is located and look after it, much to the amazement of locals. It is the last great work of the **Most Venerable Nichidatsu Fujii,** the Buddhist leader who died at the age of 100, one month before his noble and majestic temple was completed. ♦ Daily 7:30AM-dusk. Battersea Park. 081/871.7530

**32 La Tante Claire** ★★★$$$$ If you have to choose among the Tower of London, Westminster Abbey, the British Museum, or a meal at La Tante Claire, strongly consider going for the latter. This French restaurant, an outstanding treasure in London's considerable firmament, is a perfect place to stop for lunch while strolling through Chelsea. La Tante Claire was voted one of the top two London restaurants by *The Good Food Guide* in 1993. The decor is as chic and impressive as the cooking has always been, while chef **Pierre Koffman** is that rare being—a modest genius. A meal here combines simplicity with imagination: choose from first-class game, beef, fish, lamb, and vegetables in season, knowing that you will receive a revelation. Duck with two sauces, lobster roasted with spice, salmon with goose fat, roast wood-cock, or daube of beef all come highly recommended. The cheeses, from **Olivier,** are perfection, and the desserts a tour de force. If you really have no room left for the *feuilleté* of pear with caramel sauce, at least order a sorbet, for which Koffman is renowned. The generous fixed-price lunch menu is an outstanding value. Dress smartly if you're planning on dining here, as everyone else does. Reserve your table when you book your flight. ♦ French ♦ Lunch and dinner. Closed Saturday and Sunday. 68 Royal Hospital Rd. Jacket and tie required for dinner. Reservations required. 071/352.6045; fax 071/352.3257

**33 Chelsea Physic Garden** Stroll from **Dilke Street** onto **Swan Walk**, with its row of 18th-century houses, and you'll reach the handsome iron gates of the second oldest surviving botanical garden in England, founded by the **Worshipful Society of Apothecaries** in 1673 (100 years before Kew Gardens) on four acres of land belonging to **Charles Cheyne** (pronounced CHAIN-ee). In 1722, **Sir Hans Sloane,** botanist and physician to **George II** and Lord of the Manor, granted a continuous lease, requiring the apothecaries to present 50 plant species a year to the Royal Society (an organization founded in 1660 to further scientific knowledge) until some 2,000 had been acquired. Sloane was a member and eventually succeeded Isaac Newton as president of the Royal Society. After the invention of the Wardian case, a container for carrying seeds that prevented them from perishing, the Physic Garden's staff became instrumental in propagating the world's staple crops. In 1722, the first cotton seeds were exported to a garden in Georgia, in the United States, from the South Seas. **Robert Fortune,** a curator of the garden, carried tea to India from China, and Malaya got its rubber from South America. The Physic Garden opened its doors to the public in 1983 for the first time in 300 years. Now, from spring until fall and under the watchful eye of Sir Hans Sloane himself (statue by **Michael Rysbrack**), you can examine some of the 7,000 specimens of plants that still grow here. The magnificent trees include the Willow Pattern, the pomegranate, and the exotic cork oak. Plants and seeds are for sale. ♦ Admission. W-Su 2-5PM late Mar-Oct. 66 Royal Hospital Rd. 071/352.5646

**34 Chelsea Embankment** This unbeatably beautiful walk along the river, part of **Sir Joseph Bazalgette's** dual sewage/roadway system, suffers from the noise of the relentless traffic it was built to support. Still, it's worth making an effort to transcend the motorized roar to see this miraculously unchanged patch of London. The embankment begins at **Chelsea Bridge.** Built in 1934 by **G. Topham Forrest** and **E.P. Wheeler,** this graceful suspension bridge edges up to the massive and dramatic **Battersea Power Station.** The station's four chimneys are part of London's industrial archaeology. So far, the power station has successfully resisted all attempts at demolition, even after the chimneys retired. In fact, only two ever functioned: the front pair were added purely for aesthetic reasons, to provide a sense of balance. The power station currently stands empty after an abortive attempt to transform it into a leisure center, and Londoners fear the worst. ♦ Between Albert Bridge and Chelsea Bridge

**35 Cheyne Walk** Where the **Royal Hospital Road** and **Chelsea Embankment** converge, the elegant Cheyne Walk begins. The embankment (somewhat) protects the single row of houses from traffic, and the lucky residents have a view of the Thames through a row of trees. Some of the happy few who have lived in these priceless Georgian brick houses include **Rolling Stones'** guitarist **Keith Richards,** the illustrious publisher **Lord Weidenfeld** (still a resident), and the beknighted, sadly reclusive **J. Paul Getty, Jr.** But it is past residents who haunt the high windows. **George Eliot** lived at **No. 4** for 19 days after her late-in-life wedding to **John Cross;** she was 61 at the time, and died only a few months later. The pre-Raphaelite painter and poet **Dante Gabriel Rossetti** lived at **No. 16,** then known as **Tudor House,** the finest residence on the street. He led an eccentric *vie de bohème* here while mourning the loss of his wife, **Elizabeth Siddal** (the model for **Sir John Everett Millais'** painting of the dying Ophelia and the deadly beauty in *Beata Beatrix* by Rossetti—both in the Tate Gallery). Rossetti's Chelsea menagerie included a kangaroo, peacocks, armadillos, a marmot, a zebu, and he received frequent visits from fellow pre-Raphaelites **William Morris** and his wife, **Janey,** who inspired great passion in Rossetti. Today, No. 16 is known as **Queen's House,** the name inspired by the initials RC on the top of the iron gateway, long assumed to stand for **(Regina) Catherine of Braganza,** Queen of Charles II. In fact, the initials stand for **Richard Chapman,** who built the house in 1717.

Opposite the house in the Embankment Gardens is the **Rossetti Fountain,** a memorial to the artist from his friends, including Millais and **G.F. Watts,** unveiled in 1887 by **William Чolman Hunt**. The fountain is by **J.P. Seddon,** and the bust of Rossetti is by **Ford Madox Brown.** Unfortunately, the original bronze bust was stolen, so it was replaced by this fiberglass copy. The plaque on **No. 23** Cheyne Walk commemorates the site of **Henry VIII's Manor House,** which stood where Nos. 19 to 26 Cheyne Walk are now. Henry VIII became fond of the Chelsea riverside during his many visits to his friend **Sir Thomas More,** and the year after More's death, he built a palace along the embankment. Before Henry died, he gave the house to **Catherine Parr,** his last wife. One hundred years later, the house was purchased by **Lady Jane Cheyne**—the Cheynes were Lords of Chelsea Manor from 1660 to 1712 (in 1737, **Sir Hans Sloane** bought the Manor).

More's house was demolished a few years later. The gateway by **Inigo Jones** was given to the **Earl of Burlington,** who erected it in the gardens of Chiswick House, where it still stands.

**36 Cadogan Pier** Every July, the pier just east of Albert Bridge is the finishing point of one of England's oldest contests, the **Doggett's Coat and Badge Race.** The race began in 1715 to celebrate the accession of **George I** to the throne, and was sponsored by **Thomas Doggett,** actor-manager of the Drury Lane Theatre, who awarded a coat and badge to the winner. A moving ceremony reenacting the final journey of **Sir Thomas More** from his home here on the river to the Tower of London, where he was executed, also takes place at the pier in July. ♦ Cheyne Walk

**37 Albert Bridge** Lovers propose here and tired commuters refresh themselves looking at this bridge, the one Londoners love the most. Although in 1973 the Albert Bridge was strengthened, it still has a weight limit, which means that red London buses and lorries never darken its tarmac. There is even a notice telling foot soldiers to break step when crossing. The latticework suspension bridge, built by **R.M. Ordish** in 1873, is painted in ice-cream pastels—pistachio and cream—and at night is illuminated with strings of lights. The best time to view the bridge is at dusk from Chelsea Bridge (downriver), when the sun sets behind it and the bridge takes on a fairy-tale quality. At night, see it from Battersea Bridge (upriver); the red lights of Chelsea Bridge glow behind it for a lovely effect. ♦ Cheyne Walk

**38 Carlyle's House** It's a short walk up Cheyne Row to **No. 5,** now known as **No. 24** (pictured above), one of the most fascinating homes in Chelsea and one of the few that is open to the public. Set in a terrace of redbrick houses begun in 1703, this was the residence of the writer **Thomas Carlyle** and his wife, **Jane.** The rooms are almost exactly as they were 150 years ago when *The French Revolution* made its author famous, and **Charles Dickens, Robert Browning, Charles Darwin, Alfred Lord Tennyson,** and **Frédéric Chopin** were visitors. Most of the furniture, pictures, and books belonged to the Carlyles—his hat is still on the hat-stand by the door. Go down into the kitchen and see the pump, the stone trough, and the wide grate where kettles boiled. Tennyson and Carlyle used to escape to the kitchen when they wanted to smoke without provoking Mrs. C. Examine the rooms upstairs, with their four-poster beds, piles of books, mahogany cupboards, and dark Victorian wallpaper (which covers 18th-century pine paneling). Look at the double-walled attic study, carefully designed to keep out the noises of the house and the street (it was unsuccessful). The 19th-century painting, *A Chelsea Interior,* hangs in the ground-floor sitting room and shows how little the house has changed.

The tombstone in the small garden behind the house marks where Mrs. Carlyle's dog **Nero** lies buried. Carlyle was a famous Chelsea figure: the "sage of Chelsea" took solitary walks along these streets throughout his life. A bronze statue of Carlyle (by **Boehm** and erected in 1883) in the **Embankment Gardens** of Cheyne Row is said to look very much like him. Here the essayist and historian sits surrounded by a pile of books and gazes sadly at the river through an invasion of Mack trucks. ♦ Admission. W-Su 11AM-5PM Apr-Oct. 5/24 Cheyne Row. 071/352.7087

**39 Cross Keys** ★★$ This small, friendly, popular pub spills out onto the sidewalk in summer, when the pretty walled garden in the back isn't big enough to hold the thirsty clientele. The cold table—salads, meats, pâtés, and cheeses—is always fresh and good. ♦ Pub ♦ M-Sa 11AM-3PM, 5:30-11PM; Su noon-3PM, 7-10:30PM. 2 Lawrence St. 071/352.1893

**40 King's Head and Eight Bells** ★★$ It's worth coming in for a drink just to raise your glass to a pub that's 400 years old, though the 18th-century decor and engravings of Chelsea in bygone days don't date back that far. Gaze out at the river, eat at the restaurant, and try the Wethered's or Flowers bitter. ♦ Pub ♦ M-Sa 11AM-11PM; Su noon-3PM, 7-10:30PM. 50 Cheyne Walk. 071/352.1820

---

'At length they all to merry London come,
To merry London, my most kindly nurse,
That to me gave this life's first native source"

**Edmund Spenser**

---

estaurants/Clubs: Red    Hotels: Blue

ops/ ♦ Outdoors: Green    Sights/Culture: Black

**41 Chelsea Old Church** Otherwise known as **All Saints,** this church was founded in the middle of the 12th century. In spite of the heartless traffic that passes it daily and the German bombs that flattened it in 1941, this lovely old church is spiritually intact, a glorious monument to its former parishioner, **Sir Thomas More.** The chapel, restored and designed in part in 1528 by **Hans Holbein the Younger,** a friend of More's whom he enlisted to contribute to the restoration, resonates with the deep sadness of the gentle man whose conscience would not allow him either to recognize his friend **Henry VIII** as head of the Church of England, nor grant his blessing for divorce. More, who wrote his own epitaph (against the south wall to the right of the altar) two years before his death, paid for his conscience with his life. The remains of the saint are believed to be buried at Canterbury, but a Chelsea legend holds that More's daughter, **Margaret Roper,** made her way back here with her father's head, which is said to be in the Gothic tomb inside the church.

The ornate tomb with the urn in the chapel is the burial place of Chelsea's next best-known citizen, **Sir Hans Sloane.** The half-dozen chained books (books that were chained to desks to avoid theft at a time when books were a rare and valuable commodity), including the 1717 edition of the *Vinegar Bible,* which contains a printer's error converting the parable of the "vineyard" into the parable of the "vinegar," are the only such books still found in a London church. The square tower, which has since been carefully rebuilt, was the casualty of a German air raid in 1941. Off to the left side is the **Lawrence Chapel,** where Henry VIII is supposed to have secretly married **Jane Seymour** a few days before their official wedding in 1536, a year after Sir Thomas More had ceased to be a conscience to the King. On summer days, the church is the setting for happier weddings, and each July a sermon written by More is read from the pulpit. A memorial stone commemorates the American writer **Henry James,** who lived in Chelsea and died near here in 1916. ♦ M-F 10AM-1PM, 2-5PM. Guided tours: Su 1:30-5:30PM. Old Church St. 071/352.5627

**42 Roper Gardens** This garden, created in the 1960s on the site of part of **Sir Thomas More's** estate, is named after **Margaret Roper,** More's beloved eldest daughter. It replaced a garden destroyed by German bombs. See the stone relief of a woman walking against the wind by **Jacob Epstein.** ♦ Cheyne Walk

**43 Crosby Hall** Three hundred years after **Sir Thomas More** was executed, this splendid mansion he once owned was transported, stone by stone, from Bishopsgate in the City to Chelsea. Originally built in the mid-1400s, the hall was then made into a royal palace by **Richard III,** and finally purchased in 1516 by More himself. It is now the dining room of the **British Federation of University Women.** This building is no longer open to the public, which is unfortunate since the superb hammerbeam roof, the stunning oriel window, the long Jacobean table (a gift from **Nancy Astor**), and the **Holbein** painting of the More family, one of three copies made by the painter for the three More daughters, are all worth seeing. Some architecturally sensitive types lament the postwar annex and neo-Tudor building of 1925 next door. ♦ Cheyne Walk. 071/404.6447

**44 Beaufort Street** One of the busiest crossroads in Chelsea that connects the King's Road to Battersea Bridge, Beaufort Street cuts across the site of **Thomas More's** country house. The residence was demolished when **Sir Hans Sloane** acquired the estate in the 1740s. ♦ Between King's Rd and Cheyne Walk

**45 Lindsey House** Remarkable for its beauty and its survival against all odds, this large country house is the only one of its date (circa 1640-74) and size in Chelsea. The vast residence was built on the site of a farmhouse by **Theodore Mayerne,** the Swiss physician to **James I** and **Charles I.** In the 1660s, it was sold to **Robert,** 3rd Earl of Lindsey, who purchased it and substantially rebuilt it. The remarkable cast of residents in the 1770s included painter **John Martin;** engineer **Sir Marc Brunel,** who built the first tunnel under the Thames; and Brunel's son **Isambard Kingdom Brunel,** another engineer, who built many of England's suspension and railway bridges and lived at **No. 98. (Brunel House,** 105 Cheyne Walk, is named after the father and son.) **James Whistler** lived at **No. 96** from 1866 to 1878 (one of his nine Chelsea addresses). It was here that he painted the famous portrait of his mother. **Elizabeth Gaskell,** the novelist, was also born here. The gardens connected to **Nos. 99** and **100** were designed by **Sir Edwin Lutyens.** ♦ Nos. 96-100 Cheyne Walk

Summer in England means Wimbledon, the races at Ascot, the regatta at Henley, and Pimm's Cup, a favorite drink at all these events since James Pimm concocted the famous Pimm's No. 1 in the 1840s. His confection of gin, fruit liqueurs, herbs, spices, and bitters is more popular than ever today. Pimm's Cup is simple to make: take one part Pimm's No. 1 and add two to three parts mixer, plenty of ice, a thin slice of lemon or lime, and a swirl of cucumber ring. You can alter the sweetness of the drink by using soda water, tonic, ginger ale, lemonade—even champagne. And to be perfectly proper, serve it in a frosted pewter or silver mug, as it's done in clubland.

**45 Turner's House** England's greatest painter, **J.M.W. Turner,** lived in this tall, narrow house (shown above) during his last years. To remain anonymous, he adopted his landlady's surname—he was known locally as Admiral Booth. Turner died here in 1851, uttering his last words, "God is Light." ♦ 119 Cheyne Walk

**46 Chelsea Harbour** Where **Cheyne Walk** at its western end becomes **Lots Road** is now a fashionable place to live. A much sought-after condominium development called Chelsea Harbour has attracted English television, pop, and sports personalities to some of the best views and most expensive apartments in London. Houses, offices, shops, restaurants, landscaped gardens, and the **Conrad** hotel are all crushed into this tiny area set around a 75-berth yacht marina. Hoppa buses (small red buses that supplement the regular bus system from **Earl's Court** and **Kensington High Street**) visit the area regularly.

Within Chelsea Harbour:

**The Canteen** ★★★$$ Superstar British actor **Michael Caine** is famous for pulling in the glitterati to eat at his restaurants. After his success with **Langan's,** he's teamed up with mercurial **Marco Pierre White,** chef and owner of **Harvey's** restaurant, to open this 150-seat culinary mecca. The restaurant's light Mediterranean dishes, such as fillet of salmon with a crab crust and shellfish sauce, are consumed along with expansive harbor views. Meanwhile, Caine himself can gaze down on the gazers from his apartment in the adjacent residential complex. ♦ French ♦ Lunch and dinner. 071/351.7330

**Hotel Conrad** $$$$ Overlooking Chelsea Harbour Marina and apartment block, the curving all-suite hotel is a beautifully designed part of this modern complex. The quiet suites, outfitted in muted colors by well-known interior designer **David Hicks,** don't all have views of the marina. If you want a panorama, expect to pay extra for the privilege. ♦ 071/823.3000; f 071/351.6525

**47 Furniture Cave** One of London's largest places to buy antique furniture, this market contains 20 dealers selling antiques and beautiful furniture from all over the world. ♦ M-Sa 10AM-6PM; Su 11AM-4PM. 533 King's Rd. 071/352.4229

**47 Christopher Wray's Lighting Emporium** Actor-turned-shopkeeper (and later millionaire) **Christopher Wray** gave up the lure of the bright lights to make bright lights of his own, restoring and later manufacturing antique lamps, shades, and bulbs to be snapped up by the style-conscious middle class. His once-tiny shop is now the largest center of its kind in Europe, selling restored antique and reproduction Georgian, Victorian, Art Deco, and Tiffany lamps and light fittings. For the Tiffanys, he imports handmade opalescent glass from America. The shops themselves are Victoriana personified, with old-fashioned cast-iron-and-glass awnings. ♦ M-Sa 9:30AM-6PM. 600 King's Rd. 071/736.8434

**48 Chelsea Bun** $ Named after an English cake, this cafe serves good, simple food like salads, spaghetti bolognaise, fish-and-chips, and bacon and eggs, all dispensed quickly at affordable prices. It's such a bargain that the place is always full, but never of poseurs. Sip coffee or eat a full meal. ♦ British ♦ Breakfast, lunch, and dinner. 9A Limerston St. 071/352.3635

**49 Johnny Moke** Facing you at the sharp bend in the King's Road known as World's End is a men's and women's designer shoe shop that's been here since the '60s. The chap with the glasses is **Johnny,** who often serves you himself. He makes divine high-fashion shoes that show up in all the right magazines and on the feet of fashion editors and models. ♦ M-Sa 10:30AM-6:30PM. 396 King's Rd. 071/351.2232

**50 Man in the Moon** This pub marks the sharp turn where King's Road suddenly veers south. It entices crowds for more than drinks: the pub doubles as a first-rate theater club, presenting mostly modern plays. Beautiful engraved glass, a real fire in the hearth in winter, and real ale year-round, as well as lunchtime fare, add to the allure. ♦ Pub ♦ M-F 11AM-11PM; Su noon-3PM, 7-10PM. 392 King's Rd. Pub: 071/352.5075. Theater: 071/351.2876

**51 Le Shop—the Véritable Crêperie** ★★★$ Formerly called **Asterix,** after the French comic hero (Asterix's publishers asked the owners to change the name), this was London's first crêperie and the inspiration to its successors. The savory crêpes are made with buckwheat flour. Smoked salmon, chicken, mushroom, and corn are especially appetizing, or try the mozzarella and spinach, plus any of the irresistible dessert crepes. The welcoming atmosphere combined with refreshing prices make this an ideal spot for an impromptu feast. ♦ French ♦ Lunch and dinner; breakfast also on Saturday and Sunday. 329 King's Rd. 071/352.3891

**51 Natural Shoe Store** Started by an American, this might be your salvation if you are beginning to feel weary of foot. Sensible brogues and half-brogues are here, as well as loafers, lace-up boots (beautiful but they do require wearing in), clogs, **Birkenstock** sandals and shoes, **Ecco** walking shoes, and **Grenson** traditional English shoes. ♦ M-Sa 10AM-6PM. 325 King's Rd. 071/351.3721

**52 Ed's Easy Diner** ★$$ Chic teenagers and devotees of 1950s Americana congregate in this chrome-plated, New York-style diner that could substitute for a film set. You can't drink coffee without eating, and they like a fast turnover, but it's open all day. They serve delicious hot dogs, burgers, shakes, and other diner food and beer all, believe it or not, in an Anglo-American way. ♦ American ♦ Lunch and dinner; breakfast also on Saturday and Sunday. 362 King's Rd. 071/352.1956

**53 Dôme** ★$ Open all day, this authentic brasserie, part of the Dôme chain, serves reasonable French bistro classics: *salade niçoise, croques monsieur, crudités, assiette de charcuterie, mousse au chocolat,* espresso, and *citron pressé.* For breakfast, you can order coffee and a croissant or a full English breakfast. Yes, this place is crowded, but there's no need to book in advance. Service is a little on the slow side; still, it's worth waiting to bask in the lively atmosphere. ♦ Brasserie ♦ Breakfast, lunch, and dinner. Closed Sunday. 354 King's Rd. 071/352.7611

**54 Rococo Chocolates** Taste and imagination are two prime ingredients in the most eccentric chocolate shop in the world. This art gallery for chocoholics indulges both the eye and the palate with its displays of baroque and contemporary-style Belgian chocolates, ranging from sardines to Venus' Nipples (mounds of white chocolate topped with coffee beans—like those in the film *Amadeus*). ♦ M-Sa 10AM-6:30PM; Su 11AM-4PM. 321 King's Rd. 071/352.5857

**54 Chelsea Rare Books** With an excellent section of secondhand and antiquarian books on Chelsea in particular and London in general, this Chelsea institution is also the place to come for handsome bound editions of **Dickens, Scott,** and once in a blue moon, **Jane Austen.** By all means, go downstairs and have a look at the English prints and watercolors, which are usually well-mounted and reasonably priced. The shop also sells bookends and bookcases to accommodate your inevitable purchases. ♦ M-Sa 10AM-6PM. 313 King's Rd. 071/351.0950; fax 071/351.2928

# Treasure Hunt: Antiquing in London

London's vast number of private antiques and art dealers—approximately 2,000 in the 620 square miles of the Greater London area—constitute mecca for the serious collector. But first-time or occasional shoppers may find the conglomeration of antiquarians daunting. One way to narrow down the list of vendors is to look for shop windows bearing the insignia or logo of either the **London and Provincial Antique Dealers Association (LAPADA)** or the **British Antique Dealers Association (BADA).** These monikers indicate that the dealer belongs to one of these watchdog associations and is reputable. During any transaction, always ask for a receipt with the vendor's name, address, and phone number, a brief description of the item purchased (such as "early 18th-century walnut bureau-bookcase, with handles from a later period"), the price paid, and the date. If a dealer refuses to provide such a receipt, heed the warning bells that should be going off in your head.

Once you've made your purchase, getting it home to the states will involve yet another investment. The safest, though most expensive, option is door-to-door shipping, where goods leave the shop and are delivered directly to the customer's house rather than to an airport or delivery station. (Sample expense: a sideboard measuring five feet by two feet by four feet would run you roughly $1,245.00 to ship from London to San Francisco, complete with customs clearance.) Gone are the days when seagoing containers were the cheapest form of transporting antiques back to the U.S.; unless you're buying an entire houseful of furniture, the cost of using this method is prohibitive. Air freight is generally used for large items, such as furniture, with transport time taking anywhere from a week to 10 days, while smaller antiques may be shipped via Federal Express or United Parcel Service to arrive the next day, if required.

A letter from BADA (write to them at 20 Rutland Gate, London SW7 1BD or call 071/589.4128) may help expedite customs procedures if the age of an item is in question. An item over 100 years old generally can be brought or shipped into the U.S. duty free and the invoice issued at purchase (containing a description of the item, its approximate date, etc.) should be enough for customs clearance. However, if there are any questions, U.S. Customs has an Antiques Division that will value items and deal with any problems.

## Antiques Centers

Antiques centers house a number of dealers in one location, say in an indoor market. The goods may range from rare bric-a-brac to just plain junk, but most centers provide excellent browsing grounds. Some of the more well-known locations are listed here:

**Alfies Antique Market** ♦ 13-15 Church Street. Tube: Edgware Road

**Antiquarius** ♦ 135-41 King's Road. Tube: Sloane Square, South Kensington

**Chelsea Antiques Market** ♦ 245a-53 King's Road. Tube: Sloane Square, South Kensington

**Gray's Antique Market** ♦ 58 Davies Street. Tube: Bond Street

**Gray's Mews** ♦ 1-7 Davies Mews. Tube: Bond Street

**London Silver Vaults** ♦ Chancery House, 53-65 Chancery Lane. Tube: Chancery Lane

## Antiques Fairs

More than 2,000 antiques fairs take place in London during the year, and like stalls in a market, they vary greatly in both range and quality. The annual, multiday events tend to set standards for their exhibitors, and most of the better-known fairs are carefully vetted. The major events, such as the **Grosvenor House Fair** and the **Dorchester Fair,** usually take place in June. Check the weekly *Antique Trade Gazette* or the monthly *Antique Collector* for venues.

## Auction Houses

Those who prefer dealing on a large scale (both in terms of money and in size of items) should head for the auction houses. Unless you are very experienced, however, better take an expert along to do the dealing, for British auction houses are a world unto themselves. Any sales that occur at auction are defined by law as "business sales" rather than "consumer sales," which means that the auction house is not bound, as private dealers are, to provide descriptions of goods they offer for sale. This is not to say that auctioneers are less reputable in their transactions than dealers, but only that a customer has less legal protection or chance for redress if the value of an item purchased at auction turns out to be lower than expected. Also, auction houses charge commissions, or buyer's premiums, amounting to roughly 10 to 15 percent of the cost of the item (although the percentage varies with different items)—another reason to bring along an experienced bidder. The "Big Four" auction houses are:

**Bonham's** ♦ Montpelier Street. Tube: Knightsbridge, South Kensington; 071/584.9161

**Christie's** ♦ 8 King Street. Tube: Green Park, Piccadilly Circus; 071/839.9060. Also at: 85 Old Brompton Road. Tube: South Kensington; 071/581.7611

**Phillips** ♦ 7 Blenheim Street. Tube: Bond Street; 071/629.6602

**Sotheby's** ♦ 34 New Bond Street. Tube: Bond Street, Oxford Circus; 071/493.8080

## Street Markets

At the other end of the scale from the chichi auction houses lie street markets. The quality of the items varies—from pure rubbish to true treasures—and it kes a discerning eye to detect the difference. ming, however, is critical; there is no substitute for riving early. A few of the better-known markets clude:

**rmondsey Market** For glass, silver, clocks, brass, d other small items, this Friday morning market is rivaled. Officially, it opens at 7AM, but the dealers e already trading before then. ♦ F 7AM-2PM. rmondsey Square. Tube: London Bridge

**mden Passage** More than 100 dealers make this rt of north London come alive. ♦ W, Sa early orning-3PM. Between Upper Essex Road and arlton Place. Tube: Angel

**Portobello Road** This entire neighborhood turns into a market on Saturday, with hundreds of dealers in the streets, the arcades, and, of course, in the shops. ♦ Sa 7AM-5PM. Between Golbourne Rd and Chepstow Villas. Tube: Notting Hill Gate

**Note:** Don't restrict your antiquing only to London. The best places to find antiques in England are actually *outside* London at less-trafficked tourist destinations. So when you visit out-of-the-way towns, rummage through secondhand and "junk" shops, stop at "boot sales" (tag or garage-type sales), and check out local fairs. You never know what you might find.

**55 Thierry's** ★★$$ You sometimes have to ring the bell to enter this vintage restaurant, a great favorite of Chelsea dwellers who like the honest, carefully prepared, and not overly original French dishes, such as cheese soup and *cassoulet de Toulouse* (lamb stew with beans). The ambience depends greatly on the warm and efficient **Hervé Salez**, who presides over the restaurant, charming newcomers and regulars alike. ♦ French ♦ Lunch and dinner. 342 King's Rd. 071/352.3365

**56 Osborne and Little** The location is conveniently situated just across the street from the **Designer's Guild;** if you like one shop you will probably like the other. The wallpaper and fabric in florals, and clever trompe l'oeil marbles and stipples, are all in excellent taste. The shop has a range of Italian 15th-century-style wallpaper in subtle autumnal shades, complete with golden stars like those in Juliet's house in Verona. ♦ M-Tu, Th-F 9:30AM-5:30PM; W, Sa 10AM-5:30PM. 304 King's Rd. 071/352.1456

**57 Hetherington** This 12-year-old shop is so slim that it's easy to pass without noticing. However, once you've seen the colorful dresses, eveningwear, and wedding gowns that **Sasha Hetherington** purveys in her exquisite boutique, you won't be likely to forget it. Inside, her illustrious clientele, perhaps an Italian contessa or a visiting European royal, may be deciding on their outfits for the next ball. Everything can be made to order (Hetherington will even turn dresses around in a week), and dresses are available for rental. ♦ M-Sa 10AM-6PM. 289 King's Rd. 071/351.0880

**57 S. Borris** ★★$ Ignore the dingy exterior and interior: this tiny sandwich bar has been here forever. Taste the food and you'll understand why. What makes Borris the most unusual deli in London is the display of Beluga and Sevruga caviar. The contents of the fridge are worth more than the rest of the shop put together. The proprietor claims that, when he's not wrapping up poppyseed pastries and other mundane orders, he's waiting on the hostesses of Chelsea who come here to buy caviar for their dinner parties. ♦ Sandwiches ♦ Breakfast, lunch, and dinner; breakfast and lunch only on Sunday. 251 King's Rd. 071/352.8729

**57 Manolo Blahnik** Just off King's Road, this museum of a shoe shop often displays one priceless shoe in the window. **Sarah Ferguson** walked down the aisle shod in Blahnik heels and **Princess Diana,** along with every glamorous woman in London, has long worn this designer's beautiful footwear. The impeccably made shoes arrive from Italy in very limited numbers (12 to 15 pairs of each design), and are worth every considerable pound you will pay for them. ♦ M-F 10AM-6PM; Sa 10:30AM-5:30PM. 49 Old Church St. 071/352.8622; fax 071/351.7314

**58 Old Church Street** A spate of early 19th-century terraced houses surround this rambling stretch of pavement to the west of Carlyle Square. **No. 127** was home to potter/novelist **William de Morgan,** while **No. 141A** was the last London address of **Katherine Mansfield.** A small plaque on the wall of Bolton Lodge, **No. 143,** announces the address of the elusive and exclusive **Chelsea Arts Club,** founded in 1891. Inside its comfortably shabby surroundings, modern creators strive to follow in the footsteps of early members such as **James Whistler, W.R. Sickert,** and **Wilson Steer.** ♦ Between Fulham Rd and Cheyne Walk

**59 Designer's Guild** Sofas, rugs, and fabrics that are modern, timeless, and country-house comfortable all at the same time are the specialty of **Tricia Guild's** boutique. She designs and produces exquisite fabrics, which look like brilliant Impressionist watercolors of English gardens. New collections, based on African and Italian art, will appeal to those who shun anything floral and the stunning accessories, especially the pottery, baskets, and lamps, will make you want to move into a bigger home. If you're really at a loss as to how to coordinate the fabrics, there's an interior design service. ♦ M-Tu, Th-F 9:30AM-5:30PM; W, Sa 10AM-5:30PM. 271-277 King's Rd. 071/351.5775

**59 David Tron Antiques** Mr. Tron specializes in 17th- and 18th-century English and Continental furniture. This very tasteful establishment lends a distinguished tone to King's Road. ◆ M-F 10AM-5:30PM; Sa 11AM-3PM. 275 King's Rd. 071/352.5918

**59 Green and Stone** Here's one of the original shops on King's Road that hasn't gone trendy or upscale. These dealers in art supplies carry beautiful sketchbooks and a prismatic selection of oils and watercolors. A tempting assortment of old and new silver and leather frames, and a very good framing service, are available for those who have a masterpiece to hang. Green and Stone also stocks materials for creating your own decorative wall finishes, as well as for gilding and frame restoration. ◆ M-F 9AM-5:30PM; Sa 9:30AM-6PM. 259 King's Rd. 071/352.0837; fax 071/351.1098

**60 Chelsea Antique Market** Of the various antique markets on the King's Road, this one comes closest to the look and feel of a flea market; it's also the most likely to yield a bargain and claims to be the oldest in London. The stall owners are a friendly lot who specialize mainly in books. **Harrington Bros.** carries some of the best, with an emphasis on travel books, atlases and maps, natural history and color illustrations, and children's books. ◆ M-Sa 10AM-6PM. 245-253 King's Rd. 071/352.5689

**60 Johanna Booth** One of the nicest shops on King's Road, Johanna Booth carries a fine collection of tapestries, Elizabethan and Jacobean furniture, and wood carvings. She is patient and knowledgeable, and her shop speaks of taste, simplicity, and imagination. One whole wall is lined with antiquarian books, also for sale. ◆ M-Sa 10AM-6PM. 247 King's Rd. 071/352.8998

**60 Designers Sale Studio** Former Browns buyer **Andrea von Tiefenbach Savaricas** scouts the design warehouses for cancelled orders and classic end-of-line clothing, including major names like designers **Giorgio Armani, Moschino,** and **Gianni Versace.** The shop now covers two stories, one of which is devoted to menswear. ◆ M-F 10AM-7PM; Sa 10AM-6PM; Su noon-6PM. 241 King's Rd. 071/351.4171

**61 The Garage** The '50s automobiles out front are just the appetizer. Inside, the old repair shop, now oozing '90s street cool, has been turned into a shopping complex of hip clothing. Independent young designers, jewelry-makers, and proprietors of second-hand clothing stores and teen fashion outlets have joined forces to give King's Road a dose of street chic. ◆ M-Th, Sa 10AM-6PM; F 10AM-6:30PM. 350 King's Rd. 071/352.8653

**62 Givans** This shop is a reminder that King's Road was not always trend central. The Irish linen sheets, luxurious terrycloth bathrobes, and damask table linens are typical of the quality merchandise here. ◆ M-F 9:30AM-5PM. 207 King's Rd. 071/352.6352

**62 Henry J. Bean** ★$ Fifties freaks, trendies and the occasional punk join tourists and nuclear families in this Chelsea branch of ye another restaurant started by the industriou American **Bob Payton,** of **Chicago Pizza Pie** fame. He has figured out a formula for supplying the English with American-style fa food in a retro ambience they gravitate to. Bean's is an English pub converted into an American saloon, with '50s and '60s rock 'n roll as aural background. The all-star cast includes potato skins, nachos, hamburgers hot dogs, chili, pecan pie, cheesecake, ice cream, brownies, and ice-cold American bee The huge garden out back makes this a sunny-day favorite on King's Road. ◆ American ◆ Lunch and dinner. Happy hou M-Sa 5:30-7:30PM. 195-197 King's Rd. 071/352.9255

**62 Chenil Galleries** Chenil has a weighty reputation among Chelsea bohemia, includi the distinction of having hosted the first pub performance in 1923 of **Edith Sitwell's** eccentric and original *Facade* to **William Walton's** music—much to the outrage of th critics. In 1979, Chenil switched artistic genres: it's now an antique center specializi in Art Nouveau, Art Deco, and occasionally, fine art. Merchants sell antique textiles, furniture, silver, books, prints, and toys. Picture dealers and serious furniture dealers are regulars here. Look for the mural depicti the galleries' artistic history. Stop at the garden restaurant if you're feeling shopworn ◆ M-Sa 10AM-6PM. 181-183 King's Rd. 071/351.5353; fax 071/351.5350

**63 Chelsea Farmer's Market** This collectic of small food shops, open-air cafes, delicatessens, and restaurants, some of wh. stay open all night, is a welcome addition fo Chelsea residents, who drop in for a cappuccino before zipping in to the **Chelsea Gardener** to replenish their window boxes a the greenery on their tiny patios. For lunch and snacks, there are delicious sandwiches, hot pizzas, cold beer, or wine by the glass. S in the Astroturfed piazza and enjoy your repast in the English sun. There's even a homeopathic apothecary from Neal's Yard in Covent Garden, and a New Age self-improvement shop, **Hypnotic,** run by hypnotherapist **Suzanne Thomas.** Ask clairvoyant **Teresa** to read your runes! ◆ Da 9:30AM-6PM. Sydney St. 071/352.5600

---

"The attitude of the English toward English history reminds one a great deal of the attitude o a Hollywood director toward love."

**Margaret Halsey,** *With Malice Toward Som*

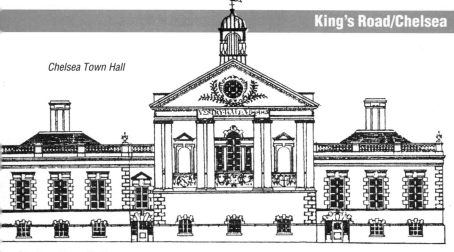

*Chelsea Town Hall*

**64 Chelsea Town Hall** On Saturday, busy shoppers trek in for the antiques fairs and jumble sales that are a regular feature. A stream of wedding parties—brides in long white gowns with their grooms and retinue—wends in and out of the **Chelsea Registry Office** throughout the day. Formal wedding photographs are usually taken on the steps outside of the hall, slowing traffic to a standstill. ◆ King's Rd

**65 Edina Ronay** *Brideshead Revisited* classicism, a French/Italian cut, and *je ne sais quoi* characterize the clothes in this small shop that prides itself on stocking only garments made of the best linens, silks, and wools. The prices may seem expensive, compared to those of other shops in this neighborhood, but the quality is Rue St.-Honoré. Ronay is famous, above all, for the handknit sweaters that established her name. ◆ M-Sa 10AM-6PM; W 10AM-7PM. 141 King's Rd. 071/352.1085

**65 Antiquarius** This is one of the earliest and best-known antiques hypermarkets, and still one of the best. You'll get agreeably lost in the maze of over 120 stalls, but you can find wonderful Georgian, Victorian, Edwardian, and Art Nouveau jewelry, antique lace, superb antique clocks, pictures, prints, and tiles; and if you shop carefully, you can expect to pay less than in an antiques shop. One of the longtime dealers, **Trevor Allen,** has irresistible antique jewelry and a good selection of Georgian and Victorian rings and earrings to offer. Slide into a seat in the cafe, where you can renew your energy with coffee and chocolate cake. ◆ M-Sa 10AM-6PM. 135-141 King's Rd. 071/351.5353

**65 Quincy** Quincy stocks high-fashion labels for men, with price tags to match. Designer jeans and casual gear compete for attention in the window before the parade of would-be owners along King's Road. ◆ M-Sa 10AM-7PM. 137 King's Rd. 071/351.5367

**66 Chelsea Potter** ★$ This King's Road pub boasts a young, lively crowd, an attractive interior, substantial lunches, and sidewalk

seating in spring and summer. ◆ Pub ◆ M-Sa 11AM-11PM; Su noon-3PM, 7-10:30PM. 119 King's Rd. 071/352.9479

**67 The Pheasantry** ★$ A beautifully restored early 19th-century building serves as the setting for this brasserie, restaurant, and nightclub. On sunny days, summer and winter, you can dine outside. Stick to pasta (which the Italian staff does particularly well) or steak, or have afternoon tea. ◆ Continental ◆ Breakfast, lunch, and dinner. Nightclub: F-Sa 10PM-2AM. 152 King's Rd. 071/351.7141

## Bests

### Baroness O'Cathain
Managing Director, Barbican Centre

London is the greatest city in the world. It's the only place I want to live. The view of the capital from my flat in the Barbican at night is spectacular.

Watching a performance by the incomparable **Royal Shakespeare Company** in the **Barbican Theatre,** or attending a concert by the magnificent resident **London Symphony Orchestra** in the **Barbican Hall.**

I adore **St. Paul's Cathedral**—it's solid, secure, and the part of London I've always loved best.

**The House of Lords**—the best debating chamber in the world (but I'm biased).

Dining at **Clarke's** on Kensington Church Street.

A window table in the **Blue Print Cafe** at the Design Museum—it's terribly romantic to see the sun setting behind Tower Bridge.

**Trooping the Colour**—When you see the splendid line of horses and the guards with their bearskins, you can't fail to have a quickening of the heart; it gives you a sense of an unchanging, solid foundation in a difficult and uncertain world.

The **Christopher Wren** architecture in the **City.** I marvel at the carvings on the facades of many City churches.

**Selfridges**—the one-stop shop for those in a hurry. Also, **Dillons,** a marvelous bookshop where I spend far too much money.

# Kensington/ Knightsbridge

Cromwell and Brompton roads gently embrace in front of the flamboyant baroque **Brompton Oratory**, the first important Roman Catholic church built in London after the Reformation, uniting at an almost imperceptible angle: two roads, two villages (Kensington and Knightsbridge), and two worlds. Victorian and high-minded **South Kensington**, with its nexus of museums, is evidence of one man's grandiose vision of the educational and moral value of art, while luxurious and high-spirited **Knightsbridge** is the province of the chic, sophisticated, and fashionable. It seems an improbable union, but the two adjoining neighborhoods bring out the best in each other, and a day spent in the company of both is unimaginably satisfying.

Together, these areas encompass everything from exhibits of dinosaurs and their living relatives to a quarter of a million butterflies, a simulation of an earthquake, a launch pad and the *Apollo 10* space capsule, an 11-foot bed for weary travelers that was mentioned in *Twelfth Night,* 10 acres of the greatest collection of antique furniture and decorative art in the world (not for sale), and 15 acres of fabulous furniture and other highly desirable goods (all for sale).

Begin at the **Natural History Museum**, a building that looks more like an ecclesiastical railway station than a museum housing more than 50 million items from the natural world. It exudes Victorian grandeur. End your tour at **Harrods**, a department store whose motto is "Omnia, Omnibus, Ubique—All Things, For All People, Everywhere," a claim now, sadly, untrue since Harrods has shifted so far upscale that it excludes more than it includes. Still, if the quantity of merchandise leaves you muddled and breathless, a detour into **Hyde Park** and

**Kensington Gardens** will help you recover from material pursuits. If you go around 10AM, you can see the Queen's horse-drawn carriages travel down **Serpentine Road;** in May or June, you can also watch soldiers practicing with their horses for **Trooping of the Colour** on **Rotten Row.** The **Hyde Park Hotel** is a worthy shrine for any Anglophile pilgrim who thinks tea in the late afternoon is a necessity for those who consider themselves civilized. Nearby is one of London's best wine bars, **Le Metro,** and a unique pub, the **Grenadier,** which was once the Officer's Mess for the **Duke of Wellington's** soldiers. If you're more gourmet and art-lover than shopper, a perfect lazy Sunday in London might begin with lunch at a French restaurant (try the excellent **Bibendum**), followed by visits to the museums. This itinerary is particularly suited for a rainy day.

**1 The Natural History Museum** If you take a taxi into London from Heathrow, this twin-towered, terracotta-and-slate-blue museum is the first real feast that greets the eye. Designed between 1873 and 1880 by **Alfred Waterhouse,** the Romanesque building looks superb in sunlight and breathtaking

**THE NATURAL HISTORY MUSEUM**

when lit up against a night sky. Animal figures grace the outside, while painted panels of wildflowers decorate the high, curved ceiling inside. As you enter the navelike central hall, you expect to see a high altar (or a diesel engine). But in this holy terminus dedicated to the wonders of Creation, rising high above the ordinary human figures below, is the 85-foot-long skeleton of **Diplodocus Carnegii,** the 150-million-year-old dinosaur believed to be the largest flesh-eating land animal to have ever existed. Would-be paleontologists will love the permanent **Dinosaurs** exhibition of robotic dinosaurs and vast skeletons of species that disappeared 65 million years ago.

The Natural History Museum used to be part of the **British Museum,** which was founded by an Act of Parliament in 1753. It houses the national collections of zoology, entemology, paleontology, minerology, and botany. With four acres of gallery space to cover and some 50 million items to see, you may have to choose among dinosaurs, humans, whales, birds, and mammals. But be sure to take time for the excellent first-floor display on the origin of the human species, including specimens from **Darwin's** historic voyage on the HMS Beagle. Also stop by the **Whale Hall** to gaze at the overwhelming model and skeleton of a blue whale. In the East Wing's bird display, parents linger in front of the extinct dodos and flightless emus and

ostriches, while children race ahead to the penguins. The **Discovering Mammals** exhibition shouldn't be missed, especially the rare giant panda **Chi-Chi,** who, having confounded early attempts at glasnost by refusing to mate with Moscow Zoo's **An-An** in the '60s, died of old age at London Zoo in 1972. She now permanently munches bamboo in the North Hall.

The museum is huge and the free pamphlet Finding Your Way Around is well worth a look. The **Ecology—A Greenhouse Effect** exhibition on global ecology makes a good introduction to the new **Plant Power** exhibit, which explores ways in which humans use and abuse plants. ◆ Admission (includes Natural History Earth Galleries); free M-F 4:30-5:50PM, Sa-Su 5-5:50PM, bank holidays. M-Sa 10AM-5:50PM; Su 11AM-5:50PM. Cromwell and Exhibition Rds. 071/938.9123

Within the Natural History Museum:

**Natural History Earth Galleries** You will not find the **Geological Museum,** designed in 1935 by **John Markham,** anymore because the Natural History Museum has engulfed it; a gallery now connects the two sites. It was originally wedged in between the Natural History and Science museums. Gaze peacefully at rubies, emeralds, sapphires, and diamonds, including a model of the Koh-i-noor diamond, cut under the supervision of **Prince Albert** and first shown at the Great Exhibition of 1851. Don't miss "The Story of the Earth," which is entered by way of a 25-foot-high "cliff" from the Highlands of Scotland. You will be taken on a journey through the first billion years on earth, complete with an erupting volcano and room-rattling earthquake. The exhibitions get more didactic as you go up, culminating in the world's largest display of metalliferous ores and a model of **Stonehenge** on the second floor. ◆ Admission (included in fee for Natural History Museum). M-Sa 10AM-5:50PM; Su 11AM-5:50PM. 071/938.9123

**The Natural History Museum Shops** These are terrific! The postcards in the first shop are the best bargain in town, with gentle gorillas, gory bugs, lavish butterflies, and fleas in costume. The shop next door carries dime-store items (plastic dinosaurs and the like), while the gift shop has more deluxe merchandise, including fossils, jewelry, minerals, replicas of skulls, and crystal goblets etched with endangered species. However, the best shop by far is the bookstore, which has an excellent collection of gardening books, beautifully illustrated guides to wildflowers, and, more specifically, **Hugh Johnson's** *Encyclopaedia of Trees,* the *Catalogue of the Rothschild Collection of Fleas* in five weighty volumes, and a replica of **Darwin's** journal of the *HMS Beagle.* ◆ M-Sa 10AM-5:50PM; Su 11AM-5:50PM. 071/938.9123

### The de Blanck Restaurant ★$ This

restaurant features main courses such as chicken Provençale and lamb curry on a menu that changes daily. The museum also houses a juice bar, serving healthy snacks and fruit juices, and a snack bar, offering goodies children love but aren't allowed to have at home. ◆ International ◆ Lunch and afternoon tea. 071/938.9123

**2  Science Museum** The Science Museum was founded in 1847, although the present building, by **Sir Richard Allison,** dates from 1913. This inspired tribute to science couldn't be more appropriately located than in the nation that gave the world **Newton, Darwin, Davy, Huxley, Thomson, Rutherford,** and **Fleming.** A visit here leaves you with the inevitable realization of just how many fundamental scientific discoveries have been British. The museum is especially enjoyable for the young, who can push, pull, and operate the countless knobs, buttons, and gadgets on display. Just like scientific theories, exhibitions change regularly, so pick up a map from the museum shop.

The lower ground floor is heaven for the small and curious. It is filled with such items as a burglar alarm to test, a model lift to operate, a take-off and landing simulator for would-be aviators, a periscope for spying on the floor above, and many more gadgets, all waiting to be tried and tested. For the more domestic, there is an authentic Victorian kitchen and a large collection of appliances.

The emphasis on the ground floor is on power, transport, and exploration, with the **Foucault Pendulum** demonstrating the rotation of the earth on its own axis. Also on display are *Puffing Billy,* which, dating from 1813, is the oldest locomotive in the world; the **Boulton and Watt** pumping engine, designed in 1777; the oldest Rolls-Royce, circa 1905; eight fire engines; a full-scale model of a moon lander; and, most popular of all, the actual *Apollo 10* capsule.

The "Launch Pad" section dominates the first floor. This hands-on gallery is where kids from 6 to 60 can test the scientific principles behind the modern technology used every day. Get a ticket at the gallery entrance before you start your visit; it's very popular. You will also find everything you ever wanted to know about map-making, time measurement, iron, steel-making and glass-making, agriculture, meteorology, and telecommunications. You'll swallow nervously as you enter "Food for Thought" in **The Sainsbury Gallery,** which reveals how science tinkers with food.

The second floor deals with the more instructive subjects of chemistry, physics, nuclear power, and computers. Be sure to see **Crick and Watson's** model of DNA, the chain of life; the larger-than-life models of cells and how they work; and the living molecules showing the work of seven Nobel prize winners.

The art of aeronautics is explored in the flight gallery on the third floor, from the hot-air balloon to jets. Of special interest is the *De Havilland Gipsy Moth,* used by **Amy Johnson** on her flight to Australia in 1930; a replica of the craft built by **Orville** and **Wilbur Wright** in 1903; and World War II aircraft. The aeronautics section shares the floor with areas devoted to a history of photography and cinematography from 1835.

The **Wellcome History of Medicine Museum** contains 43 glimpses depicting medical history, from trepanning (cutting out a circular core, as of the skull) in neolithic times to open-heart surgery in the 1980s. Clever, often spine-chilling displays cover tribal, Oriental, classical Greek, Roman, medieval, and Renaissance medicine. The vast collection of curiosities includes **Florence Nightingale's** moccasins, a microscope made especially for **Lister, Dr. Livingston's** medicine chest, and **Napoleon's** beautiful silver toothbrush. Don't miss the newly opened **King George III Collection,** otherwise known as "Science in the 18th Century," which shows just how many advances in knowledge were made during the scientifically minded Sovereign's reign.

The cafe on the third floor is only for the hungry, but the museum shop has nifty toys—gyroscopes, kites, Escher puzzles, etc.—for the gadget-minded. The *Guide to the Science Museum* (small charge) is excellent if you're in a hurry and want to find your way around easily. ◆ Admission; free M-Sa 4:30-6PM. M-Sa 10AM-6PM; Su 11AM-6PM. Exhibition Rd. 071/938.8008

**Restaurants/Clubs:** Red  **Hotels:** Blue
**Shops/ 🎋 Outdoors:** Green  **Sights/Culture:** Black

**3 Ognisko Polski** ★★$$ This Polish club (nonmembers are welcome, too) is a supposedly secret haunt of many South Kensington bohemians and intellectuals. The bar and restaurant are fairly elegant, the food is of the *zrazy, kasza,* and *pierogi* variety, and the atmosphere unbeatable. It is a kind of poor man's Russian Tea Room, with a set lunch and dinner that often includes stuffed goose and *bigos* (chopped beef or pork, cabbage, sauerkraut, and onions simmered in a spicy sauce). Wash it down with one of their lethal Polish vodkas. ◆ Polish ◆ Lunch and dinner; lunch only on Saturday. 55 Exhibition Rd. 071/589.4670

**4 Exhibition Road** If a morning of museumgoing has filled your mind with things cultural but left you craving the outdoors, continue up Exhibition Road into the refreshing greenery of **Hyde Park** and **Kensington Park Gardens.** The route is lined with monuments to the purposeful **Prince Albert,** including the **Natural History Museum Life Galleries,** the **Natural History Museum Earth Galleries,** the **Science Museum,** and the **Henry Cole Wing** of the **Victoria and Albert Museum. C.S. Freake** was the coal-seller-turned-builder who developed the area with the grand Italianate mansions that became a hallmark of mid-19th century South Kensington. The road culminates in the gargantuan **Albert Hall,** which, along with Kensington Gardens, is presided over by the **Albert Memorial.** ◆ Between Kensington Gore and Cromwell Rd

**5 Royal College of Music** Inside this elaborate building, designed by **Sir Arthur Blomfield** in 1894, is a remarkable collection of more than 500 musical instruments, ranging from the earliest known stringed keyboard instruments to some wonderfully bizarre creations of the 19th and 20th centuries. Here, **Handel's** spinet rests amiably with **Haydn's** clavichord, along with a portrait collection of more than 100 paintings and several thousand engravings and photographs, including **Burne-Jones'** portrait of **Paderewski** (1890) and **Epstein's** bust of **Vaughn Williams.** ◆ Admission. Music collection: W 2-4:30PM Sept-July. Portrait collection: M-F by appt. Prince Consort Rd (between Calendar and Exhibition Rds). 071/589.3643; fax 071/589.7740

**6 Royal Albert Hall** This stupendous piece of Victoriana is a memorial to **Prince Albert,** ordained and encouraged by **Queen Victoria.** Oddly enough, it was designed not by architects but by two engineers: **Captain Francis Fowke** and **Major-General H.Y. Darracott Scott,** who used Roman amphitheaters as their inspiration. The vast 735-foot redbrick elliptical hall with its glass-and-iron dome can hold 8,000 people, and its

acoustics are superb. Apparently the Prince approved of the design (although he wanted this site to be for another National Gallery), and it is a fitting climax to the cultural complex honoring the education of the mind and spirit in which he so strongly believed.

Albert Hall still operates under a Royal Charter and is the venue for sporting events, beauty contests, pop concerts, military exercises, and most famous of all, the annual **Henry Wood Promenade Concerts,** performed daily between mid-July and mid-September. Known as the "Proms," these performances of classical and popular pieces have an informal atmosphere and are packed with true music-lovers. The last night of the Proms is famously emotional and tickets are available by lottery. ◆ Kensington Gore. Information: 071/589.3203. Tickets: 071/589.8212

**7 Royal College of Organists** This eccentric, four-story building was designed in 1875 by **H.H. Cole,** a soldier in the Royal Engineers who preferred engineers and artists over architects. The building delights passersby with its euphoria of decoration and colors—blues, reds, and yellows—and its frieze of musicians. What's missing from this picture? Well, there is no organist . . . nor is there an organ. ◆ Kensington Gore (at Jay Mews)

**8 Albert Hall Mansions** The warm, brick mansions, built between 1879 and 1886 by **Norman Shaw,** were one of the earliest blocks of flats in London. If they weren't so utterly English—the style is Queen Anne Revival with oriels, gables, dormers, and arches—they would seem almost European in their scale and grandeur. The flats are extremely desirable because of their superb location and palatial rooms. They are occupied by an appreciative elite, including the English designer **Jean Muir,** whose flat is decorated entirely in white. ◆ Kensington Gore

**9 Royal Geographical Society** Gables and chimneys are the trademarks of the former **Lowther Lodge,** which became the home of the Royal Geographical Society in 1911. The building was designed by **Norman Shaw** between 1873 and 1875, and the statues outside are of **Sir Ernest Shackleton,** who commanded three expeditions to the Antarctic and discovered the location of the south magnetic pole in 1909, and **David Livingstone,** who discovered the Zambezi River, the Victoria Falls, and the source of the Nile, and was famously rescued by the journalist **H.M. Stanley.** Inside is an outstanding map room with a collection of more than 500,000 maps, a model of Mount Everest, and an **Expedition Advisory Centre.** The society sponsors occasional exhibitions (mainly photographic) of travel and travelers throughout the world. ◆ Map Room only open

to the public; legitimate researchers preferred. M-F 10AM-5PM. 1 Kensington Gore. 071/589.0648; fax 071/584.4447

**10 Kensington Gardens and Hyde Park** Of all the features that make London the most livable city in the world—the innate courtesy of the English, the civilized lay of the land with its squares and humane, domestic architecture, the thick layers of sympathetic history—it is the parks, the vast oases of green, that give the city an almost unique supply of urban oxygen and humanity. It is inconceivable to know London without spending time in the parks, and for many Londoners and visitors, the vast, natural wonderland of Hyde Park and Kensington Gardens in the heart of the city is not only a favorite part of London but a compulsory stopover.

Even a half-hour here is like a day in the country—a carpet of grass, the shelter of trees, a soundtrack of birds. Then there is the cast of exuberant dogs and their placid owners, joggers, pinstriped businessmen, nannies with baby carriages the size of economy cars, children briefly angelic in their school uniforms, and lovers who stroll in their own pool of private peace. The English, unlike the French and the Italians, don't look very impressive walking along city streets. But in their parks they become distinguished, their features enhanced by the blue of the sky, the green of the grass. They thrive in natural settings, even those surrounded on every side by busy roads and the relentless noise and movement of city life.

Kensington Gardens is the Eliza Doolittle of London parks: elegant, charming, and romantic, merging seamlessly into the larger green of Hyde Park. The difference between the two parks and just where they do merge is a mystery to many. But true lovers of London earth and sky can define

perfectly the area that begins at Kensington Palace and extends to **Alexandra Gate** on the south and **Victoria Gate** on the north, with the connecting **Ring Road** as the boundary.

The gardens, which were in large part laid out by **Queen Anne,** were originally the private property of **Kensington Palace,** and they still have a regal air, enhanced by the presence of the royal home. They were opened by **George III** to the public in the 19th century—"for respectably dressed people" on Saturday only—and became a fashionable venue for promenades, after **Queen Victoria** opened them fully in 1841. Many English writers, among them **Thackeray** and **Matthew Arnold,** have praised their "sublime sylvan solitude," as **Disraeli** put it. The **Round Pond,** constructed in the 18th century, was originally octagonal, and the **Broad Walk,** leading from the pond to the palace, was once lined with magnificent elm trees. Today, it's full of illicit skateboarders and rollerskaters, while the Round Pond plays host to young skippers. Neighboring Hyde Park's 390 acres are, by contrast, an informal swath of green. Once yet another hunting ground for **Henry VIII,** it was given to the public by **James I. Rotten Row,** which runs along the south side, is thought to be a corruption of "Route du Roi" or "Road of the King."

Within Kensington Gardens and Hyde Park:

**Albert Memorial** A little to the west of where the Crystal Palace once stood sits **Prince Albert,** holding the catalog of the *Great Exhibition of 1851* and gazing down on the museums, colleges, and institutions that his vision, energy, and endeavor inspired. The memorial, completed in 1872 by **Sir George Gilbert Scott,** earned its creator a knighthood. Albert's throne, crowned by a spire of gilt and enameled metal that ends in a cross rising 180 feet high, is an imposing piece of Victorian art made lovable by its sheer excess. The monument was commissioned by the Prince's mournful widow, **Queen Victoria,** and unveiled by her in 1876. Below the bronze statue of the Prince Regent are marble statues of animals representing the four continents, while allegorical figures representing Agriculture, Commerce, Manufacture, and Engineering stand at the four angles. Nearest the top of the 175-foot-high monument rest figures of Faith, Hope, Charity, and Humility.

*Albert Memorial*

On the pedestal is a magnificent procession of reliefs of the greatest artists, writers, and philosophers of the Victorian era. The memorial is a gift to Londoners and London-lovers, but it was never a gift to the Prince, who pleaded against such a remembrance. "It would disturb my quiet rides in Rotten Row," he wrote prophetically, "to see my face staring at me, and if (as is very likely) it became an artistic monstrosity like most of our monuments, it would upset my equanimity to be permanently ridiculed and laughed at in effigy." Indeed, for many years the monument was denounced as an example of the worst of Victorian sentimentality and ugly excess. But time has brought the memorial and the Prince into deserved veneration. ♦ Kensington Gore

**Serpentine Gallery** Once the **Kensington Gardens Tea House,** the beautiful building is now the ideal art gallery, ambitiously providing a setting for monthly exhibitions of contemporary art. Gallery talks Sunday at 3PM. ♦ Free. Daily 10AM-6PM. 071/723.9072; fax 071/402.4103

**The Serpentine** This 41-acre artificial lake was formed in 1730 by damming the **Westbourne,** a stream that no longer exists. The resulting riverlike lake (the name comes from its winding, "serpentlike" shape) is home to a vast range of waterfowl. The swimming hole, the **Lido,** was closed due to a health hazard, although there is a small kids' paddling pool in summer. In 1816, **Harriet Westbrook,** the first wife of the poet **Shelley,** committed suicide by drowning herself in the Serpentine. Nearby is the **Boathouse,** where rowboats may be hired by the hour for a perfect afternoon, as depicted by **Renoir.** Along the **Long Water,** that part of the Serpentine that is located within Kensington Gardens, stands **Sir George Frampton's** *Peter Pan,* the most enchanting figure in the park. The statue, erected overnight in 1912, is almost rubbed smooth by adoring little hands. Just beyond him are the **Tivoli Gardens,** four ornate shimmering fountains bedecked with flowers that will make you wonder if you are really in Italy or France, they are so out of character in London.

**11 Kensington Park Thistle Hotel** $$$ It's large but elegant, spacious yet quiet, and what's more, the location, tucked away just off the southwest corner of Kensington Gardens, puts the museums of Cromwell and Exhibition roads within walking distance. There are 323 bedrooms and 10 suites, all of which are stylishly furnished, and you can choose from light meals at the glass-topped **Moniques Brasserie** (★$$), or opt for the paneled **Cairngorm Grill** (★★$$$) for a more formal, traditionally British meal. Oddly enough, summer is not the high season for this hotel; it tends to fill up more from September to Christmas. ♦ De Vere Gardens. 071/937.8080; fax 071/937.7616

**12 White's Hotel** $$$ Squirrels will run up your legs to be fed with nuts as you stroll along the **North Flower Walk** toward **Lancaster Gate.** Here, just across Bayswater Road, is one of London's most exclusive yet virtually unknown hotels. It is a shade less expensive than the Savoy or the Inn on the Park, two hotels with which it has been ranked. The building looks like the London home of an earl, and the interior wouldn't disappoint him, either, as it's filled with crystal chandeliers, white marble, and the shades of old English roses. The Jeeves-like service is impeccable and the restaurant is rather delightful, too. ♦ 90-92 Lancaster Gate. 071/262.2711; fax 071/262.2147

**13 The Park Court Hotel** $$ Part of the International Mount Charlotte Hotels Group, the Park Court is, as you would expect, a large establishment. Many of its 432 rooms have views of adjacent Kensington Gardens, and the hotel has its own grounds as well, where, in fine weather, you can sit and enjoy a drink. If rooms are not imaginatively decorated, they are comfortably kitted out with en suite facilities, color TV, tea- and coffee-making machines, and in-house movies. The staff may give you a real Irish welcome. ♦ Lancaster Gate. 071/402.4272; fax 071/706.4156

**14 The London Toy and Model Museum** Calling all the young at heart: here's a museum that features toys from (and for) all ages, from turn-of-the-century mechanical banks to the Nutcracker himself. There are plenty of knobs to push and mechanical toys to set in motion, but what the youngsters really love is whizzing around on the carousel and garden railway rides. ♦ Admission. Tu-S 10AM-5.30PM; Su 11AM-5:30PM. 21 Craven Hill. 071/262.7905

**15 Texas Lone Star West** ★★$ It's loud and raucous, but the ribs are cooked right and the cocktails accompanying are authentic and cheap for London. If you get a hankering for enchiladas and chimichangas along with live country and western music, this is your place. ♦ American ♦ Lunch and dinner. 117-119 Queensway. 071/727.2980. Also at: 154 Gloucester Rd. 071/370.5625; 50-54 Turnham Green Terrace. 081/994.3000

**16 Kensington Place** ★★★$$$ At the top of a street brimming with antiques and history, the residents go the opposite way and favor the minimalist bare-wood-and-glass look in this the trendiest of London's brasseries. Its chef, **Rowley Leigh,** is feted by London foodies. The seats may not be that comfy, but the place is always packed. You may be expected to hurry through your delicious griddled scallops with pea purée and mint vinaigrette, followed by a roast pheasant with choucroute, carrots, and frankfurters. As you get to the finishing line, there's the obligatory steamed chocolate pudding with lashings of custard. ♦ Modern British ♦ Lunch and dinner; lunch only on Saturday and Sunday. 201-205 Kensington Church St. 071/727.3184; fax 071/229.2025

**17  Clarke's** ★★★$$$ The restaurant is classified as modern British, but the food has decidedly Californian overtones with Continental influences. Whatever you call it, it seems that **Sally Clarke** can do no wrong, thanks to such touches as her wonderful breads, which appear promptly at your table; everything is baked fresh here daily. The menu is set but lovingly matched, so you might start with the delicate fish broth, flavored with fennel and coriander, followed by a superb, slow-roasted breast of duck, with zabaglione to finish. Chocolate truffles, accompanying the coffee, add a final flourish. The only problem with Clarke's is that it is annoyingly closed on the weekend. ♦ Modern British ♦ Lunch and dinner. Closed Saturday and Sunday. 124 Kensington Church St. Reservations required. 071/221.9225

**18  The Earl of Lonsdale** ★$ After a morning spent fighting the hordes on Portobello Road, why not rest your legs in the shade of this pub's Iolanthus tree (which has white blossoms in springtime), or enjoy a pint inside the pretty conservatory. Standard pub fare—quiches, salads, sausages, and the like—is featured here. ♦ Pub ♦ Lunch and dinner. 277 Westbourne Grove. 071/727.6335

**18  Gumbo Ya Ya** ★$$ Cajun and creole specialties are the strength of this restaurant, opened in 1993 on the site of the erstwhile Gate Diner. The locals are still trying to come to terms with the chicken in coconut batter, blackened steak and fish, barbecued shrimp, and such. It isn't the best of the bayou imports, but it isn't bad, either. ♦ Cajun ♦ Lunch and dinner. 184A Kensington Park Rd. 071/221.2649

**18  Portobello Road** The mile-long stretch of street erupts in about 2,000 stalls on Saturdays, creating one of the largest open-air markets in London. From 7AM onward, thousands of tourists and bargain- and antique-hunters congregate in search of unique souvenirs or a silver teapot. Although it's packed with ethnic panache, there's loads of junk and kitsch, but then, the fun is in the search. With some dedicated rummaging, it is possible to find desirable items at reasonable prices, particularly in the surrounding shops.

♦ Sa 7AM-5PM. Between Golborne Rd and Chepstow Villas. Tube: Notting Hill Gate

**18  Geales** ★★$$ Geales was 50 years old in 1990, and its cottage dining room and rustic furniture remain loved by all who come here. The fish is fresh from Billingsgate and Grimsby, and the batter that coats it is made with beer. Try the crab soup before you tuck into a large cod and chips. If you think that's fattening, ask for the apple crumble for dessert and then try to stand up. Beer, wine, and champagne are available. No good fish shop is open on Monday (the fish would be over a day old), and Geales is no exception. ♦ Fish-and-chips ♦ Lunch and dinner. Closed Sunday and Monday. 2 Farmer St. 071/727.7969

**19  Boyd's Restaurant** ★★$$ When a self-taught chef and former professional percussionist moved into this site a few years back, the Kensington populace was skeptical about just what he would come up with. Not anymore. Now, they come to this greenhouse-style restaurant to dine on a regular basis, sampling starters like chargrilled goat's cheese on a garlic crouton or the Indian-spiced carrot and parsnip soup, followed by main courses such as roast breast of pheasant with a wild mushroom stuffing or chargrilled chicken with tarragon on vegetables. The fish of the day—often monkfish, salmon, or brill—is always a good choice. Save room for the divine iced chocolate and hazelnut soufflé; it's sheer, delightful indulgence. The set lunch is an excellent value, the wine list first-rate, and the surroundings serene and sophisticated. ♦ Modern British ♦ Lunch and dinner. Closed Sunday. 135 Kensington Church St. Reservations required. 071/727.5452

**20  The Children's Book Centre** Everything parents could ever want their child to read can be found in this immense bookshop, including literary classics such as *Velveteen Rabbit,* as well as the latest **Judy Blume.** ♦ M, W, F-Sa 9:30AM-6PM; Th 9:30AM-7PM. 237 Kensington High St. 071/937.7497

**21 Kensington Palace** If Kensington (pictured above) looks more like a grand English country house than a palace, it's because that is exactly what it once was. Known in royal circles as "KP," it is very much a living palace. Present residents include the **Princess of Wales** and the two little princes, who occupy the largest apartment, with three floors on the north side; **Prince** and **Princess Michael of Kent;** the **Duke** and **Duchess of Gloucester,** their three children, and the Duke's mother, **Princess Alice,** who have 35 rooms at their disposal; and **Princess Margaret,** who has a mere 20 rooms but the best views. The **Prince of Wales** now resides at Highgrove on weekends and Clarence House during the week. The **Duke of York** has a place in the country and lives at Buckingham Palace when he's in town. The **Queen** decides who lives in the palace, and no one pays rent. But the residents are responsible for alterations and decorating, and their own electricity, telephone, and heating bills.

The palace's historical claims are quite considerable, dating back to 1689, when **William III** commissioned **Sir Christopher Wren** to build a palace out of the existing **Nottingham House,** away from the damp conditions of Whitehall Palace, which aggravated his asthma. Past residents include five monarchs: **William** and **Mary, Anne, George I,** and **George II. Queen Victoria** was born here and stayed until she became Queen and moved into Buckingham Palace, but it was in this nonpalatial palace, then known as Kensington House, that she was awakened with the news that she was Queen. In 1899, on Queen Victoria's 80th birthday, the **State Rooms** were opened to the public; in 1975, more rooms followed.

A visit to the palace starts at the small entrance in front of the **Queen's Staircase,** where you buy tickets, guides, and cards. The steps lead to the **Queen's Apartments,** which look much as they did when Wren decorated them for William and Mary. Next door to the **Queen's Gallery,** with fine carvings by **Grinling Gibbons,** is the **Queen's Closet,** which is anything but a closet. It was the setting for the famous and final quarrel between Queen Anne and **Sarah Churchill,** the Duchess of Marlborough. After you pass the

**Queen's Bedchamber** with its tempting four poster bed, the rooms become grander. The **Privy Chamber** has Mortlake tapestries by **William Kent** on the ceiling and overlooks the state apartments of Princess Margaret; beyond are the **Presence Chamber** and the **King's Staircase.** One of the most stunning rooms is **King William's Gallery,** designed by Wren, with wood carvings by Gibbons and a Etruscan ceiling painted by Kent. This room leads into the **Duchess of Kent's** drawing room and its anteroom, which contains Queen Victoria's Georgian dollhouse and her toys. But perhaps the favorite room is **Queen Victoria's Bedroom,** where the young princess received the news of her accession. It is now filled with mementos of the long-reigning queen, including the curtained cradle where her babies, and those of queens **Alexandra** and **Mary,** slept.

The **Council Chamber** contains souvenirs and artifacts from the Great Exhibition, including the painting over the mantelpiece of **Prince Albert** holding the plans of the Crystal Palace. Also look for the extraordinary ivory throne from India, the lavish silver-gilt table pieces, some of which were designed by Prince Albert, and the centerpiece with four of Queen Victoria's dogs. There is an excellent exhibition of **Court Dress** on the ground floor. Princess Diana loaned the **Emanuel** wedding dress to the collection in 1987. The dress that once epitomized the fairy-tale quality of Princess Diana's and Prince Charles' romance now serves as a poignant reminder that for this marriage, there were once happier days. Lunches and teas are served in the **Orangery** between May and September, and in the **Winter Cafe** from October through April. ♦ Admission. M-Sa 9AM-5:30PM; Su 11AM-5:30PM. Kensington Gardens. 071/937.9561

**22 Victoria and Albert Museum** If you have a curious mind and a receptive heart, and if you like *stuff,* the Victoria and Albert Museum will become one of your favorite places on earth. It is one of the most addictive and rewarding museums in the world, covering 13 acres with items of enchantment and delight. The museum is the prodigious offspring of the **Great Exhibition of 1851,** opening a year later as the **Museum of Manufactures,** with a collection of objects purchased from the exhibition. The initial intent was to display *manufactured* art, but when great works of art were bequeathed to the museum (including the permanent loan of the **Raphael Cartoons** and the largest collection of **Constables**), the scope expanded and the intention and name were changed to the **Museum of Ornamental Art.** In her last major engagement, **Queen Victoria** laid the foundation stone for the buildings that face Cromwell Road in 1899, and at her request the museum was renamed once again. The Victoria and Albert Museum

# VICTORIA AND ALBERT MUSEUM

## Level A

Restaurant

**Henry Cole Wing**
(access to Main Museum Level A only)

Gamble Room
Morris Room
Poynter Room

Special Events Office

North Court Exhibition Gallery

11
12
Italy
13 14 15
16
17
20th Cent. Print Gallery
18
20th Cent. Exhibitions
19
20

Italy

Pirelli Garden

Northern Europe

South Court Exhib. Gallery
South Court Exhib. Gallery

Restrooms

Europe

21A
Europe

Spain, Carpets

40
Indian Art
Art of the Islamic World
Medieval Treasury
China

Plaster Casts (Northern Europe)
Textiles/Forgeries
Plaster Casts (Italy)

Japan

Dress

India
China  Plaster Casts

48
Raphael Cartoons
Shop
Information
Sculpture & Architecture

54

Europe

Main Entrance

Europe & America

## Level B

**Henry Cole Wing**

Printmaking Techniques

Conservation Dept.

Cole Gallery

Education Services
Lecture Theatre
Seminar Room

Tapestries

Metalwork Dept.
Armand Armat
Medieval

Silver
Silver

20th Cent. Textiles

Textiles

Far Eastern Colln. Offices

Church Plate

Jewelry

Trellick Textiles

Britain

Pirelli Garden

Costume/Jewelry

National Art Library

Textiles
Fans

Britain

Musical Instruments

Stained and Engraved Glass

Stained Glass

Ironwork

Modern Glass

Britain

Sculptures & Carvings

## Level C

**Henry Cole Wing**

Temporary Exhibitions

Pirelli Garden

Britain

Britain
Britain
Ceramics  China
Glass

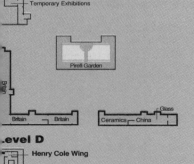

## Level D

**Henry Cole Wing**

European Painting

Portrait Miniatures

Ceramics of the Islamic World

Pirelli Garden

Ceramics

Pottery
Porcelain
Tiles
Ceramics

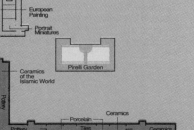

affectionately known as the **V&A,** is eclectic, idiosyncratic, and immense, yet accessible and gracious, a museum that is truly worthy of the vision and energy of its founders.

If there is such a thing as the "South Kensington Style," the V&A is its finest example. The massive building is a construction of red brick, terracotta, and mosaic, with assertions of Victorian confidence towering beside Victorian gloom. **Sir Henry Cole,** the museum's first director, preferred engineers and artists to architects. The resulting cast-iron and glass structure with corrugated-iron facings—built by **William Cubitt** in 1855—looked like a decorated factory and quickly became known as the "Brompton Boilers." The structure was moved eastward in 1867 to form the **Bethnal Green Museum of Childhood.** The buildings that make up the main quadrangle of the V&A began in 1857 with **Captain F. Fowke's Sheepshanks Gallery** along the east side, followed by the **Vernon and Turner Galleries** in 1858, and the **North, South,** and **East Courts** between 1861 and 1873. A succession of craftsmen were responsible for further additions, among them **Godfrey Sykes, James Gamble, Frank Moody,** and **Reuben Townroe. Sir Aston Webb's** Cromwell Road facade, begun in 1891 and completed in 1909, evokes the Victorian ethos of pomp and imperial importance. It is flanked by statues of Queen Victoria and **Prince Albert** by **Alfred Drury,** and **Edward VII** and **Queen Alexandra** by **W. Goscombe John.** On top of the great central tower is the figure of Fame resting upon a lantern shaped like an imperial crown.

Entering the museum is like embarking on a great, extravagant, and wonderful expedition. You will get lost in the more than 150 rooms, but don't despair. Not only is the V&A the best place in town to be lost, the guidebook actually suggests you do just that, for every cul-de-sac then becomes a treasure trove of discovery. The museum is now run by the firm hand of **Elizabeth Esteve-Coll,** but even the best-laid plans of museum curators are no substitute for a little aimless wandering.

There are two types of galleries within the museum: the **Art & Design Galleries** contain masterpieces grouped around a style, nationality, or period, while the **Materials & Techniques Galleries** revolve around a type of object, like silver or ceramics.

The V&A publishes an earnest guide that contains interesting bits of historical information on everything from the Renaissance to William Morris and divides the museum into four walks. The collections are vast, so be warned: this is one of the largest museums in the world, and you shouldn't try to see everything in one visit. The enormous collection is constantly being added to and new permanent exhibitions created. One of the newest is the **Frank Lloyd Wright Gallery** (level 2, Henry Cole Wing), with the 1936 office of **Edgar J. Kaufmann's** Pennsylvanian department store—Wright's only complete interior exhibited in Europe. ♦ Voluntary contribution. M noon-5:50PM; Tu-Su 10AM-5:50PM. Free hour-long guided tours meet at the main (Cromwell Rd) entrance: M noon, 12:30PM, 2PM, 3PM; Tu-Sa 11AM, noon, 2PM, 3PM; Su 3PM. Free gallery lectures: 2:30PM. Cromwell Rd. 071/938.8441

Within the Victoria and Albert Museum:

**Great Bed of Ware** The huge Elizabethan Bed of Ware, circa 1590, was said to have been occupied by 26 butchers and their wives on 13 February 1689. In the 1830s, **Charles Dickens** tried to purchase the bed. This is easily the most famous bed in the world, mentioned by **Shakespeare** in *Twelfth Night* and by countless writers and historians. It is nearly 9 feet high, 11 feet long, and 10½ feet wide, a size that sometimes distracts from the beauty of the carved, painted, and inlaid decoration.
♦ Room 54

**Raphael Cartoons** At press time, this gallery was undergoing restoration; it should, however, be open again by fall of 1994. The cartoons, works of art in their own right, were drawn with chalk on paper and colored with distemper by **Raphael** and his scholars in 1513, as designs for tapestrywork for **Pope Leo X.** The tapestries are still at the Vatican. Three of the original cartoons are now lost; the others are here because **Rubens** advised **Charles I** to buy them for the newly opened tapestry factory at Mortlake. After Charles' death, **Cromwell** bought them for £300, and they remained at Whitehall until **William III** moved them to Hampton Court. They have been on permanent loan at the V&A since **Queen Victoria** ruled Britain. ♦ Room 48A

**Norfolk House Music Room** This English baroque gold-and-white room was in a grand London house, situated in the 1750s on **St. James's Square.** The overmantel features a carved and gilded cluster of musical instruments. ♦ Room 58

**Morris, Gamble, and Poynter Rooms**
The original tearoom, cafe, and restaurants in the museum occupied this space until 1939; having been recently restored, they almost knock you sideways with longing for those aesthetically elaborate and civilized days. The **Green Dining Room,** decorated for the museum by **William Morris** and **Philip Webb,** features Burne-Jones stained glass and painted panels representing the months of the year. The wallpaper and furniture are by William Morris. The chimney piece in the **Gamble Room** came from Dorchester House

on Park Lane. It is surrounded by pillared a mirrored ceramicwork and a ceiling of enameled iron plates that incorporates a quotation from *Ecclesiastes*. The dazzling materials were chosen not so much for thei beauty, but because they are fire-resistant and easy to clean! The **Grill Room,** designe by **Sir Edward Poynter,** still has the original grill, set in a Dutch dream of Minton blue-a white tiles representing the seasons and the months. The three rooms form a first-class example of Victorian design. ♦ Rooms 13-1

**The Dress Collection** This recently enlarged and expanded room houses a collection of fashion dating from around 15 to the present, and draws more crowds tha any other exhibition in the V&A. The Englis and Continental male and female fashions, with outfits from the 1960s and early 1970s are strangely exotic and, some say, still eminently fashionable. ♦ Room 40

**Fakes and Forgeries** Even the floor of th gallery has criminal undertones; it was laid the women inmates of **Woking Prison.** The best fakes of their kind are housed here fro the hands of master forger **Giovanni Bastianini,** whose work is displayed among host of other bogus objects purporting to b something they are not. ♦ Room 46

**Sculpture** During the Italian Renaissance **Donatello** breathed life into stone in his marble relief, the *Ascension and the Mador and Child.* Few can match his mastery, thou **Rodin** does with his *St. John the Baptist.*
♦ Rooms 11-21A/48, Exhibition Rd entranc

**British Art and Design, 1900-60** Huge sealed glass rooms have been built to hous the objects that trace British design from th Arts and Crafts movement started by **Willia Morris** in the 19th century to the new functionalism of the 20th. You will find furniture by **Charles Rennie Mackintosh** ar **Edwin Lutyens,** as well as almost everythin from the **Omega Workshops** (the Decorativ Arts movement of Bloomsbury from 1913 t 1919), including sculptures by **Henri Gaudier-Brzesca.** ♦ 20th Century Exhibitio Gallery

**Henry Cole Wing** This splendid addition opened in 1984 and houses the **Constable Collection,** which was presented to the museum by the artist's daughter. It provide trip to the English countryside through the eyes and genius of one of England's most beloved painters. This artist, like no other, h captured this pastoral region the way the English would like to believe it still could be
♦ Exhibition Rd entrance

**V&A Restaurant** ★★$$ One of the best museum restaurants in town, with imaginative salads and tasty hot foods all freshly made. It also presents food themes t coincide with exhibitions, so you could try sushi if a Japanese exhibition is underway. The restaurant is a lovely spot for lunch, snacks, or afternoon tea. ♦ Eclectic ♦ Lunch and tea. 071/581.2159; fax 071/225.2357

**V&A Shop** Located to the left of the entrance, the shop is run separately from but for the museum by **V&A Enterprises**. The profits are all plowed back into the V&A. Exclusive to the museum are the replicas of individual works of art within the V&A, including the *Statue of Shakespeare* in terracotta, and the ceramic alphabet tiles from the **Gamble Room**, known as the *Kensington Alphabet*. There is an impressive array of stationery, diaries, and **William Morris** needlepoint cushions. The selection of postcards, books, and publications is outstanding, as are the ornaments at Christmastime. Just inside is the **V&A Crafts Shop**, a showcase for British craftspeople, with original objects in pottery, silver, gold, and glass—future treasures for the museum itself. ♦ M noon-5:30PM; Tu-Sa 10AM-5:30PM; Su 10AM-5:30PM. 071/938.8500; fax 071/938.8623

**23 Ismaili Centre** The controversial modern building opposite the V&A is a religious and cultural center for the Islamic community. South Kensington's most recent arrival, it was built in 1983 by **Sir Hugh Casson**, of **Casson, Conder & Partners**. ♦ Prayers 7:30PM. 1 Cromwell Gardens. 071/581.2071

**24 Hoop & Toy** ★$ The name of this pub refers to the game of metal hoop and wooden stick, which is now featured only in illustrated children's books. The pub has the atmosphere of days gone by, with gaslights outside, dark wood and polished brass inside, Edwardian drawings on the walls, and a menu with 18th-century dishes like beef-and-ale pie. Also known as a "Free House," the pub offers a large choice of beers and seven real ales. ♦ Pub ♦ Lunch and dinner. 34 Thurloe Pl. 071/589.8360

Earth has not anything to show more fair:
Dull would he be of soul who could pass by
A sight so touching in its majesty:
This City now doth like a garment wear
The beauty of the morning; silent, bare,
Ships, towers, domes, theatres, and temples lie
Open unto the fields, and to the sky;
All bright and glittering in the smokeless air.
Never did sun more beautifully steep
In his first splendour valley, rock or hill;
Ne'er saw I, never felt, a calm so deep!
The river glideth at his own sweet will:
Dear God! The very houses seem asleep;
And all that mighty heart is lying still!

**William Wordsworth** (1770–1850),
composed upon Westminster Bridge,
3 September 1803

**25 Daquise** ★$ For V&A regulars, the routine often includes lemon tea and apple strudel at this Polish cafe. The quality of the food varies and the surroundings are dingy, but the atmosphere's the thing. Nothing has changed since World War II: not the look of the Polish waitresses, nor the menu of *golubcy* (stuffed cabbage), *kasza* (boiled buckwheat), and *zrazy* (beef rolls stuffed with cucumber, bacon, and mushrooms). Polish émigrés meet here for morning coffee, lunch, afternoon tea, or dinner. ♦ Polish ♦ Lunch and dinner. 20 Thurloe St. 071/589.6117

**26 Rembrandt Hotel** $$$ This appropriately named hotel facing the V&A has welcomed guests since the turn of the century. It is part of the **Sarova** group and offers the kind of facilities that some travelers find very reassuring: fax, direct-dial telephones, and 24-hour food and beverage service. The jewel in the hotel's crown is access (at extra cost) to the incredibly posh **Aquilla** health club, located within the hotel. The club is a conscious attempt to re-create a Roman spa, with a marbled world of tiles, pillars, arches, and murals; inside are a gymnasium, a 50-by-20-foot pool with a Jacuzzi, a fountain, music, a grotto, a sauna, a solarium, and a salad bar. The hotel itself is more down-to-earth and contemporary, and features two restaurants: **Masters** (★★$$) serves a buffet lunch and an à la carte dinner (with hotel classics like tournedos and scampi), while the **Conservatory** (★$) offers light meals and sandwiches and afternoon tea. You can get a traditional English breakfast here, including grilled kidneys, kippers, and smoked haddock. ♦ 11 Thurloe Pl. 071/589.8100; fax 071/225.3363

**26 Period Brass Lights** In this antique shop, you'll find cast brass and Ormulu wall lights, chandeliers, Tiffany lamps, and English cut-glass lead crystal. ♦ M-Sa 9:30AM-6PM. 9A Thurloe Pl. 071/589.8305

**27 M.P. Levene Ltd.** This much-respected silver shop is a favorite with the diplomatic community in London. It carries an impressive choice of old Sheffield plates and silverware, and a beautiful selection of silver frames and objects that are the epitome of the English country house. If you ask, the salespeople will patiently explain the markings on the English silver. ♦ M-F 9:30AM-5:30PM; Sa 10AM-1PM. 5 Thurloe Pl. 071/589.3755; fax 071/589.9908

**28 Felton & Sons Ltd.** One of the many joys of life in London is that flowers don't cost a small fortune. This florist has been here since 1900, and is known for its sumptuous and rare blossoms. ♦ M-F 8:30AM-5:30PM; Sa 8:30AM-noon. 220 Brompton Rd. 071/589.4433; fax 071/589.0664

Restaurants/Clubs: Red    Hotels: Blue
Shops/ ♣ Outdoors: Green    Sights/Culture: Black

**115**

**29 London Oratory of St. Philip Neri** Built between 1880 and 1893 by **Herbert Gribble,** and better known as the **Brompton Oratory,** this was the first important Roman Catholic church to be constructed in London after the Reformation. Of the few beautiful Catholic churches in London, this one (pictured above) is sensational; following a recent restoration program, it is now even more resplendent. The smell of incense greets you upon entering the High Roman oratory, with its domes and vaults, a domed nave, and Italian ornaments and statues. Included here are Carrara marble statues of the apostles carved by **Giuseppe Mazzuoli,** a disciple of **Bernini,** which stood for 200 years in Siena Cathedral, and the altar in the **Lady Chapel,** constructed by **Corbarelli** and sons in 1693, which came from Brescia in northern Italy. In ecclesiastical and liturgical terms, an oratory is a congregation of secular priests living together without vows. The Fathers of the oratory are not monks, and thus are not bound together by the three religious vows but by the internal bond of charity and the external bond of a common life and rule. **St. Philip** founded the Institute of the Oratory in Rome in 1575.

The Oratorian Movement in England came about as the result of **John Henry Newman,** a Victorian whose conversion to Catholicism shook the Anglican establishment. It was **Father Faber** who bought the site for this building in 1853, despite protests from his fellows of it being in "a neighborhood of second-rate gentry and second-rate shops." Don't miss the triptych paintings of saints **Thomas More** and **John Fisher** (and their execution at Tyburn Gallows) by **Rex Whistler** in **St. Wilfred's Chapel,** and the dome, designed by **G. Sherrin,** with wooden ribs faced with 60 tons of lead. At 11AM on Sunday, the church is packed with nearly 2,000 people, both parishioners and visitors, for High Latin Mass with a full choir after the Italian manner (family mass is at 10AM).

Every week you can hear work from the great composers, including **Dvořák** and **Bach.** The choirmaster, **Mr. Hoban,** works for the BBC, so the singing is perfection. ◆ Daily 7AM-8PM. Mass: M-Sa 7AM, 7:30AM, 8AM, 10AM 6PM. Benediction: Tu, Th 6:30PM. Latin High Mass: Su 11AM, 4:30PM, 7:30PM. Brompton Rd (at Brompton Sq). 071/589.4811

**30 Holy Trinity** In marked and very English contrast to its neighbor, the Brompton Oratory, **T.L. Donaldson's** Holy Trinity, built 1829, is Victorian Gothic. There is no smell of incense here. Holy Trinity is an Anglican Church with an active congregation involved in healing, movements for peace, and the Alternative Service. The choir is exceptional. ◆ Cottage Pl

**31 Brompton Square** London excels at creating pretty squares, and it is hard to imagine a more humane design for urban planning. This early 19th-century square, which is not square or even rectangular but horseshoe shaped, is home to prosperous, house-proud Londoners, whose only concessions to the 20th century are the burglar alarms mounted on their perfectly maintained houses and the BMWs parked along the square. A plaque at **No. 6** honors the French poet **Stéphane Mallarmé,** who came to London to learn English and lived here in 1863. A chronically impoverished poet, however great his talent, would be unlikely to reside in this handsome square today. ◆ Off Brompton Rd

**32 James Hardy and Co.** Ring the bell first and you will be warmly welcomed by these silversmiths, whose company has been here since 1853 and still has the original storefront to prove it. The shop carries silver frames, jewelry, antiques, and silverware. ◆ M-Sa 9:30AM-5:30PM. 235 Brompton Rd. 071/589.5050; fax 071/823.8769

**32 Sun and Snow** The name heralds a snazzy sportswear shop, with the latest in fashionable ski gear, including an ample selection for kids. In summer, it carries everything you need for squash, tennis, swimming, and running. ◆ M-Tu, Th-Sa 9:30AM-6PM; W 9:30AM-7PM. 229 Brompton Rd. 071/581.2039; fax 071/584.2955

**33 St. Quentin** ★★★$$$ The food served here is excellent but variable, and you can expect no more nouvelle cuisine. Classic food is in: boeuf bourguignon and steak au poivre deserve every star available, even if you have to grouse to get served. You also won't find better cheeses or French bread than here. (The delicatessen at 256 Brompton Road has the best croissants, *pain aux* raisins, and other French treasures in town.) The decor is traditional brasserie, with a long zinc bar, mirrors, brass, chandeliers, glass, and waiters who dress the part. The tables along the banquette are uncomfortably close together, and you can't help but wish this were a real brasserie open all day. ♦ French ♦ Lunch and dinner. 243 Brompton Rd. 071/581.5131; fax 071/584.6064

**34 La Brasserie** ★★$$ This restaurant has become a permanent fixture and it looks every bit the French brasserie you'd expect to find in Paris. The waiters are friendly, the food is so-so, but London Sloanes gossip, lovers eat breakfast, and married couples steadfastly read the proffered papers here, munching their croissants and sipping hot coffee. It's a great place for noshing and watching London's glamorous residents gird their loins for an onslaught on Harrods and Beauchamp Place. The service is efficient even when it gets busy. ♦ French ♦ Breakfast, lunch, and dinner. 272 Brompton Rd. 071/584.1668

**35 Number 16** $$$ Even though the Victorians did everything in the grand manner, when four Victorian houses are smacked together it doesn't necessarily mean that the resulting hotel is large or spacious. But nostalgia buffs will forgive the occasional tiny room because, from the pretty morning room onward, all are lovingly furnished with antiques. In summer, it's sheer bliss to sit in the conservatory out in the garden. ♦ 16 Sumner Pl. 071/589.5232; fax 071/584.8615

**36 Blakes** $$$ When actress **Anouska Hempel** became an interior designer, she knew how to emphasize the dramatic in her own extraordinary hotel. Black walls and natural leather are warmed with plump cushions in rich colors, heightening the Oriental effect. Each opulent bedroom is individually styled, with matching marble bathrooms, although do ask if you prefer to stay in one, as there are standard rooms, too. The black-and-white restaurant has warrior costumes in Perspex cases, and is expensive but exquisite. ♦ 33 Roland Gardens. 071/370.6701; fax 071/373.0442

**37 San Frediano** ★★★$$ One of London's favorite Italian restaurants, this place is always packed, relaxed, and fun. There's everything here, from perennial favorites such as minestrone and spaghetti, to the very un-Italian-sounding *poussin* in herbs and brandy, and reasonably priced wines. But you do have to book. Breakfast, however, is not included in the price. ♦ Italian ♦ Lunch and dinner. Closed Sunday. 62 Fulham Rd. Reservations required. 071/584.8375; fax 071/589.8860

**38 Souleiado** In this French-owned shop, which is somehow reminiscent of the Mediterranean, brightly colored materials from 200-year-old designs are printed from original wooden blocks, and displayed and sold with TLC. ♦ M-F 10AM-5:30PM; Sa 10AM-5PM. 171 Fulham Rd. 071/589.6180; fax 071/823.9252

**39 Butler & Wilson** **Princess Diana,** when she was still a fashion leader, had been known to stop the royal entourage, nip into Butler & Wilson for a little bauble to match her newest creation, and then purr off in the royal limo. This shop sells fake jewelry to, well *dahlings,* everyone (who counts, that is). ♦ M-Tu, Th-Sa 10AM-6PM; W 10AM-7PM. 189 Fulham Rd. 071/352.3045; fax 071/376.5421

**40 Au Bon Accueil** ★★$$$ Come here for the kind of delicious, unpretentious French cooking you'd expect to get in the heart of the French countryside. Standard classics include snails in garlic butter, onion soup, and boeuf bourguignon. ♦ French ♦ Lunch and dinner; dinner only on Saturday. Closed Sunday. 19 Elystan St. 071/589.3718

**41 Zen** ★★$$$ Although it has been popular for many years, Zen often gets sour reviews, not because it's bad, but because it varies. If you like Chinese cooking à la nouvelle, it is well worth taking a chance. Regular diners and food lovers swear that the food here is excellent, and that the fish in particular is superb. Try the Peking duck, or lobster with ginger and onions, with, perhaps, the spiced braised eggplant. ♦ Chinese ♦ Lunch and dinner. Chelsea Cloisters, 85 Sloane Ave. 071/589.1781; fax 071/584.0596

**42 Bibendum** ★★★$$$$ One of London's most stylish eating places, this spectacular Art Deco building was once owned by **Michelin,** the tire company, whose mascot was an unlikely bespectacled chap called Bibendum, made entirely of white tires. The best ingredients go into every dish at this restaurant, and the food is cooked to perfection on an ever-changing menu. On Sunday, you will find mink-coated churchgoers walking through the door for lunch. Follow them, and you could find yourself eating next to someone famous, although the staff has been instructed to remain impassive. Lunchtime is recommended—it is cheaper and less ostentatious than at dinner. Make a reservation when you book your flight. ♦ French ♦ Lunch and dinner. Michelin House, 81 Fulham Rd. Reservations required. 071/581.5817; fax 071/623.7925

**42 The Conran Shop** Above, around, and to the side of Bibendum is **Sir Terence Conran's** personal apotheosis, The Conran Shop. A legend in his lifetime, Conran brought style to London in the shape of his **Habitat** chain shops back in the '60s and '70s; The Conran Shop is an extension of this. Perhaps the man no longer needs to alter the style-consciousness of the masses, for he now seems content to offer chic gewgaws to the rich. You can buy everything here, from leather-encased pencil sharpeners to bedspreads and furniture. But remember, the emphasis is on style first, quality second. ◆ M, W-Sa 9:30AM-6PM; Tu 10AM-6PM; Su noon-5PM. Michelin House, 81 Fulham Rd. 071/589.7401; fax 071/823.7015

**43 Joseph** The minimalist decor—black leather and white walls—gives a clue as to the wares on sale here. **Joseph Ettedgui's** two-floor department store contains a selection of everything that is designer chic in furnishings. Occasional tables, chairs, a sofa—some of the large goods are available only by order and can be found dotted about the women's department. There are vases everywhere, even in the men's clothing section. ◆ M-Tu, Th-F 10AM-6:30PM; W 11AM-7PM; Sa 9:30AM-6PM; Su noon-5PM. 77 Fulham Rd. 071/823.9500; fax 071/736.1644

**44 Joe's Cafe** ★★$$ Owned by **Joseph Ettedgui** (of **Joseph** shops fame), this is a pretentious, style-conscious brasserie. If you have bought clothes at his store across the street, you can sit down with an easy conscience; otherwise, it's hard to resist the inevitable temptation to dash across the street to splurge on a (pricey) little something. Try the salmon fishcake, *pomme frites*, and salad with a glass of house white. ◆ Modern British ◆ Lunch and dinner; lunch only on Sunday. 126 Draycott Ave. 071/225.2217

**45 Walton Street** Just steps away from bustling Brompton Road, Walton Street is a street in transition, a place where fashionable shops have pushed out the neighborhood hardware stores. Only the elegant window displays on the rather bare facades of the buildings at the lower end of the street reveal the array of goods inside: antique Rolex watches at **Van Petersen,** or hand-knit sweaters by **Moussie Sayer** at **Moussie.** Members of the royal family decorate their nurseries with furniture made by the carpenters at **Dragons,** and their heads with hats from **John Boyd.** Two 19th-century brick ovens turn out cookies, cakes, croissants, and even pizza at **Justin de Blanck Hygienic Bakery.** Restaurants such as **Ma Cuisine, San Martino,** and **Waltons** have loyal followings, and the only pub, **The Enterprise,** is a Walton Street institution. As you wander toward Beauchamp Place, the street's domestic side becomes apparent. The shops are less frequent and the facades grow brighter, turning into noble town houses guarded by iron gates at the more affluent end of the street. ◆ Between Hans Rd and Draycott Ave

**45 Waltons** ★★$$$$ Brompton Cross is quite a little enclave of appealing places to eat, which is hardly surprising when you consider that this is one of the most exclusive areas in London. At the height of the housing boom, someone with more money than sense paid £36,500 for what turned out to be a cupboard! Their excuse was that they wanted a London address. Dress for the occasion, because everyone else does here. Rich, up-to-the-minute cookery and opulent surroundings have conspired to keep this pricey but much-loved restaurant going for years. Try the home-cured salmon or calf's liver and bacon to see just how delicious the cooking can be. The set lunch is cheaper. ◆ British ◆ Lunch and dinner. 121 Walton St. 071/584.0204; fax 071/581.2846

**46 Van Petersen** A bijou shop on a bijou street, Van Petersen sells original '30s jewelry and **Georg Jensen** silver, old Rolex and Cartier watches, and contemporary jewelry. The quality is excellent, and it is less expensive than might be expected for the area. ◆ M-Tu, Th-Sa 9:30AM-6PM; W 9:30AM-7PM. 117-119 Walton St. 071/589.2155; fax 071/584.8165

**47 San Martino** ★★$$ Here's another much-loved, busy, and friendly Italian restaurant. For fun, why not try the spaghetti cooked in a paper bag? ◆ Italian ◆ Lunch and dinner. 103-105 Walton St. 071/589.3833

**48 The Walton Street Stationery Company** While your sheets are being stitched, pop across the street to this exquisite shop, which offers a similar service for your writing paper or invitations. If you have a style in mind, just tell them, and it will be engraved or printed to your specifications. ◆ M-F 10AM-6PM; Sa 10AM-5PM. 97 Walton St. 071/589.0777; fax 071/225.2640

**49 The Monogrammed Linen Shop** This is where the cognoscenti come to buy monogrammed Irish linen sheets, duvet covers, dressing gowns, and handkerchiefs. Everything here comes with tastefully embroidered initials. ◆ M-F 10AM-6PM; Sa 10AM-5PM. 168 Walton St. 071/589.4033; fax 071/823.7745

**50 English House** ★★$$$$ When you walk in, it feels as if you're in a private room in someone's home, gazing at mirrors, dark wallpaper, and objets d'art. Cooking extends from 18th century to Victorian, and there are some divine dishes like chicken roulade with lemon stuffing, finished off with rhubarb and cinnamon burnt cream. ◆ British ◆ Lunch and dinner. 3 Milner St. Reservations recommended. 071/584.3002; fax 071/581.2848

**51 Dragons** This enchanting shop is for grownups who want to give their youngsters the childhood they never had. Until Dragons opened, no one could have had that kind of childhood anyway! The exquisite, hand-painted children's furniture is made for royal children and other fortunate little ones; there are children's fabrics, tiny seats, and even some toys (to keep the kiddies amused while

## Walton Street Shopping Map

**DRAYCOTT AVENUE**

English restaurant **Waltons**
jewelry **Van Petersen**
French restaurant **Ma Cuisine**
Oriental knickknacks **Eastern Accents**
handknit women's sweaters **Moussie**
Italian restaurant **San Martino**
lamps **Besselink & Jones**
**The Walton Street Stationery Company**
women's dress agency **Pamela**
French restaurant **Turner's**
**Lightning Dry Cleaners**
kids' interior design **Nursery Window**
corporate apartments **Peerman**
maternity designerwear **Maman Deux**
jewelry **Kiki McDonough**
maternity and children's clothing **Balloon**
hairdressers **Ellis Helen**
pictures **Walker Bagshawe**
estate agents **Janet Osband**
womenswear **Liola**

**WALTON STREET**

**Sara Davenport Gallery** antique pet paintings
**Figure Shapers** beauty salon
**Andrew Martin** interior design
**Oasis** artificial flora
**Reenlees** leather goods
**Carew Jones** custom-made furniture
**Percy Bass Ltd.** eccentric interiors
**Anne McKee & Co.** estate agents
**Merola** jewelry
**Ozten Zeki Gallery**
**Malcolm Innes Gallery**
**Oliver Swann Galleries**
**The Monogrammed Linen Shop**
**John Campbell** framing, restoration
**Maria Andipas Icon Gallery**
**Art of Africa**
**Arabesk** African jewelry
**Durin Gallery**
**Capital Designs**

**FIRST STREET**

pub **The Enterprise**

**HASKER STREET**

kids' toys and furniture **Dragons**
tiles **Walton Ceramics**
kids' designs **Patrizia Wigan**
antique prints **Stephanie Hoppen**
interior design, furnishings **Louise Bradley**

**OVINGTON STREET**

wine merchant **Wine Rack**
interior design **Nina Campbell**
fabrics, furnishings **Les Olivadas**
deli **La Picena**
Italian restaurant **Scalini**

**LENNOX GARDEN MEWS**

Italian restaurant **Totos**

**GYNDE MEWS**

**La Reserve** wine merchant
**Tapisserie** sew-it-yourself tapestries
**Wm. Hawkes & Son** silversmith, jeweler
**Concorde of Knightsbridge** dry cleaners
**Justin de Blank Hygienic Bakery**

**OVINGTON SQUARE**

**BEAUCHAMP PLACE**

**BLENHEIM STREET**

**PONT STREET**

their parents choose). ◆ M-F 9:30AM-5:30PM; Sa 10AM-5PM. 23 Walton St. 071/589.3795; fax 071/584.4570

**52 Grill St. Quentin** ★★$$ First-rate cooking is offered here, straight from the chargrill in a brightly lit basement. The potato fries are excellent (for England, that is!). ◆ French ◆ Lunch and dinner. 2 Yeoman's Row. 071/581.8377

**52 Luba's Bistro** ★★$$ Luba's has been a fixture in the neighborhood since before World War II. Nothing much has changed in the last 30 years, including the menu and hardly even the prices. Russian classics such as borscht, *kapoostniak* (braised cabbage with prunes and sour cream), blinis, and *vereniki* all make tasty beginnings. Follow them with the *kooliebiaka* (salmon trout pie), buckwheat piroshki, or chicken Kiev. Bring your own wine for tremendous savings. If you are watching your budget, the bistro might become a regular haunt, particularly with the offer of a 10 percent discount before 8PM. ◆ Russian ◆ Lunch and dinner. 6 Yeoman's Row. 071/589.2950

**53 Patisserie Valerie** ★$ Tottering away from an exhausting shopping spree, you might expect the tea shops around here to be tourist fleecers, but for once, you will be wrong. Like its older sister in Soho, the food here is pleasant and the cakes, eclairs, pastries, and buns quite scrumptious. ◆ Cafe ◆ M-F 7:30AM-7:30PM; Sa 7:30AM-7PM; Su 9AM-6:30PM. 215 Brompton Rd. 071/823.9971

**54 Bunch of Grapes** ★$ Once upon a time, a glass partition separated the upstairs and downstairs bars in this authentic Victorian pub. Now, only the downstairs is in use and all is convivial and democratic, with tourists and locals alike welcomed and served delicious homemade food at lunchtime, snacks in the evening until 9PM, and four real ales. ◆ Pub ◆ Lunch and dinner. 207 Brompton Rd. 071/589.4944

**55 Crane Kalman Gallery** Fine quality 20th-century British and European paintings may be found inside, with works by **Degas, Dufy, Nicholson, Moore,** and **Sutherland,** to name a distinguished few. ◆ M-F 10AM-6PM; Sa 10AM-4PM. 178 Brompton Rd. 071/584.7566; fax 071/584.3843

**56 Alistair Sampson** Go to the vast room in the back of this small antique shop to find early English pottery, oak furniture, brass, primitive paintings, and unusual decorative pieces. ◆ M-F 9:30AM-5:30PM. 156 Brompton Rd. 071/589.5272

**56 Past Times** Here you'll find gifts inspired by English arts and crafts, encompassing everything from Celtic times to early 20th century. Ancient games range from Roman

Tabula to the Captain's Mistress, which **Captain James Cook** played for so long while looking for New Zealand, that the crew swore he had a woman aboard! There are Gothic playing cards, books, jigsaws; Celtic, Tudor and Stuart jewelry; and scarves and tapestries for ladies of the manor. ◆ M-Sa 9:30AM-5:30PM. 146 Brompton Rd. 071/581.7616

**57 Khun Akorn** ★★$$$ It's difficult to spot, but once you're inside this restaurant, there is a long and impressive list of classic Bangkok specialties. Try the *toong ngern yejyeung* (minced prawns and baby corn in a spicy sauce) and finish with the steamed whole banana with coconut cream. ◆ Thai ◆ Lunch and dinner; dinner only on Sunday. 136 Brompton Rd. 071/225.2688; fax 071/225.2680

**58 Montpelier Street** This Regency village between Brompton Road and Knightsbridge boasts some of the most expensive real estate in London. At **Bonham's,** an auction house founded in 1793, check out the oils, watercolors, carpets, clocks, porcelain, furniture, wine, silver, and jewelry. The firm, which has a sixth-generation Bonham on staff, normally has set days for certain items, so telephone for sale details. When special events are held in London, such as the **Chelsea Flower Show** or the **National Cat Show,** Bonham's usually holds a paintings auction to match. ◆ M-F 8:45AM-5:30PM, viewing until 7PM. Between Brompton Rd and Walton St. 071/584.9161

**59 Emporio Armani** Mr. Tailored Jacket himself now owns two stores in London. When the Bond Street shop closed, the Italian clothes mogul couldn't resist opening up in two new locations, but in the far more exclusive preserves of Knightsbridge and Sloane Street. It's a grand name for an Italian store on the grand scale, with sections for every kind of clothing—men's, women's, and *bambinis*, together with every accessory they'll need to get through life. After allowing your imagination, and perhaps your wallet, free rein, risk a healthy lunch of *pollo con radice di sedano* (strips of chicken with celery root), followed by *semi freddo* (ice-cream cake) and a cup of steaming hot java. Emporio Armani has a coffee machine that makes up to 400 cups an hour! ◆ M-Tu, Th-Sa 10AM-6PM; W 10AM-7PM. 191 Brompton Rd. 071/823.8818; fax 071/823.8854

**60 Beauchamp Place** Temptations are many on this Regency street (pronounced BEECH-am), where you can easily spend a whole day or a whole week browsing in the boutiques and smart shops. You will find the best of British designer clothes, old maps and prints, reject china and crystal (not that you will ever

## Beauchamp Place Shopping Map

**BROMPTON ROAD**

| | |
|---|---|
| *leather goods, luggage* **Mulberry** | **Reject China Shop** |
| | **Pasta Prego** *restaurant* |
| **Knightsbridge Furniture Co.** | **Chinacraft** *china, porcelain* |
| *hairdresser* **Naim** | **Janet Reger** *lingerie* |
| | **L'Aventure de Angelis** *couture womenswear* |
| *jewelry* **Bao Bijoux** | **Adèle Davis** *womenswear* |
| *jewelry* **Ken Lane** | **Shahzada** *Indian restaurant* |
| *womenswear* **Caroline Charles** | **Kanga** *womenswear* |
| *womenswear* **Johann** | **Patara** *Thai restaurant* |
| *antique prints* **The Map House** | **Mozafarian** *women's jewelry* |
| *womenswear* **Monsoon** | **Shirin** *cashmere* |
| *jewelry* **Annabel Jones** | **Creazioni Sergio Rossi** *shoes* |
| *Italian restaurant* **Ciro's Pizza Pomodoro** | **13½** *Italian restaurant* |
| *gifts* **Museum Store** | **Arthur Morrice** *optician* |
| *Portuguese restaurant* **Ofado** | **Whistles** *womenswear* |
| *womenswear* **CiBi** | **Stanley Leslie** *silver* |
| *womenswear* **Panton** | **Paddy Campbell** *womenswear* |
| *womenswear* **Elena Day** | **Old England** *womenswear* |
| | **Julie Loughnan** *children's dresses, books, model horses* |
| *Russian restaurant* **Borscht 'n Tears** | **Delia Collins** *beauty salon* |
| *jewelry* **Folli Folie** | **Hampstead Bazaar** *womenswear* |
| | **San Lorenzo** *Italian restaurant* |
| **The Grove Pub** | **Maison Panache** *womenswear* |
| *womenswear* **Michele Holden** | **Pamela Stevens** *beauty salon* |
| *beauty salon* **Beauchamps** | **Scruples** *womenswear* |
| *handmade shoes, bags* **Deliss** | **Bruce Oldfield** *womenswear* |
| *coffeehouse* **Sonny's** | |
| *Portuguese restaurant* **Caravela** | **McKenna & Co** *jewelry* |
| *Lebanese restaurant* **Maroush** | |
| *womenswear* **Hawa** | **Margaret Howell** *clothing* |
| **Reject China Shop** | |
| *designer womenswear* **Isabel Kristens** | **Verbanella** *Italian restaurant* |
| *womenswear* **Spaghetti** | |
| *wine bar/restaurant* **Bill Bentley's** | |

*(side label: BEAUCHAMP PLACE)*

**WALTON STREET**

find the flaw), antique silver, made-to-measure shoes, and lingerie fit for the Princess (who buys it here). While struggling to resist or not to resist the many covetables on the street, you can eat in restaurants that are equally stylish, fun, and delicious. ♦ Between Brompton Rd and Walton St

**60 Reject China Shops** These shops are dotted along this and many other London streets, and carry the finest porcelain, crystal, and stoneware. A certain energy, patience, and dedication is required to find the real bargains; there is a lot of truly awful stuff and the prices sometimes seem far from marked down. But if you have the stamina, you might be eating off the finest English, French, or Italian dinnerware the rest of your days, toasting with Baccharat or Waterford crystal, and gloating besides. ♦ M-Tu, Th-Sa 9AM-6PM; W 9AM-7PM. 34-35 Beauchamp Pl. 071/581.0737

**60 Janet Reger** If you are looking for crêpe de chine pajamas and the kind of silk lingerie that the finest fantasies are made of, this is the only address you'll ever need. The brassieres are brilliantly designed, amplifying or diminishing with seductive perfection, as desired. ♦ M-Sa 10AM-6PM. 2 Beauchamp Pl. 071/584.9360; fax 071/581.7946

**61 The Map House** Antique, rare, and decorative maps, botanical prints, lithographs, and aquatints line every inch of this tiny town house with honest prices. ♦ M-F 9:45AM-5:45PM; Sa 10:30AM-5PM. 54 Beauchamp Pl. 071/589.4325

**61 Caroline Charles** This top English designer still sells only the finest silks and linens. **Caroline Charles'** style is very English, but never without her own brand of sophisticated elegance. She creates clothes that you will want to wear for a lifetime. ♦ M-Tu, Th-Sa 9:30AM-5:30PM; W 9:30AM-6:30PM. 56-57 Beauchamp Pl. 071/589.5850

**62 San Lorenzo** ★★★$$$ It's comforting to think that the royal family shops and eats locally. You might even spot **Princess Diana** having lunch in the corner with some close confidantes; or **John McEnroe** dining with friends—without swearing at the waiters or throwing his cutlery about. Discretion is a watchword. The staff seems to know all the glamorous hairdos and suits personally, but service to unknowns is just as attentive and courteous. This first-class Italian restaurant attracts the kind of people who appreciate carpaccio prepared three ways, fresh game in season (pheasant with chestnuts, for example), and tripe with Parma ham. Be forewarned: credit cards are not accepted. ◆ Italian ◆ Lunch and dinner. Closed Sunday. 22 Beauchamp Pl. Reservations recommended. 071/584.1074

**62 Bruce Oldfield** What do **Joan Collins** and **Princess Diana** have in common? A passion for **Bruce Oldfield,** who creates evening dresses that embrace the figure and linger in the memories of everyone else. If you have what it takes to wear his creations, you are lucky, indeed. ◆ M-Tu, Th-F 10AM-6PM; W 10AM-6:30PM; Sa 11AM-5:30PM. 27 Beauchamp Pl. 071/584.1363; fax 071/584.6972

**63 Deliss** Come here if you do not have average feet—that is, if you suffer from chronic footache because you are impossible to fit. Among the sizable feet shod here are those belonging to **Keith Richards, Princess Michael of Kent, Jesse Norman,** and **Marvin Mitchelson.** The shoes are beautiful and at prices you can actually consider. The shop will also make shoes from your own design or copy a pair of old favorites—many make a special trip for this service alone. ◆ M-F 9:30AM-5:30PM; Sa noon-4PM. 41 Beauchamp Pl. 071/584.3321

**63 Bill Bentley's** ★★$$ Sit at the bar, order a dozen oysters and a half bottle of Muscadet, and thank your lucky stars you are in London. The proper restaurant upstairs serves British fish dishes such as Dover sole and salmon trout. ◆ Wine bar/British ◆ Lunch and dinner. Closed Sunday. 31 Beauchamp Pl. Reservations required for dinner. 071/589.5080

# Harrods

**64 Harrods** In the past, man's desire for greatness led to the creation of cathedrals and palaces. Today, it leads to department stores, and Harrods is Notre Dame, the Taj Mahal, and Blenheim Palace, all rolled into one. Even if the debate about Bloomingdales vs. Harrods rages over dinner tables, and even if the silk-scarf ladies of England vow that Harrods has gone downhill, the fact remains that this cathedral of consumerism is hard to beat.

Behind the solid and elegant Edwardian facade built between 1901 and 1905 by **Stevens and Munt,** 4,000 employees in 230 departments stand ready to fulfill your every request. You can hire a chauffeur, organize a funeral, open a bank account, book a trip around the world, reserve all your theater and concert tickets, get your lighter repaired, your clothes dry-cleaned, and your nails polished. There's even a special long-hair department in the beauty salon. And, of course, you can buy just about anything your heart desires, including a yellow labrador from the pet department, a pair of Rayne pumps (preferred by the **Queen** and **Mrs. Thatcher),** a dress by **Zandra Rhodes,** a £1million Baccharat crystal table, a set of pale-blue Egyptian cotton sheets, and a bottle of Krug Grand Cuvée to be delivered to your hotel and enjoyed whilst tallying up the bills.

Above all, don't miss the **Food Halls,** with their stunning mosaic friezes and fabulous displays of food. (The wet-fish display is a masterpiece!) For a sociological study of one of the purest slices of English life, go upstairs to the kennel, where English ladies up from the country for the day leave their labradors and Jack Russells. If you're afraid this palace of temptation will make you lose sight of the exchange rate, plan your visit around the January sale, the most famous event of the year. It is a true test of consumer stamina, but those who are tenacious and strong will be rewarded with real bargains.

Harrods has five restaurants and five bars, including a juice bar and a wine bar. The **Georgian Room** (★★$$$$) is *always* full for tea. People start lining up outside the elegant double-banquet room around 3:15PM, hoping to sit on the green-velvet furnishings and sip tea at the tables covered with pink linens and an array of buns, pastries, salads, butters, creams, and jams. ◆ M-Tu, Sa 10AM-6PM; W-F 10AM-7PM. 87-135 Brompton Rd. General information: 071/730.1234. Theater tickets: 071/589.1101; fax 071/581.0470

**65 L'Hotel** $$$ A small country inn—the kind you never seem to find—is located right in the heart of Knightsbridge. There are only 12 rooms, so you have to book well in advance in order to have pine furniture, Laura Ashley fabrics, twin beds, color TV, and clock radios all at a reasonable price. This is the stepchild of the elegant **Capital Hotel** two doors down, and is extremely popular with discriminating Americans who aren't on expense accounts. The front door is locked at 11PM during the week and 5PM on weekends, but you pick up your key from the Capital, which adds to the sense of adventure. And then there is **Le Metro** wine bar in the basement, which can be entered from L'Hotel. For the lone traveler, this is one of the best places in London to stay and feel at home. A Continental breakfast is included in the price. ◆ 28 Basil St. 071/589.6286; fax 071/225.0011

Within L'Hotel:

**Le Metro** ★★★$$ The only drawback to this wine bar is its popularity; if dozens were to pop up all over London, the quality of life would be immeasurably improved. The restaurant serves the best of things French—salad *frissée aux foies de volailles,* cheeses that are fresh and ripe, savory soups, casseroles, and tarts, and a choice of first-rate, carefully chosen wines, with a special selection of important *crus* by the glass, made possible by the *cruover* machine. Le Metro now stays open in the afternoon, when one would dearly love a hot cup of coffee and a *croque monsieur.* And it opens early in the morning for genuine espresso or frothy café crème and croissants. ♦ French ♦ Breakfast, lunch, and dinner. Closed Sunday. 071/589.6286

**65 Capital Hotel** $$$$ **David Levin,** the darling of London, is a first-class hotelier, and when he decided to open his own hotel he went about creating the very best. The Capital is small, modern, sophisticated, personal, attractive, and one minute from Harrods. **Nina Campbell** designed the 48 luxurious rooms, packed with as many of the creature comforts as could fit into the rather small dimensions, including super king-size beds with Egyptian cotton sheets, bathrobes, toothbrushes, and roses for every lady. **Margaret Levin** has furnished each room in a classic style. If you consider the elegant surroundings, perfect location, and high standard of service, even the price seems reasonable. ♦ 22 Basil St. 071/589.5171; fax 071/225.0011

Within the Capital Hotel:

**Capital Restaurant** ★★★$$$ This restaurant has put the Capital Hotel on the map. Accolades for chef **Phillip Britten** appear with delicious regularity in the British press. Decorated in delicate pinks, this is a luxury restaurant without the asphyxiating atmosphere of deluxe. The menu changes every few months but concentrates on fish, which is what Britten loves to cook and you will love to eat: try the steamed langoustines and cod in a butter sauce. The set lunch is a real value. The French wine list draws serious oenophiles from far and wide. ♦ Haute cuisine ♦ Lunch and dinner. 071/589.5171

**66 Basil Street Hotel** $$$ Traditional English charm abounds at the Basil Street Hotel, which has been owned by the same family since it was built in 1910. It rambles eccentrically from floor to floor and is full of antiques; the place is an old-fashioned delight. It has a loyal clientele of English country folk who make twice-yearly trips to London to shop and see plays. The prices appeal to the British sense of economy, the location is ideal, and the service is proper. Afternoon tea in the lounge is an institution, and it's served in a room that looks like a setting for an Agatha Christie novel, with the characters and the tea seemingly untouched by the passage of time. Also popular with the frugal English is the restaurant upstairs, though the salad bar, buffet, and selection of hot dishes are just a cut above the category of English school food. ♦ 8 Basil St. 071/581.3311; fax 071/581.3693

**67 Pearl** ★★$$ The dim sum here is delicious and well worth seeking out. Otherwise, on a trip back for supper, a good choice is the crispy roast chicken. ♦ Chinese ♦ Lunch and dinner. 22 Brompton Rd. 071/225.3888

**67 Scotch House** Believe it or not, if you want a cashmere sweater or scarf, you will do better here in terms of quality and price than at Harrods. The shop has a huge selection of the best Scottish woolens, including 300 kilts and a book that can match names with patterns. There's also a considerable children's department with kilts and jumpers and even those tiny Burberrys that make kids look like dwarves. The French (astute shoppers that they are) come here as soon as they arrive in London. ♦ M, Th-F 9:30AM-6PM; Tu 10AM-6PM; W 9:30AM-7PM; Sa 9AM-6PM. 2 Brompton Rd. 071/581.2151; fax 071/589.1583

**67 Mr. Chow** ★★★$$$ The restaurant's popularity dates back to the '60s, when the owner decided to combine the style and exuberance of an Italian restaurant, complete with Italian waiters, with the innate nouvelle cuisine of the finest Chinese cooking. Yes, Mr. Chow owns a restaurant in Beverly Hills and another in New York, so you'll know what to expect in the way of old-style opulence. The decor is chrome and dimmed glass with the flair of another era, and the inventive menu is explained in down-to-earth language. Try the imitation crab, velvet chicken, or Mr. Chow's noodles—your taste buds will never be the same again. A bottle of Gewürztraminer goes well with the subtly spiced food. ♦ Chinese ♦ Lunch and dinner. 151 Knightsbridge. Reservations recommended. 071/589.7347; fax 081/563.0588

**68 The Lanesborough** $$$$ Overlooking the hurly-burly traffic chaos of Hyde Park Corner, The Lanesborough is London's newest hotel. It was built originally in the classical/Greek revival style of Portland stone in 1829. Texan billionaire **Caroline Rose Hunt,** whose **Rosewood Hotels** bought this former hospital, flew in the face of prudence by spending a reputed $1.7 million on each of the 95 guest rooms, including 46 suites, during the recession. Well, she's created a sumptuous temple of luxury, according to the *Times,* and a stunning landmark has been transformed. Inside are polished marble floors, neo-Georgian furnishings, and your own personal butler for the duration of your stay. ♦ 1 Lanesborough Pl, Hyde Park Corner. 071/259.5599; fax 071/259.5606

Within The Lanesborough:

**The Dining Room** ★★$$$ Swagged in deepest green, red, and gold with pink columns and walls, The Dining Room is so flamboyant that it's almost like being in the boudoir of an 18th-century French courtesan. The English take this kind of decoration in stride, but with difficulty. The food is delicious; try the mousseline soufflé of Arbroath smokies (divine smoked haddock from Scotland) with langoustines. Mmmm! ♦ Continental ♦ Lunch and dinner. Closed Saturday and Sunday. 071/259.5599

**The Conservatory** ★★$$$ The setting is perfect for hot summer nights, with a high glass roof, giant potted palms, candlelight, and piano music setting a serene mood as you eat your meal. The smoked duckling carpaccio with sweet ginger crisps is a favorite here, and the vegetarian food comes recommended. ♦ Continental ♦ Breakfast, lunch, afternoon tea, and dinner. 071/259.5599

**69 Hyde Park Hotel** $$$$ More a stately home than a hotel, the Hyde Park (pictured above) is a Knightsbridge institution. The Edwardian splendor of the marble entrance hall, gilded and molded ceilings, and Persian carpets the size of cricket fields leaves you wondering how Buckingham Palace can hold a candle to it; at any rate, one suspects the service is far better here. Guests have included **Winston Churchill** and **Mahatma Gandhi,** for whom a goat was milked each day. In the last few years, the hotel has been completely refurbished with no expense

spared. Bedrooms are country house size, individually decorated, and furnished with antiques, recalling the tranquility of a country château. **Madonna** stays here on publicity trips to London, along with bodyguards who jog protectively beside her along Hyde Park's Rotten Row. There is also a fitness center. ♦ 66 Knightsbridge. 071/235.2000; fax 071/235.4552

Within the Hyde Park Hotel:

**Park Room** ★★$$$ This grandly proportioned restaurant overlooks the greenery of Hyde Park's Rotten Row. Underneath the crystal chandeliers, a new style of northern Mediterranean cooking has been introduced, one that avoids butter and cream. (Dessert is the exception!) At midday a sumptuous self-service buffet of appetizers is laid out in the center of the room, with salads of artichoke, cold fish, or meats like *bresaola* and pâtés amid the silver and fine china. Follow this with a tempting *escalope* of salmon or breast of chicken filled with zucchini and fontina cheese. A Park Room breakfast might include scrambled eggs wrapped in smoked salmon. A pianist accompanies the traditional afternoon high tea (jacket and tie required), and dinner. ♦ Continental ♦ Breakfast, lunch, and dinner 071/235.2000

**The Restaurant** ★★★$$$$ Since the hotel's refurbishment, popular young chef **Marco Pierre White** has come on board for the opening of his latest restaurant. It's still early, but judging by his past performance at The Canteen in Chelsea Harbour, White's culinary ways will help turn The Restaurant into yet another yuppie hot spot. **Michael Caine** and **Claudio Pulze** are partners in the venture. ♦ Continental ♦ Lunch and dinner; dinner only on Saturday. Closed Sunday. Reservations recommended. 071/259.5380

**Ferrari Bar & Lounge** Adjoining the Park Room restaurant, the bar is open 24 hours a day for drinks (coffee, tea, or cocktails) and snacks, all served in a relaxing setting. ♦ Daily 24 hours. 071/235.2000

**69 Harvey Nichols** Like two guards at each end of Sloane Street, the **General Trading Company** at Sloane Square and Harvey Nichols at Knightsbridge are the arbiters of London's jet set chic. "Harvey Nix," as it's lovingly called, is a department store devoted solely to fashion—you'll find only designer labels here. Menswear is in the basement, fashionable accessories on the ground floor, big-name designers on the first. Watch the prices drop marginally as you ascend the moving stairs. ♦ M-Tu, Th-F 10AM-7PM; W 10AM-8PM; Sa 10AM-6PM. 109 Knightsbridge. 071/235.5000; fax 071/259.6084

Within Harvey Nichols:

### The Fifth Floor at Harvey Nichols ★★$$
Revive your flagging spirits at this chic eatery by watching others spend lots of money in the food department through a glass wall the length of the restaurant. This is a pleasant place to take an eating break during a shopping trip. Try the fillet of cod with tapenade for a taste of perfection, followed by the pear sable. ◆ Cafe ◆ Lunch and dinner. 071/235.5000

**69 Sheraton Park Tower** $$$$ The modern exterior looks like a brick ear of corn, and it hasn't improved with age. But this circular luxury hotel offers that marvelously egalitarian notion of equal-size rooms with a view (the higher up the 17 stories, the better the room *and* the view), and you can count on spacious comfort and reliable service. There is even a complimentary valet who will unpack your suitcase. ◆ 101 Knightsbridge. 071/235.8050; fax 071/235.8231

Within the Sheraton Park Tower:

### Restaurant 101 ★★$$$ Facing
Knightsbridge, this restaurant is within a conservatory, which gives it a commodious, airy feeling. The food is light and healthy, too. Try the cold buffet at lunchtime. ◆ Continental ◆ Lunch and dinner; lunch only on Sunday. 071/235.8050

### The Bar, Champagne Bar, and Rotunda
Service is as simple as the names of the establishments. ◆ Daily 9AM-7:30PM. 071/235.8050

**69 The Berkeley** $$$$ It is pronounced the "BARK-lee," and despite the pervasive theme of wealthy elegance, the hotel has a personality of its own. It is known for providing amenities to suit every whim, including a rooftop indoor-outdoor swimming pool, a sauna, a small, exclusive cinema, and a florist. Such distinguished luxury is usually associated with things of the past, but this Berkeley is relatively new, built in 1972. The old Berkeley, which sat on the corner of Berkeley Street and Piccadilly, wasn't left behind; the charming reception room, designed by a young and then-unknown architect named **Edwin Lutyens,** was re-erected here. It is this incredible attention to detail that makes the hotel one of the most popular in London. ◆ Wilton Pl. 071/235.6000; fax 071/235.4330

Within The Berkeley:

### Berkeley Restaurant ★★$$$ Bartolozzi's
18th-century reproductions of the Queen's **Holbein** collection adorn the paneled walls of this very English room furnished in Colefax and Fowler chintzes and lime-oaked paneling, with a portrait of **Sir Thomas More** observing the elegant surroundings. The food is very tasty indeed, with skillful handling of veal,

game in season, and fish. ◆ Continental ◆ Lunch and dinner. 071/235.6000

### Perroquet ★$$ Chief among the merits of
this restaurant is the magnificent fresh fish display that allows you to choose the fish of your choice from the menu. At lunchtime, there is a tempting Italian hot-and-cold buffet, as well as à la carte fare. The evening brings sensational steaks, pasta dishes, and more seafood. ◆ Italian ◆ Lunch and dinner. Closed Sunday. 071/235.6000

### Minema Café ★$$ This brasserie serves
Mediterranean style lunches and suppers, drinks and light snacks. ◆ Cafe ◆ Lunch and dinner. 071/235.6000

**Minema** The unique cinema has regular film showings (well-chosen foreign films in particular) and is available for private screenings. It is comfortable, small (68 seats), and much-loved by cinema buffs. ◆ 45 Knightsbridge. 071/235.4225

**69 Grenadier** ★★★$ The atmosphere of this pub is as old and military as in the days when it was the Officer's Mess for the **Duke of Wellington's** soldiers, complete with a ghost of an officer who was flogged to death for cheating at cards. Service in either the à la carte restaurant or, more simply, in the bar provides excellent officer's fare in the finest British tradition. But if at the end of a long day spent in South Kensington and Knightsbridge all you want is a bitter, you can count on the best, and a warm welcome as well. ◆ British ◆ Lunch and dinner. 18 Wilton Row. Reservations recommended. 071/235.3074

## Bests

### Dame Judi Dench
Actress

**Edward Stanford,** Covent Garden—I particularly love this shop because I am fascinated by maps, and here one can find all kinds—city maps, road maps, ordinance survey maps—of practically anywhere in the world. I go whenever I have the time.

### John J. Otterpohl
Teacher, The American School in London

**Shama Restaurant,** Cricklewood—Great Indian food for under seven pounds.

**Peach Blossom Restaurant,** Cricklewood—Quality and quantity Chinese food.

**Old Bailey,** near St. Paul's—Free, real live drama every time. Best show in town, but no clapping, flowers, eating, or drinking allowed.

**Big Ben,** Westminster—The 336 steps are a stimulant to the heart, while the clock and bells are nothing like what you would expect.

The 18th-century house of **Dennis Severs**—Meet everyone who has ever lived there in three hours.

# Marylebone/ Camden Town

A sedate, almost feminine feel characterizes this elegant section of London. Perhaps this charm should come as no surprise, since a woman, **Margaret Harley**, daughter of **Edward Harley**, the Earl of Oxford, originally inherited the land, which has frequently been owned by and passed on to women. **J.M.W. Turner** and **Allan Ramsay** were just two of the artists who exercised their talents on **Harley Street**, and **Elizabeth Barrett** scribbled in secret while waiting for her true love, **Robert Browning**, to take her away from nearby **Wimpole Street**. Today, enigmatic **Marylebone** displays a doppelganger personality. On the one hand, it's cultured and refined: you can stroll through the royal lawns at **Regent's Park**, take in **Shakespeare** at the **Open Air Theatre**, or visit **The Wallace Collection**, a mansion containing an astounding array of 18th-century French furniture and old master paintings among its artistic treasures. On the other hand, the neighborhood is playful and whimsical: there's the **London Zoo, Madame Tussaud's, Lord's Cricket Grounds**, and **Baker Street**, home to the most famous (make-believe) detective ever to have sleuthed through London: **Sherlock Holmes**.

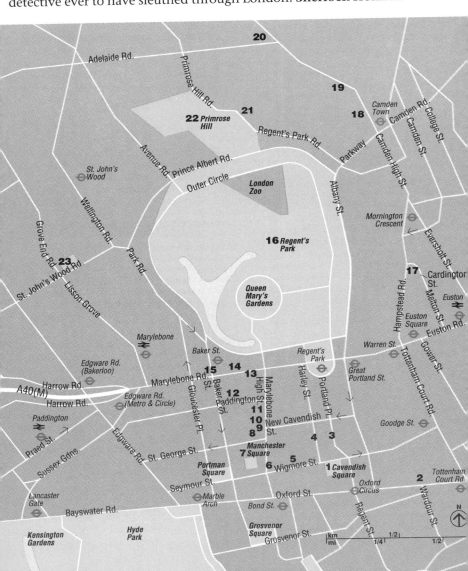

Northeast of Marylebone (a shortened version of the church name, **St. Mary by the Bourne**—Bourne being an alias for the **Tyburn River**) lies **Camden Town,** which also originally belonged to a woman—in this instance, the wife of the first Earl of Camden. Once pastures and coal wharfs, Camden Town is now a qualified yet slightly bohemian neighborhood, its cottages furnished to overflowing with antiques and cellular phones. When not converting Victoriana, the occupants, who range from novelists to spiritual seekers, wander down to **Camden Market,** one of London's most interesting street-markets, and to the burgeoning artists' and craftsmen's colony, **Camden Lock.**

**1 Cavendish Square** It's always so cold and windy in this stately square that it's almost possible to feel the tears of **Mrs. Horatio Nelson,** the woman the admiral continually left for the sea, when she lived here in 1791. **John Prince** laid the square out in 1717, but it wasn't until 1761, when **George II's** daughter **Amelia** came to live at **No. 16,** that it really came into its own. Standing among the trees you can see **Jacob Epstein's** sculpture, the *Madonna and Child.* ◆ Between Wigmore St and Henrietta Pl

**2 100 Club** Smoky and slightly seedy, the underground venue for the 100 Club is not famed for its decor, characterized by plastic tables and hard chairs, but for its musicians. The live jazz ranges from classic to Latin and African rhythms (**Charlie "Bird" Parker** is just one of the names reputed to have played here), with the occasional lapse into the blues. Beer and bar snacks round off a "must" for the serious jazz fanatic. ◆ Cover. Daily 7:30PM-closing. 100 Oxford St. Tube: Tottenham Court Rd. 071/636.0933

**3 Portland Place** When **Robert Adam** laid out this thoroughfare between 1776 and 1780, it was considered one of the finest of London's streets architecturally—part of the reason **John Nash** came to add **Regent Street** to its southern end. To the right, next to the curve of Langham Street, stands the BBC's **Broadcasting House,** built by **George Val Myers** and **F.J. Watson-Hart** in 1931. Sculpture by **Eric Gill** decorates the outside, including the Shakespearean figures of Prospero and Ariel from *The Tempest;* this was Gill's way of showing Ariel, who has become the symbol of broadcasting, being sent out into the world. ◆ Between Park Crescent and Langham Pl

**4 Harley Street** This area is one gracious band of stately Georgian houses, all designed with the eye for proportion and attention to detail that this era left as its architectural legacy. Artists such as **Joseph Turner** and **Allan Ramsay** lived here first; then, beginning in the 1840s, private doctors took it over, and today it is wall to wall with specialists catering to the ills of the wealthy. ◆ Between Marylebone Rd and Cavendish Sq

**5 Wigmore Hall** **Friedrich Beckstein** built this concert hall in 1901 as an afterthought to his spacious piano showrooms. Recently refurbished, its near-perfect acoustics make it a regular venue for classical concerts, particularly those performed by chamber orchestras. ◆ Box office: M-Sa 10AM-7PM. 36 Wigmore St. 071/935.2141

**6 Button Queen** They don't call this shop the Button Queen for nothing: it's a vision of an old sitting room, but filled with sewing boxes. ◆ M-F 10AM-6PM; Sa 10AM-1:30PM. 19 Marylebone Ln. 071/935.1505

**7 The Wallace Collection** Though little publicized, this museum houses one of the finest collections of French furniture and porcelain, old master paintings, and objets d'art in the world. It is arguably one of the major museums in London—and one of its best-kept secrets. Visiting this grand town house, built in 1776-88, and seeing its owner's private art collection is a much more intimate experience than going to a museum, however. The rich and varied collection was acquired by successive marquesses of Hertford during the 18th and 19th centuries. The first marquess was partial to **Canalettos;** the second, who lived between 1743 and 1823, added **Gainsborough's** *Mrs. Robinson* and **Reynolds'** *Nelly O'Brien.* He acquired the lease on **Hertford House** (the name of the present building) in 1797. The third marquess, 1777-1842, was a close friend of the Prince of Wales (later **George IV**), and collected French furniture and porcelain and 17th-century Dutch paintings. But it was the fourth marquess, who lived from 1800-70, who transformed the family's art collection into what you see today.

An eccentric recluse in Paris who declared, "I only like pleasing pictures," he collected 18th-century French paintings by **Watteau, Boucher, Fragonard,** and **Greuze,** among others, as well as old masters (including masterpieces by **Rembrandt, Rubens, Poussin,** and **Velázquez**). He also made lavish purchases of 18th-century French furniture by **Boulle, Crescent,** and **Riesener,** including the chest of drawers made for **Louis XV's** bedroom at Versailles and various pieces made for **Queen Marie Antoinette,** not to mention what is now the richest museum collection of **Sèvres** porcelain in the world. Don't miss the exquisite collection of gold boxes or the wrought-iron and gilt-bronze staircase balustrade, which was made in about 1720 for Louis XV's Palais Mazarin (now the Bibliothèque Nationale). It was sold around 1870 as scrap iron but rescued by **Sir Richard Wallace,** the fourth marquess' illegitimate son, who inherited the collection and brought it to Hertford House, adding the European arms and armor and medieval and Renaissance works of art. When Wallace died in 1890, his widow bequeathed the collection to the nation. ♦ Free. M-Sa 10AM-5PM; Su 2-5PM. Hertford House, Manchester Sq. Tube: Bond St. 071/935.0687

**8 Stephen Bull** ★★★$$$ Bull's is probably the most stylish restaurant in London, with innovative, no-nonsense food: turbot is paired with smoked bacon, and the vegetables are a celebration. Owner **Stephen Bull** is continually adding frequent and astonishing inventions to his menu. The wine list, running to 100 bottles, is superb. ♦ Modern British ♦ Lunch and dinner; dinner only on Saturday. Closed Sunday. 5-7 Blandford St. Reservations required. 071/486.9696

**9 Marylebone Lane and High Street** An old village at heart, this area is full of expensive specialty food shops and boutiques that cater to the wealthy (and healthy) relatives of the ill who pay court to the good doctors of nearby **Harley Street.** Charles Dickens, who lived all over London, wrote 11 books when he resided here.

**10 Patisserie Valerie at Maison Sagne** ★★★$ This is a gathering place of great cachet—everyone is someone at Valerie's on Saturday morning. **Stanley Comros** organizes his customers with care and diplomacy—it takes five years to be considered a regular. **Ray Hall** creates butterfly-light croissants and cakes of imaginative genius in a tearoom that has become a Marylebone institution. ♦ French ♦ Breakfast, lunch, and afternoon tea. 105 Marylebone High St. 071/935.6240

**11 Villandry** Jean Charles and his wife, **Rosalind,** have brought St.-Germain-des-Près to Marylebone with the charm and character of their French food shop. Delicacies range from 20 kinds of French and Italian breads—from dried tomato to Parisian sourdough—to 80 jams and 35 olive oils, original salads, picnic baskets, and pastries from **Le Manoir aux Quat'Saisons.** The neighborhood gathers in its best tweeds every Wednesday when fresh produce arrives from Paris. ♦ M-F 8:30AM-7PM; Sa 9:30AM-5PM. 89 Marylebone High St. 071/487.3816

**11 Villandry Dining Room** ★★$ Get here early for lunch; it's so popular, they run out of main courses by 2PM, and you'll be forced to fall back on their oysters, charcuterie, or smoked salmon. *Quel dommage!* ♦ French ♦ Breakfast and lunch. Closed Sunday. 89 Marylebone High St. 071/224.3799; fax 071/486.1370

**11 Daunt** Tall and effete, **James Daunt** was a Cambridge graduate-turned-New York City banker before he started this travel bookshop, a place that makes it seem unnecessary to travel

anywhere else. The shop takes you back in time to a turn-of-the-century galleried Bloomsbury studio, where books are arranged by nation: fiction, poetry, and nonfiction together. What you have is the so and spirit of the land housed in the only "bui for the purpose" bookshop left in London. ♦ M-Sa 9AM-7:30PM. 83 Marylebone High S 071/224.2295

**12 Le Muscadet** ★★$$ The atmosphere and the food inspire the kind of intense conversation you always imagined you woul have in a great French bistro. Try the *salade du mâche* with crisp bacon and impressive cheeses; if nougatine is available, have two slices. And don't miss the ginger sorbet. ♦ French ♦ Lunch and dinner; dinner only on Saturday. Closed Sunday. 25 Paddington St Reservations required. 071/935.2883

**13 St. Marylebone Parish Church** Built by **Thomas Hardwick** between 1813 and 1817, this church is splendidly ornate on the outside, with gold caryatids on the steeple. Halfway through its construction, plans shifted, turning what had begun as a chapel into a parish church. The resulting interior was thus quite dramatic—much more like a theater than a church—but today its simplicity gives the place a tranquil atmosphere. **Elizabeth Barrett** and **Robert Browning** were married here. These days, th building doubles as an active holistic healin center. ♦ M-Sa 10AM-7PM. Marylebone Rd. 071/935.7315

**14 Madame Tussaud's**

In Florence, you can wait for two hours before opening time at the fabulous Uffizi Gallery, filled with the Renaissance grand masters. In England, the lines are just as long, but the grand masters (and mistresses) are made of wax. Forget whatev you may have against waxworks—there is nothing ordinary about Mme Tussaud's. It h been a British institution since 1765 and recently completed a five-year, $30 million transformation. Once you see it you will understand why it attracts more than two an a half million visitors a year. Part of the fun i watching the Brits themselves, who love to visit this museum and can be observed speaking their minds to the wax images of controversial trade union leaders, or standin with hushed respect before the figures of th royal family.

Mme T learned her trade making death mask during the **French Revolution,** and those of **Louis XVI** and **Marie Antoinette** are displaye on spikes beside the actual blade that beheaded them. The oldest surviving likeness, dating from 1765, is that of **Mme du Barry,** also known as *The Sleeping Beauty.* A mechanism hidden in the bodice of her dress allows the figure to "breathe." **Henry VIII** is surrounded by all six of his wives, and there is a full re-creation of the ill-fated wedding party of the **Prince** and **Princess of Wales.** The wax likenesses are most often modeled from life and are never displayed behind glass. They stand in small tableaux, grouped as figures from history, politics, literature, sports, and entertainment, and are regularly joined by new figures.

One room is devoted to **Contemporary Heroes,** where **David Bowie's** hair moves and **Elvis** talks; they have recently been joined by **Arnold Schwarzenegger** and **Bill Clinton.** The **Chamber of Horrors,** featuring the likes of **Hitler, Jack the Ripper,** and **Charles Manson,** is not the attraction it once was, outclassed these days by the rival **London Dungeon** on Tooley Street. Still, the great and the good are spookily immortalized. Culture buffs can admire **Luciano Pavarotti,** while lowbrows can smile at **Dudley Moore.** In a 1940s Hollywood set, you can see **James Dean, Humphrey Bogart,** and **Marilyn Monroe.**

The newest attraction, costing some $15 million, is the **Spirit of London** exhibition. Here, London's heritage is brought alive by modern technology: animated 3-D figures take you through London's great events. There are museum guards made of wax, and an incredibly lifelike, exhausted tourist who dozes in a chair with guidebook in hand. Unlike him, however, you can revive yourself in the cafe and gift shop. On the same site as Tussaud's, **The London Planetarium** is probably the only place you'll be able to see stars in the London sky. It offers a high-tech "Space Trail" exhibition, as well as the usual star show. ◆ Admission (combined tickets available). M-F 10AM-5:30PM; Sa-Su 9:30AM-5:30PM. Marylebone Rd. Tube: Baker St. 071/935.6861; fax 071/465.0862

**15 Baker Street** The street is named after **William Baker,** who built it in 1790, but everyone knows it as the home of the fictional sleuths **Sherlock Holmes** and **Dr. Watson,** who lived at **No. 221b.** Their house no longer exists; instead, there's the **Abbey National Building Society** (by Baker Street tube), which employs someone full-time just to answer letters still written to the great detective! In 1951, Holmes' flat was re-created for the **Festival of Britain.** It can now be seen at the **Sherlock Holmes Pub** on Northumberland Avenue (see page 166).

**16 Regent's Park** London is a city of parks and squares, and nowhere do nature and the man-made environment meet more gloriously than at Regent's Park. The essence of **John**

Nash's original plan of 1811 to turn the almost 500 acres of farmland into a park survived eight years of government commissions. His spectacular terraces, iced with stucco and lined with columns, surround the park, making it look like a gigantic wedding cake; the terraces are named after the titles of some of **George III's** children. **Cumberland Terrace** is the most splendid, with its magnificent pediment and 276-yard facade lined with Ionic columns; **Chester Terrace,** constructed two years before, is the longest, stretching 313 yards with 52 Corinthian columns. The elegant **Clarence Terrace,** designed by **Decimus Burton** in 1823, is the smallest.

The neo-Georgian **Winfield House,** now the residence of the U.S. Ambassador, is located on the site of **St. Dunstan's Lodge,** designed in 1825 by Decimus Burton; the house was donated by **F.W. Woolworth** heiress **Barbara Hutton,** and now forms one of the few private areas of the park. The curiously shaped boating lake, reaching out in every direction and surrounded by ash groves, is undeniably romantic, as is the exquisite **Queen Mary's Garden,** which contains 40,000 rose bushes laid out in large beds, each with a different variety. **Regent's Canal** skirts the northern boundary of the park and runs for eight miles from Paddington to Limehouse and passes by the animals at **London Zoo.** ◆ Daily 5AM-dusk. Bounded by Prince Albert Rd and Albany St, and Marylebone and Park Rds

Within Regent's Park:

**London Zoo** As the oldest zoo, created in 1826, the gardens of the **Zoological Society of London** (the first society to shorten its name to "zoo") now spread over 36 enchanting acres of Regent's Park. Most of the 6,000 animals have been released from depressing iron cages and roam in settings similar to their natural habitats—separated from the public by moats.

Soon the **Mappin Terraces** will reopen as the gorilla enclosure, while Britain's largest aquarium and the children's zoo will be redesigned to make the animals more accessible. Ask on arrival about the times for feeding the lions, sea lions, penguins, and, of course, bathing the elephants. On Friday, see the snakes fed on whole dead animals (ugh!). The zoo's focus is now on captive breeding of endangered species; hence the admission charge to keep this most worthy of charities afloat. ◆ Admission. Daily 10AM-dusk. 071/722.3333; fax 071/483.4436

**Open Air Theatre** This delightful outdoor theater, which seats 1,187, presents a summer season (May-August) of **Shakespeare,** as well as the occasional musical. For refreshments, there's barbecue and salad, or you could opt to bring along a

Harrod's hamper. That old theatrical adage "The show must go on" is taken as gospel here—it always does, despite rain, roaring jets, and hay fever. Go prepared, then, and enjoy the Bard on sunny days and starry nights. ◆ Box office: M-Sa 10AM-8PM. 071/486.1933

**17 The Kennedy Hotel** $$ Conveniently located close to **Euston Station,** the Kennedy is a modern hotel and not to be touched if all you seek is tradition. While **Regent's Park** and **Madame Tussaud's** are in close proximity, the hotel is convenient for easy access to most of central London; it also has air-conditioning— which an older hotel may lack. All 360 rooms are fully equipped with shower, hair dryer, TV, and tea and coffee-making facilities. **Spires Restaurant** (★$$) within the hotel is informal and serves everything from light snacks to international cuisine. ◆ Cardington St. Tube: Euston. 071/387.4400; fax 071/387.5122

**18 Camden Markets** Camden Town has three kinds of markets covering two large sites. On the one hand, you have **Camden Market,** a huge weekend affair beginning in the northern reaches of **Camden High Street** where stall-holders gather to sell designer clothes and jewelry, as well as all sorts of artistic items. Across the street at **Camden Lock Place** is the site of what used to be known as **Dingwalls Market** but is now dubbed **Camden Lock Market.** During the week, this area is a craftsperson's paradise, featuring working artists selling handmade furniture, rugs, pottery, baskets, and an abundance of high-quality gift items.

On the weekends, it changes its face, and the stallholders invade to lure tourists with everything from secondhand clothing to New Age crystals. Don't worry if you get lost; that's half the fun of Camden, since as long as you keep walking, you're bound to stumble onto something worth opening your pocketbook for. You can also find out about canal trips from here to **London Zoo** (and farther afield) at the **Regent's Canal Information Centre,** housed in an old lockhouse on the quayside. ◆ Canal Information Centre: daily 10AM-1PM; 2-5PM. 289 Camden High St. 071/482.0523. Camden Market: Sa-Su 8AM-6PM; times vary, call for exact hours. Camden High St and surroundings. Camden Lock Market: M-F 10AM-6PM; Sa-Su 8AM-6PM. Camden Lock Pl. 071/485.4457

**19 Jongleurs** The comedy/cabaret show at Jongleurs has spawned a wealth of British talent. **Lenny Henry, Ben Elton, Ruby Wax, Stephen Fry,** and **Hugh Laurie** (to name just a few) have all walked the boards here, and the club prides itself on providing the "Best of British Comedy." It is generally well worth the £19.85 admission, which includes temporary membership, reserved seating, a drink from the bar, main meal, and entrance to the

Jongleurs disco. ◆ Admission. F-Sa 7:30PM closing (occasionally open during the week; call ahead). Middle Yard, Camden Lock (inside Ted's Bar). 071/267.1000. Tube: Camden Town. Also at: 49 Lavender Garden Battersea (above The Cornet Pub). 071/924.2766

**20 Belgo** ★★$ This is a must for *moules* this side of Brussels, so if you can't make it to th Continent, come here. The setting is austere and the reservation system faulty, but Belgc regulars don't mind, as many are here for th Belgian beer, which is flavored with fruit juices like strawberry, raspberry, and blueberry. Prices are amazing for the quality of food, so roll up for a portion of wild boar sausages and mash. ◆ Belgian ◆ Lunch and dinner. 72 Chalk Farm Rd. Reservations required. 071/267.0718

**21 Cecil Sharp House** Across from **Primros Hill** lies the headquarters of the **English Fol Dance and Song Society** and England's **National Folk Centre,** otherwise known as Cecil Sharp House. It was built in 1929 by **H.M. Fletcher** in honor of Cecil Sharp, who pioneered techniques of collecting and preserving folk songs. Inside, the **Vaughan Williams Memorial Library** houses more than 11,000 books on folklore, folksongs, a related interests, as well as more than 3,00 recordings. The House is busy, with dance and music sessions of all types taking place every day. If you'd like to learn to Morris Dance or clog or to take part in a Celtic singer's night while you're here, then stop ▶ The small shop inside sells tapes, books, ar other folksy items. ◆ Shop: M-F 9:30AM-5PM. Vaughan Williams Library: M-F 9:30AM-5:30PM. 2 Regent's Park Rd. 071/485.2206

**22 Primrose Hill** Sixty-two acres seem superfluous in comparison to its larger neighbor to the south, yet Primrose Hill is beloved and well-used by nearby residents for everything from kite flying to druidical ceremonies (seriously!). The grounds were once owned by **Eton College,** but in 1841, t site was made public, given in return for roy land closer to the school in **Windsor.** On a clear day, you can get a fantastic view from the top of the park—the summit measures around 219 feet—both of **Regent's Park** an of the whole vista of central London. No wonder **Alan Bennett, V.S. Pritchett,** and other literati have moved in.

When a proud mother said her baby looked liked Churchill, he replied: "Madam, all babies look like me."

**Restaurants/Clubs:** Red          Hotels: Blue
Shops/ 🌳 **Outdoors:** Green          **Sights/Culture:** Bl

**23** **Lord's Cricket Ground** The gentle pop of leather on willow (ball on bat) characterizes a game that remains a mystery to many Americans, and to many Brits. In England, if not around the world, Lord's beats at the very heart of the cricket scene, particularly once a year, when English teams attempt to overthrow current Australian or Pakistani dominance in the game. Lord's current site was established in 1811, following a move by founder **Thomas Lord** from a situation originally located around **Dorset Square.** You'll find the entrance to this hallowed ground farther along **St. John's Wood Road,** where the **W.G. Grace Memorial Gates** open onto the **Marylebone Cricket Club (MCC),** as Lord's is officially known. Visit the museum of memorabilia dedicated to the sport but don't pretend to understand it. ◆ Cricket season: M-Sa 10AM-5PM May-Sept. Tours (including gallery and museum) by appointment. St. John's Wood Rd. 071/289.1611

# Petite Retreats: London's Best Small Hotels

If you like the intimacy of a bed-and-breakfast but prefer the amenities of larger lodgings, consider booking a room at one of London's small hotels. Following is a guide to noteworthy establishments that will charm you with their attention to detail.

### In Kensington/Knightsbridge:

**The Beaufort** $$$ Pastel colors, fresh flowers, original watercolors, and comfy armchairs welcome Beaufort guests. Other amenities range from access to a health club to drinks from a 24-hour bar, all included in the tariff. Best of all, you'll find no hidden charges on your bill, and tipping isn't necessary! ◆ 33 Beaufort Gardens. 071/584.5252; fax 071/589.2834

**The Knightsbridge Green Hotel** $$ Friendly, efficient, and reasonably priced, this hotel features whitewashed walls and rich fabrics. Most of the bedrooms have sitting rooms. Tea and coffee are available all day in the public room. ◆ 159 Knightsbridge. 071/584.6274; fax 071/225.1635

**Pelham Hotel** $$ The Pelham overlooks a busy street but has lovely decor and a pretty, spacious restaurant to recommend it. This attractive small hotel has been described as the epitome of Englishness. ◆ 15 Cromwell Place. 071/589.8288; fax 071/584.8444

### In King's Road/Chelsea:

**Eleven Cadogan Gardens** $$ You'll love this gabled, redbrick Victorian house with paneled staircases and sedate portraits gazing from the walls. Plush sofas and a bridge table greet the weary traveler in the lounge, but there's no restaurant or bar. Cozy bedrooms offer welcome respite to the footweary. ◆ 11 Cadogan Gardens. No credit cards. 071/730.3426; fax 071/730.5217

**The Fenja** $$ Rooms are named after notable English artists and writers—ask for the J.M.W. Turner Room if you'd like to sleep in an enormous four-poster bed. Service is very good: staff members carry your suitcases, polish your shoes, and bring drinks in decanters to your room. Although there's no restaurant in the hotel, you can have breakfast brought to your room until 2PM, or order both breakfast and light meals in the small drawing room. 69 Cadogan Gardens. 071/589.7333; fax 71/581.4958

**Sydney House Hotel** $$ Baccarat chandeliers sparkle in the lobby of this ultrachic hotel where, upstairs, themed rooms are furnished with Bugatti furniture. Red walls and a canopied bed set the tone in the Paris Room while the India Room abounds in gold stars and Oriental swirls. ◆ 9 Sydney Street. 071/376.7711; fax 071/376.4233

### In Marylebone/Camden Town:

**Dorset Square Hotel** $$$ This hotel, under the same management as the **Pelham,** splices two Georgian town houses together. The country house decor, with antique furniture and marble and mahogany bathrooms, is different in each room. Some rooms are small, and the double beds remarkably slim. Unfortunately, traffic noise intrudes from one side. ◆ 39-40 Dorset Square. 071/723.7874; fax 071/724.3328

### In Mayfair/Piccadilly:

**47 Park Street** $$$$ A small lounge in the lobby is the only public room in this old Edwardian town house with high ceilings and a splendid staircase. Spacious rooms are designed by **Monique Roux,** wife of **Albert,** one of the co-owners of the famous **Le Gavroche** restaurant on Upper Brook Street. If you're traveling on a budget, you'll approve of the suites because they have kitchens, but these lodgings really appeal to gourmets: the Roux brothers' restaurant provides room service. ◆ 47 Park Street. 071/491.7282; fax 071/491.7281

### In St. James's:

**22 Jermyn Street** $$ Like tiny apartments, the rooms here are filled with comfortable chairs and antiques. You'll have breakfast and light snacks (but no restaurant), and a fridge stocked by **Fortnum & Mason** across the street. ◆ 22 Jermyn Street. 071/734.2353; fax 071/430.0750

### In Soho/Covent Garden:

**Hazlitt's** $$ Three carefully preserved 18th-century terraced houses make up Hazlitt's. Oak and pine furniture, claw-foot baths, and sloping floors add authenticity to the ambience. Room service is available at breakfast only. Alas, some of the light and airy rooms seem cramped, as do the beds. ◆ 6 Frith Street, Soho Square. 071/439.1524; fax 071/434.1771

# Bloomsbury/ Holborn

**Bloomsbury** is the Oxford of London, a sheltered kingdom of scholars that is ruled both by the past, in the form of the **British Museum**, and by the future, which is constantly being shaped in the halls of the **University of London**. In between these institutions lie spacious squares filled with shade trees and rosebushes. Illustrious ghosts haunt the streets where **Clive Bell** struggled with literary criticism, where **W.B. Yeats** struggled with poetic philosophy, and where **Virginia** and **Leonard Woolf** struggled with themselves and each other—and with **T.S. Eliot**, whenever he came to tea. Though a bookish air pervades the neighborhood, Bloomsbury is not devoid of everyday pleasures. Modern minds swap theories over a pint in the **Plough**, head tutors munch chips in the **Museum Cafe**, and unripe novelists buy pullovers in **Westaway & Westaway**.

In striking contrast, **Holborn** is decidedly Dickensian, almost as if the author himself still resided at **Dickens House**. His footsteps are easy to follow, through the ancient legal byways of two **Inns of Court**, into the **Bleeding Heart Yard** of *Little Dorritt*, and finally to the **Old Bailey**, and the largest meat market in the world, **Smithfield**, with their grim associations of crime and slaughter. Since this area covers so many miles of terrain, you should pick and choose your stops. Like **Holborn Viaduct**, the world's first "flyover" (that's British for overpass), you can always skip what does not appeal.

**1 University of London** In 1826, a group of enlightened sponsors decided to establish a center of higher learning that would not be tied to the Anglican Church and would offer a more liberal and wide-ranging curriculum than other universities. Opponents said it wouldn't last. Yet more than a hundred years later, the "godless college in Gower Street" has built a formidable reputation and a full-time student body that exceeds 40,000, scattered among 50 colleges as far afield as Egham, Surrey, and Queen Mary's in the East End. Although the university received its charter relatively late, it has made up for lost time, scoring a string of firsts over the years. Medical research in its facilities led in 1846 to the first use of ether and in 1867 to the first antiseptic surgery (by **Joseph Lister**, a Quaker who had been refused admission to Oxford). In 1878, it became the first British university to admit women. Today, **Princess Anne** is its chancellor.

Many university buildings are in the area around Gower and Malet streets. The best-known is **Charles Holden's Senate House,** which was begun in 1932. The huge Portland stone structure contains the university's massive library, with its specialist collections of Elizabethan books and music. ♦ Tube: Russell Sq, Goodge St

**2 Russell Square** The west side of London's second-largest square is lined with huge plane trees and houses once favored by lawyers and merchants. Readers of **Thackeray's** *Vanity Fair* may recognize this as the turf of the Sedleys and Osbornes. The square was laid out between 1800 and 1814 by **Humphrey Repton** and named after the Russells, Dukes of Bedford, who owned the land. The elaborate statue of **Francis Russell**, Fifth Duke of Bedford, created in 1809 by **Sir Richard Westmacott,** shows the Duke leaning on a plow. Some of the original houses by **James Burton** remain, including **Nos. 25 to 29,** which now contain the **Institutes of Commonwealth Studies** and **Germanic Studies,** branches of the University of London. The great law reformer **Sir Samuel Romilly** lived and died by his own hand at **No. 2. Sir Thomas Lawrence**

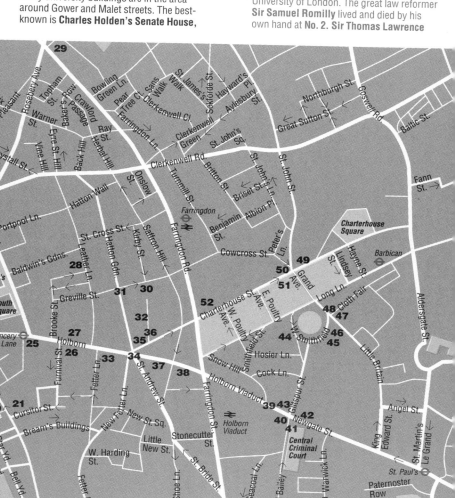

had his studio at **No. 67** (it was later demolished) from 1805 until his death in 1830. Here he painted his portrait series of princes, generals, and statesmen who helped bring about **Napoleon's** downfall; these works now hang in the Waterloo Chamber at **Windsor Castle.** Stop at the Italian cafe on the square's northern tip for a frothy cappuccino. ♦ Tube: Russell Sq

**3 Hotel Russell** $$ This rambling Bloomsbury institution looks and feels like it should be attached to the Great Western Railway. Built by **Charles Fitzroy Doll** in 1898, it tempers the Victorian appetite for size with modesty. The stairway is grand, but the 320 rooms are not. The best rooms are on the seventh floor, and all have been prettily refurbished with jolly fabrics. Book fairs are held here on Sunday and Monday mornings once a month; phone for dates. ♦ Russell Sq. Tube: Russell Sq. 071/837.6470; fax 071/837.2857

**4 Thomas Coram Foundation for Children** Known as the **Foundling Hospital,** this is one of the most unusual small museums in London. It owes its existence to sea captain **Thomas Coram,** who lived from 1668 to 1751 and made his name as a colonizer of America. Returning to London, Coram was shocked at the number of abandoned infants. He enlisted 21 noblewomen, 11 earls, and 6 dukes to petition **George II** for help in establishing a home for the foundlings.

**William Hogarth** was one of the original governors; he and his wife served as foster parents to the children. A major Hogarth work, the *March to Finchley* (1746), and the superb portrait of a robust *Captain Coram* (1740) are two of the treasures in the museum's picture collection, which includes works by **Gainsborough** and **Reynolds.** The composer **Handel** was also an early benefactor. He not only donated a pipe organ and gave performances to raise money for the children but also bequeathed his own copy of the *Messiah* manuscript, which is now on display.

An unforgettable collection is found in the lovingly preserved 18th-century **Courtroom.** Mothers left these mementos in the baskets of their abandoned infants: coral beads, locks of hair, a section of a map of England, earrings, watch seals, coins, a crystal locket, a single lace glove, the letter "A" cut in metal, and a message scratched on mother of pearl: "James, son of James Concannon, late or now of Jamaica, 1757." These tokens were the foundlings' only clues to their personal histories. ♦ Admission. M-F 9:30AM-4PM; call ahead because days are subject to change. 40 Brunswick Sq. Tube: Russell Sq, King's Cross. 071/278.2424

Restaurants/Clubs: Red    Hotels: Blue
Shops/ 🌳 Outdoors: Green    **Sights/Culture: Black**

# BRITISH MUSEUM

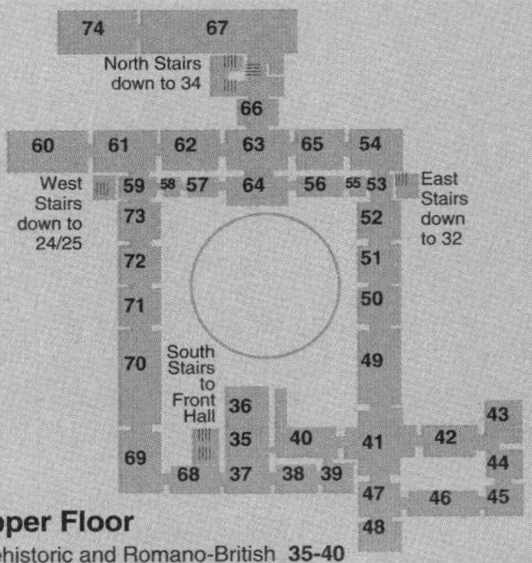

**Upper Floor**
Prehistoric and Romano-British **35-40**
Medieval and Lateral **41-48**
Special Exhibitions **49**
Coins and Metals **50**
Western Asiatic **51-59**
Egyptian **60-66**
Prints and Drawings **67**
Greek and Roman **68-73**
Oriental

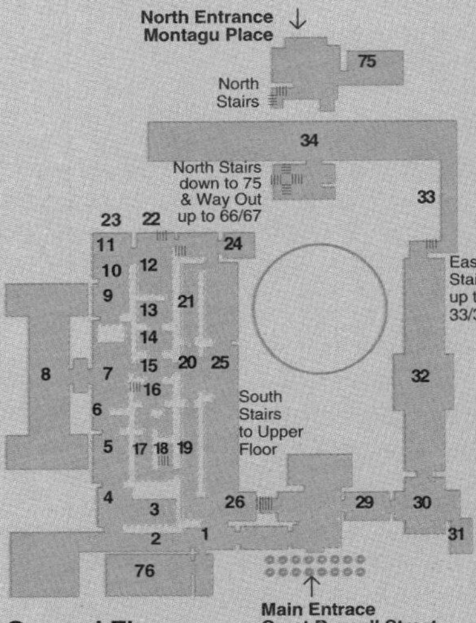

**Ground Floor**
Greek and Roman **1-15**
Western Asiatic **16-26**
Egyptian **25**
British Library **29-33**
Oriental **34, 75**
Special Exhibitions **76**

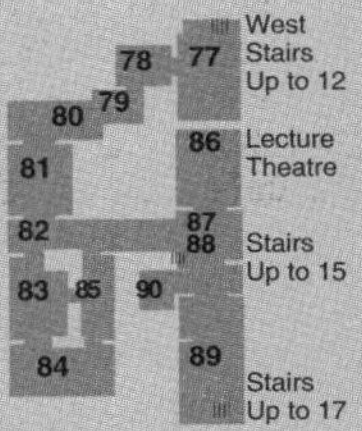

**Basement**
Greek and Roman **77-87**
Western Asiatic **88-90**

## Objects of Special Interest

| | |
|---|---|
| Assyrian Lionhunt Reliefs **17** | Lindisfarne Gospels **30** |
| Clocks and Watches **44** | Magna Carta **30** |
| Egyptian Mummies **60, 61** | Mildenhall Treasure **40** |
| Egyptian Sculptures **25** | Parthenon Sculptures **8** |
| Hull Grundy Gift of Jewelry **47** | Portland Vase **14** |
| Indian Sculptures **34** | Rosetta Stone **25** |
| Lewis Chessman | Sutton Hoo Treasure **71** |

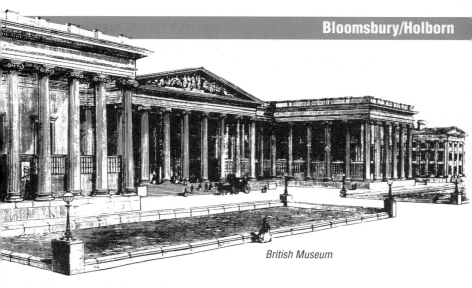

*British Museum*

**5 St. Margaret's Hotel** $$ Friendly, small, and quiet for central London, the hotel is part of a Bloomsbury estate owned by the **Duke of Bedford** and has been managed by the same Italian family for 40 years. Although some of the rooms are small, all are sparkling clean and have TVs and phones. Prices include a full English breakfast, but if you want a private bath or shower, book in advance and be prepared to pay the premium. If you're flying in to Heathrow, you can take the Piccadilly line straight to the nearby Underground stop (although those with heavy bags may need a taxi to cope with the six-minute walk between station and hotel). ♦ Bedford Pl. Tube: Russell Sq, Holborn. 071/636.4277, 071/580.2352.

**6 British Museum** "Ennui," wrote the lyricist of an old song, "was the day when the British Museum lost its charm." For those still excited by history, the British Museum is as charming as ever; the only problem is managing to see the exhibitions through the crowds.

When physician and naturalist **Sir Hans Sloane** died in 1753, his will allowed the nation to buy his vast collection of art, antiquities, and natural history for £20,000—less than half of what it cost to assemble. With the additions of **Robert Cotton's** library and antiquities and the manuscripts of **Robert Harley,** Earl of Oxford, the collection grew, and when **George II's** 12,000-volume library was dedicated in 1823, it filled **Montagu House,** where it had been on display since 1759. A decision was then made to build new quarters for the burgeoning national collection. **Sir Robert Smirke** designed a large quadrangle with an open courtyard behind Montagu House, then surrounded the house with a fine neoclassical facade, adding an Ionic colonnade in 1847 and a pediment decorated with **Sir Richard Westmacott's** figures representing the progress of civilization. The architect's brother, **Sydney Smirke,** began the courtyard's conversion

into the beautiful, blue-domed **Reading Room** in 1852 according to a plan by **Sir Anthony Panizzi,** the principal librarian. Space problems were alleviated in the 1880s, when the natural history exhibitions moved to the **Natural History Museum,** and in 1970, when the ethnographic exhibitions were moved to the **Museum of Mankind.**

Start with the **Egyptian Sculpture Gallery** (Room 25) on the ground floor. The massive granite figures can be seen over the heads of any number of people. To the left of the door is the **Rosetta Stone,** not so much fascinating in itself (it is an irregularly shaped, tightly inscribed piece of black basalt) as in the way it changed man's understanding of history. Written in Greek and in two forms of ancient Egyptian script, the stone's Greek translation provided the key to hieroglyphics undeciphered for 1,400 years. Enormous sculptures, intricate pieces of jewelry, and carvings give an overwhelming introduction to the ancient Egyptians. There is a haughty bronze cat from 600 BC, sacred to **Bastet** (an Egyptian deity); a large reclining granite ram with a tiny figure of **King Taharqa** tucked beneath his chin; and from the **Temple of Mut in Thebes,** carved in about 1400 BC, are four huge granite representations of the goddess **Sakhmet,** with the body of a woman and the head of a lion. The rest of the Egyptian exhibitions are on the upper floors (Rooms 60-64 and 66).

The Etruscans, the Italian civilization that reached its peak of power in the seventh and sixth centuries BC, were fine metalworkers and potters. Here their achievements in jewelry and ornamentation are revealed, some so intricate that even today jewelers cannot copy them (Rooms 70 and 71).

Before climbing the stairs, visit Rooms 1 through 15, which hold the museum's collection of **Greek and Roman Antiquities,** including the hotly contested **Elgin Marbles** (Room 8), sculptures from the Parthenon and the Erechtheum that **Lord Elgin** brought to England in 1816 and which the government of Greece is seeking to have returned. Mostly fragments, they are described in the diary of an attendant, **John Conrath,** who helped move them into the museum and was assigned to the gallery where they were displayed. This diary can be seen in the **British Library Galleries.** "Northside," he wrote, describing the frieze that had been inside the great colonnade, "a young man almost naked, putting a Crown on his head, another ready to mount, attended by his grooms, around the west corner a single person, a magistrate or director, two Chariots . . . South frieze, Seven more Bulls, a man Crowning himself." Although the eroded and broken state of the marbles disappointed some early visitors, they also attracted such illustrious fans as the **Grand Duke Nicholas,** later Czar Nicholas I of Russia, who spent two days looking at the marbles in 1817.

At the head of the stairs in Room 35, the well-preserved body of Celtic **Lindow Man** (discovered in a Welsh bog) lies in an airtight chamber; even the brutality of his death as a religious sacrifice cannot detract from the gleaming artistry of the golden torques in the rest of the Celtic collection. The upper floors also hold **Medieval and Later Antiquities from Europe** (Rooms 41-48), with lethal bronze weapons and the extraordinary **Lycurgus Cup,** a Roman goblet carved from a single block of green glass that shows the tortured face of the Thracian **King Lycurgus,** imprisoned by the tendrils of a vine. The rooms also contain remarkable displays of jewelry. The **Gallery of Clocks and Watches** (Room 44) exhibits a range of timepieces from the Middle Ages to the beginning of this century.

On the ground floor, to the right of the entrance, are the British Library Galleries (Rooms 29-32a), where illuminated historical, musical, and literary manuscripts and maps are displayed in glass cases. Here is where the large, firm signature of **Elizabeth I** appears on the order sentencing **Robert Devereux,** Earl of Essex, to death by beheading. On permanent display are two of the four surviving copies of the **Magna Carta** issued in 1215 by **King John;** the **Lindisfarne Gospels,** written and illuminated in 698; a **Gutenberg Bible;** the 15th-century **Canterbury Tales;** and **Shakespeare's First Folio.**

Visitors may view the **British Library Reading Room,** with its domed ceiling and 30,000 reference books, every hour on the hour from 11AM Monday through Friday. The library has been used by readers as diverse as **Marx, Lenin, Gandhi, George Bernard Shaw,** and **Thomas Carlyle**, though Carlyle was so irked at the amount of time it took to receive his books that he stalked off and helped found the **London Library.** For a fee, there are daily 90-minute guided tours of the highlights of the British Museum collections.

The British Museum occupies the site of the first **Duke of Montagu's** house. Needing to replenish a fortune ravaged by the extravagances of building this mansion, he set out to win the hand of the extremely rich and quite mad second **Duchess of Albemarle.** The Duchess, who insisted that she would marry only a crowned head of state, happily offered her hand when the Duke convinced her that he was the Emperor of China. The ghost of the erstwhile Empress must roam contentedly through the museum's collection of Oriental antiquities, located in Rooms 33 and 34 on the ground floor and Rooms 90 through 94 on the upper floor. Ask at the information desk on the ground floor for details of free gallery talks and lectures. ♦ Free. M-Sa 10AM-5PM; Su 2:30-6PM. Great Russell St. Tube: Russell Sq, Holborn, Tottenham Court Rd. General information: 071/636.1555. Recorded information: 071/580.1788

Within the British Museum:

**British Museum Shop** There are two excellent shops—one for books and cards, left of the main entrance; the other for replicas, jewelry, and coins, left of the Reading Room entrance. You won't need a degree in archaeology or a rich benefactor to take home fabulous pieces of (well-replicated) antiquity. ♦ M-Sa 10AM-4:45PM. 071/636.1555

**Museum Cafe** $ Sometimes the temperature in the museum seems hotter than the Egyptian deserts, and following in the footsteps of **Howard Carter** becomes hungry and thirsty work. Revitalize yourself with delicious snacks and soft drinks. ♦ International ♦ Lunch and afternoon tea; afternoon tea only on Sunday. 071/636.1555

**7 Westaway & Westaway** London's largest, most reliable, and most affordable dealer in woolens carries scarves, blankets, hats, suits, and socks—everything for keeping warm. The variety of Scottish cashmeres, woven in Scotland from the wool of cashmere goats in China, gives you a better selection here than you're likely to find in Scotland. ♦ M-Sa 9AM-5:30PM; Su 11AM-6PM. 62-65 Great Russell St. 071/405.4479. Tube: Holborn, Russell Sq. Also at: 92-93 Great Russell St. 071/636.1718

**7 L. Cornelissen** This is an old-fashioned shop with old-fashioned and very special art supplies—cobalt blues, British and French gold leaf, L. Cornelissen's own brand of violin varnish (Dragon's Blood), pure squirrel-mop brushes, and quill brushes. At the back of the store you will find "His Nibs," **Philip Poole,** who had to move from his beautiful shop in Drury Lane because of rent increases. The white-haired Poole still runs the spectacular scribbler's emporium himself, selling every make and age of fountain pen, many of them collected when Biros (ballpoints) became fashionable, as he was convinced they were a passing fad. Every kind of ink is available, along with beautiful pencils, paper, and objects related to aesthetic writing. ♦ M-F 9:30AM-5:30PM; Sa 9:30AM-5PM. 105 Great Russell St. Tube: Holborn, Russell Sq. 071/636.1045

**8 Print Room** Specializing in prints of London, prints by **Hogarth,** and caricature prints of the 18th and 19th centuries, the shop also has a large, tempting, and reasonably priced collection of botanical prints. Its staff is friendly and helpful. ♦ M-F 10AM-6PM; Sa 10AM-4PM. 37 Museum St. Tube: Holborn, Tottenham Court Rd. 071/430.0159

**9 Plough** ★$ The feel of Bloomsbury lingers in this literary pub, perhaps because it has remained popular with publishers and writers for so long. They appreciate its coziness in winter and the outdoor tables in summer, as well as the bar lunch and wide selection of traditional ales. ♦ Pub ♦ M-Sa 11AM-11PM; Su noon-3PM, 7-10:30PM. 27 Museum St. Tube: Holborn, Tottenham Court Rd. 071/636.7964

**10 The Central Club Hotel (YWCA)** $ An affordable option for anyone, the newly refurbished YWCA facilities are clean, well-located, and much like a hotel. Most rooms have TV, radio, telephone, and beverage facilities. Rates differ according to whether you opt for room only, room and breakfast, or half board. All guests can use the swimming pool, lounge, writing room, and launderette; also on the premises are a hairdressing salon, a gym, and a solarium. Those who don't like heavy pub grub can get fresh salads, health food, and vegetarian fare at the coffee shop. Family rooms and student discounts are available. ♦ 16-22 Great Russell St. Tube: Tottenham Court Rd. 071/636.7512.

**11 Museum Street** Cross the broad intersection of New Oxford Street, High Holborn, and Bloomsbury Way to this narrow, friendly street, lined with some of the best antique-print dealers, bookshops, and jewelers in London. ♦ Tube: Holborn, Tottenham Court Rd

---

"Hell is a city much like London—
A populous smoky city.
There are all sorts of people undone,
And there is little or no fun done,
Small Justice shown, and still less pity."

**Percy Bysshe Shelley,** 1819

**11 Museum Street Cafe** ★★$ There's no smoking, no license to serve alcohol, and no frills here—the tables are wooden, the napkins paper—but the breads are freshly baked, the meats chargrilled to perfection, and the homemade ice cream and cheeses come from **Neal's Yard** in Covent Garden. No wonder it's packed to the rafters. The day's list of simple, freshly cooked dishes is on the blackboard. ♦ British ♦ Lunch and dinner. Closed Saturday and Sunday. No credit cards. 47 Museum St. Reservations recommended. Tube: Holborn, Tottenham Court Rd. 071/405.3211

**11 S.J. Shrubsole** A distinguished dealer in old English silver, Shrubsole offers outstanding pieces of old Sheffield plate at honest prices. ♦ M-F 9AM-5PM. 43 Museum St. Tube: Holborn, Tottenham Court Rd. 071/405.2712

**12 Stefania's Delicatessen** ★$ Order sandwiches, lasagna, and pizza to go. ♦ Italian deli ♦ Breakfast, lunch, and snacks. Closed Saturday and Sunday. 184 Drury Ln. Tube: Holborn, Covent Garden. 071/831.0138

**13 New London Theatre** The West End's newest theater, built in 1973 by **Michael Percival,** sits on an old foundation: a place of entertainment that's been here since Elizabethan times. The New London is ultramodern, with movable seats, lights, walls, and stage—all surrounded by lots of glass. The seating was expanded from 952 to 1,102 to accommodate the crowds for **Andrew Lloyd Webber's** feline phenomenon, *Cats.* ♦ Drury Ln. Tube: Holborn, Covent Garden. Box office: 071/404.4079

**14 Anello & Davide** The best ballet and tap shoes are stocked here, along with old-fashioned leather lace-up boots with pointy toes. While most of the women's shoes don't look as though they're made to last more than the average run of a West End show, the more traditional leather-lined shoes will last years and years. The Victorian-style button boots are a great buy. ♦ M-F 9AM-5:30PM; Sa 9AM-5PM. 35 Drury Ln. Tube: Holborn, Covent Garden. 071/836.1983. Also at: 92 Charing Cross Rd. Tube: Tottenham Court Rd, Leicester Sq. 071/836.5019

**15 Freemason's Hall** The imposing headquarters of the **United Grand Lodge of England,** built by **H.V. Ashley** and **F. Winton Smith** in 1933, boasts a central tower rising 200 feet above the street. The Art Deco building was conceived as a memorial to Masons who died in World War I. Today, it houses an exhibition on the history of English Freemasonry, which may help to dispel the suspicion surrounding the "funny handshake brigade." This is the largest collection of Masonic regalia, medals, art, and glassware in the world, though few of the sect's secrets are divulged. Look for angels and pyramids, both Masonic symbols. ♦ Free. M-F 10AM-5PM; Sa

10AM-noon. 60 Great Queen St. Tube: Holborn, Covent Garden. 071/831.9811

**15 Bhatti** ★★$$ This award-winning restaurant occupies a 17th-century "listed building" that retains original paneling, stenciling, and fireplaces (listed buildings have been deemed important to England's heritage; they cannot be knocked down nor can the interiors be altered). Try the lamb *pasanda* or the chicken *jalfrezi*. Also a fine value is the vegetarian *bhojan*—that's simply the Gujarati word for "meal." The owners have a second restaurant, **Royals** (★$$; 7-8 Bow St, 071/379.1099), near Covent Garden, which offers the same fare. ♦ Indian ♦ Lunch and dinner. 37 Great Queen St. Reservations recommended. Tube: Holborn, Covent Garden. 071/831.0817

**16 Great Queen Street** This once-fashionable thoroughfare, named in honor of **Henrietta Maria,** the devoted wife of **Charles I,** is now lined with restaurants, including the private advertising and media club, **Zanzibar,** at **No. 30.** ♦ Between Drury Ln and Kingsway. Tube: Holborn, Covent Garden

**17 Sir John Soane's Museum** Go out of your way to visit this museum. **Sir John Soane,** the eminent architect of the **Bank of England,** chose the largest square in central London for the site of his house, which was actually three domestic residences. He required an appropriate setting for his enormous collection of international antiquities and art, and the result is a fascinating dwelling that is unique in London. Moving through rooms of unusual proportions, built on varying levels with cantilevered staircases and hundreds of mirrors, you will feel that time has been suspended and that you are experiencing the mind of a brilliant and eccentric master builder. Incorporated within the house are a sculpture gallery, a crypt, and a mock ruin of a medieval cloister.

In the **Picture Room,** you can see **William Hogarth's** *The Rake's Progress* (1732-33) and *The Election* series; the latter is ingeniously mounted by Soane so that the first paintings pull away from the wall to reveal hidden panels with subsequent paintings. A well-known highlight of the collection, found in the **Sepulchral Chamber,** is the magnificent **Sarcophagus of Seti I.** Discovered at Thebes in 1815, it dates from 1300 BC—Soane snapped it up when it was passed over by the British Museum. The collection contains unpredictable juxtapositions of fragments salvaged from various buildings (such as the original House of Lords) destroyed during Soane's lifetime. Glancing through a window into the court known as the **Monk's Yard,** it is possible to glimpse a huge melancholy tomb inscribed, "Alas, Poor Fanny"—a monument to **Mrs.**

**Soane's** favorite dog. At last the colored glass in the skylights, bombed out during World War II, has been replaced to re-create the ingenious lighting effects so beloved by Soane. ♦ Donations welcome. Tu-Sa 10AM-5PM; free guided tour Sa 2:30PM. 13 Lincoln's Inn Fields. Tube: Holborn, Chancery Ln. General information: 071/405.2107. Recorded information: 071/430.0175

**18 Lincoln's Inn Fields** When property developer **William Newton** won the right to build here in 1620, angry lawyers appealed to the House of Commons and won: the space was left open. Adjacent to Lincoln's Inn, the largest rectangular square in central London is surrounded by tennis courts, flower beds, and a bandstand, and is graced by many distinguished houses, including stately **Lindsey House** (Nos. 59-60), which may have been based on plans by **Inigo Jones,** and its imitative younger neighbor (Nos. 57-58) by **Henry Joynes.** In contrast to these grand mansions with Ionic pilasters, rows of pitifully inadequate tents are now pitched here by London's homeless. ♦ South of High Holborn and Kingsway junction. Tube: Holborn, Chancery Ln

**19 Her Majesty's Stationery Office** "HMSO," as it is known to Londoners, carries a remarkable collection of maps, charts, guides, cards, diaries, and travel books on every inch of the British Isles. The shop also stocks the latest copies of laws passed in **Parliament,** replicas from the **British Museum,** and attractive copies of English country maps. ♦ M-F 8:15AM-5:15PM; Sa 9AM-1PM. 49 High Holborn. Tube: Chancery Ln. General inquiries: 071/873.0011. Ordering service (24 hour): 071/873.9090

**20 Lincoln's Inn** Of the four great **Inns of Court** (Lincoln's Inn, Inner Temple, Middle Temple, and Gray's Inn), this is the most unspoiled and the only one to have escaped World War II without major damage. The inns were formed in the Middle Ages to provide lodgings for lawyers and students of law. They now belong to barristers' societies, which control the admission of students to the bar, finance, law reform, legal education, and the maintenance of professional standards for lawyers. Lincoln's Inn was established on the site of the **Knights Templar's** tilting ground after the dissolution of the order in the early 14th century. Reflecting the times when most highly educated people became lawyers, the rolls of the inn contain famous names: **Sir Thomas More, John Donne, Oliver Cromwell, William Penn, Horace Walpole, William Pitt, Benjamin Disraeli, William Gladstone.** The brick-and-stone buildings, arranged in a collegiate plan, date from the 15th century.

Enter through the gatehouse, facing Chancery Lane, which dates from 1518 and bears the arms of Lincoln's Inn: a lion rampant. The Tudor redbrick **Old Buildings** date from the early 16th century, and the **Old Hall**, built around 1491 and approached through the archway and small courtyard, contains a superb wooden roof, linen-fold paneling, and **William Hogarth's** painting, *St. Paul Before Felix*, completed in 1748. The hall was the **Court of Chancery** from 1737 to 1883; the fictional case of Jarndyce vs. Jarndyce in *Bleak House* took place here. Built in the 1840s, **Philip Hardwick's** redbrick **New Hall** contains the vast mural by **G.F. Watts**, *Justice, a Hemicycle of Lawgivers;* Hardwick's library is the oldest and most complete law library in England, with nearly 100,000 volumes. **Henry Serle's** 1697 **New Square,** which faces toward **Lincoln's Inn Fields,** is on a tranquil and pretty courtyard of solicitors' offices; this is where 14-year-old **Charles Dickens** was once employed as a solicitor's clerk. The rebuilding of the Gothic chapel was finished in 1623. **John Donne** laid the foundation stone and gave the first sermon. ◆ Chapel and gardens: M-F 12:30-2:30PM. Tube: Holborn, Chancery Ln. 071/405.1393

**21 London Silver Vaults** English silver deserves its rich reputation: the silver content, marked with the hallmark of the British lion, is the highest in the world, and the tradition of design has been consistently strong. Unless you're familiar with hallmarks, makers, and dealers, however, buying silver is bound to be an unnerving experience, and coming to this underground prison with 159 silver vaults and 49 shops containing the greatest concentration of silver dealers in London certainly won't set you at ease. You have to make your way through a lot of junk in the beginning and encounter taciturn dealers once you come across desirable silver. If you persevere, though, and have a clear idea of what you want, you will eventually find prices lower here than elsewhere. Study a simple hallmark card, the guide to hallmarks (on sale here), or the hallmark plaques on the wall before making a major purchase. ◆ M-F 9AM-5:30PM (last entry 5:20PM); Sa 9AM-1PM (last entry 12:50PM). Chancery House, 53-64 Chancery Ln. Tube: Chancery Ln. 071/242.3844

**22 Cittie of Yorke** ★★$ One of the largest pubs in London with the largest bar, this 17th-century establishment must have served most of Holborn in days gone by. A capacious three-sided fireplace and little cubicles keep the place warm and intimate. The bar lunches are excellent and the real ales much appreciated by the legal clientele. ◆ Pub ◆ M-F 11:30AM-11PM; Sa 11:30AM-3PM, 5:30-11PM. 22-23 High Holborn. Tube: Chancery Ln. 071/242.7670

Dickens House
Doughty Street

**23 Dickens House** The sheer quantity of Dickensiana crammed into this Victorian row house (shown above) is all the more amazing because the structure is one of four Dickens houses open to the public. (The others are outside London, although he did live and work at other city addresses.) The author lived here from 1837 to 1839, writing the last part of *The Pickwick Papers*, all of *Oliver Twist* and *Nicholas Nickleby,* and the beginning of *Barnaby Rudge.* He also penned some 550 letters here. In the sitting room, Dickens' 17-year-old sister-in-law, **Mary,** died in his arms, an emotional blow from which he never recovered. Visitors can see the writer's desk, the china monkey he kept on it for good luck, and the family Bible, as well as portraits, illustrations, autographed letters, and other personal relics. The first-floor drawing room has been reconstructed to appear as it did in Dickens' time, as have the study and basement. ◆ Admission. M-Sa 10AM-5PM (last admission 4:30PM). 48 Doughty St. Tube: Russell Sq. 071/405.2127

**24 Gray's Inn** In the 14th century, the manor house of **Sir Reginald le Grey,** Chief Justice of Chester, was located here. By 1370, the grounds had developed into a hostel for law students, which was expanded during the Tudor period. Unfortunately, Gray's Inn was badly damaged during World War II; despite much restoration, it lacks the authentic feeling of its neighbor to the south. But be sure to walk through the passage in the southwest corner of the 17th-century **Gray's Inn Gardens.** Laid out by **Bacon** in 1606 and known affectionately as "The Walks," these sloping, tree-filled lawns delighted **Samuel Pepys,** who noted "fine ladies" promenading there, while **Charles Lamb** called them the "best gardens of the Inns of Court." ◆ The Walks: daily noon-2:30PM May-Sept. Tube: Chancery Ln

# Color It Blue: A Mini-Guide to London's Historic Houses

More than 600 blue ceramic plaques on buildings and sites throughout London identify where the distinguished once lived. **English Heritage,** an arts/preservation society (funded by the government) that preserves architectural and archaeological sites, decides who "deserves" a plaque, following certain guidelines: the person must have died at least 20 years ago and made some important contribution to human welfare or happiness. The *Blue Plaque Guide*—an historical and cultural who's who—lists all the plaques that have been placed since the first was affixed in 1867 on the house where **Lord Byron** was born on Holles Street in Westminster; it's available at large bookshops. Following is a guide to some choice venues once inhabited by the illustrious:

**James Boswell** lived and died on the site of 122 Great Portland Street.

**Elizabeth Barrett Browning** lived on the site of 50 Wimpole Street.

**Charlie Chaplin** lived at 287 Kennington Road.

**Sir Winston Churchill** resided at 28 Hyde Park Gate.

**Samuel Taylor Coleridge** lived at 7 Addison Bridge Place, and at 71 Berners Street.

**Charles Darwin** lived on the site of 110 Gower Street.

**Charles Dickens** lived at 48 Doughty Street.

**Benjamin Disraeli,** born at 22 Theobalds Road, died at 19 Curzon Street.

**Sir Edward Elgar** lived at 51 Avonmore Road.

**George Eliot (Mary Ann Evans)** lived at Holly Lodge, 31 Wimbledon Park Road, and died at 4 Cheyne Walk.

**T.S. Eliot's** house, where he died, is at 3 Kensington Court Gardens.

**Benjamin Franklin** lived at 36 Craven Street.

**Sigmund Freud** lived at 20 Maresfield Gardens.

**William Ewart Gladstone** lived at 11 Carlton House Terrace, at 10 Street, James's Square, and at 73 Harley Street.

**Joseph Grimaldi** lived at 56 Exmouth Market.

**David Ben Gurion's** former residence is at 75 Warrington Crescent.

**George Frederick Handel** lived and died at 25 Brook Street.

**Thomas Hardy** lived at 172 Trinity Road, and at Adelphi Terrace.

**William Hazlitt** lived on the site of 6 Bouverie Street, and died at 6 Frith Street.

**Henry James** lived and penned his novels at 34 De Vere Gardens.

**Jerome K. Jerome** lived at 91-104 Chelsea Gardens, Peabody Buildings.

**Amy Johnson** lived at Vernon Court, Hendon Way.

**Dr. Samuel Johnson** lived at 17 Gough Square, Fleet Street, and at Johnson's Court, Fleet Street.

**John Keats** was born on the site of The Swan and Hoop public house at 85 Moorgate, and lived at Wentworth Place, Keats Grove.

**Rudyard Kipling's** home was at 43 Villiers Street.

**D.H. Lawrence** lived at 1 Byron Villas, Vale of Health, Hampstead Heath in 1915.

**T.E. Lawrence (Lawrence of Arabia)** lived at 14 Barton Street.

**Katherine Mansfield** lived at 17 East Heath Road.

**Karl Marx** lived at 28 Dean Street.

**W. Somerset Maugham** lived at 6 Chesterfield Street.

**Wolfgang Amadeus Mozart** composed his first symphony at 180 Ebury Street.

**Napoleon III** lived at 1c King Street.

**Lord Horatio Nelson's** domiciles included the site of 147 New Bond Street, and 103 New Bond Street.

**Sir Isaac Newton** lived on the site of 87 Jermyn Street.

**Florence Nightingale** lived and died on the site of 10 South Street.

**Sir Robert Peel** lived at 16 Upper Grosvenor Street.

**Samuel Pepys** resided at the site of 12 and 14 Buckingham Street.

**Sylvia Plath** lived and committed suicide at 23 Fitzroy Road (**Yeats'** former home).

**Captain Robert Falcon Scott** lived at 56 Oakley Street.

**George Bernard Shaw** lived at Adelphi Terrace.

**Percy Bysshe Shelley** lived unconventionally at 15 Poland Street.

**William Makepeace Thackeray** lived at 16 Young Street, at 2 Palace Green, and at 36 Onslow Square.

**Anthony Trollope** lived at 39 Montague Square.

**Joseph Mallord William Turner** lived at 23 Queen Anne Street, and at 119 Cheyne Walk.

**Mark Twain (Samuel L. Clemens)** once resided at 23 Tedworth Square.

**H.G. Wells** lived at 13 Hanover Terrace.

**James Abbott McNeill Whistler** lived at 96 Cheyne Walk.

**Oscar Wilde** lived at 34 Tite Street.

**P.G. Wodehouse** lived at 17 Dunraven Street.

**Virginia Woolf** lived with her husband, Leonard, at 29 Fitzroy Square.

**William Butler Yeats** lived at 23 Fitzroy Road.

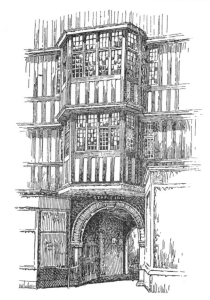

**28 Leather Lane Market** You can reach this lunchtime street market via a passage down the east side of **Alfred Waterhouse's** Gothic **Prudential Assurance Building** (known as "The Pru"). Shop for new clothes at bargain prices—lamb's wool sweaters, shoes, jeans. Some plants, fruit, vegetables, and glassware are also sold. However, the only leather that can be found is at a stall that sometimes offers genuine chamois. ♦ M-Sa noon-3PM. Between Greville St and Holborn. Tube: Chancery Ln, Farringdon

**29 Quality Chop House** ★★$$ For 120 years, the old-fashioned working-class dining room here moldered unnoticed, but in 1989 Le Caprice's former chef, **Charles Fontaine,** bought it, gave it a scrub, and made it fashionable. The experience is now worth the trek up Farringdon or down King's Cross Road. You'll share hard pews with *Guardian* journalists from the neighborhood and nibble on egg and chips or salmon fish cakes with sorrel sauce. Gaslight enhances the ambience. ♦ British ♦ Lunch and dinner. 94 Farringdon Rd. Reservations recommended. Tube: Farringdon. 071/837.5093

**30 Bleeding Heart Yard** ★$ Bleeding Heart Yard is featured in **Charles Dickens'** *Little Dorrit.* Bookshelves with the author's first editions line the walls of this brasserie, wine bar, and restaurant. The spooky, underground restaurant is also lined with bottles of wine— which may explain why the wine list takes up 27 pages. One of the rooms has a grand piano. Try the *gigot d'agneau aux flageolets* (roast leg of lamb with kidney beans) or a simple *omelette avec frites;* then consider the excellent *tarte au citron* for dessert. As one would expect, the restaurant is a little pricier than the brasserie. In summer, there is a terrace with its own menu, but you'll be jostled by lots of City workers. ♦ French ♦ Lunch and dinner. Closed Saturday and Sunday. Off Greville St. Reservations recommended for lunch. Tube: Chancery Ln. 071/242.8238

**31 Hatton Garden** Named for **Elizabeth I's** chancellor, the center of the diamond trade isn't what it used to be. Office blocks have descended and ascended, and most of the shops look so vulgar or so impenetrable that you'd have to be an expert shopper to take them on. The impressive building that houses the **London Diamond Club** is not open to the public, but many of the dealers within buy and sell on a commission basis. The monthly auctions of silver and jewelry have been discontinued, perhaps temporarily (call for updates). ♦ M-F 9:30AM-5:30PM; Sa 9:30AM-1PM. 70 Hatton Garden. Tube: Chancery Ln, Farringdon. 071/242.6452

**25 Staple Inn Buildings** A pure, domestic remnant of Elizabethan London, this pair of houses (one of which is pictured above) dates from 1586 and displays black-and-white timber and plaster, gables, overhangs, and oriels. Badly damaged by a bomb in 1944 and then carefully restored, the inn now comprises offices and old-world shops, including the **Institute of Actuaries,** which is one of the Inns of Chancery affiliated with **Gray's Inn. Dr. Samuel Johnson** moved into **No. 2** in 1759, following his wife's death and his departure from Gough Square. The silver griffin on the stone obelisk in front marks the boundary of the City of London. ♦ Holborn (opposite Gray's Inn Rd). Tube: Chancery Ln

**26 Barnard's Inn** On the south side of Holborn lies the City's oldest surviving secular building, which incorporates the remains of the **Inn of Chancery** where **Pip** and **Herbert Pocket** shared rooms in *Great Expectations.* The 14th-century hall has 16th-century paneling and fine heraldic glass. From 1894 to 1958, this was the hall of **Mercer's School.** ♦ Passage to hall beside Nos. 20-23 Holborn. Tube: Chancery Ln

**27 Prudential Assurance Building** This is an example of what the late **Sir John Betjeman,** poet laureate and longtime resident of the neighborhood, admired, defended, and fought to save: high Victorian architecture. The Gothic redbrick immensity, built by **Alfred Waterhouse** between 1879 and 1906, no doubt infuses passersby with confidence in the large insurance company. It stands on the site of **Furnival's Inn,** where **Charles Dickens** lived and wrote part of *The Pickwick Papers.* Only the facade remains. ♦ 142 Holborn Bars. Tube: Chancery Ln

| **Restaurants/Clubs:** Red | **Hotels:** Blue |
| --- | --- |
| **Shops/ 🌳 Outdoors:** Green | **Sights/Culture:** Black |

**32 St. Etheldreda (Ely Chapel)** When this church was built in 1290, it was, of course, Catholic, and like all churches in England during the Reformation, it became Protestant. In 1874, the Roman Catholics bought it back and named it St. Etheldreda, making it the first pre-Reformation church to return to the fold. This masterpiece of the 13th-century Early Decorated style has a mood of great antiquity and quotidian warmth thanks to **Sir Giles Scott's** sensitive restoration in 1935. You enter to the smell of soup and incense; the former wafts in from the small adjoining cafe run by the church. The windows at the east and west ends are noted for their superb tracery; the west window, which dates from around 1300, is one of the largest in London. Modern stained-glass windows by **Charles** and **May Blakeman** depict English martyrs. Very much a living church, St. Etheldreda's is active in such organizations as **Amnesty International** and in the community. The vaulted crypt, dating from circa 1252, serves as a nicely chaotic meeting room/Sunday school/storage area. ♦ Ely Pl. Tube: Chancery Ln, Farringdon

**33 Daily Mirror Building** This was built in 1960 by **Sir Owen Williams & Partners,** with **Anderson, Forster and Wilcox** as consultants. It's as if an aggressive, vulgar newspaper has been translated into its architectural equivalent. ♦ New Fetter Ln. Tube: Chancery Ln

**34 Holborn Circus** The almost whimsical statue of **Prince Albert** on a horse in the middle of a traffic island is unworthy of the man who worked tirelessly for his adopted country, left a legacy of great museums, and introduced the Christmas tree to Britain. The monument was created by **Charles Bacon** in 1874 and heralds the beginning of **Holborn Viaduct.** ♦ Tube: Chancery Ln, Farringdon

**35 Ye Olde Mitre Tavern** ★★$ Tucked away in the narrow alleys of Ely Place, this 18th-century pub was built in 1546 as lodgings for the servants of the Bishops of Ely. The sign probably came from the bishops' gatehouse, and medieval tiles were discovered during road repairs in 1985. If you can find the tavern, it's a perfect choice for a half-pint of bitter to quench your thirst after a salty breakfast at the **Fox and Anchor.** But it is very small, so come early if you want to avail yourself of sausages and sandwiches. ♦ Pub ♦ M-F 11AM-11PM. 1 Ely Ct. Tube: Chancery Ln, Farringdon. 071/405.4751

**36 Ely Place** A watchman in a small gatehouse still guards this charming cul-de-sac of 18th-century houses. As the land belongs to **Ely Cathedral** in Cambridgeshire, the street remains legally under the jurisdiction of the Bishops of Ely, meaning London police cannot automatically enter—perhaps a more useful edict now that the lovely doorways by the **Adam** brothers lead to lawyers' and accountants' offices rather than to private houses. Sadly, as with many other parts of historic London, the developer's ax threatens to fall here. ♦ Off Charterhouse St. Tube: Chancery Ln, Farringdon

**37 St. Andrew Holborn Sir Christopher Wren** built his largest parish church in 1690, on the remains of a church founded in the 13th century. In 1704, he refaced the medieval tower of the original church, which miraculously survived the five bombs that destroyed its interior during World War II. In the 1960s, the furnishings were replaced with treasures from the **Foundling Hospital Chapel** in Bloomsbury, including the gilded 18th-century organ that **Handel** gave to the hospital and the 18th-century font and altar rails. The church records show the 1770 burial of **Thomas Chatterton,** the poet who committed suicide by poison at the age of 18 after despairing over his poverty and lack of recognition (he later became a symbol of the Romantic movement). Essayist **William Hazlitt** was married here in 1808, with **Charles Lamb** as his best man and **Mary Lamb** as a bridesmaid. **Benjamin Disraeli** was baptized here in 1817 at the age of 12. The tomb of **Captain Coram,** founder of the Foundling Hospital, withstood the bombing of World War II, and a weeping cherub watches over the good man. ♦ Holborn Circus. Tube: Chancery Ln, Farringdon

**38 City Temple** Opened by the famous preacher **Dr. Joseph Parker** in 1874, this Congregational church was gutted during an air raid in 1941. It was lavishly rebuilt in 1950, incorporating the old facade by **Lord Mottistone** and **Paul Paget.** ♦ Not open to visitors. Holborn Viaduct. Tube: Chancery Ln

"Oranges and lemons
Ring the bells of St. Clement's
When will you pay me?
Ring the bells at the Old Bailey
When I am rich
Ring the bells at Fleetditch
When will that be?
Ring the bells at Stepney
When I am old,
Rings the great bell at Paul's."

—from "London Bells," an anonymous
18th-century poem

Claude Du Vall, a highwayman hanged at Tyburn, is buried in St. Paul's Church.

"Here lies Du Vall: Reader, if male thou art
Look to thy purse; if female to thy heart."

**39 Holborn Viaduct** The Holborn Viaduct is the world's first overpass, 1,400 feet long and 80 feet wide, constructed between 1863 and 1869 by **William Haywood** to bridge the valley of the River Fleet and to connect Holborn with Newgate Street. The cost was 4,000 dwellings and £2.5 million. Its elaborate cast-iron work is best seen from Farringdon Street. Four bronze statues representing Agriculture, Commerce, Science, and Fine Art grace the north and south sides of the bridge section, and at the corners are four City heroes: **Henry FitzAilwin,** first lord mayor of London; **Sir Thomas Gresham,** founder of the Royal Exchange; **Sir Hugh Myddelton,** who brought fresh water to London; and finally antihero **Sir William Walworth,** who stabbed rebellion leader **Wat Tyler.** Before the viaduct was built, the steep banks of this part of the river were very difficult to negotiate. Steps lead down to Farringdon Street and **Holborn Viaduct Station,** a small railway depot that serves commuters to the southern counties.
♦ Tube: Farringdon, St. Paul's

**40 Magpie and Stump** ★★$ The secret passage between this illustrious old pub and the jail has been bricked up, and the windows upstairs are no longer hired out for viewing public hangings, but friends and family of the accused still gather here to fortify themselves during trials and to toast or console each other following commutations and acquittals. In the quiet bar in back, crime reporters and barristers enjoy a drink after a day's work at the Old Bailey, though presumably any conversation between the two professions is strictly off the record. Have lunch here before sitting in on a trial at the Old Bailey. ♦ Pub ♦ M-F 11AM-10PM. 18 Old Bailey. Tube: St. Paul's. 071/248.5085

**41 Old Bailey** The figure of Justice, neither blind nor blindfolded but holding scales, stands atop the dome, a bronze-gilded prelude to countless TV and film thrillers. The carved inscription over the main entrance, "Defend the Children of the Poor and Punish the Wrongdoer," proves as difficult a combination today as it was when **Fagin** went to the gallows on this very site in chapter 52 of *Oliver Twist.* The Old Bailey is the other name for the **Central Criminal Court,** which serves Greater London and parts of Surrey, Kent, and Essex; it's where the most serious, dramatic, and celebrated criminal cases are heard. A medieval gatehouse where murderers and thieves were imprisoned originally stood on this site. It was part of **Newgate Prison,** which for centuries played an important and dreadful role in London life, especially during the late-18th and 19th centuries when it was London's chief penitentiary. Methods of execution were particularly horrible, including death by pressing. The conditions, despite numerous

extensions and the installation of a windmill on the roof to improve ventilation, were just as notoriously barbaric. In 1750, a plague of "gaol fever"—actually a nasty strain of typhoid—swept through the prison, killing more than 60 people, including the lord mayor, members of the jury, and three judges. This was the origin of a tradition still honored today whereby judges carry nosegays on the first day of each session to protect against vile smells and diseases.

The first Old Bailey (or **Sessions House**) was built in 1539 for trials of the accused. Those tried here include the men who condemned **Charles I** in 1660; **Oscar Wilde** (for homosexual offenses) in 1895; and famous 20th-century murderers **Dr. Crippen, J.R. Christie,** and **Peter Sutcliffe** (the Yorkshire Ripper). In 1973, a terrorist bomb went off in the building during a trial of members of the **Irish Republican Army,** which led to fortresslike security during IRA trials. Public executions were held outside the Old Bailey from 1783 until 1868, replacing Tyburn as the site of the gallows. The road was widened to accommodate the large number of spectators.

The present building with an elaborate Edwardian frontage (built in 1907) and its extension (built in 1972) accommodate 19 courts. Ten of them are in the old building, entered on Newgate Street, which has a very unassuming door with the words "Ring bell hard" written above the doorbell; the other nine courts are in the new building entered from the Old Bailey. Visitors watch trials from the public gallery, as few experiences are more fascinating than seeing the English judiciary at work, with the judge and barristers in their white wigs and the accused in the dock. Major trials held in courts one through four attract large numbers, so you may have to wait in line. ♦ No children under 14, cameras, tape recorders, large holdalls, or bags allowed. Free when court is in session. Old Bailey and Newgate St. Tube: St. Paul's. 071/248.3277

**42 Viaduct Tavern** ★★$ A fascinating pub, this one was built over cells of the old **Newgate Prison** and named for **Holborn Viaduct,** the world's first overpass. The interior is lavished with gold mirrors, an ornate metal ceiling, and large paintings. Light lunches are served. ♦ Pub ♦ M-F 11AM-11PM; Sa 11AM-3PM, 7-11PM; Su noon-3PM, 7-11PM. 126 Newgate St. Tube: St. Paul's. 071/606.8476

"Christopher Wren
Went to dine with some men.
'If anyone calls,
say I'm designing St. Paul's.'"

**Anonymous**

**43 Holy Sepulchre** Often referred to as "St. Sepulchre's," the spacious church (shown above) was originally dedicated in 1137 to East Anglian **King Edmund.** It was rebuilt in the 15th century, restored after the Great Fire (possibly by **Sir Christopher Wren**), heavily Victorianized in 1878, and sensitively repaired after World War II. Known as the "Musicians Church," Holy Sepulchre has a long tradition of memorial services for composers and singers; a **Musician's Chapel** with windows in memory of opera singer **Dame Nellie Melba** and composer **John Ireland,** and exquisite kneelers with names of great musicians, bars of music, and musical instruments in fine needlepoint. **Sir Henry Wood,** the founder of the **Promenade Concerts,** was baptized here, became assistant organist when he was 12, and is remembered in **Gerald Smith's** central window of the north chapel, which is dedicated to **St. Cecilia,** the patron saint of music. Every year on St. Cecilia's Day (22 November), a festival is held, with the choirs of **Westminster Abbey** and **St. Paul's.**

American associations with the church inspired the south aisle's stained-glass window of **Captain John Smith,** who led the expedition to Virginia that began in 1606. Taken prisoner by Native Americans, he was saved by a chief's daughter, **Pocahontas,** just as he was about to be killed. The English captain became governor of Virginia, and his savior married another settler, **John Rolfe,** who brought her to England. Sadly, Pocahontas' health declined during the damp English winter and she died. Smith is buried here, but the resting place of his rescuer is still not certain.

Not all the annals of the church are as life-affirming as its musical history. To the right of the altar, a small glass case encloses a hand bell that was tolled outside the cell of a condemned man at midnight on the eve of his hanging. The bellman recited the following verses: "All you that in the condemned hole do lie; Prepare you, for tomorrow you shall die; Watch all and pray; The hour is drawing near. That you before the Almighty must appear; Examine well yourselves; in time

repent. That you may not to eternal flames be sent. And when St. Sepulchre's Bell in the morning tolls, Lord have mercy on your souls." All this, including the ringing of the great bell of St. Sepulchre on the morning of the execution, was arranged and paid for by an endowment of £50 made by parishioner **Robert Dowe** in 1605. ♦ M-F 9AM-4PM. Snow Hill Ct. Tube: St. Paul's. 071/248.3110

**44 Bishop's Finger** ★★$ This pub used to be called the **Rutland,** but Bishop's Finger is the name of one of the beers made by the brewer **Shepherd Neame,** to which the pub is tied, and the name stuck. Meat carriers from the market, doctors and medical students from Bart's, lawyers and reporters from the Old Bailey, and money-makers from the City all drink in the two bars, which spill over into the park opposite on sunny days. ♦ Pub ♦ M-F 11:30AM-11PM. 9-10 West Smithfield. Tube: Barbican, St. Paul's. 071/248.2341

**45 St. Bartholomew the Less** This octagonal chapel for St. Bartholomew's Hospital was founded in the 12th century, rebuilt 300 years later (two 15th-century arches survive under the tower), rebuilt again in 1789 and 1823, and restored in 1951 following damage suffered during World War II. The register dates back to 1547 and indicates that **Inigo Jones** was baptized here in 1573. ♦ Open 24 hours for friends and families of hospital patients. West Smithfield Sq (between Giltspur St and Little Britain). Tube: Barbican St. Paul's

**46 St. Bartholomew's Hospital** When **Wat Tyler** was stabbed by **Sir William Walworth** during the 1331 peasants' confrontation with **Edward II,** he was brought to Bart's, as this institution is commonly called, and died in the "emergency room." Though still treating patients these days, Bart's is under threat of closure—despite the fact that it's the oldest hospital in London and the only one of London's medieval foundations to remain on its original site. Like the church of St. Bartholomew the Great, the hospital was founded in 1123 by **Thomas Rahere,** although **Henry VIII** is regarded as a kind of second founder after he dissolved the adjacent priory during the Reformation and granted a royal charter refounding the hospital in 1546. The gateway, built in 1702 by **Edward Strong the Younger,** is topped by a statue of Henry VIII by **Francis Bird.** The collegiate-style building inside the great quadrangle were added by **James Gibbs** between 1730 and 1770. *The Pool of Bethesda* and *The Good Samaritan,* two large murals painted in 1737 by **William Hogarth,** a governor of the hospital, line the staircase that leads to the Great Hall. The **Medical School,** which is a vital part of the hospital, is the oldest in London, founded in 1662. Now part of the **University of London,** Bart's has expanded into a new building in nearby Charterhouse. ◆ West Smithfield Sq (between Giltspur St and Little Britain). Tube: Barbican, St. Paul's

**47 St. Bartholomew the Great** For lovers of antiquity and lovers of London, St. Bartholomew's is a shrine. It's the oldest parish church in London (only **St. John's Chapel** in the Tower of London exceeds it in age) and the city's only surviving Norman church. **Thomas Rahere,** a favorite courtier of **Henry I,** built it as a priory in 1123, along with St. Bartholomew's Hospital, as an act of gratitude after he had a vision during a fever in which St. Bartholomew saved him from a monster. The building's simple majesty and ancient beauty quicken the hearts of all who enter: an inexplicable power comes from the stones, the strong pillars, the pointed windows, the tomb of Rahere, and the miracle of survival to which the church is witness. Today's visitors do not see it quite as Rahere, first canon and first prior, saw it. The massive nave was the choir of the original church; the original nave is now part of the courtyard; and the 13th-century entrance gate was originally the west entrance to the south aisle. But the choir and vaulted ambulatories, crossing, chancel with apse, two transepts, and at least one bay of the nave have changed little since Rahere's time. The music sung during the choral service on Sunday seems to reach back in time, forming a heavenly connection among stones, centuries, saints, and angels.

The restored **Lady Chapel** dates from the 14th century and contains the only medieval font in the City; **William Hogarth** was baptized here in 1697. The five pre-Reformation bells in the tower peal before Evensong on Sunday. The crypt and cloister have been restored, and the large chamber is dedicated to the **City of London Squadron of the RAF,** which holds a memorial service here each year.

During the Reformation, the church was sold and fell upon hard times. The cloisters became a stable, the crypt was used for storing coal and wine, and the Lady Chapel became a printer's office where a young **Benjamin Franklin** worked in 1725. There was a blacksmith's forge in the north transept.

In the 1860s, architect **Sir Aston Webb** began the Parliament-funded restoration of the church. With the assistance of his colleague, **F.L. Dove,** Webb saved both the reality and the spirit of St. Bartholomew's. The gateway has been restored in memory of the two architects—notice their coats of arms. The wooden figure of Rahere was carved from a beam taken from the church and placed here in memory of Sir Aston's son, **Phillip,** who was killed in action in France during World War I. ◆ Daily 8:30AM-4:30PM summer; daily 8:30AM-4PM winter. Services Su 9AM,

11AM, 6:30PM. West Smithfield Sq (east side). Tube: Barbican. 071/606.5171

**48 Cloth Fair** This street in the heart of old London retains the style that the whole City of London had before it was destroyed by money, the Great Fire of 1666, and World War II. **No. 41** is the only house in the City built before the fire. **Sir John Betjeman,** a beloved poet laureate, once resided at **No. 43.** Now the short terrace of 18th-century houses is owned by the **Landmark Trust,** a charity that rescues minor buildings in distress before they are knocked down by vandals or developers. **Nos. 43** and **45A** are available for short holiday rentals (to book, write to Landmark Trust, Shottesbrooke, Maidenhead, Berkshire, SL6 3SW, or call 062/882.5925 a year ahead). ◆ Off Little Britain. Tube: Barbican

**49 Fox and Anchor** ★★$ Bleary-eyed medical students, young doctors and nurses, and bummarees from the meat market are here in the morning eating huge platters of eggs, bacon, sausages, black pudding, baked beans, and fried bread. The special early morning market license that allows alcohol to be served between 6AM and 9AM is for bona fide market workers; visitors get coffee. The facade is Art Nouveau, and the interior was recently refurbished to match, but the ambience is the real attraction—best appreciated after working up a hearty appetite. Surprisingly, you can also get a vegetarian breakfast here. ◆ Pub ◆ Breakfast and lunch; breakfast only on Saturday. Closed Sunday. 115 Charterhouse St. Tube: Barbican, Farringdon. 071/253.4838

**50 Stephen Bull's Bistro & Bar** ★★$$ Young City men and women gather at this trendy canteen to see who else is here and to sample the daily soups, salads, and pastas. The brown sugar meringue with fudge sauce is divine. ◆ Modern British ◆ Lunch and dinner; dinner only on Saturday. Closed Sunday. 71 St. John St. Tube: Farringdon, Barbican. 071/490.1750

"Royalty is a government in which the attention of the nation is concentrated on one person doing interesting actions. A Republic is a government in which that attention is divided between many, who are all doing uninteresting actions. Accordingly, so long as the human heart is strong and the human reason weak, Royalty will be strong because it appeals to diffused feeling, and Republics weak because they appeal to the understanding."

**Walter Bagehot**

Restaurants/Clubs: Red     Hotels: Blue
Shops/ 🌳 Outdoors: Green     Sights/Culture: Black

**51** **Smithfield Market** At midnight, the vans start arriving at the oldest and largest "dead meat" market in Europe. Covering 10 acres and two miles of shop frontages, this wholesale market is still on its original medieval site. Unloading, weighing, cutting, marking, and displaying all take place before selling begins at 5AM. Starting the day at dawn amid the orderly bustle of city life makes you feel like both an honorary and ordinary citizen, wherever you are. When you start a day at Smithfield Market, surrounded by white-coated butchers and "bummarees" (porters at the Smithfield Market) effortlessly conveying pink, red, purple, and brown carcasses, you may feel like a background figure in a surreal painting; you'll see calves by Georgia O'Keeffe, piglets by Mother Goose, rib cages by Francis Bacon. Feathered chickens, geese, and turkeys hang alongside furry rabbits. A pervasive sense of the history of this trade allows guilt and nausea to recede: life depends on death, markets depend on life.

Signs announcing beef from Australia, New Zealand, and Scotland hang between the shining hooks. The arches, pillars, ornaments, and swirls of ironwork that adorn the trading halls are worthy of a City church. Though the animated atmosphere is pure Gothic, the long iron-and-glass building, modeled on **Sir Joseph Paxton's** Crystal Palace, is mid-Victorian; designed by **Horace Jones,** it opened in 1868 with a meaty banquet for 1,200 people. With typical Victorian high-mindedness, a small park was built in the center of Smithfield where the bummarees could rest, but predictably, they choose now, as they chose then, the pubs in the area, which have special licenses to open in the early-morning market hours.

The site has far more sinister associations than the slaughter of animals for consumption. Originally, it was a grassy "smooth field," or level, just outside the City walls for citizens' entertainment and exercise (hence the name, a corruption of Smoothfield). Executions were held here as early as 1305, when **William Wallace,** the Scottish patriot, was put to death on St. Bartholomew's Day. **Roger Mortimer,** who murdered **Edward II** and loved his Queen, was executed here on the orders of **Edward III,** and it was here, in 1381, that the confrontation over a poll tax took place between **Wat Tyler** with his band of revolutionaries and the 14-year-old **Richard II.** The young King calmed the angry mob and promised them mercy and justice. The crowd took him at his word and peacefully dispersed, but Richard II delivered neither justice nor mercy, and Tyler, stabbed by **Sir William Walworth** during the confrontation, died a few hundred yards away at **St. Bartholomew's Hospital.** From the 15th century onward, Smithfield was the execution place for all who were convicted of heresy, including the Catholics set ablaze by **Henry VIII** and most of the 277 Protestant martyrs who died for their faith during the reign of **Mary I,** when they, too, were burned alive.

Smithfield's history is not entirely grim. The great **St. Bartholomew's Fair** was held here every August, from Henry II's time until 1855. The three-day event was the most important cloth fair in England, expanding as the export of wool and fabric grew. The **Royal Smithfield Show** (now held at Earl's Court) had its origin here in 1799, and as far back as medieval times there was a large horse-and-cattle market; live animals were herded across the streets of London to reach it. The days of gre

*19th-Century Smithfield Market*

fairs have passed, but the area has been kept vital by the remarkable and ironic juxtaposition of its two principal institutions: the meat market and the hospital. Both are under threat, however. The former may be moved elsewhere, while the latter is struggling against government cutbacks. ♦ M-F 5-10:30AM. Bounded by Farringdon Rd, and West Smithfield/Long Ln, and Lindsey and Charterhouse Sts. Tube: Barbican, Farringdon

**52 Bubbs** ★★$$$ You'll have to go down the stairs to the side of the Holborn Viaduct to find this bistro, a series of connecting rooms packed with City ladies and gents. The fish specials change daily, but meat lovers should stick with the entrecôte béarnaise. Mont Blanc makes a delicious dessert if you're still a tad hungry after any of the entrées. ♦ French ♦ Lunch. Closed Saturday and Sunday. 329 Central Market. Tube: Farringdon, Barbican. 071/236.2435

## Bests

### Roger Ebert
Film Critic

The walk across **Hampstead Heath** from Parliament Hill to the **Spaniard's Inn,** and then down the road to **Kenwood House.**

The corner table next to the fire in the front room of the **Holly Bush,** Hampstead.

The Thames-side walk from **Hammersmith Bridge** to **Chiswick House.**

**Jermyn Street,** particularly the **Paxton & Whitfield** cheese shop.

The **London Library** in St. James's Square.

**Highgate Cemetery.**

Houses: **Sir John Soane's Museum** in Lincoln's Inn Fields, **Lord Leighton's House** in Holland Park, and **Dr. Johnson's House** in Gough Square.

Bookstores: **Heywood Hill,** Curzon Street; **Fisher & Sperr,** Highgate High Street; **Skoob,** Sicilian Avenue; **Bernard Stone's Bookshop,** Lamb's Conduit Street.

Books: *Ian Nairn's London* (Penguin), the fierce, passionate, affectionate book about the best and worst things in the city, ranging from the ugliest house to the most stygian Underground passage to Soane's breakfast room.

Galleries: the **Catto Gallery,** Hampstead; **Chris Beetles,** Ryder Street; **Agnew, Thomas & Son,** and the **Fine Arts Society,** Bond Street; **Abbott and Holder,** Museum Street; **Pomeroy-Purdy,** Southwark.

Restaurants: **Rules, Le Caprice, Langans, Ken Lo's Memories of China,** and **Dino's** at the South Kensington tube stop.

### Margaret Daubney
Calligrapher/Editor

The **King's Library** in the British Museum is, I suppose, one of my natural homes and a particularly elegant room. I usually pause in the adjacent manuscript room to look at **The Stonyhurst Gospel,** which is almost 1,300 years old.

The **St. Bride's Printing Library** houses an amazing collection that should be cherished as a national treasure.

**Cornelissen** on Great Russell Street supplies real materials to artists and craftsmen.

The beautiful old lampposts all over London—I particularly like the fishy ones on the **Embankment.**

The poems on the **Underground.**

The view across **Blackheath** of people exercising their dogs and children flying their kites is a scene out of a **Lowry** painting.

The **National Gallery's Sainsbury Wing,** especially watching Trafalgar Square from the restaurant. The staircase, and its carved letters, are very handsome, and the **Bellini** portrait of *Doge Leonardo Loreda* is not to be missed.

**The Festival Hall**—I like the building, the space and light, the concert hall, the view across the river, and the **Poetry Library.** It's massive but comfortable.

The tiles on the facade of **Battersea Dogs' Home** always make me laugh. So does **Albert Bridge.**

The weather vane on **No. 2 Temple Place.**

Most things about **Greenwich.** The park here is particularly spectacular in autumn colors and magical in snow. Walk up to the statue of *General Woolfe* and look down over Greenwich, the river, and London as far as Hampstead on a clear day. It's definitely the best view in London.

### Zaqueline Souras
Artist/Biologist

Cycling, walking, listening to a band, and horseback-riding in the parks of London.

Seeing the **City** and **Embankment** lights after the theater.

Eating at the **Michelin Building** with its Art Nouveau decor, either at the cafe or at **Bibendum.**

Seeing the **Changing of the Guard** horses looking down from their personal balconies at around 10AM at **Hyde Park Barracks.**

Watching the English participate in a peaceful demonstration.

"Swan upping"—an ancient ceremony in which the **Watermen** and **Lightermen** mark all the swans along the Thames that don't belong to the Queen.

A carol service in a City church.

The annual London to Brighton vintage car rally.

The quaint way in which the English decide to carry out repairs on London's bridges in the middle of the tourist season.

# Soho/ Covent Garden

The whole of Covent Garden revolves around the **Piazza,** an open square with a covered arcade modeled on Italian lines by **Inigo Jones.** But of the 1631 original, only **St. Paul's, Covent Garden**—the church that Jones built between 1631 and 1633—survives. By 1830, it was fashionable for the rich to mingle in the square alongside farmers and flower girls, and this is where **George Bernard Shaw** got his inspiration for *Pygmalion.* Walk along these streets, once haunted by the poor, and you will tread in the footsteps of **Dickens** and **Chippendale,** who both lived and worked in the area for years. Nowadays, designers, ad execs, and PR people make their living in this area, and they are the clientele that so many excellent restaurants here strive to impress (all the better for visitors to London, who are typically drawn to the warren of boutiques, colorful street stalls, and sidewalk entertainment in Covent Garden). By day, the quaint streets of this tiny area are packed and noisy; by night—except in the height of summer—it falls back into local hands.

West of Covent Garden is Soho, a neighborhood that began as a royal park but deteriorated into squalor, slums, and sex shops. In the last 10 years, however, the cheap rents have attracted a more fashionable sort: filmmakers, whose releases are screened in the giant cinemas on **Leicester Square;** music companies, whose employees hang out in **Denmark Street,** London's answer to Tin Pan Alley; and designers, whose clothes are displayed in the side-street boutiques. Catering to these trendy new residents are a variety of excellent restaurants and brasseries, including the huge number of Oriental restaurants flourishing in **Chinatown.** Sit down at virtually any table in these parts and you'll find yourself staring at a TV producer and perhaps even a movie star. *So-ho!,* incidentally, was an ancient hunting cry that rang out in this area when **Henry VIII** used to kill game here.

**1 Theatre Royal Drury Lane** The present theater (shown above) is the fourth on the site since 1663; two were destroyed by fire and one was demolished. "What, sir," said owner **Sheridan,** as his life's work went up in flames, "may a man not warm his hands at his own fireside?" Few London theaters have so illustrious or lengthy a past as Drury Lane. **Nell Gwyn** made her debut in *Indian Queen* in 1665 with **King Charles II** in the audience. **King George II** was shot at in the theater in 1716, and his grandson **George III** was shot at here in 1800. One of **Gainsborough's** favorite models, **Mary Robinson,** was discovered here by the **Prince of Wales** while she was playing Perdita in *A Winter's Tale* in 1779, and this is where the **Duke of Clarence,** later

**William IV,** first saw **Dorothea Jordan,** the Irish actress who became his mistress and mother of 10 of his children. Drury Lane was also the scene of riots over admission prices and impromptu duels that spilled over from the pit onto the stage. Today, it is the safer home of musicals, most recently *Miss Saigon, A Chorus Line,* and *Sweeney Todd.* Unlike so many of his ancestors, **Prince Charles** has yet to be seen in the audience. **Benjamin Wyatt** modeled the present theater, which seats 2,245 people, after the great theater at Bordeaux in 1811. The interior was added in 1931, the portico in 1820, and the pillars came from **Nash's** quadrant on Regent Street. ♦ Catherine St. 071/494.5001

**2 Taste of India** ★★$$ The vegetarian *thali* or the fashionable Bangladeshi entrées are the dishes to try in this bustling Indian restaurant. There's also a set buffet lunch that provides a couple of curries, freshly made onion *bhajis,* and *pilau* rice for a very reasonable price. A wine bar downstairs serves food from the main kitchen. ♦ Indian ♦ Lunch and dinner. 25 Catherine St. 071/836.2538; fax 071/240.2951

**3 Luigi's** ★★$$ After the show, Luigi's becomes a crowded Italian bistro full of the actors and singers whose signed photographs line the wall. The atmosphere is lively and the food authentic, especially the cannelloni. Booking for the late evening is essential. ♦ Italian ♦ Lunch and dinner. Closed Sunday. 15 Tavistock St. 071/240.1795; fax 071/497.0075

**3 Cafe du Jardin** ★★★$$ Rescued from bankruptcy in 1993 by **Robert Siegler,** the beloved cafe's new chef is **Tony Howarth,** whose touch used to grace Le Caprice. The menu now has a more Mediterranean feel, with starters such as sun-dried tomato risotto, and a grilled monkfish with Sicilian ratatouille as a main course. The usual bourgeois dishes—entrecôte steak, etc.— are still there, however, and the reasonable prices haven't changed. ♦ French ♦ Lunch and dinner. 25 Wellington St. Reservations advised for lunch. 071/836.8769; fax 071/836.4123

**4 Joe Allen** ★★$$ This is one of London's favorite American restaurants, known for its big burgers and salads, good cocktails, and an extensive blackboard of unchanging favorites like chili. It's not as popular as it used to be (there have been complaints about rude staff), but you should still book ahead. ♦ American ♦ Lunch and dinner. 13 Exeter St. 071/836.0651

**5 Orso** ★★$$$ Much beloved by those in the know, this flourishing first-class trattoria is a haven for good food and attentive service. The food is flown in fresh from Italy and varies from the extravagant—such as dandelion, radicchio, and Pecorino salad—to the homey (*tagliatelle* with sausage, herbs, and tomatoes), with some excellent Italian wines to boot. ♦ Italian ♦ Lunch and dinner. 27 Wellington St. Reservations required. 071/240.5269; fax 071/497.2148

**5 Penhaligon** Princess Di was once spotted in this shop buying perfume. Who can blame her? Straight from the world of *Brideshead Revisited*, it's filled with silver mirrors and dressing-table treasures. The bottles are exclusive and as exquisite as the scents; you won't find them elsewhere. Bluebell, in particular, is divine. ♦ M-F 10AM-6PM; Sa 10AM-5:30PM. 41 Wellington St. 071/836.2150

**6 London Transport Museum**
Old-fashioned buses, trams, trolley buses, and trains demonstrate how London's transport system works both above and below ground. Londoners will add that some of the exhibits are still in use on the Northern Line. ♦ Admission. Daily 10AM-6PM. 39 Wellington St. 071/379.6344; fax 071/836.4118

**7 Christopher's** ★★★$$$ Owner **Christopher Gilmour** once lived in Chicago, where he fell in love with American cuisine (i.e., clam chowder, Maine lobster, and New York strip steak). At his London restaurant, you can sample grilled chicken with lemon salsa, beautifully cooked fillet steak, and vegetables such as red cabbage with apple or mashed potatoes with nutmeg. The wine list includes a good American selection, and the desserts are a sure cure for the homesick blues. ♦ American ♦ Lunch and dinner; dinner only on Saturday. Closed Sunday. 18 Wellington St. Reservations required. 071/240.4222; fax 071/240.3357

**8 Theatre Museum** The 20-foot-high golden statue of *Gaiety* that dominates the ground floor of this museum gives a hint of what's to come. Here Britain proudly displays her theater collections, showcasing the history of her stage from **Shakespeare** to today, with regularly changing performing arts exhibitions. You can see theater, ballet, circus, opera, mime, puppetry, rock, and pop. A gift shop sells posters, postcards, and the like, and a tiny theater features regular shows. You can also book tickets for the Barbican, West End shows, concerts, and the National Theatre. ♦ Admission. Tu-Su 11AM-7PM. Russell St. 071/836.7891

**9 Covent Garden Market** The Garden produced fruits and vegetables for a 13th-century abbey in Westminster, and a market was established here in the 1700s. Immortalized by **George Bernard Shaw's** *Pygmalion* and the cockney flower girl **Eliza Doolittle,** who sold violets to rich operagoers here, today the market has more in common with the luxurious tastes of **Henry Higgins.** It is nonetheless a brilliant example of urban survival: the restored central market is a tantalizing structure of iron-and-glass roofs covering a large square, which was designed in 1831 by **Charles Fowler.**

The market's revitalization has dramatically improved this part of London, providing shops, restaurants, cafes, and pubs. At the same time, it has freed the area of the wholesale fruit and flower market that, for all its sentimental charm, clogged the surrounding streets. Although the shops in the piazza are mainly boutique-size branches of existing chain stores, the surrounding stores are often one-offs (merchandise that is sold in one shop only, for a limited period). There is an antiques market within the piazza on Monday, a crafts market Tuesday through Saturday, and a permanent fairground. ♦ Bounded by King and Bedford Sts, and Henrietta St and Covent Garden

Within Covent Garden Market:

**Opera Terrace** ★★$$ Gazing out across the piazza, this glorious glass restaurant provides a lovely escape from the crowds in spring and summer. It's great for the health conscious, too, as there's no high-cholesterol food on the menu. Try the steamed fingers of turbot and crayfish. For lighter lunches and suppers, go to the cafe. ♦ Continental ♦ Restaurant: lunch and dinner. Cafe: lunch; dinner also on Saturday and Sunday. 45 E. Terrace. 071/379.0666; fax 071/497.9060

**Culpeper** Mrs. C.F. Leyel founded Culpeper back in 1927, naming it after **Nicholas Culpeper,** an herbalist from 1616-52. The products, which include lotions, soaps, and the like, are nice, natural, and not tested on animals. ♦ M-Th 10AM-8PM; F-Sa 9AM-8PM; Su 10AM-7PM. Unit 8. 071/379.6698

**Penguin/Puffin Bookshop** Puffin is the children's imprint of **Penguin Books,** and there's everything here that you would expect from the publisher whose aim in life was to sell good-quality literature at a price anyone could

afford. ◆ M-Sa 10AM-8PM; Su 11AM-5PM. Unit 10-11. 071/379.7650; fax 071/836.1340

**Edwina Carroll** This unique shop specializes in collector's quality and hand-knit sweaters. ◆ M-Sa 10:30AM-6:30PM; Su 1-4PM. Unit 16. 071/836.9873

**Crusting Pipe** ★★$$ Candlelight, a sawdust floor, and a limited menu await you in this establishment. Treat yourself to the smoked salmon and salad or, if you are really hungry, the game pie and potatoes followed by excellent English cheese and good wines. ◆ British ◆ Lunch and dinner; lunch only on Sunday. Unit 27. 071/836.1415

**Doll's House** These are the kind of dolls you dream about; some look like museum pieces, and some are. ◆ M-Sa 10AM-7PM. Unit 29. 071/379.7243

**The Cabaret Mechanical Theatre** The Cabaret Mechanical Theatre is full of toys both old and new, including a fascinating selection of "Mechanicals"—many of the handmade wooden variety. ◆ M-Sa 10AM-7PM; Su 11AM-7PM. Unit 33. 071/379.7961

**Bar Creperie** ★$ Situated at the western corner of the market, the Creperie's terrace and outside tables afford fine views of the piazza; the only problem is that when the sun is out you may not want to move for the rest of the day. There *are* tables downstairs, but the dark interior is made up of all shades of pink, which may detract from the otherwise tasty meal set before you. This is one of the few places in London to find such a good selection of crepes—both sweet and savory. ◆ French ◆ Lunch and dinner. Unit 21. 071/836.2137

**Museum Store** Here you'll come across a bizarre collection of the best items from museum shops around the world. Sissinghurst watering cans, statues of Egyptian cats, and Mackintosh cards and prints compete for space. ◆ M-Sa 10:30AM-6:30PM; Su 11AM-5PM. Unit 37. 071/240.5760

**Benjamin Pollock's Toy Shop** Traditional toys, hand-stitched teddies like you had when you were a child, and toy theaters can be found in this gem of a shop. ◆ M-Sa 10:30AM-6PM. Unit 44. 071/379.7866

10 **Jubilee Market** Pay a fraction of the price you would in a regular shop for homemade silk lingerie, hand-knit sweaters, pottery, handcarved wooden salad bowls, etc. Poke around (there are 180 stalls) and the cream will rise to the top. The prices seem particularly good after shopping at the smart boutiques in the area. There are even a few fruit and vegetable stalls for old time's sake. ◆ Antiques: M 9AM-5PM. General: Tu-Sa 9AM-5PM. Bounded by Southampton St, Tavistock St, and Covent Garden Piazza

11 **Boulestin** ★★$$$ This restaurant is like an old gents' club in a time warp; ancient oils, over-rich colors, and swags serve as decor. The food, however, prepared by chef **Kevin Kennedy**, is highly praised, as is the wine cellar, particularly the Burgundies. Try the tournedos Rossini—beef with foie gras and a truffle sauce. ◆ Continental ◆ Lunch and dinner; dinner only on Saturday. Closed Sunday. 1a Henrietta St. Reservations required. 071/836.7061; fax 071/836.1283

12 **St. Paul's, Covent Garden** When the thrifty Fourth Earl of Bedford was developing Covent Garden, he asked **Inigo Jones** to design an economical church not much bigger than a barn. Jones complied, creating what he called the handsomest barn in Europe. The redbrick church (pictured above) with pitched roof, overhanging eaves, and the famous Tuscan portico was the setting for the opening scene in **George Bernard Shaw's** *Pygmalion;* the interior is now frequented by artists and actors, while the portico serves as a backdrop for many of the street performers who play here, especially during summer. Gutted by fire in 1795, the church was carefully restored by **Philip Hardwick.** Today, it is known as the actors' church because of its close association with the theater; numerous plaques inside commemorate actors and playwrights. ◆ The Piazza

13 **Rules** ★★$$$ Nearly 200 years old, London's oldest restaurant has always been a museum of London's literary and theatrical beau monde, and it still is today. The Prince of Wales, later **Edward VII**, and Lillie Langtry drank champagne behind a special door on the first floor, and **Dickens** had a regular table across the room. Paintings, prints, and yellowing playbills still cover the walls. Rules is a compulsory stop for visitors to London, but the secret to a good meal is selective ordering. Stick to very English dishes such as Scotch beef with Yorkshire pudding, pheasant and grouse in season (the game comes from Rules' own estate in the Pennines), and the weekday specials. ◆ British ◆ Lunch and dinner. 35 Maiden Ln. Reservations required. 071/836.5314; fax 071/497.1081

14 **Porters** ★★$$ Owned by **Richard,** the Seventh Earl of Bradford, this deservedly successful restaurant serves high-quality,

traditional English fare: pies, sausages, and delicious nursery puddings like jam *roly-poly* (a suet-based, dumpling-style dessert with jam rolled inside it), spotted dick (a sponge cake baked with currants or raisins), and sherry trifle. The prices are honest and it's fun for babies and toddlers, too. ◆ British ◆ Lunch and dinner. 17 Henrietta St. 071/836.6466; fax 071/379.4296

**15 TGI Friday's** ★$ Tiffany lamps hang in this cavern of a place. You can munch on big burgers, chunky chicken wings, and there is also a special children's menu. The cocktail selection will make grown-ups feel right at home. ◆ American ◆ Lunch and dinner. 6 Bedford St. 071/379.0585

**16 Naturally British** Stop here for hard-to-resist creations by British designers and craftspeople, including clothes, furniture, pottery, table linens, pewter, baskets, toys, and food. If you are looking for presents not to be found in department stores, this shop is a gold mine. ◆ M-Sa 11AM-7PM; Su noon-5PM. 13 New Row. 071/240.0551

**16 White Swan** $ This rambling old Queen Anne pub had a fiercely loyal clientele who fought to keep the managers, **Mr.** and **Mrs. England,** who had been there for years. They failed and the pub is all the poorer for the loss of the warm, friendly atmosphere. Draft Bass washes down the sandwiches and hot pub grub. ◆ Pub ◆ M-Sa 11AM-11PM. 14 New Row. 071/836.3291

**17 Garrick Club** Dickens, Trollope, Millais, and **Rossetti** met actors and "men of education and refinement" sitting in this gloriously ornate gentlemen's club, which was founded in 1831 and named in honor of actor **David Garrick.** The walls are lined with portraits of famous actors from the British stage, said to be the best collection of theatrical paintings in Britain. Today's armchairs hold members from the worlds of arts and law. ◆ 15 Garrick St

**18 Lamb & Flag** ★★$ The cobbled courtyard of this lovely 1627 pub is always full of office workers, who love its ancient charm. But it wasn't always so nice. It used to be called the "Bucket of Blood" because local fighters came here. In 1679, the poet **John Dryden** was beaten up nearby for writing nasty things about the Duchess of Portsmouth, **Charles II's** mistress. ◆ Pub ◆ M-Sa 11AM-11PM. 33 Rose St. 071/497.9504

**19 Moss Bros.** England's gentry held their breath when Moss Bros. closed its flagship store. Luckily, it only moved across the street to a space with a higher ceiling, thicker carpets, and the same top designer labels. The rentals department, much beloved by Ascot and the charity ball set, bridegrooms, and best men, still remains. ◆ M-W, F-Sa 9AM-6PM; Th 9AM-7PM. 27 King St. 071/497.9354

**20 Calabash** ★★$$ Exotic and delicious African food in a laid-back atmosphere is distinctly appealing after the hectic tourism of Covent Garden. Masks, headdresses, and batik cloths decorate the walls and tables. Choose from Ghanaian ground-nut stew, Tanzanian beef stew with green bananas and coconut cream, vegetarian *kukus,* and excellent Zimbabwean and Algerian wines. ◆ African ◆ Lunch and dinner. Africa Center, 38 King St. 071/836.1976

**20 Palms Pasta on the Piazza** ★★$ Light, airy, and generally superior to the pasta restaurants in the same price range proliferating all over London, the food here is generally fresh and delicious. Start with the *bagna cauda* (raw vegetables served with a warm anchovy-and-walnut sauce). They don't take bookings, so get here early or after 2PM ◆ Italian ◆ Lunch and dinner. 39 King St. 071/240.2939

**21 Fielding** $$ This is a rare hotel in London: small, inexpensive, and quiet. It attracts performers from the **Royal Opera House,** a stone's throw away, and media and arts clientele, who are drawn by the discreet charm and perfect location. The rooms are modest—most have showers instead of baths—and small, but the pedestrian street below spares you from the sounds of cars at night. It's an ideal place if you are a music-lover or theatergoer, as the manager also sells theater tickets, but not a good idea if you wish to do more than sleep there. The hotel is named after **Henry Fielding,** the author of *Tom Jones* and a magistrate at **Bow Street Court** nearby. ◆ 4 Broad Ct. 071/836.8305; fax 071/497.0064

**22 Bow Street** Look again, this street really is shaped like a bow. Covent Garden's cafe society reads like a Who's Who of English history and literature. But most of it happened in just two spots—the **Garrick Club** and in **Will's Coffee House,** where you could expect to meet **Pepys, Dryden, Pope, Swift, Johnson, Boswell, Sheridan,** and **Fielding,** though not all together! When things got too unruly in the area (which was poor and dangerous by the late 18th century), Fielding set up the forerunners of today's police force to catch thieves; they were called the "Bow Street Runners." Today, in **Bow Street Magistrates Court,** it's illegal aliens who are put on trial.

**23 Royal Opera House** Three theaters have stood on this site since 1732. The great dome and regal red, gold, and cream auditorium you see today (shown above) is **E.M. Barry's** 1858 design, capable of seating 2,154. The frieze under the portico, *Tragedy and Comedy* by **Flaxman,** was salvaged in 1855 from a fire at the theater. In 1946, Covent Garden became the home of the Royal Opera and Ballet companies. Some of the great names who have played here are **Patti, Melba, Caruso, Gobbi,** and **Callas.** The opera and ballet companies will have to move in 1997, when the site is redeveloped. ♦ Bow St. Box office: 071/240.1066. Recorded information: 071/240.1911

**24 Paul Smith** Even restrained men go wild in this shop, trying on stylish suits, sportswear, sweaters, and shoes. Meanwhile, partners sit around in comfort, gazing at the expensive designer accessories—mirrors, hip flasks. It's a beautifully designed, surprisingly cozy shop, and *so* fashionable. The clothes, which don't date, are created by Smith using English materials; they're made in England, too. ♦ M-Sa 10:30AM-6:30PM; Th 10:30AM-7PM. 41-44 Floral St. 071/379.7133

**24 R. Newbold** The first-ever R. Newbold shop features a collection that draws on influences from British clothing over the past 100 years. Designs include actual styles and garments the R. Newbold factory is famous for having produced in the past. The range of clothing should appeal to the customer in search of something different: especially if it's for traditional styles with a modern twist. ♦ M-Sa 10:30AM-6:30PM; Th 10:30AM-7PM. 7-8 Langley Ct. 071/240.5068

**25 Sanctuary** One of the few drawbacks to traveling is the unhealthy feeling that stems from extra meals and lack of exercise. Some dedicated travelers continue to jog or swim, but, for a woman in London, the Sanctuary is one of the most idyllic and essential indulgences. Restore your spirits and health in the sauna, Turkish steam room, swimming pool, and Jacuzzi, or make use of the sun bed. Shampoo, conditioner, towels, soap, body lotion, and cologne are provided free of charge. Indulge further with top-to-toe beauty treatments, including a massage, a facial, and a healthy lunch at the food bar. ♦ Daily membership fee; evening rate available from 5-10PM. M-Tu, Sa-Su 10AM-6PM; W-F 10AM-10PM. 11 Floral St. 071/240.9635; fax 071/497.0410

**25 Agnes B.** White walls and pine floors showcase unfussy, practical clothing for men, women, and children. Choose from colorful sweaters and wool suits, or invest in a definitive pair of leather jeans. ♦ M-Sa 10:30AM-6:30PM; Th 10:30AM-7PM. 35-36 Floral St. 071/379.1992

**26 Edward Stanford** The largest collection of maps, guides, charts, atlases, and travel books in the world is located in this Edwardian shop, built in 1901. **David Livingston** had his maps drawn here, and today's customers include mountain climbers and actress **Dame Judi Dench.** ♦ M, Sa 10AM-6PM; Tu-F 9AM-7PM. 12-14 Long Acre. 071/836.1321

**27 Blazer** The British version of preppy clothes can be purchased here at reasonable prices. ♦ M-W, F-Sa 9:30AM-6:30PM; Th 9:30AM-7:30PM; Su noon-6PM. 36 Long Acre. 071/379.6258

**27 Long Acre** Once the medieval market garden (a place where people grew crops such as potatoes or apples for sale) of **Westminster Abbey's** monks, this street became the center of both coach and furniture-making by the middle of the 18th century. **Chippendale** worked here, and it's easy to imagine him walking to his workshop from his home in St. Martin's Lane.

**27 Dôme** $ The Dôme chain of restaurants is good for snacks, coffees, teas, and a glass of wine, but the food is not very inspiring. The goat cheese and sun-dried tomato salad is tasty, for instance, but a bit on the dull side. ♦ Brasserie ♦ Breakfast, lunch, and dinner. 38 Long Acre. 071/836.7823

**28 Emporio Armani** Meet the man who put the gold into the golden triangle of streets that are Covent Garden. The arrival of Armani is even welcomed by the competition—now, darlings, everyone will come to find men's and women's clothing and accessories, casual gear, and jeans. ♦ M-W, F-Sa 10AM-6:30PM; Th 10AM-7:30PM. 57-59 Long Acre. 071/917.6882; fax 071/917.6881

**28 Magno's** ★★$$ Hidden away at the end of Long Acre, this restaurant is a favorite of theater buffs, who come for coq au vin or Roquefort in puff pastry. There's a spectacular wine list, and a set menu at lunch (a better value, as otherwise vegetables are charged separately). ♦ French ♦ Lunch and dinner; dinner only on Saturday. Closed Sunday. 65a Long Acre. Reservations recommended. 071/836.6077; fax 071/379.6184

| | |
|---|---|
| **Restaurants/Clubs:** Red | **Hotels:** Blue |
| **Shops/ 🍃 Outdoors:** Green | **Sights/Culture:** Black |

**29 Cafe des Amis du Vin** ★★$$ This Continental-style establishment is actually three eateries in one. The upstairs restaurant is intimate and hushed, the better for formal lunches; the ground floor is characterized by squashed-together tables and a lot of noise; downstairs is *vrai parisienne,* with great atmosphere and lots of media folk, wine drinkers, and French snack eaters. It's vital to book. You must arrive very early to get a table downstairs. ◆ French ◆ Restaurant: lunch and dinner; dinner only on Saturday. Cafe: lunch and dinner. Wine bar: M-Sa 11:30AM-11PM. All three closed Sunday. 11-14 Hanover Pl (off Long Acre). 071/379.3444

**30 Ajimura** ★★$$ Japanese food in London can be very expensive, but the Ajimura has kept its prices reasonable—hence the crowds. This versatile and relaxed restaurant offers sashimi, sushi, tempura, sukiyaki, *shabu-shabu,* and an endless variety of set meals and menu specials. Try the beef teriyaki. Book for supper. ◆ Japanese ◆ Lunch and dinner; dinner only on Saturday. Closed Sunday. 51-53 Shelton St. 071/240.0178

**31 Diana's Diner** ★$ Fall into Diana's for cheap, good, but standard British/Italian cafe grub. Pig out on the liver and bacon with chips followed by one of Diana's filling puddings, then adjust your waistband, but not your wallet. Try sightseeing after this! ◆ Anglo-Italian ◆ Breakfast, lunch, and dinner; breakfast, lunch, and afternoon tea only on Sunday. 39 Endell St. 071/240.0272

**31 Rock & Sole Plaice** ★★$ Considered one of London's finest fish-and-chips joints, this place is clean, inexpensive, and, sadly, rather small. Eat outside when the weather's fine, munching on delectable plaice, or cod, wrapped up in a crisp, golden batter and accompanied by the required bowl of "mushy peas" and a "wodge" of chips. Wash it all down with a spot of tea. ◆ British ◆ Lunch and dinner. Closed Sunday. 47 Endell St. 071/836.3785

**32 World of Difference, The London Ecology Centre** In England, going green used to mean envious; now it means environmentally friendly. This shop has some highly unusual green gifts, like a heap of useless ordinance survey maps converted into exquisite writing paper. ◆ M-Sa 10AM-6PM. 21 Endell St. 071/379.8208

**33 Muji** The English have now decided they like everything Japanese. Following in the footsteps of **Issey Miyake** comes Muji, with affordable, functional yet desirable cotton clothes, housewares, and stationery. ◆ M-W, Sa 10:30AM-7PM; Th-F 10:30AM-7:30PM. 39 Shelton St. 071/379.1331

**34 Flip** Designer prices getting you down? Then come here and flip out at the secondhand leather jackets, shirts, trousers, coats and more that hang upon endless rails at this haven for upmarket "secondhand roses." Don't expect mint conditions, but seek and ye shall find the bargains. A Southampton Street branch features mainly army gear. ◆ M-W 10AM-6:30PM; Th 10AM-8PM; F-Sa 10AM-7PM; Su noon-6PM. 125 Long Acre. 071/836.4688

**34 Neal Street East** Everything Asian is sold here, from Afghan tribal jewelry to tiny Chinese pin cushions. ◆ M-Sa 10AM-7PM; Su noon-6PM. 5 Neal St. 071/240.0135

**34 The Tea House** If you like London policemen, you can buy a ceramic one here and he will pour your tea forever. The shop is packed with eccentric and absurd teapots and more than 40 teas, from decaffeinated and jasmine to spiced Christmas teas. ◆ M-Sa 10AM-7PM; Su 11AM-6PM. 15 Neal St. 071/240.7539

**35 Food for Thought** ★★$ This tiny restaurant classes itself for "gourmets on a budget." If you don't mind being hurried and eating practically in someone else's lap, try the carrot, orange and ginger soup, cauliflower quiche or penne pasta Milano. The menu changes each day: there is always soup three types of salad, and either a stir-fry, casserole, or hot bake. Look out for the Scrunch, a legendary dessert with a thick, oaty base, plus fruit, yogurt, cream, and/or honey. ◆ Vegetarian ◆ Breakfast, lunch, and dinner; lunch and tea only on Sunday. 31 Neal St. 071/836.0239

**35 Thomas Neal's** Like a modern Burlington Arcade, this is a barrel-vaulted brick mall on a diminutive scale with more than two dozen small, idiosyncratic specialty shops and three restaurants. ◆ Shorts Gardens

Within Thomas Neal's:

**Sol e Luna** ★★$ Hot off the streets of Manhattan, Aspen, and Beverly Hills, this restaurant imports all its own ingredients fresh from Italy. ◆ Italian ◆ Lunch and dinner 071/379.3336; fax 071/379.3340

**Lunn Antiques** Risk the temptation of dreamy antique lace nightdresses and blissful christening gowns lovingly made by someone's grandmama a long time ago. Everything, including the linen tablecloths and bedspreads, is fabulously expensive. ◆ M-Sa 10:30AM-7PM. 071/379.1974

**Interlude** Right in the heart of adland is a pen shop designed for closet typographers and calligraphers to slide into for that vital little present to themselves—a new **Mont Blanc,** a **Parker & Cross,** or an old-fashioned quill pen. ◆ M-F 10:30AM-6PM; Sa 10:30AM-6:30PM. 071/379.3139

**36 The Donmar Warehouse** This is one of the most important fringe theaters in London, mainly because it serves as a proving ground and springboard to the bigger West End venues. Once used by the **Royal Shakespeare Company** for experimental productions, it now hosts all sorts of theater. The seating capacity is 200. ◆ Thomas Neal's, Earlham St (between Shorts Gardens and Endell Sts). Box office: 071/867.1150. Credit card bookings: 071/867.1111

**36 Head over Heels** For up-and-coming Italian ladies' designer clothes and lingerie, and a helpful staff to boot, drop in here. ◆ M-F 11AM-7PM; Sa 10:30AM-6:30PM. 27 Neal St. 071/240.7737

**37 Neal's Yard** This quaint little courtyard is jammed with tiny shops specializing in top-quality food popular with health nuts. An apothecary sells herbal medicines packaged in old-fashioned blue-glass jars and bottles. ◆ Bounded by Monmouth St, Short Gardens, and Neal St

Within Neal's Yard:

**Neal's Yard Dairy** Everything is British here, from the blue sheep's cheeses to the little round goat cheeses and the glorious, well-matured cheddars. It's like walking into an edible map of England: Caerphilly, Red Leicester, Sage Derby . . . all with their own names and from those parts of the country that provided them. Move over France, the British cheesemakers are coming. ◆ M-Sa 9AM-7PM; Su 11AM-5PM. 071/379.7646

**Neal's Yard Bakery Co-operative** Quiches and salads can be eaten in the upstairs tearoom, while the **Farm Shop** sells organic vegetable juice and Indian vegetarian curries to take home. ◆ M-F 10:30AM-5PM; Sa 10:30AM-5:30PM. 071/836.5199

**38 Neal Street Restaurant** ★★$$$$ Brick walls hung with abstract art have made this restaurant famous, along with its wild mushrooms, which are on display in profusion as you walk in. There's other wild produce, too, such as dandelion tart. Try the carpaccio of beef with truffle cheese; it's quite delicious. Tread carefully through the menu though, for it can become quite pricey. ◆ Italian ◆ Lunch and dinner. Closed Sunday. 26 Neal St. 071/836.8368

**39 Natural Shoe Store** This shop has been here forever, selling well-made traditional English shoes for men and women. They also do "Jesus boots": healthy shoes with thick soles and straps for people who believe that feet, not looks, come first. ◆ M-Tu 10AM-6PM; W-F 10AM-7PM; Sa 10AM-6:30PM; Su noon-5:30PM. 21 Neal St. 071/836.5254

**39 The Kite Store** Drop in here for brightly colored kites, Frisbees, boomerangs, and all else that flies. ◆ M-F 10AM-6PM; Sa 10:30AM-5:30PM. 48 Neal St. 071/836.1666; fax 071/836.2510

**39 Sheep Shop** If you're into fleeces, "sheepy" gifts, and sweaters, this one's for you. ◆ M-Sa 10AM-6PM. 54 Neal St. 071/836.4094

**39 Plumline** For men's and women's shoes you won't find anywhere else, Plumline is a real treasure. The merchandise is classy. ◆ M-Tu 10AM-6PM; W-Sa 10AM-6:30PM; Su noon-5PM. 55 Neal St. 071/379.7856

**39 The Hat Shop** As the name indicates, this is a brilliant place to buy hats: everything from flying hats to straw boaters. ◆ M-Th 10AM-6PM; F 10AM-7PM; Sa 10:30AM-6PM. 58 Neal St. 071/836.6718

**39 S. Fisher** Here's a menswear shop packed with traditional English clothes like Aran sweaters and cashmere jackets at competitive prices. ◆ M-Sa 10:30AM-7PM. 72 Neal St. 071/836.2576

**39 Equinox** Astrology has gotten big in London since the start of the recession. Although this is a very "straight-looking" shop, quasi-scientific horoscopes can be prepared while you wait in trepidation, or you can rummage among the astrology books, cassettes, videos, and prints. ◆ M-Sa 9AM-7PM; Su 10AM-6PM. 78 Neal St. 071/749.1001; fax 071/497.0344

**40 Arthur Beale** Yacht chandler **Arthur Beale** could trace his origins back to a company of ropemakers on the Fleet River at the start of the 16th century. Dream of the sea, as you look at the bright-yellow macs and boots. ◆ M-F 9AM-6PM; Sa 9:30AM-1PM. 194 Shaftesbury Ave. 071/836.9034

**41 Mysteries** New Agers and the wholly holistic dip in to buy their crystals, books, a new tarot pack, or to get in touch with the future—resident clairvoyants, palmists, and crystal ball gazers are happy to help, of course. ◆ M-Sa 10AM-6PM. 9 Monmouth St. 071/240.3688

**42 Mon Plaisir** ★★$$ An authentic bistro and pre-theater haunt, Mon Plaisir presents good food and service to match. Garlic-laden frogs' legs, coq au vin, and escargots all star on the menu, along with vegetarian options. ♦ French ♦ Lunch and dinner; dinner only on Saturday. Closed Sunday. 21 Monmouth St. 071/836.7243; fax 071/379.0121

**42 Monmouth Coffee House** Taste the delicious freshly ground coffee here, and then buy some to take home with you. Monmouth keeps a limited range of top-quality coffees like Colombian Medellin, Kenyan, and Papua New Guinea mild. ♦ M-Sa 9AM-6:30PM; Su 11AM-5PM. 27 Monmouth St. 071/836.5272

**42 Natural Leather** Bags, blousons, biker jackets, and leather accessories fill this shop to overflowing. Watch out for the pigskin rucksacks. ♦ M-Sa 11AM-7PM; Su noon-6PM. 33 Monmouth St. 071/240.7748

**43 Mountbatten** $$$$ Theater lovers flock to this hotel, named after **Lord Louis Mountbatten** of Burma, the much-beloved uncle of **Prince Charles.** The Edwardian-style hotel could almost be Broadlands, the family seat, it's so full of Mountbatten's memorabilia, comfy sofas, chandeliers, and marble. ♦ 20 Monmouth St, Seven Dials. 071/836.4300; fax 071/240.3540

**44 Seven Dials** A tall column stood in the center of this junction of seven streets, and each of the column's seven faces contained a sundial—hence the name. The area was once a notorious thieves' quarter—**Dickens** described it in *Sketches by Boz,* published in 1834—and when word got out that the column was built by **Thomas Neale,** Master of the Mint (where British coins are struck), a legend grew that treasure was buried at the bottom of the column. It was actually dug up in 1773, but nothing was there. The pillar went to Weybridge in Surrey, and it took until 1989 for some locals to band together to pay for a new Seven Dials to go in its place. ♦ Intersection of Monmouth and Mercer Sts, and Earlham St and Short Gardens

**45 Dar & Dar** While not exactly of the porno ilk, the designer leather and rubber gear sold here is definitely on the pop-star side of daring. ♦ M-Sa 11AM-7PM. 53 Monmouth St. 071/240.7577

**46 St. Martin's Lane** Furniture builder **Thomas Chippendale** once lived here, but that didn't stop the city from knocking down the buildings to make way for **Trafalgar Square.** Unfortunately, they didn't renumber the street, so it starts at No. 29!

**46 Beotys** ★★$$ An old Covent Garden favorite and one of the oldest Greek restaurants in town (it opened the year World War II ended), Beotys is known for its charming, competent waiters, delicious

*dolmas,* and succulent lamb. Stick to the Greek-Cypriot side of the menu, and delicious food will be yours. ♦ Greek ♦ Lunch and dinner. Closed Sunday. 79 St. Martin's Ln. 071/836.8768

**47 The Photographer's Gallery** This is probably the best gallery for photographic art in London, usually running two or three exhibitions by international photographers at a time. ♦ Tu-Sa 11AM-7PM. 5-8 Great Newport St. 071/831.1772

**48 New Shu Shan Divine** ★★$$ You'll like this place if you're a fan of Pekinese or hot Szechuan cooking. The fish in black-bean sauce is definitely worth trying, or, for hotpot lovers, sample the stewed crab with bean vermicelli casserole. ♦ Chinese ♦ Lunch and dinner. 36 Cranbourn St. 071/836.7501

**49 Sheekeys** ★★★$$$ This is another of London's oldest and best-loved seafood restaurants, tucked away on St. Martin's Cou alongside Wyndham's and Albery theaters. Immaculate lobster, potted shrimps, flambée scallops, Dover sole—you name it, they serve it, and even the humble fish cake tastes dreamlike here. Have a dozen oysters with a bottle of house wine or a full meal at the long oyster bar. Pre-theater dinners and set lunches offer the best value. ♦ Seafood ♦ Lunch and dinner; dinner only on Saturday. Closed Sunday. 28-32 St. Martin's Ct. 071/240.2565; fax 071/491.2477

**50 Giovanni's** ★★$$$ Pictures of the West End stars who pop across after the show fill this good old-fashioned Italian restaurant. Giovanni has been here for years. ♦ Italian ♦ Lunch and dinner; dinner only on Saturday. 10 Goodwin's Ct, 55 St. Martin's Ln. 071/240.2877

**51 Coliseum** This 2,358-seat theater is home to the **English National Opera,** which sings only in English. It has a very splendid interior, complete with chariots, granite columns, and 20 boxes. The globe on top was designed to revolve, but an obscure legal ordinance deemed this illegal; the flashing lights on the globe are the next best thing. ♦ St. Martin's Ln. 071/836.3161. Credit card bookings: 071/240.5258

---

"Nearly all people in England are of the superior sort, superiority being an English ailment."

**D.H. Lawrence,** *The Last Laugh*

---

"Everyone likes flattery and when you come to royalty you should lay it on with a trowel."

**Benjamin Disraeli** to Matthew Arnold

---

Restaurants/Clubs: Red          Hotels: Blue
Shops/ 🌳 Outdoors: Green          Sights/Culture: Blac

**51 Cafe Pelican** ★★$$ A firm fixture as one of London's favorite Parisian-style bar/brasseries, the Pelican gets busy at lunchtime, so get there early. At the front they serve coffee, *croque monsieur,* baguettes, salads, and delicious *pommes frites.* At the back in the restaurant it's less crowded, so you can eat at a more leisurely pace. Try to stick to the brasserie menu or it gets expensive. ♦ French ♦ Lunch and dinner. 45 St. Martin's Ln. 071/379.0309

**52 Droopy & Browns** This dreamy wedding gown, party dress, and ball gown designer set up shop here with opera and ballet-goers in mind. As they leave the Coliseum opposite, next week's "first night outfit" beckons from the window displays. Lace, velvet, satin, and silk—all are available at a price. ♦ M-W 10:30AM-6:30PM; Th 10:30AM-7:30PM; F 10:30AM-7PM; Sa 9:30AM-5:30PM. 99 St. Martin's Ln. 071/379.4514

**53 Dance Books** This shop sells volumes, videos, CDs, cards, and pictures covering all aspects of dance and movement. ♦ M-Sa 11AM-7PM. 9 Cecil Ct, St. Martin's Ln. 071/836.2314; fax 071/497.0473

**53 David Drummond at Pleasures of Past Times** Showtime is captured forever in the books sold here, or you can buy printed Victoriana—the greeting cards are a real find. ♦ M-F 11AM-2:30PM, 3:30-5:45PM; any other time by arrangement. 11 Cecil Ct. 071/836.1142

**53 Bell, Book and Radmall** This shop is reserved for the dedicated bibliophile only. Expensive first editions reside in locked glass cabinets tended by a knowledgeable staff. ♦ M-F 10:30AM-5:30PM; Sa 10:30AM-4PM. 4 Cecil Ct. 071/240.2161

**53 Quinto and Francis Edwards Bookshop** Look at the glorious leather-bound first editions and antiquarian books here, or study the impressive collection of old military maps and prints. There's every kind of secondhand book, too. ♦ M-Sa 9AM-9PM; Su noon-8PM. 48a Charing Cross Rd. 071/379.7669

**53 Books of Charing Cross Road** It's a wonder the floors don't give way under the myriad ancient books crammed into every conceivable cranny. There's a super-cheap bargain basement where you'll pay pennies (40p!) for a book, and a vast selection on the ground floor, where you can wax lyrical over the poetry and history, or grow hot under the collar in the political section. ♦ Daily 10:30AM-9:30PM. 56 Charing Cross Rd. 071/836.3697; fax 071/240.1769

**53 Any Amount of Books** Here you'll find just what it says—this bookstore catches the overflow from nearby Books of Charing Cross Road. ♦ Daily 10:30AM-7:30PM. 62 Charing Cross Rd. 071/240.8140

**54 Shipley Specialist Art Booksellers** This specialist art bookseller is just up the road from the National Gallery and, as might be expected, they've got fine art books as well as titles on every kind of working art: graphics, design, fashion, architecture, photography, interior design, and furniture. ♦ M-Sa 10AM-6PM. 70 Charing Cross Rd. 071/836.4872

**54 Zwemmers** Picasso, Mondrian, Warhol, Gainsborough . . . this art historians' mecca sells the most fabulous, opulent art books; students at the nearby St. Martin's School can only wish and start saving. ♦ M-Tu, Th-F 9:30AM-6PM; W, Sa 10AM-6PM. 26 Litchfield St. 071/379.7886

**55 The Ivy** ★★★$$ There's so much art—mirrors, wood panels, stained glass, and diamond lattice windows—in this utterly trendy, upmarket brasserie, which was designed with designers in mind, that you half expect your scallops with shiitake mushrooms to be served by a trainee architect. The Ivy is sister to **Le Caprice,** which explains why the food is as good as the decor. ♦ Modern British ♦ Lunch and dinner. 1 West St. 071/836.4751; fax 071/493.9040

Mark Twain on family hotels: "They are a London specialty. God has not permitted them to exist elsewhere. The once spacious rooms are split into coops which afford as much discomfort as can be had anywhere out of jail for any money. All the modern inconveniences are furnished, and some that have been obsolete for a century. The prices are astonishingly high for what you get. . . . The rooms are as interesting as the Tower of London, but older I think. Older and dearer. The lift was a gift from William the Conqueror, some of the beds are prehistoric. They represent geologic periods. Mine is the oldest."

**56 St. Martin's** Agatha Christie's *The Mousetrap*, the world's longest-running play ever, transferred here from the nearby Ambassador in 1974. The play premiered in 1952 and, since everyone who sees it is sworn to secrecy, the whodunit factor has never been revealed. There's a minimum six-week waiting list for this one, and "no reduced prices at any time from any source," but it's well worth it, and is a popular show with families. The theater seats 250. ◆ West St, Cambridge Circus (at St. Martin's Ln). Box office/credit card bookings: 071/836.1443

**57 No. 84 Charing Cross Road** When **Helene Hanff** began writing letters here in 1945, it was the site of **Marks & Co.'s** bookshop. When the letters became a film, the bookshop disappeared!

**58 Murder One** Budding super sleuths will have a field day in this bookshop, with its volumes of mysteries and all sorts of crime fiction. If you're looking for tips from the great detectives, you can also find **Sherlock Holmes** and **Agathie Christie** lurking among the shelves. ◆ M-W 10AM-7PM; Th-Sa 10AM-8PM. 71-73 Charing Cross Rd. 071/734.3483

**58 Foyles** Walt Disney and George Bernard Shaw were just two of the illustrious customers of this British institution. It's chaotic and crammed from floor to ceiling with books, but they can be as hard to find as a knowledgeable assistant. Don't knock it, though, as the British defend this oddity to the hilt. ◆ M-Sa 9AM-6PM. 119 Charing Cross Rd. 071/437.5660

**58 Waterstones** This chain store is eminently refined and sensible—in other words, it's packed with all the latest books, *and* they're easy to find. ◆ M-Sa 9:30AM-8PM; Su noon-7PM. 121-129 Charing Cross Rd. 071/434.4291

**59 Break for the Border** ★$ If you suddenly long for some guacamole or chili, this is the place. It's loud, young, and packed. ◆ Mexican ◆ Dinner. 5 Goslett Yard, Charing Cross Rd. 071/437.8595

**60 Soho Square** Begun in 1677 in honor of **Charles II**—that's his statue in the center—Soho Square was one of the first squares laid out in London. The Elizabethan hut in the middle is actually a folly tool shed built in 1870. Look out for **Paul McCartney,** who occasionally visits his offices in the square.

# Viewing London from Aloft

Given its many facets, London should be viewed from all angles, including from on high. Only by rising above street-level can you grasp a broad perspective of this vast and sprawling metropolis. Sadly, two of the best vantage points, **Canary Wharf** and the **National Westminster Towers,** are no longer open to the public. That said, there are still several breathtaking panoramas from which to choose, among them:

**Kenwood House** The beautiful landscaped gardens of this 17th-century house offer 180-degree panoramic views of London. A driveway leads to the house and grounds. ◆ Free. Daily 10AM-6PM Apr-Sept; daily 10AM-4PM Oct-Mar. Hampstead Ln. 081/348.1286

**The Monument** The stone column built by **Sir Christopher Wren** between 1671-77 to commemorate the **Great Fire of London** in 1666 is 202 feet high and 202 feet west of the baker's shop on Pudding Lane where the fire started. The steep spiral staircase with 311 steps (there are no elevators) offers stunning views of the City. ◆ Admission. M-Sa 9AM-5:40PM Apr-Sept; Su 2-6PM May-Sept; M-Sa 9AM-3:40PM Oct-Mar. Monument St. 071/626.2717

**Primrose Hill** The top of this north London summit—where, incidentally, not one primrose is to be seen—rises roughly 219 feet in the air, and affords fine views across Regent's Park to the south, as well as (on a clear day) central London. Wear comfortable shoes for the climb to the top.

**Royal Observatory** In **Greenwich Park,** the Royal Observatory looks over the Thames to London's east end and the Isle of the Dogs, with the National Maritime Museum and 17th-century Queen's House in the foreground. You'll have to climb some stairs, as there isn't an elevator. Unbeatable. ◆ Admission. M-Sa 10AM-5PM, Su 5PM Nov-Mar; M-Sa 10AM-6PM, Su noon-6PM Apr-Oct. Greenwich Park. 081/858.4422

**St. Paul's Cathedral** Be prepared to trudge up 560 steps (there are no elevators) to reach this 280-foot-high vantage point. The reward is a 360-degree vista from the **Golden Gallery** at the apex of the dome. ◆ Admission. M-Sa 8:30AM-4:15PM. 071/248.2705

**Tower Bridge** Fabulous views over the Tower of London and of river life on the Thames. Ascend by the **North Tower** and traverse the river in an enclosed 140-foot-high walkway before descending by the **South Tower.** Elevators to the covered walkway are available if you're not up for the hike. ◆ Admission. Daily 10AM-5:45PM Apr-Oct; daily 10AM-4PM Oct-Apr. Tower Bridge. 071/403.3761; fax 071/357.7935

**Westminster Cathedral** The 352-and-a-half-foot-high **St. Edwards Tower** allows a general 360-degree panorama over London. You might want to call ahead, as the elevator isn't always in working order. ◆ Admission. Daily 6:30AM-7PM winter; daily 6:30AM-8PM summer. Ashley Pl. 071/834.7452

**61 The Gay Hussar** ★★$$ Famous for its old-fashioned, discreet service, The Gay Hussar is a bastion of Hungarian food; try the Transylvanian stuffed cabbage, veal goulash, or the chicken *paprikash*. Well-known politicians dive in here to gossip in private. ♦ East European ♦ Lunch and dinner. Closed Sunday. 2 Greek St. Reservations required. 071/437.0973

**61 Au Jardin des Gourmets** ★★$$$ This haven of traditional French cooking now has a *salle á manger* (brasserie) on the ground floor that offers a good set lunch. In both it and the main restaurant, you can sample the best of French cooking, with dishes such as a confit of duck on Puy lentils, and lamb with tarragon sauce. The excellent wine list includes delicious older clarets. ♦ French ♦ Brasserie/Restaurant: lunch and dinner; dinner only on Saturday. Closed Sunday. 5 Greek St. Reservations required. 071/437.1816; fax 071/437.0043

**62 L'Escargot** ★★$$ London's adland comes to this Soho institution to gossip in public, and be overheard. After a rough time in the past few years, L'Escargot is now in the capable hands of chefs **David Cavalier** and **Garry Hollihead.** You can order snails or sole Veronique in the brasserie downstairs, and a different but equally French selection in the more expensive dining room upstairs. ♦ French ♦ Brasserie/Restaurant: lunch and dinner; dinner only on Saturday. Closed Sunday. 48 Greek St. Reservations recommended. 071/437.2679

**63 Ming** ★★$$ Pekinese recipes inspired by the Ming dynasty are the specialty in this pale-blue restaurant. Try the eggplant and duck hotpot or the Hong Kong-style king prawns in cheese sauce. For lunch, there's fresh carp, eel, and lobster. ♦ Chinese ♦ Lunch and dinner. Closed Sunday. 35 Greek St. 071/734.2721

**64 Il Pollo** ★$ Cheap, filling food and fast service are the hallmarks of Il Pollo, a haven for students and budget diners. ♦ Italian ♦ Lunch and dinner. Closed Sunday. 20 Old Compton St. 071/734.5917

---

Another street created as part of the massive slum clearance in Victoria's day, Charing Cross Road has been known for its antiquarian and secondhand bookshops for nearly a century. Dedicated bibliophiles may peruse the quaint pedestrian walkway of Cecil Court and Bertram Rota in Covent Garden during the workweek, only; these old-fashioned antiquarian stores don't open to the sticky hands of the hoi polloi on weekends.

---

"Courtesy is not dead; it has merely taken refuge in Great Britain."

**Georges Dunhamel**

**65 Coach & Horses** Most of Soho's pubs are hot, smoky, and cozy, but have nothing much to distinguish them from one another. This one has cartoons all over the walls, London's rudest landlord, and lots of drunken journalists; the satirical magazine *Private Eye* holds regular lunches here. Last but not least, **Jeffrey Barnard** (who had a West End play written about him) is a regular. ♦ Pub ♦ M-Sa 11AM-11PM; Su noon-3PM, 7-10:30PM. 29 Greek St. 071/437.5920

**65 Maison Bertaux** Don't be fooled by the spartan surroundings: Maison Bertaux has been here since 1871, and even when the ovens weren't working well (for about five years), it still turned out the lightest croissants in town. Only fresh butter and cream are used, so cholesterol counters should avoid the scrumptious French cream cakes and meringues. All patisserie is baked on the premises by **Michael Young,** who has been with Bertaux for about 20 years. ♦ Daily 9AM-8PM. 28 Greek St. 071/437.6007

**66 Kettners** ★$$ Once **Oscar Wilde's** favorite club, it then became **Frank Sinatra's.** The dining rooms and piano bar are beautifully decorated, but the fare is fairly standard: pizzas, burgers, and salads. Don't let them put you upstairs unless you want cold food. Young, glittery advertising types froth and flutter in the champagne bar here, swallowing copious quantities of champagne cocktails. This room gets unbearable at lunchtime and from 6:30-7:30PM. ♦ Pizzeria ♦ Restaurant: lunch and dinner. Champagne bar: M-F noon-3PM; 5:30-11PM; Sa 5:30-11PM. 29 Romilly St. 071/437.6437

**67 Shaftesbury Avenue** Named after the beloved and loving **Seventh Earl of Shaftesbury,** whose Eros memorial stands at the bottom on Piccadilly Circus, this avenue opened up in 1886, and instantly became home to a host of London theaters; many are still here. For a British playwright to get a play "in the West End" is considered the pinnacle of success. Just walk down Shaftesbury Avenue at dusk when the hoardings light up and you'll feel the magic draw you in. There's just one intrusion of the modern age: the **Cannon** cinema in a modern block right in the middle.

**67 Ed's Easy Diner** ★★$ This is the perfect '50s retro-diner, with good, genuine American-style diner fare, including decent doughnuts. It's the place to be seen eating fast food and what's more, it's very good. ♦ American ♦ Lunch and dinner; breakfast also on Saturday and Sunday. 12 Moor St. 071/439.1955. Also at: 362 King's Rd. 071/352.1956

**67 The Palace Theatre** Located at Cambridge Circus, the Palace is indeed a palace of a theater, designed as it was by **Collcutt and**

**Holloway** in 1891 as the home of the **Royal English Opera.** This is where **Sarah Bernhardt** played *Cleopatra,* and where **Pavlova** made her London debut in 1910. In recent years, the 1,480-seat Palace has hosted mega-hits such as *Les Misérables.* It is now owned by **Andrew Lloyd Webber.** ♦ Shaftesbury Ave (at Charing Cross Rd). Box office/credit card bookings: 071/434.0909

**68 Cork & Bottle** ★★$ Central London's slightly sleazy Leicester Square area hasn't stopped lots of Londoners from frequenting this basement haunt. The food is simple, good, and plentiful. Try a wedge of the raised ham and cheese pie with a glass of New World or French wine. ♦ Wine bar ♦ Lunch and dinner. 44-46 Cranbourn St. 071/734.7807

**69 Man Fu Kung** ★★$$ This huge establishment claims to be the largest of London's Chinese restaurants. Dim sum snacks are wheeled around until 6PM, when the full menu and matching prices suddenly appear. Try the chicken thighs wrapped in bean curd. ♦ Chinese ♦ Lunch and dinner. 29-30 Leicester Sq. 071/839.2957

**70 Poon's** ★★$$ Wind-dried ducks, sausages, and bacon hang from the window. This restaurant is cheap, clean, attractive, and packed with a loyal following. ♦ Chinese ♦ Lunch and dinner. Closed Sunday. 4 Leicester St. 071/437.1528

**71 Jade Garden** ★★$$$ This is an elegant mirrored restaurant with a wide range of stir-fried, steamed, and roasted dishes served in clay pots. At lunchtime, try dim sum (perhaps paper-wrapped king prawns or steamed beef and ginger dumplings). At night, go for the mixed seafood noodles with squid and giant prawns. ♦ Chinese ♦ Lunch and dinner. 15 Wardour St. 071/437.5065

**71 Chuen Cheng-Ku** ★★$$ It seats 400 but it still gets crowded. Opt for dim sum at lunch, or try the lemon-sauced roast duck in the evening. ♦ Chinese ♦ Lunch and dinner. 17 Wardour St. 071/734.3281

**72 Dragon's Nest** ★★$$ Beware: the chefs here do jellyfish with shredded duck and tripe with preserved vegetables. Apart from that, there are conventional Chinese yummies on the menu. ♦ Chinese ♦ Lunch and dinner. 58-60 Shaftesbury Ave. 071/437.3119

**73 Wong Kei** ★$$ The rudest waiters in London await you here. The food is okay, but the restaurant is packed because it's so cheap. Offer a check or, even worse, credit cards, and they get very angry indeed. ♦ Chinese ♦ Lunch and dinner. 41-43 Wardour St. 071/437.6833

**74 China** ★$ While it's a shabby cafe, China offers those giant bowls of noodle soup that hungry Chinese people tuck into while the uninitiated wonder what they're eating. Ask

for *choi sum* to go with it. No one drinks or smokes here, and there are plenty of good snacks. ♦ Chinese ♦ Lunch and dinner. 3 Gerrard St. 071/439.7511

**75 Mr. Kong** ★★$$ A foodie's Chinese restaurant crushed into three little floors, Mr. Kong offers innovative food combinations. Bu it's the more usual fare, such as chow mein, that brings in the crowds. The noodles are sti fried to perfection, enhancing the delicacy of the flavor. ♦ Chinese ♦ Lunch and dinner. 21 Lisle St. 071/437.7341

**75 Fung Shing** ★★$$ Avoid the set meals and go for a delicious chicken with preserved clams on the specials section of the menu, or try a hotpot. It's a big menu, but half the fun is reading it in a comfortable restaurant. ♦ Chinese ♦ Lunch and dinner. 15 Lisle St. 071/437.1539

**76 New World** ★★$ Like Man Fu Kung, this Chinese restaurant stakes a claim as London largest, with the same quality and slightly lower prices. Dim sum is the specialty. ♦ Chinese ♦ Lunch and dinner. 1 Gerrard Pl. 071/734.0677

**77 Dean Street** Mozart's father advertised his child prodigy here in 1763; he asked the publi to test his son's ability to sight read. The seven-year-old boy and his four-year-old sister gave a performance at **No. 21** (then it was **Caldwell's Assembly Rooms;** now it's the **Ben Uri Art Gallery**). **Karl Marx** lived at **No. 28,** above what is now **Leoni's Quo Vadis** you may ask at the restaurant, or call 071/437.4809 to see the two rooms Marx called home.

**78 The French House** This pub was known affectionately as "The French" until *le patron,* Gaston, renamed it the French House, at whic point all the regulars (or cognoscenti) started calling it the York Minster (just to tease the landlord). It was the official headquarters of t Free French in World War II, and the decor hasn't changed since then. There are still signed photos of famous French people on th walls. M. Gaston, the landlord, who retired in 1989, had a policy of serving beer in half-pint measures only. Dirty, dingy, and sleazy, this bar is, needless to say, packed to the gills wit aging Soho reprobates and trendy young poseurs. ♦ Pub ♦ M-Sa noon-11PM; Su noor 3PM, 7-10:30PM. 49 Dean St. 071/437.2799

Within The French House:

**French House Dining Room** ★$$ Situate over a traditional Soho pub, the French House Dining Room serves a mixture of traditional and contemporary British food, including stuffed quail with mashed celeriac. It's a tiny room with a jolly atmosphere, so be sure to book. ♦ British ♦ Lunch and dinner; lunch on on Sunday. 49 Dean St. 071/437.2477; fax 071/287.9109

**78 Amalfi** ★$ It still has Chianti bottles hanging from the ceiling and does a good plate of spaghetti (by London standards) with salad for a reasonable price. Have a full meal or go to the patisserie for Italian coffee and delicious cakes. ♦ Italian ♦ Restaurant: lunch and dinner. Patisserie: breakfast, lunch, and dinner. 29-31 Old Compton St. 071/437.7284

**79 Le Bistingo** ★★$$ You'll find a country-rustic look and solid portions of French food in this restaurant, so don't worry: there is no nouvelle cooking here. ♦ French ♦ Lunch and dinner; dinner only on Sunday. 57-59 Old Compton St. 071/437.0784

**80 Algerian Coffee Stores** One hundred years old in 1983, this shop doesn't seem to have changed at all, apart from the funny, newfangled coffee makers in the window—try a rich house blend like Gourmet Noir. Interestingly, flavored teas and tisanes outnumber coffees by 130 to 30. ♦ M-Sa 9AM-7PM. 52 Old Compton St. 071/437.2480

**80 A. Moroni & Son** Homesick? Then dive into this 100-year-old shop for a copy of your favorite read—it's bound to be here. But make it fast: A. Moroni won't allow browsers because all of the stock leaves very little room. If you can, make up your mind before you go in. ♦ M-Sa 7:30AM-7:15PM. 68 Old Compton St. 071/437.2847

**81 The Vintage House** This is a tippler's delight: an enormous range of more than 180 whiskies—there's even a single malt, the Spring Bank, that costs £6900. You'll also find a tremendous variety of wines, 800 miniatures, and a full range of Havana cigars. ♦ M-Sa 9AM-11PM; Su noon-2PM, 7-10PM. 42 Old Compton St. 071/437.2592

**81 Patisserie Valerie** It's fabulous, fattening, and full of Soho wannabes and cussing regulars squashed for space—they all come for the cakes. Try the chocolate-truffle cake, but be prepared: there is never a time, day or night, when this pastry shop isn't packed. ♦ M-F 8AM-8PM; Sa 8AM-7PM; Su 10AM-6PM. 44 Old Compton St. 071/437.3466

---

"For 57 nights without let-up, the Luftwaffe attack continued. Every night during that September and October bombers flew over, at least 200 strong. London was caught off-balance. Defense was impossible, devastation enormous. The death toll: 9,500. By this, the first mass civilian attack in history, the Germans hoped to force a surrender. It failed."

*London: 2000 Years of a City and its People*
by Felix **Barker** and Peter **Jackson**

---

staurants/Clubs: Red    Hotels: Blue
ops/ 🌳 **Outdoors**: Green    **Sights/Culture**: Black

**82 Frith Street** On another trip in the 1760s, **Mozart's** papa took rooms here at **No. 20.** Later, in 1926, **John Logie Baird** brought the street into the 20th century when he gave the first public demonstration of TV at **No. 22;** the equipment is now in the Science Museum.

**83 Ronnie Scott's** This is *the* place to go for jazz/contemporary music fans in the know, as it's one of the best-known venues in the world. **Sarah Vaughan, George Melly,** and **Maynard Ferguson** are just some of the names who have played here, not to mention the legendary **Ronnie Scott** himself. It's a good place to kick back, relax, and occasionally enjoy a meal while you listen to the rhythm, though eating is not compulsory. Membership brings reductions in door fees. ♦ M-Sa to 3AM; starting times vary. 47 Frith Street. 071/439.0747

**84 Chiang Mai** ★★$$$ This black-and-white trend-setting restaurant is a stylish place to eat delicious Thai cuisine. Try the hot-and-sour seafood salad in chili sauce. ♦ Thai ♦ Lunch and dinner. 48 Frith St. 071/437.7444

**84 Alastair Little** ★★★$$$ Another haunt of London foodies, Alastair Little is a restaurant where people go for serious eating. The decor is stark and minimalist, but there's an ever-changing modern Continental menu, featuring such entrées as grilled tuna with tomato sauce, or risotto with morels, and a good selection of wines. As you tuck into your bouillabaisse, try the Pouilly Fumé. ♦ Continental ♦ Lunch and dinner; dinner only on Saturday. Closed Sunday. 49 Frith St. 071/734.5183

**84 Gopal's of Soho** ★★★$$ Chef **Pittal** (nicknamed **Gopal**) worked at the best Indian restaurants before opening his own place five years ago. The resulting delicately spiced dishes are among the best in the West End. Try the curry, the fish in coconut curry, the chicken *jalfrezi,* or the delectable king prawns with spring onions. The wine list is also good. ♦ Indian ♦ Lunch and dinner. 12 Bateman St. 071/434.0840

**85 Kaya Korean** ★$$$ In this highest of high-class Korean restaurants, a friendly staff guides you through one of the more exotic menus in London. The food—spicy soups, marinated and barbecued meats—is tasty, but it's hard to justify the extortionate prices. ♦ Korean ♦ Lunch and dinner; dinner only on Sunday. 22-25 Dean St. 071/437.6630

**86 The Red Fort** ★★★$$$ Named after the red sandstone fort built by **Emperor Shah Jahan,** the cooking, by chef **Manjit Gill,** is definitely fit for the Moghuls. They will tandoori anything in the swankest surroundings. ♦ Indian ♦ Lunch and dinner. 77 Dean St. 071/437.2525; fax 071/434.0721

**87 Berwick Street Market** Lots of cheap fruits and vegetables are on sale in this traditional London street market. Herbs are sold lower down, on Rupert Street. There's been a market here since the 1700s as well as a Blue Posts pub. ♦ M-Sa 9AM-3:30PM

**87 Fratelli Camisa and Lina Stores** Soho's Italian delis go on forever, selling delicious fresh pasta, hundreds of cheeses, and *panettone*. Salamis hang from the ceilings, while breads are stacked in baskets on the floor. ♦ Fratelli Camisa: M-Sa 9AM-6PM. 071/437.7120. Lina Stores: M-F 8AM-6PM; Sa 8AM-5PM. 18 Brewer St. 071/437.6482

**88 Melati** ★★★$ Cheap and cheerful (the weekend lines are full of people who are long on fine food but short on cash), this restaurant offers Malaysian and Indonesian cuisine. Try the *ayam percik* (grilled chicken in spicy coconut sauce) or the excellent *tahu goreng* (fried bean curd and vegetables covered in peanut sauce). You can book, but you'll probably still wait. Warning: do *not* confuse this Melati with the one on Peter Street; they're no relation, and the latter is awful. ♦ Asian ♦ Lunch and dinner. 21 Great Windmill St. 071/437.2745

**89 Just Games** For a variety of old favorites, including Scrabble or chess, plus the largest selection of imported European games outside the Continent, visit this shop. It's more suitable for older children and teenagers. ♦ M-Sa 10AM-6PM. 71 Brewer St. 071/734.6124; fax 071/437.4541

**90 Beau Monde** Women's "power gear" (emphasis on the shoulder pads, please) shares shelf space with made-to-measure shirts in this tiny shop. ♦ M-W, F 10:30AM-6:30PM; Th 10:30AM-7PM; Sa 10:30AM-6PM. 43 Lexington St. 071/734.6563

**90 Andrew Edmunds** ★$ This wine bar/restaurant is a homey little place with a friendly staff serving hearty soups, casseroles, and *tiramisù*. Beware, it's hard to get a seat at lunch. ♦ British ♦ Lunch and dinner. 46 Lexington St. 071/437.5708

**91 Ben de Lisi** New York tries to wow impoverished Londoners in the shape of fashion designer **Ben de Lisi**, who displays his low-key European clothing here with an American twist. ♦ By appointment only. 6A Poland St. 071/734.0089

**92 The John Snow** In 1854, Londoners were dropping like flies from cholera until **Dr. John Snow** figured out that the bacteria was carried by water. The water pump he turned off, thereby saving countless lives, was near the site of this pub. There's a giant model of a steam train named after the good doctor and all sorts of memorabilia in the rather shabby pub. ♦ M-F 11AM-11PM; Sa-Su noon-2:30PM. 39 Broadwick St. 071/437.1344

**93 Contemporary Ceramics** This stunning shop has been doing a brisk trade in Soho since 1960, selling the pottery and ceramics created by members of the **Craft Potters Association.** Throw out your ideas of quaint, cottagey, chunky pottery; what's on sale here is exquisite and infinitely collectible. ♦ M-W, F-Sa 10AM-5:30PM; Th 10AM-7PM. William Blake House, 7 Marshall St. 071/437.7605

**93 Cranks** ★$ This branch of the 10-store-strong chain has vegetarian takeout and sit-down meals, and there's a shop for wholefoodies. ♦ Vegetarian ♦ Restaurant: breakfast, lunch, and dinner. Closed Sunday. Shop: M-F 8:30AM-6:30PM; Sa 9:30AM-5:30PM. 8 Marshall St. 071/437.9431

**94 Carnaby Street** For a flashback, walk dow this street—one of the centers of modern fashion during the '60s. Carnaby Street attracted scores of hippies with its shops full flared jeans and psychedelic patterns, and personalities such as **The Beatles** and **Mary Quant.** Sadly, the Carnaby Street of 30 years ago no longer exists; today, it's laden with shops selling tourist kitsch and horribly expensive leather goods. Still, take a stroll he for nostalgia's sake. ♦ Between Foubert's Pl and Beak St

**95 Phood** ★$ Phood provides sandwiches and light snacks for the peckish on the move, but you've got the time and/or appetite, opt for th crispy duck with plum sauce or the noisette of lamb with spinach at the restaurant. ♦ International ♦ Breakfast, lunch, and dinner. Closed Sunday. 29-31 Fouberts Pl. 071/494.4192

**96 London Palladium** On Sunday nights duri the '50s and '60s, most people in Britain tune their radios in to "Sunday Night at the Londo Palladium," broadcast from this luxurious 1910 music hall, able to seat 2,325. This remains the home of great variety shows suc as the **Royal Variety Performance,** though a the moment it's *Joseph and the Amazing Technicolor Dreamcoat.* ♦ Argyll St (betweer Oxford Circus and Great Marlborough St). B office/credit card bookings: 071/494.5020

**97 The Copper Chimney** ★★$$$ The food is somewhat expensive and the interior is cavernous to an extreme, but all those Indiar families you see eating here can't be wrong. Dishes like *dhal majhani*—dark lentils with cumin and saffron-flavored rice—are both delicious and beautifully presented; no wond service always comes with a smile. The set dinner provides a range of dishes and is a go value. ♦ Indian ♦ Lunch and dinner. 13 Hedd St. 071/439.2004 ests

## rol Gould
evision/Film Producer

nch at **L'Escargot** on Greek Street, Soho, where dine in a heavenly room surrounded by stars, and get chocolate snails with your coffee.

ner at **Simpson's on the Strand,** where the waiter eels the large cut of meat to your table.

thing at **Le Gavroche** on Upper Brook Street—*the* te cuisine of London.

ma Minsky's Buffet at the Hilton, St. John's Wood.

mple every flavor of religion in one square mile at famous **Mosque** in Regent's Park, the gorgeous eral Jewish Synagogue opposite Lord's Cricket und, the **Church of Our Lady** on Lisson Grove, **St. rk's Hamilton Terrace** (**Alan Bates** is known to quent it), the **St. John's Wood Roundabout** rch, plus orthodox Judaism with the Chief Rabbi reat Britain on Abbey Road.

international **Doll's House and Miniatures Fair** ord's Cricket Ground, which takes place every vember.

ultimate in Britishness—**Lord's Cricket Ground** a weekday in June, when men who are usually sible sit from dawn until dusk in suits and ties, king hot tea from a thermos in the blazing sun (or ally rain) watching cricketers more overweight n the **Philadelphia Phillies** playing with red balls.

vent Garden Market any day. The **Houses of rliament** and **Westminster Hall,** where **Henry VIII** aid to have played tennis. It is said 400-year-old s have been known to fall from the rafters. tching the **House of Commons** from the Public lery when they are in session.

pping on **Bond Street, Brompton Road,** and **High eet,** St. John's Wood—and stopping at any nch of **Richoux** for exquisite pastries and superb vice, where bevies of ancient, demanding nese ladies gather to torment daintily aproned tresses.

oping the Colour in mid-June. **Speakers' Corner** yde Park, off Park Lane, on a Sunday. mbledon tennis if you don't mind queueing for rs in the traditional June rain.

## bin Simon
tor, *Apollo* (an international arts magazine)

rdon's Wine Bar, Villiers Street—Licensed since Middle Ages, and feels it. It is not *wholly* ossible to find.

Old Watergate—Carved in the 17th century, it is w stranded 50 yards from the river (**Pepys** used it; house is in the adjoining street).

h Mass on Sundays at **All Saints Church,** rgaret Street—the only place to hear, say, zart's "Coronation Mass," superbly sung *within* context of full High Church ritual.

nsong at **Westminster Abbey.**

**Sir John Soane's Museum**—Just as **Sir John** left it in the early 19th century. Mad architecture, great paintings, and an unforgettable surprise.

**The Dove** at Hammersmith—Lovely old riverside pub, with Fuller's "London Pride" beer (it's brewed just downstream).

**Pizzeria Amalfi,** top of Southampton Row—Cheap, friendly, and simple, when visiting the British Museum (or Sir John Soane's Museum).

**The Law Courts,** the Strand—A secular cathedral infinitely more appealing than the Old Bailey.

**Lincoln's Inn**—"New Court" was built here in 1698.

**Abbott and Holder,** Museum Street—Easily the best, cheapest, and friendliest dealers in historic original drawings, prints, watercolors, and paintings. Your money back and a box of chocolates is the guarantee on everything.

The **Wilton Diptych** in the **National Gallery**—Early in the day, with coffee and a croissant in the brasserie. Then the rest of the National Gallery.

## Sunny Stout
Training and Marketing Consultant/Author

**Notting Hill,** my multicultural quarter of London, famous for its three-day **Carnival.** On Saturdays, **Portobello Road** is a mile-long antiques bazaar and flea market, with buskers and street performers. Favorite lunch places for buzzy atmosphere, light cuisine—**The Brasserie du Marché Aux Puces** (349 Portobello Road) and **192** (192 Kensington Park Road).

In the heart of London's Financial District, the futuristic **Lloyds of London Building** towers over **Leadenhall Market,** a bustling Dickensian arcade.

From **Buckingham Palace** (wonderful **Canalettos** at the small **Queen's Gallery**) take a short walk through leafy **Green Park** (passing imposing 18th-century **Spencer House,** which proves **Princess Diana** wasn't a commoner) to the **Royal Academy.**

Five minutes walk west: **Shepherd's Market,** a cobbled pedestrian quarter-island of calm in elegant Mayfair. For exquisite Lebanese *mezé,* the friendly **Al Hamra,** or the more elegant **Al Sultan.** For a classic film, slip round the corner to the **Curzon Cinema.**

End the day with a cocktail at the **Hilton's Roof Bar** on Park Lane—book a table by the window and watch the sun set over this amazing metropolis.

**Theatreland:** immediately south of **Shaftesbury Avenue** is **Chinatown;** north is **Soho**—not just the red light district, but cafes and delis. For Austro-Hungarian velvet and intimacy, the **Gay Hussar** on Greek Street, haunt of journalists and politicians. Later, world-class jazz at **Ronnie Scott's.**

Over the Thames, **The Royal National Theatre** is currently on a dazzling, artistic high. After, a savory meal at the National's **Ovations**—last time I spotted **Dustin Hoffman.**

# The Strand/Fleet Street

For the curious, the city lover, the history-minded, and the Dickensian-spirited, the treasures of **The Strand** and **Fleet Street** are many. This seamless thoroughfare that runs parallel to the River Thames has connected the center of government (the **City of Westminster**) to the center of finance (the **City of London**) for more than a thousand years and through 16 reigns. Fleet Street has fashioned a reputation for itself as London's journalistic hub. Despite the computer age, these areas all depend upon one another, and journalists, politicians, and financiers continue to keep the path well-trodden.

Gone, too, are the days when the mansions of wealthy bishops, surrounded by gardens that led down to the river's edge, lined the Strand. Gone too are the days of elegance, when magnificent hotels, sophisticated restaurants, and

glamorous theaters reflected in the glory of the newly opened **Charing Cross Station.** Although the Strand survived the Reformation, when aristocrats, not bishops, lived in the great houses, it failed to triumph over another type of reformation: the building in 1867 of the **Victoria Embankment,** which reclaimed land from the Thames (and removed its stench) but isolated the Strand from the river. Yet the revitalization of **Covent Garden** to the north and a thriving theater scene kept the many massive office blocks from dehumanizing this extraordinary thoroughfare, which continues to hum with media folk, shoppers, and tourists by day, and theater and restaurant patrons by night.

Fleet Street has changed as well. **William Caxton** printed the first book in English here, and England's first daily newspaper, *The Daily Consort,* was issued from **Ludgate Circus** around 1702. Most of the city's major newspapers have moved from their Fleet Street location; but despite changes of address, journalists continue to return to their old watering holes and gaze at the buildings they once occupied 24 hours a day, now home to stockbrokers and computers.

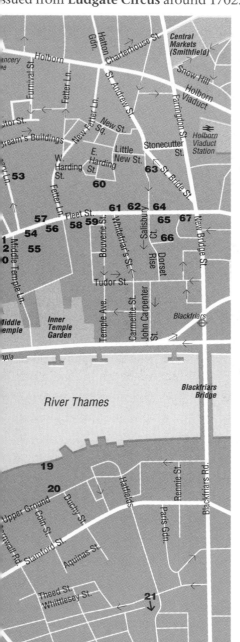

Those who stroll down the Strand and Fleet Street follow in the footsteps of an impressive list of walkers and talkers: **Sir Walter Raleigh, William Congreve, Richard Sheridan, Samuel Johnson, James Boswell, Samuel Coleridge, Charles Lamb, Henry Fielding, William Thackeray, Mark Twain,** and the omnipresent **Charles Dickens.** Along the way, stop for a port in London's oldest wine bar (**Gordon's**); have lunch in a 17th-century pub (**Ye Olde Cheshire Cheese**); peek in on the **Law Courts;** examine the building in which the first English dictionary was written (**Dr. Johnson's House**); buy tea from the shop that supplies the Queen (**Twinings**); visit the best Impressionist collection this side of Paris at the **Courtauld Institute;** catch a show in surroundings that helped make **Gilbert & Sullivan** famous (the **Savoy Theatre**); or attend a concert, play, or movie just across the river at Western Europe's largest arts complex (**South Bank Centre**), which also offers perhaps the best vantage point to gaze at the stretch of London that **Henry James** called "a tremendous chapter of accidents."

**1 Charing Cross Station** With the arrival of the railway at Charing Cross Station in 1863, the Strand became the busiest street in Europe, lined with enormous hotels, restaurants, and theaters built in the euphoria of the age. In the early 1990s, British Rail reconstructed the cobbled driveway to the station and rebuilt the exterior walls as they were originally, adorned with 21 cast-iron lanterns. In the station yard stands what is known as an **Eleanor Cross** (see **Charing Cross Monument** at the top right of this page), designed by **E.M. Barry.** Charing Cross is the mainline station closest to the heart of London—and one of the busiest. More than 110,000 people use the station each weekday, and if you're here in the morning during rush hour, you'll come face-to-face with nearly half of them. ♦ Strand (between Villiers and Caxton Sts). Tube: Charing Cross

**2 Charing Cross Hotel** $$$ The hotel, designed by **E.M. Barry** and built from 1863 to 1864, sits over the train tracks of **Charing Cross Station** and houses its waiting room. Railway hotels have a certain mystique, appealing to writers with vagabond souls and melancholy hearts. Trouble is, they always look better from the outside. Inside, you have to face hideous attempts at modernization, unmanageable legions of tour groups, and a tired, unhappy staff. The Charing Cross Hotel is no different, but it does have a few redeeming features: appealing Renaissance motifs on the facade, an old-fashioned and tranquil room on the first floor for morning coffee and afternoon tea, an immense staircase that the insensitive converters of this hotel have not yet managed to demolish, and one of the better carveries in town. ♦ Strand (between Villiers and Caxton Sts). Tube: Charing Cross. 071/839.7282; fax 071/839.3933

Within the Charing Cross Hotel:

### The Betjeman Craving Restaurant

★★$$ If you're traveling on a shoestring with a large family, this could be the answer to a few prayers: a set three-course meal including coffee, dessert, and service. The cafeteria-style service features all-you-can-eat helpings of roast beef, lamb, and pork, and though the vegetables tend to be overcooked and the desserts lacking in taste, the place is full of foreigners enjoying English roast beef. Children between the ages of five and 10 eat for half-price. ♦ British ♦ Lunch and dinner. Reservations recommended. 071/839.7282

**3 Coutt's Bank** The bank of the royal family, established in 1692, has occupied this site of **John Nash** buildings since 1904. In a daring and skillful act of restoration in 1979, **Sir Frederick Gibberd & Partners** created an ultramodern building behind Nash's neoclassical stucco facade and pepper-pot corner cupolas. ♦ 440 Strand

**4 Charing Cross Monument** In 1290, a sad and devoted **King Edward I** placed 12 **Eleanor Crosses** along the route of the funeral cortege of his beloved consort, **Queen Eleanor,** from the north of England near **Lincoln** to **Westminster Abbey.** The final stopping place was a few yards from here, where the statue of **Charles I** now stands looking down Whitehall. But the octagonal Eleanor Cross placed here was torn down by Puritans in 1647. The Charing Cross you see in the forecourt of **Charing Cross Station** was designed by **E.M. Barry** in 1865; it is a memorial, not a replica of the original Charing Cross. ♦ Strand and Whitehall. Tube: Charing Cross

**5 Craven Street** The street forms the western border of **Charing Cross Station,** with Villiers Street on the east, and reaches down to the Embankment. Its greatest claim to fame is that **Benjamin Franklin** lived at **No. 36** from 1757 to 1762 and then again from 1764 to 1772. Currently, an effort to open the house as a **Benjamin Franklin Museum** is nearing completion.

**6 Sherlock Holmes Pub** $ Stuffed to the gills with Sherlock Holmes memorabilia presented by the **Sherlock Holmes Society,** including the great detective's study, this pub is where the sleuth supposedly met his adversaries from the underworld. Although it seems to be a tourists' pub, it's frequented by local office workers who love the eccentricity of it all. ♦ Pub ♦ M-F 11AM-11PM. 10 Northumberland Ave. Tube: Charing Cross, Embankment. 071/930.2644

**7 Playhouse Theatre** In 1987, Londoners blinked in surprise when the Playhouse lit up again after 12 years of darkness. Founded by **Sefton Parry** in 1882, the theater's first production, **George Bernard Shaw's** *Arms and the Man,* was staged in 1894. Tragedy struck 11 years later, when part of **Charing Cross Station** collapsed on the theater, killing six people. Actress/manager **Gladys Cooper** ran the Playhouse until 1933, and it was taken over by the BBC as a radio sound studio from 1951 to 1975, with the **Beatles,** among others, broadcasting from here. Now owned by millionaire **Ray Cooney,** the 786-seat theater has established itself as home of the one-(wo)man show. The Playhouse has a restaurant as well, so you can buy a show ticket and book a meal at the same time, a boon to hungry theatergoers. ♦ Restaurant: dinner; late lunch also on Thursday and Saturday. Closed Sunday. Northumberland Ave and Northumberland St. Tube: Charing Cross, Embankment. 071/839.4401; fax 071/839.8142

---

**Restaurants/Clubs:** Red  **Hotels:** Blue
**Shops/** 🌳 **Outdoors:** Green  **Sights/Culture:** Black

**8 Sir Joseph Bazalgette Statue** It's sad that a man who had such a profound effect upon London and its people should be so totally forgotten, but such is the fate of the chief engineer, depicted in this statue by **George Simonds.** It was under Bazalgette that the solid granite Albert, Victoria, and Chelsea embankments were built between 1868 and 1874. The project reclaimed 32 acres of mud and cost a cool £1.55 million, but unlike most new developments, was welcomed. Bazalgette had an even more important role, however: he built London's original sewer system between 1858 and 1875, saving the citizens from utterly disgusting conditions, including an overpowering stench, regular sewage floods, and cholera epidemics. ◆ Embankment Pl (opposite Northumberland Ave). Tube: Embankment

**9 Villiers Street** Named for **George Villiers,** Duke of Buckingham (see also **Buckingham Street**), whose fabulous **York House** covered the street, Villiers Street has a feeling of the past, with flower, fruit, and newspaper sellers, and two special attractions: the **Players Theatre Club** and **Gordon's Wine Cellar.** Villiers was a clever opportunist, but not quite clever enough. A favorite of **James I** and his son **Charles I,** the Duke progressed from plain George Villiers to viscount, marquis, and, finally, Duke of Buckingham in less than 10 years. His ruthless behavior led to his assassination in 1628 and probably set the stage for Charles I's estrangement from Parliament and the Civil War—and the King's own execution. ◆ Embankment Pl and Strand

**10 Players Theatre Club** This was once the site of **Craven Passage,** immortalized in the **Flanagan and Allen** song "Underneath the Arches" and in **George Orwell's** *Down and Out in Paris and London.* The 300-seat Players Theatre was built in its place as part of the massive rebuilding program at Charing Cross. Visitors enjoy Victorian music hall entertainment at its best, with the same high-spirited sense of humor and fun that delighted audiences in the days before radio, television, and canned laughter. The club has two bars and a supper room, and drinks and snacks are served during the performances. How civilized! Above the station complex are pristine new offices and shops in the giant and appropriately tunnel-like glass and concrete landmark called **Embankment Place.** ◆ Dinner: Tu-Su 6PM-closing. Shows: Tu-Su 8PM. Craven Passage, Villiers St. Tube: Charing Cross, Embankment. 071/839.1134

**11 Gordon's Wine Cellar** ★★★$ Even though Gordon's looks every bit its 300 years, it feels very 1940s, like a film set of London during the War with dim vaults stretching back beneath the street. The bottles are stored behind a locked grill; the tables and chairs don't match; and the food is basic but good, laid out the way it must have always been, with homemade terrines, smoked hams, roasted birds, first-class English cheeses (Stilton, Red Windsor), and a large choice of fresh salads. Hot meals are served in winter. Sherries, ports, and Madeiras poured by the glass straight from the cask are impressive, as are the house wines. Once discovered, Gordon's could become your favorite London haunt, but be warned—it gets very crowded, so arrive early. ◆ British ◆ Lunch and dinner. Closed Saturday and Sunday. 47 Villiers St. 071/930.1408

**12 Embankment Underground Station** For the best route to **Hungerford Bridge,** walk into the station from Villiers Street, out the other side, turn right, and go up the flight of stairs to the bridge. ◆ Villiers St

**13 Hungerford Bridge** Built in 1863 by **John Hawkshaw,** this bridge replaced one by **Brunel** of the 1840s, and the current paint job makes it a handsome red tapestry of trussed iron across the Thames. The only bridge in central London for trains and people, it's a useful pedestrian walkway to the concert hall and theaters on the South Bank. Do pause on your way across to appreciate the stunning views toward the City and Waterloo Bridge. ◆ Embankment

**14 South Bank Centre** At the southern end of **Hungerford Bridge** lies the largest arts center in Western Europe. The South Bank Centre's massive concrete structures are much prettier than their **Barbican** counterpart in the City; the **Royal Festival Hall** is the first building you'll encounter. In addition to hosting performances by visiting musicians, singers, and the like, it's the permanent home of the **London Philharmonic Orchestra.** Inside the hall are a **Farringdons** record shop, the ever-wonderful **Waterstones** bookstore, the **RFH Shop** for musically related items, and the **Festival Buffet,** where you can eat lunch or have a drink to the strains of free music in the foyer.

The smaller **Queen Elizabeth Hall** and the **Purcell Room** are also housed within the center, as is the **Voicebox,** used mainly for literary events. The **Poetry Library** on level five offers free membership and access to more than 4,500 poetry books, so drop in and wax lyrical. ◆ Main buildings: daily 10AM-9PM. Poetry Library: daily 11AM-8PM. South Bank. Tube: Embankment, Waterloo. General information: 071/928.0639. Box office: 071/928.8800. Recorded information for standby tickets, from 10AM: 071/633.0932

**15 The Hayward Gallery** Located in its own separate concrete bunker, the Hayward usually hosts two art exhibitions. Also within are a permanent cafe and an art bookshop. ◆ During exhibitions: M, Th-Su 10AM-6PM; Tu-W 10AM-8PM. South Bank. 071/928.3144. Recorded information: 071/928.0177

# MUSEUM OF THE

# MOVING IMAGE

**16 Museum of the Moving Image (MOMI)**
Londoners rave about this museum, which
showcases everything from pre-cinema
experiments, European cinema, and cartoons
to the technical wizardry of a modern TV
studio. Visitors can be interviewed, fly across
the Thames, read the news, and see how
special effects are created, all with the help of
guides who are actors by trade. Even if you
arrive early, expect to stand in line to get in.
New acquisitions include a huge model of
**Frankenstein's** monster and **Marilyn
Monroe's** dress from *Some Like It Hot.* Allow
at least two hours for a visit. ♦ Admission.
Daily 10AM-6PM (5PM last admission). South
Bank (off Upper Ground). Recorded
information (24 hours): 071/401.2636

**17 National Film Theatre** More than 2,000
films a year are screened here in three
cinemas. ♦ Box office: daily 11:30AM-
8:30PM. South Bank. Recorded information:
071/633.0274 (24 hours). Box office:
071/928.3232

**18 Royal National Theatre** The world-famous
**National Theatre Company** was created in
1962 under **Sir Laurence Olivier** and opened
with **Peter O'Toole** in *Hamlet* in the **Old Vic.**
In 1951, construction of a new concrete
cultural paradise for the company, designed
by **Denys Lasden,** was started on the South
Bank, and the curtain was finally raised in
1976, with **Sir Peter Hall** as artistic director
and Olivier as proud papa of the company.
Incorporated under one vast roof are three
theaters, eight bars, a restaurant, modern
workshops, paint rooms, wardrobes,
rehearsal rooms, and advanced technical
facilities. The theaters differ in design, but all
have first-class acoustics and good seats, and
the tickets are reasonably priced, with the
added bonus of magnificent views of the
Thames, the Houses of Parliament, and
St. Paul's.

The **Olivier** seats 1,160 people in its fan-
shaped auditorium. The dark-walled,
rectangular **Cottesloe,** named after **Lord
Cottesloe,** the chairman of the South Bank
Board and Council, is the smallest and most
flexible, with removable seating for 400.

Experimental plays and fringe theater are
performed here. The 890-seat **Lyttleton** is a
proscenium theater, with roughly finished,
shuttered concrete walls for better acoustics.
Insightful backstage tours are available for a
nominal fee from the Lyttleton information
desk. Buy tickets at the main box office on the
day of the performance, or book ahead. The
theater holds tickets for same-day sale, and
you may be able to nab one if you get in line
by 8:30AM (the box office opens at 10AM).
Forty cheap "day" seats (20 on press nights)
are sold for both the Olivier and Lyttleton. You
can also join the mailing list and reserve seats
from anywhere in the world. Friday and
Saturday nights are usually sold out, but
inexpensive seats are often available for the
rest of the week. Wednesday matinees are
half-price. ♦ Foyers: M-Sa 10AM-11PM.
South Bank. 071/928.2033

**19 East of the Sun, West of the Moon**
★★★$$ From the Royal Festival Hall, a five-
minute stroll along the riverfront leads to
**Gabriel's Wharf** (home of designer crafts at
designer prices) and a restaurant with one of
the best views of London across the Thames.
Owned by American **Jerry Gotel** (who also
owns **Studio Six**), the upstairs dining
room/downstairs brasserie combination
shares a decor reminiscent of the 1920s
colonial era. The food is a mix of European
and Oriental dishes, with Gotel's favorite
Ploughman's Burger thrown in for good
measure. The house white is a perfect
companion to the sweet and sour tiger
prawns. ♦ Eclectic ♦ Lunch and dinner (to
1AM). 56 Upper Ground, Gabriel's Wharf.
Tube: Embankment, Waterloo. Reservations
recommended. 071/620.0596

# Studio Six

**20 Studio Six** ★★$ One of the South Bank's
best-kept secrets, this laid-back little eatery at
the southern end of **Gabriel's Wharf** is a
favorite with the media folk at the nearby
**London Weekend Television** tower. (LWT
has just five studios, hence the restaurant's
name). The decor blends a beachfront bar
with a stylish conservatory, while the
cosmopolitan menu plucks items from the
Continent and the United States and serves
them at fantastic prices (for London). Try the
vegetarian crepes of the day, followed by
home-baked cheesecake. Tip: Arrive early or
late for lunch to avoid the crunch of "journos."
♦ Eclectic ♦ Lunch and dinner. 56 Upper
Ground, Gabriel's Wharf, South Bank. Tube:
Embankment, Waterloo. 071/928.6243

**21 Meson Don Felipe** ★★$ Of all the trendy tapas bars that hit London in a wave of Spanish popularity during the late 1980s, Meson Don Felipe is one of the originals and still one of the best—and it's the most authentic in London. Perch on stools at the high wooden bar or squeeze around one of the closely packed tables, but arrive early to be sure of a seat of some kind. Popular with businesspeople at lunchtime and theatergoers in the evening, the bar serves a wide assortment of delicious, traditionally cooked tapas, ranging from Spanish omelets to peppers stuffed with chicken and herbs in a cream sauce. The Pan Catalán (a do-it-yourself toasted bread with garlic, tomatoes, and olive oil) is highly recommended. Also, don't miss the chilled *fino* or *oloroso* Sherry, served as it should be, to experience true Spanish style. The final flourish is a live flamenco guitarist every night from 8:30PM. ◆ Spanish ◆ Lunch and dinner. 53 The Cut, Waterloo. Tube: Waterloo. 071/928.3237

**21 Old Vic** From 1962 to 1976, the Old Vic was the temporary home of the **National Theatre Company,** under the direction of **Sir Laurence Olivier.** Though the foundation stone, taken from the demolished **Savoy Palace,** dates from the theater's opening in 1818, the rest of the Old Vic has changed interiors and owners many times, most recently in 1982, when Canadian entrepreneur **"Honest" Ed Mirvish** took over and gave it a £2.5 million face-lift. Now that Renaissance man **Jonathan Miller** has become director of the 1,037-seat theater, its great days have returned. ◆ Waterloo Rd (corner of The Cut and Waterloo Rd). Tube: Waterloo. Box office: 071/928.7616

**22 Waterloo Bridge** Designed by **Sir Giles Scott,** completed in 1939, and opened in 1945, the current bridge replaced a Regency river crossing opened on the second anniversary of the **Battle of Waterloo.** In fact, the name of the bridge was changed in honor of the great battle. The original design was supposed to have been more elegant than Scott's cantilevered concrete construction. But no one can deny the splendor of both City and Westminster views from the bridge itself. On the right of the bridge is the only floating police station in London, manned by the **Thames Division,** which patrols the 54-mile precinct of river in police-duty boats 24 hours a day. ◆ Victoria Embankment

**23 Cleopatra's Needle** Rising 68 feet high and weighing 180 tons, this pink-granite obelisk is one of a pair created around 1500 BC by **Thothmes III** in Egypt on the edge of the Nile. **Cleopatra** had nothing to do with the obelisk, but some say it was named after the Queen when it was moved to Alexandria, the royal city of Cleopatra, during the Greek dynasty in 12 BC. Others claim it was named after the barge that transported it to Britain in 1819 after it was given to the country by the **Viceroy of Egypt.** The obelisk was placed here by the river in 1878, and its companion is now in New York City's **Central Park.** ◆ Victoria Embankment (between Hungerford and Waterloo Bridges). Tube: Embankment

**24 Victoria Embankment Gardens** During summertime, office workers and tired tourists relax in deck chairs, children sprint along the grassy slopes, and bands play in this secluded and charming riverside garden. This is excellent picnic territory, with a considerable population of 19th-century statues among the dolphin lamp standards and camel and sphinx benches. One of the best statues is of **Arthur Sullivan,** who wrote the Savoy operas with **Gilbert.** The inscription "Is life a boon?" is from *Yeoman of the Guard.* Another favorite is the World War I memorial to the **Imperial Camel Corps,** complete with a fine miniature camel and rider. ◆ Victoria Embankment (between Horseguards Ave and Savoy Hill). Tube: Embankment

**25 York Water Gate** Located in the western corner of **Victoria Embankment Gardens,** this is a fairly ironic monument for the corrupt **Duke of Buckingham.** Built in 1626 in the Italian style with Buckingham's motto in Latin, *Fidel Coticula Crux* (which means "The Cross is the Touchstone of Faith"), and the Duke's coronet, the gate marks where the Thames reached before the Embankment was built. ◆ Victoria Embankment Gardens and Buckingham St. Tube: Embankment

**26 Buckingham Street** The street runs parallel to Villiers Street and is named after the same **Duke of Buckingham,** whose mansion was built here in 1626 on land formerly occupied by the Bishops of Norwich and York. One of the street's most famous residents, philosopher **Francis Bacon,** was evicted by Buckingham during his expansionist building program. Yet many other famous names have stayed here, among them **Samuel Pepys, Henry Fielding, Jean-Jacques Rousseau,** and **Samuel Taylor Coleridge.** In place of the Duke's mansion stands **Canova House,** an 1860s Italian-Gothic structure with redbrick arches built by

*Waterloo Bridge*

**Nicholas Barbon.** The Duke of Buckingham's entrance to his gardens from the Thames at the bottom of the street is marked with the **York Water Gate.**

**27 The Adelphi** Parallel with the Strand is John Adam Street, the site of the late, lamented Adelphi, a stunning architectural and engineering achievement and London's first grand speculative housing development. It was built between 1768 and 1774 by the **Adam** brothers, **William, James,** and **Robert,** with **John** as economic advisor. The scheme was a testament to fraternal genius (the word *adelphos* is Greek for brother), but it proved a financial disaster. With brilliant vision and dreamy optimism, the brothers leased the land between the Strand and the Thames and built a quay above the river, with four stories of arched brick vaults for warehousing. On top of this structure they created four streets—**Adelphi Terrace, John Adam Street, Robert Street,** and **Adam Street**—and a terrace of 11 four-story brick houses that faced the Thames, inspired by the fourth-century Palace of Diocletian at Spalato, as well as by Pompeii and Athens.

The project almost ruined the Adam brothers, and the houses were eventually occupied by a £50-per-ticket lottery sponsored by Parliament in 1773. In the 19th century, the Adelphi was popular with artists and writers, and it became home for such literary celebrities as **Thomas Rowlandson, Charles Dickens, John Galsworthy, Thomas Hardy, Sir James Barrie, H.G. Wells,** and **George Bernard Shaw. Richard D'Oyly Carte** lived at 4 Adelphi Terrace while producing the comic operas of **Gilbert & Sullivan.** In 1936, most of the Adelphi was demolished, a wanton act still lamented by architects and lovers of fine buildings. The legacy of the visionary speculation consists of the streets that the Adam brothers named after themselves, as well as a few fragments: **1-3 Robert Street,** with the honeysuckle pilasters that were the trademark of the Adelphi; **7 Adam Street,** which is pure Adam in style; and **4-6 John Adam Street,** which still contains features of the original scheme. The Adam brothers remained sufficiently undaunted to go on to speculate and build **Portland Place** north of Oxford Street. ♦ John Adam St

**28 Royal Society of Arts (RSA)** The RSA is easily the most interesting building in the maze of once-**Adelphi** streets. Completed by **Robert Adam** in 1754, it has all the noble tranquility, purity, and order that epitomize Adam architecture, complete with a Venetian window with a scalloped stone arch and acanthus-leaf capitals. The society was founded in 1754 with the aim of encouraging art, science, and manufacturing, and it employed talented artists and craftspeople of the day. The fine hall is decorated with six

vast paintings by **James Barry** depicting the progress of civilization. The paintings can be seen by applying to the society librarian after 9:30AM. ♦ 8 John Adam St. 071/930.5115

**29 Adelphi Theatre** Paternal devotion created the Adelphi Theatre, built in 1806 by **John Scott** to help launch his daughter's acting career. From 1837 to 1845, many of **Charles Dickens'** novels were performed here. But a real drama took place out front in 1897, when leading actor **William Terris** was shot by a lunatic. The theater's simple interior, with its straight lines and angles and deep-orange paneling, dates from extensive remodeling by **Ernest Schaufelberg** in 1930. Today the 1,500-seat Adelphi is the home of popular musicals. ♦ Strand (near Bedford St). Tube: Charing Cross. 071/836.7611

**30 Steven Scott and G.B. Stamps** These two stamp companies in one building have friendly staffs who are as helpful to young collectors as they are to those looking for the finest and the rarest. ♦ M-F 9:30AM-5:30PM; Sa 10AM-4PM. 77 Strand. 071/836.2341

**30 Shell-Mex House** Beyond Adam Street, the vista changes dramatically to the cold-white bulk of Shell-Mex House and its mantelpiece clock, larger than Big Ben, ticking away the time. The immense building, built by the **Messrs Joseph** in 1931, stretches from the Strand all the way to the Embankment. The Strand front of red brick and stone is all that remains of the **Hotel Cecil,** once the largest hotel in Europe, with 800 rooms, built in 18 and demolished in 1930 to make way for the Deco-style office block. The front is best seen from the other side of the river on the South Bank, a favorite view for theatergoers during intermissions at the National Theatre. ♦ Strand (near Adam St). Tube: Aldwych

**31 Vaudeville Theatre** Opened in 1870, the Vaudeville was completely refurbished in 1969 and is now one of the most delightful theaters in London, with an elegant gold-and-cream decor, plum-covered seats, and a beautiful chandelier in the foyer. Built by **C. Phipps,** the 694-seat theater has many long runs to its credit, including the first performances of **Ibsen's** *Hedda Gabler,* **Barrie's** *Quality Street,* and a record run of **Julian Slade's** *Salad Days* from 1954 to 1960. ♦ Strand (near Southampton St). Tube: Aldwych. 071/836.9987

**31 Stanley Gibbons International** Since Stanley Gibbons moved here in 1874, this has become the largest stamp shop in the world and, quite naturally, *the* shop for British and Commonwealth stamps. Two huge floors are filled with stamps, albums, hinges, magnifying glasses, and Stanley Gibbons stamp catalogs. Stamp auctions are held regularly. ♦ M-F 8:30AM-6PM; Sa 10AM-4PM. 399 Strand. 071/836.8444

**32 Savoy Theatre** Londoners feared the Savoy Theatre would never open again after it was destroyed by fire in 1990. Built in 1881 by **Richard D'Oyly Carte**, it was the first theater (and first public building) in the world to be lit by electricity, providing audiences with opulence and comfort as well as wonderful **Gilbert & Sullivan** comic operas. Happily, it has reopened with a re-creation of its 1929 Art Deco interior: Chinese lacquerwork, a five-shade color scheme, and cream fluted walls. If you're in the mood for a small and worthwhile splurge, book a pre- or post-theater supper at the **Savoy Grill,** right next door in the Savoy Hotel on Savoy Court, and tickets for the Savoy Theatre. Savoy Court is the only road in England with driving on the right, allowed by a special Act of Parliament to provide easier access for carriages delivering their passengers to the theater. ◆ Savoy Ct (at Strand). Tube: Aldwych, Embankment. 071/836.8888

# THE SAVOY

**32 Savoy Hotel** $$$$ In 1246, **Henry II** presented **Peter,** Earl of Richmond, with a splendid piece of land overlooking the Thames. Here the Earl, who was also the Count of Savoy, built a magnificent palace where he entertained beautiful French women, organized politically advantageous marriages into the Anglo-Norman aristocracy, and created a feudal center of considerable power. The grand manor later came into the hands of **Simon de Montfort,** founder of the House of Commons, and the man who led the barons in their revolt against **Henry III.** The illustrious past of this palatial site reached a fiery climax when a mob of angry peasants under the leadership of **Wat Tyler** stormed the palace, destroying everything of value, ripping tapestries into shreds, flattening the silver and gold, and, finally, burning the palace to the ground. The flames were watched from the Tower of London by 14-year-old **Richard II,** who was planning a swift and ruthless repression of the peasant revolt. But the site seems to have been ripe for palaces, and in 1889, a luxurious hotel was built by entrepreneur **Richard D'Oyly Carte,** discoverer of **Gilbert & Sullivan,** for whom he built the still-existing **Savoy Theatre** on the same plot of land.

The seven-story building took five years to complete and combined American technology with European luxury—the concrete walls, electric lights, and 24-hour elevators were all new to hotel construction in England. Tiny, bearded D'Oyly Carte outdid Peter of Savoy: he persuaded **Cesar Ritz** to be his manager and **Escoffier** his chef (his pots and pans are still at the hotel). **Johann Strauss** played

waltzes in the restaurant and **Caruso** sang. After having tea here, **Arnold Bennet** wrote his *Grand Babylon Hotel.* **Whistler** stayed here with his dying wife, sketching her and the river from his room. The first martini in the world was mixed in the **American Bar,** which has long been a favorite meeting place of Americans in London.

The Savoy has fully recovered from its decline in the 1950s and 1960s. Now it wins guests' hearts with its Art Deco marble bathrooms and their dazzling chrome fixtures, afternoon tea in the **Thames Foyer,** and Edwardian riverside apartment suites, which are filled with antiques, arched mirrors, fine plasterwork, Irish linen sheets, and a gracious atmosphere that even kings and queens can't resist. Illustrious names have lived in these apartments, including **Noel Coward** and more recently **Elaine Stritch,** who lived here until her husband died. **Liza Minnelli** and **Frank Sinatra** also maintain apartments at the Savoy. ◆ Strand. Tube: Aldwych, Embankment. 071/836.4343; fax 071/240.6040

Within the Savoy Hotel:

**River Restaurant** ★★★$$$ With fine views through the trees to the Thames, this spacious salmon-pink room rates as one of the prettiest places to dine in London. The elegant setting is matched with worthy cuisine, and if you have *le déjeuner au choix* (the set lunch) you can expect to eat well, feel rather grand, and survive the arrival of the bill. Even though you're surrounded by the daunting prospect of businesspeople and media folk lunching on expense accounts, it's well worth it. Under the auspices of chef **Anton Edelman,** the menu features more choices than ever, including a menu *de regime naturel* (simply cooked food), smoked salmon, and decaffeinated coffee. At dinner, the menu changes and the prices rise, but you can work off your anxiety about the coming bill while dancing to a live band. One way to feel truly right with the world is to have breakfast in this sumptuous setting: freshly squeezed fruit juices, prunes, eggs, bacon, kippers, toast and marmalade, and the famous Savoy coffee in the company of cabinet ministers, opera singers, tycoons, and movie stars who have made this *the* place for the business breakfast in London. Book your reservation at least a day or two in advance. ◆ French ◆ Breakfast, lunch, and dinner. Closed Sunday. Jacket and tie required. Reservations required. 071/836.4343

**The Savoy Grill** ★★★$$$ Certain French food critics give the Grill Room a thumbs down, a decision hard to comprehend. This very British paneled room offers English classics prepared with a delicate touch and rare imagination. The daily lunch specialties feature farmhouse sausages, creamed potatoes and fried onions (bangers, mash, and onions), shepherd's pie, Irish stew, and roast beef and Yorkshire pudding. At supper, the menu is more expensive, richer, and just as traditional, with roast pheasant, Dover sole, chateaubriand, roast partridge, or native oysters, and the waiters will flambé steak Diane in front of you. Power brokers can be seen sampling the classic omelet Arnold Bennett and lobster Thermidor, or being adventurous with the sauté of lamb with aubergine and parsnip mousse and a grain mustard sauce. The cooking is everything that you would expect from this, one of the premier hotels in the world. There are some excellent wines, although they aren't cheap, and special pre- and after-theater dinner menus that are a good value for this part of town. ♦ British ♦ Lunch and dinner; dinner only on Saturday. Closed Sunday. Jacket and tie required. Reservations required. No children under 14. 071/836.4343

**32 Simpson's-in-the-Strand** ★★★$$ Only a meal at Eton or Harrow could be more English than this, with tables arranged in long rows, dark-wood paneling, and, at lunchtime during the week, a sea of dark-suited men watching as joints of beef and lamb are wheeled to their tables on elaborate silver-domed trolleys and carved to their specifications. Roast beef served with cabbage and roasted spuds, and saddle of lamb and Aylesbury duck are classic British meals, and the waiters who bring them to your table are like old family retainers. Approach a meal here as an authentic English experience, and enjoy the Stilton, treacle tart, and house claret. While all the English tradition takes place downstairs, the first-floor **Chandelier Room** (★★★$$$) has quietly transformed itself into a vegetarian and fish restaurant serving such delicacies as cream of mussel soup with coriander, or skate with black butter. Shhhh! Word might get out to those below! ♦ British ♦ Lunch and dinner. 100 Strand. 071/836.9112; fax 071/836.1381

**33 Strand Palace Hotel** $$$ Opposite the Savoy, this hotel is more hotel than palace, but the location is hard to beat and the price makes it one of the best values in London. With the money you save, you can walk across the street and have an elegant lunch in the Savoy overlooking the Thames. The Strand Palace doesn't have room service, but does have those very English electric kettles in all 777 rooms, a coffee shop, a pasta bar, and a cocktail bar. ♦ 372 Strand. 071/836.8080; fax 071/836.2077

**34 The Russian Shop** Capitalism, Russian-style, comes to the Strand in the shape of this delightful shop bearing Russian gifts, including reasonably priced wooden dolls, pretty china, boxes encrusted with semiprecious stones, and brightly colored peasant shawls. The lacquerwork is something else, and so are the prices. ♦ M-Sa 9:30AM-6PM. 99 Strand. 071/497.9104

**34 Smollensky's on the Strand** ★$$ Micha Gottlieb must have designed this tongue in cheek, making the outside exactly the same Simpson's just up the street. Although it's actually located underground, Smollensky's on the side of a steep hill with a view of the delightful Queen's Chapel at the Savoy, whic is sometimes lit up at night. This large Prohibition Era Deco-themed restaurant offe American-style food, steak sandwiches, steaks, and corn-fed chicken with matching U.S. service and the guarantee of a hearty meal. Finish off with a chocolate-peanut cheesecake or chocolate mousse, and, on Saturday evenings at least, dance off all the added calories on the spot. Londoners love i and rumor has it that **Princess Di** takes the little Princes to **Smollensky's Balloon** (★★: Dover Street) for lunch on weekends when Smollensky puts on a kids' treat day with clowns, Punch and Judy, face-painting, magicians, and bedlam. ♦ American ♦ Lunc and dinner. 105 Strand. 071/497.2101; fax 071/836.3270

**35 Queen's Chapel of the Savoy** This have of tranquility belongs to the **Duke of Lancaster,** who is in fact the Queen (the reigning monarch keeps this title, which goe back to **Henry IV,** who was Duke of Lancaste before he usurped the throne from **Richard I** Erected in 1505 in the late perpendicular styl on the grounds of the **Savoy Palace,** the chapel has been used by royalty since the reign of **Henry VII.** The present building is almost entirely Victorian, rebuilt by **Sir Robe Smirke** in 1820 and restored by his brother **Sydney Smirke** after a fire in 1864. The original chapel was once part of the **Order o St. John** (1510-1516), and since 1937, it ha been part of the **Order of Chivalry** and the **Royal Victorian Order.** The heraldic plaque the vestibule is made of gilded marrow seed crushed into the seductive forms of the leopards of England. The stained-glass window commemorates **Richard D'Oyly Ca** (1844-1901), and another window is in memory of **Queen Mary,** who died in 1953. The window with heraldic designs of the Roy Victorian Order was designed in part by **King George VI.** ♦ Tu-F 11:30AM-3:30PM Oct-Ju Savoy Hill (at the bottom of Savoy St). Tube Aldwych, Temple

**36 Lyceum** ★★★$ The tap room downstairs pours real ale; the ground floor serves good salads, terrines, and tarts; and the bar upstai has views over the Strand. A passage leads from the pub to a former disco, which was once the **Lyceum Theatre,** where theater history was furthered in great performances by **Henry Irving** and **Ellen Terry.** ♦ British ♦ Lunch and dinner. 354 Strand. 071/836.71

---

| **Restaurants/Clubs:** Red | **Hotels:** Blue |
|---|---|
| **Shops/** 🌶 **Outdoors:** Green | **Sights/Culture:** Bl |

# That's the Ticket: How to Get Theater Seats in London

Unlikely as it may seem, the safest and ultimately cheapest way to buy theater tickets in London is at the theater box office; most are open from 10AM throughout the day until the evening performance. The only hitch is that, without advance booking, you'll have to choose from the seats that remain. Advice? Go early. Also, ask to see a diagram of the seating arrangements and check whether seats have restricted viewing or you could find yourself behind a pillar or to one side of the stage. If it's summer, check whether the theater in question is air-conditioned, and, if necessary, ask about disabled access. When in doubt about the latter, call **Artsline** (071/388.2227) for full information on facilities for the disabled. Many theaters have sound systems for the hearing impaired.

Another bargain is the **Leicester Square Ticket Booth** (opposite the Hampshire Hotel), at the core of the Theater District, which sells half-price tickets the day of the performance—M-Sa noon-2PM for matinees, 2:30-6:30PM for evening shows. There is a small booking fee and a four-seat maximum per person. Cash only is accepted; purchases must be made in person. Of course, tickets for hit shows are rarely available. If you aren't able to stop by the theater or Leicester Square, call the box office and reserve your tickets with a major credit card; you must pay for them by mail or in person (be prepared to show your credit card for identification purposes) within three days.

You can also purchase tickets from one of the agencies scattered throughout London and other large cities, including New York. Most charge an additional booking fee of at least 10 to 20 percent. Be careful when choosing where to buy tickets, as some ticket agencies have recently been investigated for exorbitant rates on popular shows. **First Call** (071/497.9977), a 24-hour credit-card service for London's top shows, concerts, and movies, offers a wide range of tickets at all prices and tries to provide a real choice of seating. Tickets are delivered by mail or, if there isn't time, by courier to the box office for later collection. The booking fee is up to 70 percent less than the fee charged by most other services. **Ticketmaster** (071/344.4444) also offers some shows without any booking fee. Other respected agencies include **Edwards and Edwards** (071/379.5822), **New York Freefone** (800/223.6108),

London Theatre Booking (071/439.3371), and Premier Box Office (071/240.2245).

In London, scalpers are called "ticket touts," but they're the same the world over. Usually operating in and around last-minute queues for West End shows, they pose a major problem for London's theaters because they fuel the idea that tickets are expensive. Be careful: people have paid up to $200 for a ticket only to find out they have a seat behind a pillar. The **Society of West End Theatre (SWET)** is collecting files on the touts and will prosecute, so write to this organization (Bedford Chambers, The Piazza, Covent Garden, London WC2E 8HQ) if you lose out, but better still, either buy the tickets before you come to the U.K., try the major ticket agencies, or go and see another show—there are at least 50 to choose from in the West End. It is worth noting that London theater differs from New York in that last-minute booking for shows is often possible, since some theaters reserve seats to be sold on the day of a performance.

**Theatreline** provides essential West End theater information, including daily seat availability. The six categories:

**Children's** 0836/430963
**Comedies** 0836/430961
**Musicals** 0836/430960
**Opera/Ballet/Modern Dance** 0836/430964
**Plays** 0836/430959
**Thrillers** 0836/430962

Alternatively, the **London Tourist Board** offers its own guide to theater as follows:

**Comedy & Thrillers** 0891/505472
**Musicals** 0891/505473
**New Productions/How to Book** 0891/505477
**Non West End Productions** 0891/505476
**Plays** 0891/505475
**Shakespeare** 0891/505474

Theater buffs who want to keep current on London theater happenings can subscribe to *London Theatre Guide,* a monthly newsletter that includes theater listings, reviews, interviews, backstage chatter, and restaurant tips. Subscriptions include access to a telephone ticket service. For more information, write to London Theatre Guide, SWET, Bedford Chambers, The Piazza, Covent Garden, London WC2E 8HQ, or call 071/836.0971.

Note: Most theaters are closed on Sunday.

OPEN AIR THEATRE
REGENT'S PARK · LONDON, N.W.1

Monday JUNE 28
LOWER TIER £6.00
B 10
No money refunded. If performance is cancelled this ticket is exchangeable for any other performance of the season.

AMXC
£10.00
11-FEB-86
20 FEBRUARY 1986 at 7:30 PM
GRAND TIER
A14
GLC SOUTH BANK CONCERT HALLS

**37 Courtauld Institute/Somerset House**

Architect **Sir William Chambers** designed this Georgian stronghold from 1776 to 1786 to replace the 16th-century Renaissance palace that occupied the site. As one of London's premier neoclassical buildings, it stands facing the Thames east of Waterloo Bridge and is one of the few Georgian buildings still gracing the riverside. Like the old Adelphi, Chambers' Somerset House rose out of the Thames before the construction of the Embankment. The great palace of the **Protector Somerset** (1547-1572), with its magnificent chapel by **Inigo Jones** and riverside gallery by **John Webb,** originally stood on this site and was lived in by **Elizabeth I** when she was a Princess, as well as the Queens of **James I, Charles I,** and **Charles II.** Until recently, the present building enjoyed a less-than-illustrious existence, housing administrative offices and institutions and the **Registry of Births, Deaths, and Marriages.** Now it is home to the exquisite modern art collection of the Courtauld Institute.

It's particularly appropriate that the **Fine Rooms,** designed between 1776 and 1780 by Chambers, should now be occupied by the Courtauld Institute. The original inhabitants of this block were the **Royal Society,** the **Royal Academy of Arts,** and the **Society of Antiquaries,** who finally left in 1850 and were replaced by the **Registrar General** until the 1970s. The rooms then remained empty for 20 years.

The Courtauld is one of the galleries that most people mean to visit but don't quite get around to, yet it has the best Impressionist and post-Impressionist collection in Britain, not to mention a fabulous Classical collection. The major collections were assembled by **Samuel Courtauld** and **Viscount Lee** of Fareham (the British versions of the Guggenheims), who founded the institute in 1931.

Resist all temptations to use the lift and take the magnificent spiral staircase instead, dubbed the "Rowlandson" after a painting by **Thomas Rowlandson,** showing revelers falling down it at a party. Known as the **Prince's Gate Collection,** the first four galleries contain Italian Renaissance and Dutch art from the 15th and 16th centuries given to the institute in 1978 by **Count Antoine Seilern.** The range of art is extraordinary, from **Palma Vecchio's** lush *Venus in a Landscape* and **Van Dyck's** *Portrait of a Man in an Armchair* to **Botticelli's** *Holy Trinity* and **Albertinelli's** *Creation.* Gallery 2 contains **Rubens'** spectacular baroque work, *Descent from the Cross,* which was the model for the altarpiece in **Antwerp Cathedral,** while Gallery 3 is mainly given over to the Rubens school and *The Bounty of James I Triumphing Over Avarice,* a *modello* for the ceiling corners at **Banqueting House,** Whitehall. The haunting *Landscape by Moonlight,* at one time owned by **Sir Joshua Reynolds,** inspired both **Sir Thomas Gainsborough** and **John Constable.**

The Impressionist works are so familiar and frequently reproduced that they seem almost like icons of a world religion called 19th-century art. The surprise is that all the major Impressionist and post-Impressionist artists are here, beginning with **Boudin, Daumier, Manet, Monet, Degas, Renoir, Pissarro, Sisley, Cézanne, Gauguin, van Gogh, Seurat, Toulouse-Lautrec, Bonnard, Vuillard,** and **Modigliani.** Exhibitions change regularly, but don't miss the following:

**Modigliani's** *Female Nude,* which even thousands of reproductions have failed to spoil. ♦ (G10)

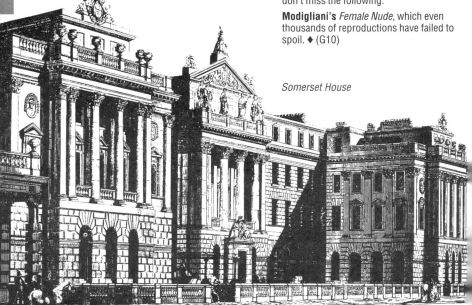

*Somerset House*

Renoir's *La Loge,* with a man staring at the stage through opera glasses while the viewer stares with equal intensity at his voluptuous partner, her neck wound round with crystal beads, her boldly striped opera cloak falling open to reveal the rose tucked between her breasts. ♦ (G5)

Monet's *Vase of Flowers,* full of pink and mauve mellows and so evocative of summer light that it cuts through the grayest London day. ♦ (G8)

Gauguin's *Nevermore.* **Paa'ura** was Gauguin's 14½-year-old mistress, and this naked South Sea beauty somehow sums up his reaction against Impressionism. This painting and his *Te Rerioa* (The Dream) will make you want to cut loose and fly to the islands. ♦ (G8)

Van Gogh's *Peach Blossom in the Crau* and *Self-Portrait of the Artist with a Bandaged Ear,* which together sum up van Gogh at his happiest and his most despairing. Van Gogh left Paris for Arles in 1888, and almost immediately the orchards of Provence became a foaming cascade of blossom. Here, he spent the happiest eight months of his brief life. Nearby is the tragic self-portrait, painted a few months earlier when he was recovering from a fit during which he had attacked Gauguin, then cut off his own ear. ♦ (G5)

Manet's *A Bar at the Folies-Bergère.* Manet was an inspiration to the Impressionists and this is his last major work. His blond barmaid is instantly recognizable, and after looking at this work, no tawdry barroom can ever be quite the same again. ♦ (G5)

Cézanne's *Mont Ste.-Victoire.* Cézanne was the artist who inspired **Braque** and **Picasso** during their Cubist period. In this painting, the green, gold, and blue of the landscape form a geometric pattern so exquisite that you feel you could step into the frame and walk away. ♦ (G5)

Upstairs on the second floor in Galleries 7, 8, and 9 are Gainsborough's lovingly crafted portrait of his wife as well as paintings by **Allan Ramsay, George Romney, Roger Fry,** and the **Omega Workshop's** collection, along with **Oscar Kokoschka's** huge painting, *Prometheus Triptych.* Gallery 10 is more sedate, with 19th- and 20th-century works by such artists as **Sickert** and **Ben Nicholson.**

The gold treasures from the Italian and Netherlands collections of the 14th, 15th, and 16th centuries are found in Gallery 11. These are not jewels but tiny gold-ground panel paintings such as the *Madonna* by **Fra Angelico's** workshop and an exquisite triptych by **Bernardo Daddi** of 1338, the *Master of Flemalle Deposition.*

The Courtauld Collection also contains magnificent old master drawings by

Michelangelo, Rubens, and **Rembrandt** on the ground floor. You must make arrangements in advance to view some of the 25,000 old master prints. If you need a moment to sit and contemplate all this wonderful art, there is a coffee shop, as well as a bookstore for mementos. ♦ Admission. M-Sa 10AM-6PM; Su 2-6PM. Lancaster Pl and Strand. Tube: Aldwych, Temple. 071/873.2526

**38 The King's College** Founded in 1829 by the **Duke of Wellington,** archbishops, and 30 bishops of the Church of England, King's College adjoins the east wing of **Somerset House** and has formed part of the **University of London** since 1898. ♦ Strand. Tube: Aldwych, Temple

**39 Statue of Isambard Kingdom Brunel** Son of the equally famous **Marc Isambard Brunel,** he was the brilliant engineer who designed the **Great Western Railway** and built the *Great Eastern,* the first steamship to make regular voyages between Britain and America. His statue is by **Baron Marochetti** and dates from 1871. ♦ Victoria Embankment and Temple Pl

**40 Roman Bath** Tucked away down Strand Lane along the east side of **Somerset House** under a dark archway, this 15-foot enigma is certainly not Roman, possibly Tudor, but more likely 17th century. Built over a tributary of the **River Fleet,** it fills each day with 2,000 gallons of icy water that flow into a pipe and down into the Thames. David Copperfield used to take cold plunges here, but now the bath belongs to the **National Trust** and can be seen by appointment, although it's partially visible through a window. Be alert—this alleyway has become the territory of a number of homeless people who wish to be left alone. ♦ W 1-5PM May-Sept. Surrey Ct, Surrey St. 071/798.2063

**41 St. Mary-le-Strand** St. Mary-le-"Stranded" is the sadder, more apt name for this jewel of a church once half surrounded by houses on the north side of the Strand, but, since 1910, isolated by the widening of roads. This is the first major work built between 1714 and 1717 and the first of its kind for Scottish architect **James Gibbs.** St. Mary's is essentially a baroque church with its half-domed porch and numerous vertical pediments. As though in a self-fulfilling prophesy, the upper order contains the windows, while the lower order is solid to keep out the noise from the street. In an act of continuing faith, the church is being restored. The splendid five-stage steeple, weakened by wartime bombing, pollution, traffic vibration, and rusting iron clamps that bind the Portland stone, is being dismantled stone by stone. The hours are erratic because of the restoration, but if you get in, the barrel vault has ornate plasterwork and a coffered ceiling. **Thomas à Becket** was lay rector of the medieval church that originally stood on the site, and the parents of **Charles Dickens** were married here. One-time poet laureate **John Betjeman** made it his life's work to save this beautiful church from demolition. Who can blame him? ♦ Strand (opposite Strand Ln). Tube: Aldwych

**42 Aldwych** The crescent, identified mainly by the name on the street wall, sweeps around an immense stone fortress occupied by **Australia House, India House,** and **Bush House,** the latter decorated with symbolic figures of England and America. The word Aldwych is Danish for "an outlying farm." Its familiarity in London is enhanced by being the name of a tube station and a theater, the Aldwych. ♦ Between the Strand and Kingsway

**43 Duchess Theatre** With seating for 474, the Duchess is one of the best-designed theaters in London, with excellent views from every seat. ♦ Catherine St. Tube: Aldwych. Box office: 071/494.5075

**44 Fortune Theatre** The immortal line "There is a time in the affairs of men which, if taken at the tide, turns to fortune" is embossed on a highly polished brass plaque in the foyer of this theater. Though built after World War II, the delightful marble-and-copper foyer shows little evidence that money and materials were scarce. The Fortune is a lovely, intimate (432 seats) theater that puts on a wide selection of plays. But do watch out: there are pillars in the stalls, so be sure you aren't sitting behind one. ♦ Russell St and Drury Ln. Tube: Covent Garden, Aldwych. Box office: 071/836.2238

**45 Strand Theatre** The Strand and the **Aldwych** theaters sit like bookends on either side of the mighty **Waldorf Hotel.** Built as a pair, they are both quite magnificent. The proscenium above the arch in the 925-seat Strand depicts **Apollo** drawn by horses, with goddesses and cupids, and the whole is so ornately decorated that it's almost wanton to ignore it and rush out for that interval drink. ♦ Catherine St and Aldwych. Tube: Aldwych. 071/930.8800

**45 Aldwych Theatre** Slums between Drury Lane and Lincoln's Inn were razed to make room for Aldwych and Kingsway roads, and in 1905, the Aldwych became one of the first theaters to take up residence. Designed by **W.G.R. Sprague** for **Charles Frohmant,** the 1,089-seat Georgian theater is handsome and ornate, uncomfortable and wonderful. This was the home of the **Royal Shakespeare Company** from 1930 until 1982, when it moved to the **Barbican,** and its absence is much lamented. The smash hit *Nicholas Nickleby* began here. ♦ Aldwych. Box office: 071/836.6404

**45 Waldorf Hotel** $$$ Old-world charm, excellent service, and a refurbished interior, with marble floors, coral-and-white walls,

crystal chandeliers, and palm trees and fern characterize **A. Marshall Mackenzie's** Waldorf, built between 1907 and 1908. Tea the **Palm Court Room** (★★$$$) is one of London's greatest treats. You have a choice Balijen India, Lapsang Souchong China, or Waldorf's own blend of India Darjeeling, followed by an endless sequence of sandwiches, muffins, scones and clotted cream, pastries, and cakes. Tea dancing take place Saturday and Sunday, and smart dres is preferred between 3:30PM and 6:30PM. ♦ Catherine St and Aldwych. Tube: Aldwych 071/836.2400; fax 071/836.7244

**46 Bush House** Namesake American **Irving T Bush** wanted a trade center with shops and marbled corridors, but it didn't work out th. way. Since 1940, **BBC World Service,** one the most important broadcasting institution in the Western world, has used the building for its worldwide transmissions. "To the Friendship of English Speaking Peoples" is carved into the stonework of this vital build erected in 1935 by **Harvey W. Corbett.** The entrance for both officeworkers and shoppe is opposite St. Mary-le-Strand. Inside is **Penfriend,** a rather splendid pen shop offer the kind of personal service you just don't g in department stores. If you have a penchar for early radio recordings, stop by the **BBC and Radio Shop.** Access is to the shopping arcade only. ♦ Montreal and Melbourne Pls Tube: Aldwych

**47 Statue of W.E. Gladstone** The statue designed by **Sir Hamo Thronycroft** in 1905 looks out bravely onto the sea of uncaring traffic from the middle of the roadway wher the Strand is rejoined by the Aldwych. Gladstone, a liberal statesman, was prime minister four times. He introduced educational reform in 1870, the secret ballo in 1872, and succeeded in carrying out the Reform Act of 1884. But he failed to gain support for home rule for Ireland, which would no doubt have made the history of th 20th century in these islands more tranquil. This statue shows him robed as Chancellor the Exchequer with Brotherhood, Education Aspiration, and Courage represented at the base. ♦ Strand

**48 St. Clement Danes** Now the church of th **Royal Air Force, Sir Christopher Wren's** oranges-and-lemons church (so called because the church's bells play the tune fro the nursery rhyme "Oranges and Lemons") was built from 1680 to 1682, blitzed during World War II, and skillfully rebuilt by **W.A.S** **Lloyd** in 1955. (The steeple, added in 1720, was designed by **James Gibbs.**) The floor is inlaid with slabs of Welsh slate carved with the 735 units of the RAF, and the rolls of honors contain the 125,000 men and wome of the RAF who died in World Wars I and II. The original pulpit by **Grinling Gibbons** was shattered in the bombing and painstakingly pieced together from the fragments. The organ was a gift from members of the U.S. Air Force, and there is a shrine to the USAF under the west gallery. Each March, oranges and lemons are distributed to the children of the parish in a special service. **Samuel Johnson** worshiped here and is now silenced in bronze behind the church, where he gazes nostalgically down the street he believed to be unequaled: Fleet Street. ♦ Strand (opposite Milford Ln). Tube: Aldwych

**9** **Royal Courts of Justice** Better known as the **Law Courts,** this dramatic Gothic ramble of buildings, with a 514-foot frontage along the Strand, was built in a period of Victorian reorganization of the legal system and opened by **Queen Victoria** in 1882, with the power and glory of the law architecturally proclaimed. The main entrance is flanked by twin towers and slate roofs. **Solomon** holds his Temple above the entrance on the left, and on the right is the founder of English law, **Alfred the Great.** The lofty **Great Hall** (238 feet long and 80 feet high) contains a monument to the original architect, **G.E. Street,** who, in the Victorian tradition of tutelage, was a pupil of **George Gilbert Scott** and teacher of **Philip Webb** and **William Morris.**

The buildings house 64 courts spread over seven miles of corridors and 1,000 rooms. They are reached by way of the hall, and when the courts sit, the public is admitted to the back two rows. Take time out for a visit if you're at all interested in seeing the English justice system at work, visually enhanced by the wigged presence of judges and barristers and undisguised solicitors. Read the *Daily Lists* in the central hall to decide what appeals to you in the still faintly Dickensian world of probate, bankruptcy, and divorce. You're free to enter any court except those marked "court in camera" or "chambers." ♦ M-F 10:30AM-1PM, 2-4PM. Strand (between Clement's Inn and Bell Yard). Tube: Aldwych

**50** **George Public House** ★★$ Named after **George III** and once frequented by **Dr. Johnson** and **Oliver Goldsmith,** the author of the *Vicar of Wakefield,* this famous timbered tavern has one long-beamed and cozy room that serves buffet lunches, salads, tarts, and puddings. The excellent lunchtime restaurant upstairs is frequented by journalists, lawyers, the innocent, the guilty, and the tourist. A pantry snack bar is located downstairs. ♦ British ♦ Tavern: M-F 11AM-11PM. Restaurant: lunch and dinner. Closed Saturday and Sunday. 213 Strand. 071/353.9238

**50** **Twinings** Chinese Mandarins guard the Georgian entrance to London's narrowest shop and oldest business still on its original site. (Twinings has been paying taxes longer than any other business in Westminster.) **Thomas Twining** opened the shop in 1716 as **Tom's Coffee House,** and the store has been selling tea ever since it became the national drink. Alas, you can't drink a cup of tea here; you can only buy it or find out about it in the small museum in the back of the shop. ♦ M-F 9:30AM-4:30PM. 216 Strand. 071/353.3511

**50** **Wig and Pen Club** ★★$$ As the name indicates, this is a private club for lawyers and journalists, located in a modest 17th-century house that is the only building on the Strand that survived the Great Fire of 1666. Black timber-framed windowpanes hold old cartoonist drawings of law court characters and the second story juts out over the street. You can have a look around before noon and, amazingly, obtain a free temporary membership, which is especially

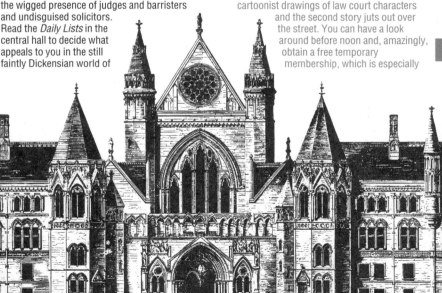

*Royal Courts of Justice*

nice for visiting lawyers and journalists. (This special privilege extends only to foreigners, as Britons can't become instant members.) Men must don a jacket and tie, and women are required to wear skirts. The club has an all-day alcohol license. ♦ British ♦ Lunch and dinner. Closed Saturday and Sunday. 229-230 Strand. 071/583.7255; fax 071/583.6608

**51 Temple Bar Monument** The spiky griffin, created in 1880 by **Horace Jones,** stands on the site of **Sir Christopher Wren's** fine three-arched gateway, which was here from 1672 to 1878. (The gate was dismantled because it obstructed traffic and moved to **Theobald's Park** in Hertfordshire.) The griffin is a mythical beast famous for its voracious appetite and, appropriately, it marks the boundary between the City of Westminster, impelled by restraint, and the City of London, inspired by acquisition. The Temple Bar's griffin also marks the end of the broad, dozy Strand and the beginning of congested, lively Fleet Street. The figures on either side of the griffin are **Queen Victoria** and **Edward VIII,** Prince of Wales. ♦ Fleet St at the Strand

**51 Fleet Street** This lively, crowded street has a glorious and eclectic mix of styles and levels and a tremendous skyline defined by the tower and pinnacles of the **Law Courts,** the tower of **St. Dunstan-in-the-West,** and the dome of **St. Paul's Cathedral,** best seen from the north side of the street. Sadly, the editorial offices of the nation's newspapers have left Fleet Street. The last to go was the *Daily Express* from the "Black Lubyanka" (the **Daily Express Building,** so named for its glossy black tile facade) at **Nos. 121-128** in 1989, which moved to a gray Lubyanka crowded onto Blackfriars Bridge. ♦ Between Middle Temple Ln and Ludgate Circus

**52 Royal Bank of Scotland** Founded in 1671, this is the oldest bank in London, and it was the inspiration for Tellson's Bank in **Dickens'** *A Tale of Two Cities*. The nonfictional list of early customers includes **Charles II,** the **Duke of Marlborough, Nell Gwyn, Samuel Pepys, Oliver Cromwell,** and **John Dryden.** The bank is now part of **Williams' and Glyn's Bank.** ♦ 1 Fleet St

**53 Public Record Office** Once a favored haunt of genealogists, the 84 miles of records stored here today consist mainly of government and legal texts. (The genealogy bits have moved to the huge modern complex at Kew.) The museum in the old **Rolls Chapel,** however, is worth a look, since it houses the 11th-century *Domesday Book,* **William the Conqueror's** survey of England. Other items include the wills of **Shakespeare** and **Jane Austen,** and **George Washington's** letters to **George III.** ♦ Free. M-F 9.30AM-5PM. Chancery Ln (near Fleet St). Tube: Temple, Chancery Ln. 081/876.3444

**54 Prince Henry's Room** Located above th archway leading to the Temple, the timber house containing Prince Henry's Room wa built in 1610 as a tavern with a projecting upper story. The great treasure inside is th Jacobean ceiling, one of the finest remaini enriched plaster ceilings of its time in Lon with an equally enriched set of stories to g with it. The most persistent tale claims tha the initials **P.H.** and the **Prince of Wales' Feathers,** which decorate the ceiling, commemorate the 1610 investiture of **Hen** eldest son of **James I** and elder brother of future and luckless **King Charles I.** The Pri died two years after his investiture from a caught after playing tennis. The room also contains mementos of one of London's m important figures, the diarist **Samuel Pepy** who was born in 1633 in nearby **Salisbury Court,** Fleet Street, baptized in nearby **St. Bride's Church,** educated at **St. Paul's Cathedral,** and lived most of his life close **Tower Hill.** His remarkable shorthand diar recording the period between 1660 and 16 fills many volumes and is the liveliest and fullest account of London life ever written, including the Plague of 1665 and the Great Fire of 1666. The wide oriel windows looki down over Fleet Street and across to Chan Lane manage to frame London's timelessn in a prism of light—the way one longs to s it. ♦ Free. M-Sa 11AM-2PM. 17 Fleet St. 071/936.2501

**55 The Temple** An oasis of calm between th traffic of the Embankment and the bustle o Fleet Street, the Temple was originally the headquarters of the **Knights Templar,** a monastic order founded in 1119 during the Crusades to regain Palestine from the Saracens for Christianity. They settled at the Temple in 1160, but were suppressed by the Pope, and all that remains of their monastery is the Temple Church and the Buttery.

Since the 14th century, the buildings have been leased to lawyers. Today, they house two of England's four **Inns of Court (Inner Temple** and **Middle Temple),** the voluntary legal society that has the exclusive privilege of calling candidates to the bar. Visitors are free to stroll through the warren of lanes, courtyards, and gardens and to admire the buildings, each composed like an Oxford or Cambridge college, with chambers built around steep stairways, communal dining halls, libraries, common rooms, and chapels. The tranquility of the setting is disrupted by the speed with which the lawyers, either wearing their gowns or carrying them over their arms—loaded down with books and papers—race between their chambers and the Law Courts, the vast Gothic world that stretches from Temple Bar to the Aldwych.

The **Temple Church,** located within the precincts of the Inner Temple, was badly damaged during the Blitz, but has been skillfully repaired. The beautiful round nave, completed in 1185, is modeled after the Church of the Holy Sepulchre in Jerusalem. It's the only circular nave in London, and one of only five in England, all connected with the Knights Templar. The chancel was added in 1240, and the rib vaulting within the Gothic porch is original.

The **Middle Temple Hall,** also painstakingly restored after the Blitz, is a handsome Elizabethan building with a splendid double-hammerbeam roof and carved-oak screen. Here, aspiring barristers are called to the bar upon passing their examinations. Lunch and dinner are served in the hall, and though residence at the inns has become vestigial, the students must eat three dinners during each term here. **Shakespeare's** *Twelfth Night* is said to have been performed in the hall in 1602, and the round pond amid the mulberry trees outside in **Fountain Court** was featured in **Dickens'** novel *Martin Chuzzlewit*.

The **Inner Temple Gateway,** leading back to the Strand, is a half-timbered three-story house that looks suspiciously like a stage set, but it is the real 17th-century thing, with **Prince Henry's Room** on the top floor. ♦ Bounded by Middle Temple Ln and Crown Office Row, and Mitre Court and Embankment. Tube: Temple

**S. Weingott** This traditional tobacconist to the lawyers nearby keeps a large humidifier on the premises that contains a few thousand cigars, including some costing $20 apiece that come in their own polished box. Weingott also sells the best pipes in London. Since its beginnings in 1859, very little has changed inside the shop: S. Weingott still weighs and blends tobaccos, and the 119 brands and 50 loose varieties are still stored in old wooden drawers. The proprietor is also a wine merchant, and if you're lucky, he may have a bottle of Château d'Yquem on hand. ♦ M-F 8:30AM-6PM. 3 Fleet St. General information: 071/353.7733. Wine Merchants: 071/583.2472

**L. Simmonds** The journalists may have left Fleet Street, but this bookseller remains. For books on journalism from all over the world, L. Simmonds has the best stock in the U.K. The store is also probably the slimmest shop on the street—reach out and both hands will touch the book-stacked walls on either side. ♦ M-F 9AM-6PM. 16 Fleet St. 071/353.3907

**56 Ye Olde Cock Tavern** ★★$$ Another illustrious role call of former regulars—**Nell Gwyn, Pepys, Goldsmith, Sheridan,** and **Garrick**—once drank in this small tavern, which still serves tradition, an excellent bar lunch, and delicious roasts and puddings in the dining room. The original sign, carved by **Grinling Gibbons,** is happily preserved behind the bar upstairs, and the modern clientele is a civilized mix of journalists and barristers. ♦ Pub ♦ M-Tu 11AM-9:30PM; W-F 11AM-10:30PM. 22 Fleet St. Reservations recommended for lunch in the restaurant. 071/353.8570

**56 Hoare's Bank** The only private bank left in London is still as old fashioned, discreet, and attractive as when it was founded in 1672. It's well worth a peek inside. ♦ 37 Fleet St

**57 St. Dunstan-in-the-West** This architectural gem—London's Romanian Orthodox patriarchal church—is beautifully situated on the north side of the curve in Fleet Street. Designed by **John Shaw,** the Victorian church, with its octagonal tower, openwork lantern, and pinnacles, was built in 1831 at the beginning of the Gothic Revival movement on the site of an earlier church whose great treasures were saved when it was demolished to widen Fleet Street.

The church is unusually placed, with the tower and entrance on the south and the brick octagon of the sanctuary and altar on the north. Treasures from the original church include the communion rail carved by **Grinling Gibbons** and the old wooden clock dating from 1671, with two wooden giants that strike each hour. In 1830, the **Marquis of Hertford** bought the clock for his house in Regent's Park. **Viscount Rothermere,** a British newspaper proprietor, later purchased the clock and returned it to the church in 1935 to commemorate **King George V's** Silver Jubilee. The statue of **Elizabeth I** over the door (believed to be the oldest outdoor statue in London) and the statues of **King Lud** and his sons came from the Ludgate when it was torn down in 1760. The bronze bust of **Lord Northcliffe,** who lived from 1865 to 1922 and was newspaper proprietor and founder of the *Daily Mail,* was sculpted by **Lady Scott** in 1930. ♦ Fleet St (between Chancery and Fetter Lns). Tube: St. Paul's

> "You cannot hope to bribe or twist, thank God! the British journalist! But seeing what the man will do unbribed, there's no occasion to."
>
> **Humbert Wolfe,** "The Uncelestial City"

**58 El Vino's** ★$ Whoever said "in vino veritas" didn't hang out at El Vino's. This masculine institution is packed daily with journalists, lawyers, and City businessmen. A lot of history has been written over bottles of wine in this haunt of boozy journalists. What starts as a piece of gossip, idle speculation, or a mischievous rumor and becomes an item in the *Standard Diary* or an article in *Private Eye,* progresses to "something worth checking" in more serious papers. Women weren't allowed to drink at the bar until 1982, and few do today. The wine list is long and the menu consists of such simple foods as Scottish salmon and Smithfield beef. No jeans are allowed. ◆ Wine bar ◆ Bar: M-F 11:30AM-3PM, 4:30-8PM. Restaurant: lunch. Closed Saturday and Sunday. 47 Fleet St. Reservations recommended. 071/353.6786; fax 071/936.2367

**59 Printer's Pie** ★$ In addition to the beer, this pub is famous for the Queen Victoria mixed grill and such traditional English fare as shepherd's pie, sausages, mash, and onions. ◆ Pub ◆ Lunch and dinner. Closed Saturday and Sunday. 60 Fleet St. 071/353.8861

**60 Dr. Johnson's House** London is full of great men's houses, lovingly bought and preserved, restored, rearranged, and revitalized in the spirit of the departed. They usually possess an orderliness that the former inhabitants would find astonishing, especially in the houses of writers. Among the most tempting for the London lover is the house of **Samuel Johnson,** one of three of his London residences and the place where he produced the first complete dictionary of the English language, published in 1755. Until he moved to Gough Square, Johnson had lived in miserable lodgings, taking whatever literary hackwork he could find. But with the advance he was given to write the *Dictionary,* he leased 4 Gough Square in 1748. On the day he signed the contract to write the *Dictionary,* he composed the following prayer: "Oh God, who hast hitherto supported me, enable me to proceed in this labour, and in the whole task of my present state; that when I shall render up, at the last day, an account of the talent committed to me, I may receive pardon. For the sake of Jesus Christ, amen." Johnson installed his assistants in the huge attic, and for the next 11 years, they worked at their task. In 1759, when his beloved wife, **Tetty,** 15 years his senior, died, he left his house, melancholy and impoverished, and went to live in **Staple Inn.** ◆ Admission. M-Sa 11AM-5:30PM May-Sept; M-Sa 11AM-5PM Oct-Apr.17 Gough Sq. 071/353.3745

**61 Dombey & Son** No, there never was a Mr. Dombey, so there couldn't have been a son, either. No one is quite sure, but this tailor was believed to have been named after **Charles** Dickens' book. Look through the window at the dying art of Savile Row-trained tailors cutting and sewing the bespoke suits they make for City workers. ◆ M-F 8:30AM-5PM. 151 Fleet St. 071/353.2940

**62 Ye Olde Cheshire Cheese** ★★★$$ This 17th-century hostelry is probably the most profitable institution on Fleet Street and one of the few remaining of its kind in London. "The House," as it's also known, has witnessed 1[?] reigns and hardly changed since it was rebu[?] after the Great Fire of 1666. The 14th-centur[?] crypt from **Whitefriars** monastery is beneat[?] the cellar bar, and is available for private parties. The sawdust on the floor, changed twice daily, and the oak tables in "boxes" wit[?] benches on either side enchant foreigners, who long to have their England frozen in tim[?] Considering the unrivaled popularity of the place, the food is pretty good, although the famous pudding of steak kidney, mushroom[?] and game, which celebrated its bicentenary 1972, no longer feeds 90 people nor require[?] 16 hours to cook. Nor does it contain oyster[?] and lark, but it's sustaining and flavorful. Th[?] biggest pies now serve up to 35 people with steak kidney, venison, and game packed under a delicious pie crust. Rich game puddings are served in autumn and winter. Follow the pudding with Stilton or lemon pancakes and relish the Englishness of it all. ◆ British ◆ Bar: M-F 11:30AM-11PM; Sa noon-3PM, 6-9PM. Restaurant: lunch and dinner; lunch only on Sunday. 145 Fleet St. Reservations recommended. Tube: St. Paul[?] Blackfriars. 071/353.6170

**62 Daily Telegraph Building** This massive modernish neo-Greek building designed in 1928 by **Elcock**, **Sutcliffe, and Tait** once housed London's most sensible, conservati[?] paper. The *Telegraph* was the capital's first daily penny paper, founded in 1855. The pa[?] moved to Docklands, but the building's faca[?] remains. ◆ 135 Fleet St

**63 Cartoonist** ★★$ A Fleet Street "local" and[?] headquarters of the **Cartoonist Club of Grea[?] Britain,** every square inch of wall space in th[?] pub and restaurant is covered in framed original cartoons. The telephones are used b[?] members of the press, who are the regulars here. ◆ Pub ◆ Lunch and dinner. 76 Shoe Ln[?] 071/353.2828

**64 Daily Express Building** Nicknamed the "Black Lubyanka," this building's black-gla[?] tiles and chrome represent one of the finest examples—inside and out—of Art Deco in London. It was designed by **Ellis Clarke an[?] Atkinson,** with **Sir Owen Williams,** and bui[?] in 1932. ◆ 121-128 Fleet St

**65 Old Bell Tavern** ★★$ Sir Christopher Wren built this intimate and warm pub in 1670 to house and serve the workmen rebuilding St. Bride's nearby after it was destroyed in the Great Fire. ◆ Pub ◆ M-Sa 11AM-11PM; Su 11:30AM-3PM. 95 Fleet St. 071/583.0070

**66 St. Bride's Church** Wedged in between ponderous newspaper offices is **Sir Christopher Wren's** "madrigal in stone," one of his grander creations, with the tallest of his steeples (226 feet), the origin and inspiration of the wedding cake, resting on a plain, squarish nave. The church was damaged in the Blitz and beautifully restored in the 1950s. Optimistic journalists marry and attend memorial services for fellow journalists here. The crypt—established in memory of **Lord Beaverbrook**—is now a museum of Fleet Street's printing history. ◆ Daily 8:30AM-5:30PM. Recitals: Tu-W, F 1:15PM, 1:45PM. Fleet St. 071/353.1301

**66 Wynkyn de Worde** ★★$$ Everyone's heard of **Caxton,** but **Wynkyn de Worde** was almost forgotten until now. A blue plaque calling him, rather unfortunately, the "Godfather of Fleet Street," is located just off **Ludgate Hill** on the **Stationers Hall.** This is the man who invented the printer's blocks without which the mighty Caxton presses would not have worked. Almost on the site where Wynkyn worked is this new restaurant and brasserie, which has been decorated with antique stone, church pews, a confessional box, and even an altar. It's frequented by City folk who appreciate homemade cooking with a modern touch. The spinach-and-salmon roulade is delicious, as are the traditional homemade pies and the smoked chicken. ◆ British ◆ Lunch and dinner. Closed Saturday and Sunday. 1 St. Brides Passage, Bride Ln. 071/936.2554; fax 071/583.4742

**67 Reuter's and The Press Association** The headquarters of two famous international news agencies are located at No. 85 Fleet Street, where the genius of **Sir Edwin Lutyens** comes through as always in this, his last commercial building in London. It's located next door to **Wren's** beautiful **St. Bride's,** and the Edwardian architect was wisely inspired by and respectful of the wedding-cake church, conceiving his L-shaped plan as a backdrop and linking the building to the west door of the church by a high vaulted passage. The building dates from 1935. ◆ 85 Fleet St

## Bests

### J.P. Donleavy
Writer

It was always my unfailing custom to perambulate to at least one of London's mainline stations every day. These included, in order of their attraction: **Paddington, Victoria, Charing Cross,** and **Liverpool Street.** In such places, I usually spent one and a half hours around peak arrival time meeting trains off which no one ever came that I knew. But it is astonishing at how excited I could get in such hope. Next, I would snatch a taxi from in front of some intending, weary traveler and rush to teatime, usually at **Fortnum's** for their China Lapsang Souchong tea and Sacher torte chocolate cake. Over the years, as the Jermyn Street part of Fortnum's would get thronged, I also repaired to the emptier fourth-floor venue. **Christie's,** on King Street, was also a nice place to stop off to use the gents' convenience and to take pleasure in other people's possessions, as well as to partake in the sad atmosphere of mature ladies depositing their pearls for appraisal.

Sometimes, on a variation of a theme of friendship, I would take tea with one **William Donaldson** (a.k.a. **Henry Root**) in either of two places: **Basil Street Hotel** or **Brown's.** These discreetly sedate places were chosen because there were often indiscreet matters to discuss. Mr. Donaldson was always a marvelous pleasure to see, and he was always as prompt to the split second as I was, which meant we would confront each other two minutes early. On occasions when our conversation was extremely indiscreet, the venue was changed to a suite at the **Grosvenor House.**

However, my most stable standby, following a walk through **Mayfair** after tea, was champagne at **Claridge's,** followed by either a stroll under the massive plane trees in **Berkeley Square** or a visit to **Farm Street Church.** Then, with absolutely nowhere to go or no one to see, I would repair back to **Victoria Station,** meet the trains for a couple of hours, and then either take an apple out of my pocket to eat or go dine on game pie and beer at one of the **Pall Mall** clubs.

### Robin Gibson
Curator of the 20th-Century Collection and Exhibition Organizer, National Portrait Gallery

**Queen Mary's Rose Garden,** Regent's Park, followed by a performance at the **Open Air Theatre** on a (dry) evening in late June.

An exhibition at **Agnews,** unchanged for the last hundred years.

Crossing **Waterloo Bridge** and seeing the city skyline at dusk on the way to a concert at the **Royal Festival Hall**—still the best piece of '50s architecture I know.

Window shopping on **Cork Street,** which has most of the best modern art galleries in London.

Lunch at **Rules;** afternoon tea at **Claridge's.**

Mingling with the British gardener at one of the monthly flower shows at the **Royal Horticultural Society's New Hall**—itself a gem of 1920s architecture.

A trip by river bus to **Ham House,** the best 17th-century interior in Britain.

# The City/ The Thames

The love affair between England's capital and its host waterway dates back more than 2,000 years, when the origins of what is now the City of London took root on the banks of the river. London began in the so-called **Square Mile**, today the site of the **Lloyds of London Building**, the **National Westminster Tower**, and other skyscrapers, and now known simply as the City.

Commerce gave birth to the city and commerce was possible mainly because of the Thames. What the Roman conquerors called "Londinium" in AD 43 had been a hub of trade between Britain and the Continent since the Bronze Age. Commerce thrived as everything from spices and jewels to silks and tea from China arrived on the wharves of the Thames, brought to Britain by explorers and captains who forged a seafaring tradition for their island nation.

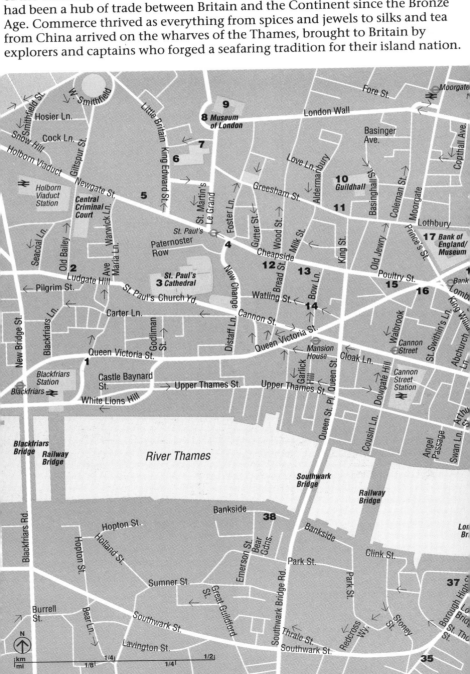

In the midst of this incessant trade governed by a powerful merchant class, the river fulfilled another function: it was the highway of sovereigns, as well as of those who served or displeased them. Barges plowed slowly through the dark waters, ferrying king to castle, bishop to church, and prisoner to the execution block. They also ferried actors to theaters, for on the south bank the likes of **William Shakespeare** and **Richard Burbage** were shaping the history of English language drama in **Southwark**.

Today, the Thames is quiet. The cargo ships have all but vanished, and the populace has largely turned its back on the river. Yet, despite modern face-lifts, its two banks are remarkably unchanged. Theater is flourishing again in Southwark, thanks to the **International Shakespeare Globe Centre**. Finance still rules the City, though computers in the **Stock Exchange** now clinch deals once made with handshakes in coffeehouses or on the docks. The

**Docklands** area is still a center of commerce, but the commodity it handles is no longer crates of tea. Instead, offices and tourist attractions are its mainstay. Finally, the merchant class's struggle for dominance (they jousted with the crown and the church for centuries) is still evident in the buildings of the **Bank of England**, the **Guildhall**, and the **Tower of London**, a prison for traitors in medieval times, though the latter is now devoted to peaceful concerns. In the midst of it all stands stately and solemn **St. Paul's Cathedral** London's epicenter. Like the City over which it presides and the river that flows past it, **Sir Christopher Wren's** splendid cathedral has weathered countless changes, but has always managed to keep its soul intact, just as London itself has.

**1 Mermaid** This is the City's only theater outside of the Barbican complex, as well as the most ignored one in town, which is sad because it's the dream-come-true of **Sir Bernard Miles,** who had always wanted to build his own stage and did so in 1959. Nonetheless, those in the know love it because it livens up the **Puddle Dock** area, once the site of a Norman castle given to the Black Friars Dominican Order. The Mermaid also keeps dramatic tradition alive; in the 16th and 17th centuries, this part of London became an artists' quarter, attracting playwrights such as **Ben Jonson** and **William Shakespeare.** Modern audiences needn't fear Elizabethan conditions, however: today's Mermaid is comfortable, with excellent views from every seat (all 610 of them), and is easy to get to (next to Blackfriars tube). ◆ Puddle Dock. 071/410.0000; fax 071/410.0202

**2 St. Martin Ludgate** The sharp, dark obelisk spire is accent and prelude to St. Paul's Cathedral, a City prayer away. **Sir Christopher Wren's** design, dating from 1677, centers around a cross inside a square, which is defined by two sets of stairs in the vestibule and four tall Corinthian columns that support two intersecting tunnel vaults. A magnificent brass candelabra hangs in the middle of the crossing, and there is a pale, concerned pelican above the font. ◆ Daily 10AM-4PM May-Oct; daily 11AM-3PM Nov-Apr. Ludgate Hill

**3 St. Paul's Cathedral** The glimpses you'll have of St. Paul's while walking up Ludgate Hill are inspiring, reassuring, and awesome. But when you're within a few yards, the cathedral grows smaller, the road veers too close, and the statue of **Queen Anne** seems dumpy and distracting. It's worth stepping back a moment when you reach **Sir Christopher Wren's** greatest masterpiece to try and see what the architect himself intended: the slight curve of the road; the scale, monumental in the context of the medieval perspective; the magnificent dome, second only in Christendom to St. Peter's; and the skyline, uncluttered and harmonious. Even as late as 1939, before the Germans

chose St. Paul's as a primary bombing target, the cathedral stood in a tapestry of streets, courts, squares, and alleys, and medieval London was still recognizable.

Five churches have stood on this site. The first, founded by **King Ethelbert** of Kent for **Bishop Mellitus** in AD 604, was destroyed by fire, and rebuilt between 675 and 685 by **Bishop Erkenwald.** This church, in turn, was destroyed by a ninth-century Viking raid, but was rebuilt in 962. In 1087, this Saxon structure also burned, but rebuilding began almost immediately, at the behest of **William Rufus,** son of **William the Conqueror.** It was this great wooden cathedral, unfinished until 1240, that became known as **Old St. Paul's.** But the magnificent cathedral, with one of the tallest spires in Europe, fell into desperate decay, and after the Great Fire of 1666, lay in ruins. Six days after the fire, Wren, then 31, submitted his plan for rebuilding the City and the cathedral. It was rejected, but Wren remained undaunted, and in May 1675, his design was approved. He laid the first stone on 21 June 1675, and the last was set by his son, 33 years later.

Wren managed to get an important concession attached to the design that gave him the freedom to make "ornamental rather than essential" changes during construction. He took full advantage of the clause, modifying his design considerably—including deleting a tall spire—during the three decades spent building the church. When it was complete, Wren, who was retired and living in Hampton Court, would still come and sit under the dome of his monument: "If I glory, it is in the singular mercy of God, who has enabled me to finish a great work so conformable to the ancient model."

St. Paul's was the first building in London to have an exterior of Portland stone, and when it was cleaned in the 1960s, Londoners were astonished to discover a dazzling, honey-colored building. In front of the cathedral stands the statue of Queen Anne looking down Ludgate Hill. The original statue, carved in 1712 by **Francis Bird,** suffered from decay and occasional attacks—she lost her nose, orb, and scepter—and was removed to the grounds of a girls' school in East Sussex in 1884. The Queen and the forecourt were originally inside a railing, which was sold at auction in 1874. At the same time, the road was expanded, bringing St. Paul's closer to the hellish stream of traffic en route to the City.

The spacious 78,000-square-foot interior accommodates tourist groups more readily than Westminster Abbey and, in spite of its 300 years and large population of statues and monuments, there is a lack of clutter, unique in cathedral design. The focal point is the huge dome-space at the crossing. The dome rises 218 feet above the floor and is supported by eight massive double piers with Corinthian capitals. Wren actually created three domes: a brickwork inner dome supports the lead-covered outer dome as well as the painted inner one, also made of brick. The spandrels under the **Whispering Gallery** contain 19th-century mosaics executed by **Antonio Salviati,** depicting the four Evangelists (Matthew, Mark, Luke, and John) and the four Prophets (Isaiah, Jeremiah, Ezekiel, and Daniel). The surface of the dome is decorated

with eight large monochrome frescoes by **Sir James Thornhill,** depicting scenes from the life of St. Paul. The epitaph to Wren, who is buried in the crypt, is written in Latin on the pavement under the dome, and the plaque to **Winston Churchill,** also on the floor beneath the dome, was unveiled in 1974. If you are sound of breath and limb, it is well worth inspecting the dome more closely. For a small fee, you can climb the 259 steps to the Whispering Gallery, thus named because if you stand at the entrance you can hear what is being said in a normal voice on the other side 107 feet away. The gallery offers spectacular views of the concourse, choir, arches, clerestory, and the interior of the dome. If you're still feeling fit, climb the steeper spiral to the **Stone Gallery,** which surrounds the top of the drum outside. From here you can see all of London. For the heartiest, the **Golden Gallery** at the top of the dome takes you to the lantern and the golden ball.

The best place to start a tour of the monuments in the cathedral is at the west entrance in the small **Chapel of All Souls,** a 1925 memorial to Field Marshall **Lord Kitchener,** who died in 1916, and "all others who fell in 1914-18." Behind the splendid ornamented wooden screen—carved by **Jonathan Maine,** one of Wren's great craftsmen, in 1698—is **St. Dunstan's Chapel,** reserved for private prayer. Beyond the chapel in the main aisle are various monuments, though Wren did not want memorials in the cathedral and none were added until 1790. Most impressive is the monument to the **Duke of Wellington,** which fills the central bay. Painter and sculptor **Alfred Stevens** spent 20 years creating the huge equestrian statue of the Duke on top of a canopy, and it still wasn't completed until 1912, nearly 40 years after Stevens's death. The third bay in the aisle contains an eerie Victorian monument to **Lord Melbourne, Queen Victoria's** first prime minister, who died in 1848. The inscription above the double doors guarded by two angels reads: "Through the Gate of Death we pass to our Joyful Resurrection." The **North Transept Chapel,** also called the **Middlesex Chapel,** is reserved for private prayer and contains a large marble font carved by **Francis Bird** in 1726-27. Beyond the crossing is the **North Chancel,** with a memorial screen that lists the names of former St. Paul's choristers who died in the two World Wars. The carved paneling on the right is the work of **Grinling Gibbons.** The aisle ends in the **Altar of the**

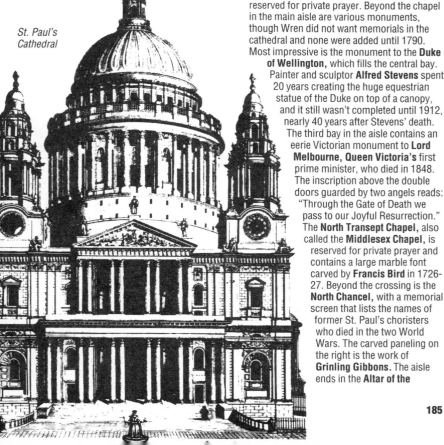

*St. Paul's Cathedral*

**Modern Martyrs,** where the names of all known Anglican martyrs since 1850 are recorded in a book kept in a glass-topped casket. Pass through the fine ironwork gate by **Jean Tijou** and enter the **American Memorial Chapel,** paid for entirely by contributions of people all over Britain as a tribute to the 28,000 members of the American forces who lost their lives in Britain or in active service from Britain during World War II. The names fill 500 pages of illuminated manuscript, bound in a red-leather volume and presented to St. Paul's by **General Eisenhower** on 4 July 1951.

The choir is enclosed by a low screen made from the original altar rail by Jean Tijou, and contains the exquisite carved choir stalls made in the 1690s by Grinling Gibbons. The carved oak *baldacchino* (canopy) above the high altar was created from some of Wren's unused drawings by **Godfrey Allen** and **Stephan Dykes Bower.** It replaced the reredos damaged in 1941, and serves as Britain's memorial to the more than 324,000 men and women of the Commonwealth who died in the two World Wars.

The **Lady Chapel,** in the eastern end of the south choir aisle, contains the cathedral's original high altar. Nearby is a statue of **John Donne,** the poet who became one of the finest preachers the Anglican church has ever produced and the most famous dean of St. Paul's, serving from 1621 to 1631. When Donne believed he was about to die, he called for sculptor **Nicholas Stone the Elder** to come and draw him in his shroud. It is the only effigy that survived the Great Fire intact.

On the second pillar in the south aisle hangs a version of **William Holman Hunt's** most famous painting, *The Light of the World,* depicting a pre-Raphaelite Christ knocking at a humble door overgrown with weeds. The door has no handle and can only be opened from the inside; this is the door of the heart. Nearly life-size, it is the third and largest version of the painting Hunt produced and was presented to the cathedral by wealthy shipowner **Charles Booth** in 1908.

The **Chapel of the Order of St. Michael and St. George,** with its beautiful woodwork by **Jonathan Maine** and colorful banners, can only be entered on a 1 1/2 hour **Supertour** (conducted from the **Friends' Table** near the west door). The order was instituted in 1818 for those who had given distinguished service to the Commonwealth. The chapel was dedicated in 1906 by **Bishop Henry Montgomery,** with the stirring words: "You who represent the best of the Anglo-Saxon race at work beyond the seas are now made the guardians of the west door of the cathedral."

If you leave the chapel and continue westward along the aisle, you will reach the **Geometrical Staircase,** designed by Wren and built with a

railing by Jean Tijou. Each stone step is set in the wall only a few inches, the weight at each level carried by the step below.

The crypt, entered from the South Transept and covering the whole length of the cathedra is probably the largest in Europe. Many famo people are buried here, including **Nelson** in t elegant black tomb **Cardinal Wolsey** had bui for himself before he fell out of royal favor, a well as Wellington, and Wren and his family. The artists' corner commemorates **Van Dyck, Blake, Turner, Reynolds, Constable,** and many others. Noteworthy are the memorial t **John Singer Sargent,** designed by the artist himself, and the memorial to **George Frampton,** which includes a small replica of t statue of Peter Pan he sculpted for Kensingtc Gardens. ♦ Admission (includes crypt). Daily 7:15AM-6PM; daily 8:30AM-4:15PM for sightseeing. For details about services and guided Supertours: 071/248.2705

**4 Balls Brothers** ★★$ Judiciously avoid the sandwich bars at the front of St. Paul's. The sandwiches and coffee are okay, but the meal are everything that you'd expect from cafes that cater to tourists en masse. Instead, go around the back of the cathedral to what looks like an insurance office—this is Balls Brothers an underground bar where huge sandwiches (for England) are served, with at least three ounces of meat. This is a traditional-style bar, with wooden paneling, glass screens, and brie a-brac. The only drawback: too few seats. ♦ Bar food ♦ Lunch and dinner. Closed Saturday and Sunday. 6 Cheapside. 071/248.2708

**5 London Chief Post Office and National Postal Museum** If you could save up all yc postcards and letters and mail them in just o spot, it would have to be here: the most sumptuous place to stick a stamp on a letter London. It makes such a minuscule task feel like an important occasion. This building, constructed between 1907 and 1911 by **Sir Henry Tanner,** was one of the first in Londor to have a reinforced concrete structure, whic gives the tremendous white, marbled, and cavernous interior an immensely safe and reassuring feel.

The National Postal Museum was started in 1965 by **Reginald M. Phillips** of Brighton. H wanted to create a national home for postal history, so he gave to the post office his own unique collection of 19th-century British postage stamps, documents, drawings, and proofs, together with a lot of money to get th whole thing going. The museum houses the **Phillips** and **Post Office Collections** and the **Berne Collection** of stamps from countries belonging to the **Universal Post Union.** Modern stamp history began with the penny-black, tuppenny-blue, and penny-red postag stamps on 6 May 1840, but the collections g back in history and forward to the present day, worldwide and maritime. The most popular countries' stamps are on display; those from more exotic locales may be seen by prior arrangement, as can the collection of letter boxes. Outside on the pavement stands the man who started it all: a granite **Sir Rowland Hill,** the founder of the **Penny Post;** the statue was made in 1881 by **R. Onslow Ford.** ♦ M-F 9:30AM-4:30PM. King Edward Building, King Edward St. 071/239.5420

**6 Postman's Park** The City of London is long on big buildings and short on green spaces, so this tiny emerald enclave is all the more welcome. The park got its name because it is next to the Post Office. On one wall of the park is a monument to heroic deeds, dedicated in 1900 and covered in plaques with stories that bring tears to your eyes: "William Fisher aged 9 lost his life on Rodney Road, Walworth, while trying to save his little brother from being run over." (12 July 1886)

**7 St. Botolph's Without Aldersgate** One of four churches in London built in the 10th century for the spiritual comfort of travelers, this church is dedicated to St. Botolph, a seventh-century Saxon abbot, the traveler's patron saint. It has been rebuilt twice, the last time by **Nathaniel Wright** in 1788-91, and once again the interior is in urgent need of restoration. Despite its dull exterior, it is quite lovely inside because of its preserved 18th-century architecture, with big plaster rosettes covering the ceiling, three wooden galleries, a barrel-vaulted roof, and exquisite stained-glass windows (including the *Agony in the Garden*). Methodists will love this church because, close by in Little Britain, **John** and **Charles Wesley** were converted back in 1736, a fact that is commemorated outside the church and on a big bronze scroll outside the nearby **Museum of London.** ♦ M-F 8:15AM-6PM. Aldersgate and Gresham Sts. 071/606.0684

# ondon: A City Wren-dered

**Christopher Wren** was a brilliant Latinist, onomer, mathematician, engineer, and itect in Elizabethan England. In spite of this utation as a remarkable polymath, Wren saw plan for rebuilding the City after the Great Fire 666 rejected. Eventually, however, he put his ature on London by building 52 City rches and **St. Paul's Cathedral,** a tribution unparalleled in architectural ory. During the Second World War, when e than one-third of the City was destroyed, rly all of Wren's churches were severely aged. But because elaborate plans had n preserved, many have since been utifully rebuilt; today, 23 remain. The ous epitaph, composed in Latin by n's son, that identifies the architect's at in St. Paul's Cathedral reads: neath lies the founder of this church city, Christopher Wren, who lived more ninety years, not for himself but for public good. Reader, if you seek his ument, look around you."

le a good portion of Wren's legacy rged intact from the Blitz, another ault is currently in progress. troversy surrounding the City of don's redevelopment erupted in the Os and 1970s when elopers, with complete egard for the historic ine, began closing in St. Paul's and ounding **Paternoster are.** Britons of all ses were alarmed at ng developers run

roughshod over these beloved landmarks. A fireman who had braved the World War II bombings to keep the cathedral from going up in flames sent in a letter to the *Times:* ". . . we might as well have let it burn. It would have saved the grabbers and developers a lot of trouble and money and made it much easier for the 'architects.' Certainly many a good fireman we lost in the City those nights might now be drawing his well-earned fire brigade pension."

On 1 December 1987, **Prince Charles** joined the fray on behalf of St. Paul's by delivering a well-aimed speech to the Corporation of London Planning and Development Committee. The Prince's attack on what he called "the rape of Britain" made front-page news. "St. Paul's," he declared, "is not just a symbol and a mausoleum for national heroes. It is also a temple which glorifies God through the inspired expression of man's craftsmanship and art. . . . As a result of technological change, places like Paternoster are obsolete. Here, surely, is a heaven-sent opportunity to build a model of real quality, of excellence, next to so great a building in the heart of our capital city. I, for one, would love to see the London skyline restored, and I am sure I am not alone in feeling this."

Indeed. Since this speech, architects have submitted new plans for the area, many of which are still under consideration by the Department of the Environment.

*St. Martin Ludgate*

**8 Museum of London** Two thousand years of London's history have been immortalized on this site, along the line of the old City wall. The Romans took up residence in AD 43 and built a wall that was 3.25 miles long with six main gates; this wall was finally demolished during the 18th century, although bits of it still survive. The explanation of how London came to be as it is today can be found here, starting with a model Roman village and ending with the spectacular **Lord Mayor's Coach,** which is wheeled out on state occasions. There are four main themes within the museum: Prehistoric and Roman, which includes sculpture from the Temple of Mithras; Medieval spans a thousand years from the fifth-century Dark Ages to the 15th century; Tudor and Stuart contrasts those glittering eras against the Great Plague of 1665 and contains a re-creation of the Great Fire of 1666, which destroyed 80 percent of London, and, in turn, allowed **Christopher Wren** his prolific church-building career. In the Modern galleries, which cover Georgian and Victorian periods, and the 20th century, the museum dubs London the world's first megalopolis and shows how the City is surviving the tremendous transition of the last 200 years. It is amusing to think that most of the artifacts have been dug up, either physically or metaphorically, around the city somewhere. Watch out for school parties—there are lots of them. The shop here is stacked with London paraphernalia, including more than 400 books on the mighty city. ◆ Admission. Tu-Sa 10AM-6PM; Su noon-6PM. 150 London Wall. 071/600.3699; fax 071/600.1058

Within the Museum of London:

**Museum Restaurant** ★$ In summer, you can sit outdoors here as a lot of Londoners do—arrive by 12:30PM to get a spot. The food is decent enough, but it is the sun and fresh air that are worth coming for, not the cold drinks, sandwiches, and salads. ◆ Cafe ◆ Tu-Sa 10AM-5PM; Su noon-5PM. 071/600.3699

**9 Barbican Centre** When **Queen Elizabeth II** opened the Barbican in 1982, she called it one of the wonders of the modern world, and, as usual, the Queen was not exaggerating. Designed by architects **Chamberlin, Powell and Bon** on a site that was heavily bombed during the Blitz, this walled city within the City covers 20 acres, rises 10 levels, descends 17 feet below sea level, and caps it all with the most extensive flat roof in Europe. The **Royal Shakespeare Company,** which is Britain's leading subsidized company and is based in Stratford-upon-Avon, moved to the Barbican from the Aldwych in 1982. The theater, reached from levels three through six, has 1,166 seats, with raked stalls and three circles projecting toward the stage, putting every

guest within 65 feet of the action. The 109-foot, double-height fly-tower above the stage, used for scenery storage, is believed to be the tallest in the world. A remarkable stainless-steel safety curtain descends during intermissions.

Small productions of **Shakespeare,** revivals and new plays are performed in the **Pit,** which was originally a rehearsal space but has been redesigned as a flexible auditorium for 200 people. The **Concert Hall** (on levels five and six) is the home of the **London Symphony Orchestra.** The area around the Barbican is slowly acquiring restaurants and cafes but is still a windy wasteland at night, and the catering in the Barbican is appalling, so eat before you come; by the time you get back to the center of town all the restaurants will have closed. Getting to the Barbican can be a drag, too. One strategy is to arrive by taxi and leave by the tube, but the most practical way is to take the tube both ways. It would help if the Barbican were better marked (en route and inside), but at least the tickets are now sold central London at the **Theatre Museum** (at Wellington Street, and Covent Garden). Do go see at least one of Shakespeare's plays by this brilliant company. There are usually some standby seats available. ◆ M-Sa 9AM-11PM; Su noon-11PM. Silk St. Box office and credit card bookings: 071/638.8891

**10 Guildhall** The first lord mayor, **Henry FitzAilwin,** was installed in 1192. The Gothic porch, which is still the entrance to the hall from Guildhall Yard, was finished in 1430; the main structure was finished in 1439. The most extensive medieval crypt in London today still exists beneath the hall and it has one of the finest vaulted ceilings in London. The building is the largest hall after Westminster Hall and was once used for treason trials, such as that of **Lady Jane Grey.** Nowadays, it is used for state occasions. It survived the Great Fire but was bombed out in World War II and repaired by **Sir Giles Gilbert Scott,** who also worked on the Houses of Parliament. The newer buildings were designed by **Sir Giles Scott, Son & Partners,** and seem to match the Gothic classical front in a '60s way. It is open to the public, except when booked for state occasions, so call and check. ◆ Free. M-Sa 10AM-5PM. Aldermanbury (at Basinghall St) 071/606.3030; fax 071/260.1119

**10 Guildhall Library** **Dick Whittington,** thrice lord mayor of London, left enough money to start this library in 1423. The entire contents were pilfered by the **Duke of Somerset** in 1549 and recovered as recently as 1824. The library is the greatest source of information on England's capital, with genealogical histories, parish registers, and heraldic histories of important Londoners. ◆ M-F 9:30AM-5:30PM; Sa 9:30AM-4:45PM. Guildhall. 071/606.3030

Within the Guildhall Library:

**The Clock Museum** Within the library's precincts, this museum contains clocks from many centuries, as well as books dating back to 1814. There are 700 exhibits under one roof, including a pocketwatch said to have belonged to **Mary, Queen of Scots,** making it one of the foremost horological museums in the country. ♦ Free. M-F 9:30AM-5:15PM; Sa 9:30AM-4PM. 071/606.3030

**11 St. Lawrence Jewry** On the wall of this church is one of the few remaining blue police phone boxes in London. The lord mayor and corporation worship here because it is close both to Mansion House and Guildhall, not because it is particularly beautiful inside, having suffered great damage during World War II. ♦ Gresham and King Sts

**12 Le Poulbot** ★★$$$ Considering the amount of money sloshing around in the coffers of the Square Mile, the City is quite low on first-class eating establishments. This is one of the exceptions, and somehow most of the power-lunchers gravitate here to toy with such delicacies as the *saumon poché au beurre rouge* followed by the *tarte au citron.* ♦ French ♦ Lunch. Closed Saturday and Sunday. 45 Cheapside. Reservations required. Jacket and tie required. 071/236.4379

**13 St. Mary-le-Bow** Every true Cockney is born "within the sound of Bow Bells," which were smashed to smithereens never to ring again after a bombing raid during World War II. The church, on this spot since 1091, has a very bloody history: the tower collapsed sometime in the 12th century, killing 20, and people seeking sanctuary here got short shrift and usually death, too. **Sir Christopher Wren** rebuilt it in 1670, and the exterior is rather stunning, but the interior, which was rebuilt in the late '50s, is not all that exciting. ♦ M-W, F 6:30AM-4PM; Th 6:30AM-6PM. Cheapside. 071/248.5139

Within St. Mary-le-Bow:

**The Place Below** ★★$$ What a find! In the crypt of the church, this restaurant serves lots of coffee, tea, and lashings of homemade lemonade for breakfast and throughout the day. Soups, salads, and a hot dish that changes daily are absolutely delicious. No corkage charge means that you can bring your own bottle to the more sophisticated evening meal, which includes inventive recipes such as a casserole made with butternut squash. ♦ Vegetarian ♦ Breakfast and lunch; dinner also on Thursday and Friday. Closed Saturday and Sunday. 071/329.0789

**14 Bow Lane and Watling Street** This is one of the oldest parts of London. Watling Street was first mentioned in 1230, but it is believed to have been part of the main Roman road between Dover and St. Albans, built nearly 1,000 years earlier. The tiny streets here show graphically just how chaotic the City is, lacking any formal plan. After the Great Fire of 1666 (which destroyed the plague rats as well as 80 percent of London's buildings), Londoners were desperate to get back to work and to make money. **Sir Christopher Wren** and many others drew up spectacular plans for a beautiful city. But changing the street plan would have taken a long time and cost a lot of money, so to this day the medieval plan remains. The only difference is that the buildings are made of stone, not wood. Today, Bow Lane is quaint and kitsch. Still, ancient pubs like **Ye Olde Watling** (built from ships' timbers by Wren in 1668) and **Williamson's Tavern and Library Bar** (an old lord mayor's house dating back to the 17th century) seem to be left intact; and the **Bow Wine Vaults,** the haunt of City businesspeople, and the old bookshop, **Jones & Evans** on Cannon Street, haven't suffered, either—at least not yet.

Henry VIII is indelibly engraved on the memory as a robust man who had six wives—and went to excessive lengths in order to do so. A truer picture is of a brilliant, gifted, scholarly, athletic, musical, and devout man who was handsome in youth—more than six feet tall with blond hair—and who had a great appetite for life. Sir Thomas More described him as a man "nourished on philosophy and the nine muses." He is also the monarch who, more than any other, created the look of central London, even more than George IV and his architect, John Nash.

| | |
|---|---|
| **Restaurants/Clubs:** Red | **Hotels:** Blue |
| **Shops/ 🌳 Outdoors:** Green | **Sights/Culture:** Black |

**15 Mappin & Webb** Rumbling away underneath this building is the District Line underground, which was built at the same time as the street. This Gothic-style structure, designed by **J.& J. Belcher** in 1870, faces one of London's busiest intersections and has become the subject of considerable controversy. Make the most of it; no one knows how long it will stay here. This building is both charming and eccentric, and a perfect place to buy discreetly beautiful jewelry in the company of some of London's most successful businesspeople. ◆ M-F 9AM-5:30PM. 2 Queen Victoria St. 071/248.6661

**16 Mansion House** Lord mayors in London get just one year in office, and so a mere 365 days to live and work in the splendor of this Palladian mansion, constructed between 1739 and 1753 by **George Dance the Elder.** There are a series of superb state rooms leading to an Egyptian banqueting hall with giant columns along each side on the first floor and the ballroom on the second. Note the pediment frieze depicting London defeating Envy and bringing in Plenty. ◆ Open by arrangement. Bank. 071/606.2500

**17 Bank of England/Museum** In 1797, **Richard Brinsley Sheridan** referred to "An elderly lady in the city of great credit and long standing" in the House of Parliament, and the name stuck. The bank is still called the "Old Lady of Threadneedle Street" to this day, and looks after the nation's gold and the National Debt, issues banknotes, and acts as the government's and bankers' bank. A figure of a woman holding a model of the building on her knee rests above the portico but is considered merely an ornament.

The "Old Lady" is the bank itself, according to those who work there. Established in 1694, it moved to Threadneedle Street 40 years later, where architect **Sir John Soane** rebuilt it between 1788 and 1808. Today, it has 2.25 million accounts, and prints (and destroys) five million banknotes daily. The museum holds gold bars, coins, interactive videos, and even Roman mosaics, found beneath the site. ◆ Free. M-F 10AM-5PM; Su 11AM-5PM. Threadneedle St. Tube: Bank. 071/601.5792

**18 Royal Exchange** A building where merchants can meet and conduct business has been on this site since 1566 and received royal approval from both **Queen Elizabeth I** and, later, **Queen Victoria.** This classical building, designed in 1844 by **Sir William Tite,** is the third Royal Exchange, as the other two were razed. Financial landmarks like this used to be open to the public, but the IRA bombs put an end to that. These days, the receptionist won't even tell you what companies have offices here! On the Threadneedle Street side, note the statue of **Dick Whittington,** the famous City merchant

who became three-time lord mayor. As part of a longstanding tradition, the outside steps are used to proclaim a new sovereign. ◆ Bank

**18 Searle & Co.** Clustered on the side of the Royal Exchange are a set of bijou shops. This jeweler has been based in the City since 1893 and on this spot since 1932. The wooden exterior and interior are original, and each evening the 60 tiny bejeweled gold and silver animals on display are lovingly tucked away for the night. Businesspeople come here to buy gifts, and Searle's ducks have even been seen swimming across the **Queen Mother's** dining table from time to time. ◆ M-F 9AM-5:15PM. 1 Royal Exchange. 071/626.2456

**18 Hermès** This little branch of the chic Paris and Bond Street store sells the same classic women's scarfs and accessories that set its style apart. ◆ M-F 10AM-6PM. 3 Royal Exchange. 071/626.7794

**18 Halcyon Days** Charming enameled boxes and brooches decorate every available shelf in this offshoot of the Brook Street store. It says a lot about the area that Bond Street has set up shop here. ◆ M-F 10AM-5:30PM. 4 Royal Exchange. 071/626.1120

**18 Royal Exchange Art Gallery** This cozy gallery specializes in marine art—watercolors and etchings from 1800 to the present—which is hardly surprising, given that **Lloyd's of London** is no more than a quarter of a mile away. ◆ M-F 10:30AM-5:15PM. 14 Royal Exchange. 071/283.4400

**19 George Peabody Statue William Wetmore Story's** bronze statue of American philanthropist **George Peabody** was erected in 1869, the year of Peabody's death. Peabody spent most of his life in Britain building 5,000 homes for the poor, which still stand today, and he is the only American buried in Westminster Abbey. ◆ Royal Exchange

**19 St. Mary Abchurch** This is one of the best-preserved **Sir Christopher Wren** churches in London, built between 1681 and 1686 with almost everything left unspoiled by overzealous renovators of ensuing centuries. The war wreaked havoc here, but everything has been painstakingly restored to its former beauty. The limewood reredos by **Grinling Gibbons** dates from 1686. St. Mary Abchurch is now a center for psychic research. ◆ Abchurch Yard (off Abchurch Ln)

---

"Englishman—a creature who thinks he is being virtuous when he is only being uncomfortable."

**George Bernard Shaw**

---

Clink Street's name comes from the "Clink"—a squalid prison in Southwark owned by the bishops of Westminster. Destroyed in 1780, it's been immortalized by the word clink, slang for jail.

**20 Cornhill** Once a grain market, this is the highest hill in the City. Today, it is packed with office workers, bankers, and stockbrokers; a century ago, these streets were traversed by authors like **Mrs. Gaskell, Thackeray,** and the **Brontës.** ♦ Between Bank and Gracechurch Sts

**21 St. Michael's Alley** Here is one of the few places in London that makes you draw in your breath, for it is Dickensian London as you will rarely see it anywhere else. There's no need to rush along this alley, though—it ends where your eye rests and becomes modern London again. Just two buildings, the **Jamaica Wine House** and the **George & Vulture,** lean across the street, sharing experiences of days gone by. ♦ Between Birchin Ln and Gracechurch St

Within St. Michael's Alley:

**Jamaica Wine House** A regulars-only pub, keeping strict City hours. It got its name from customers back in the 1670s who were trading in Jamaica. Once you could get the best rum here; see what you think now. ♦ Daily 11:30AM-8PM. 071/626.9496

**George & Vulture** ★★$$ This is a restaurant, not a pub, so make reservations the day before, at least, if you're thinking of coming here. Once a live vulture was used as a pub sign. **Charles Dickens** used the pub in *Pickwick Papers* for the Bardell vs. Pickwick trial. The brass plate outside is worn thin from its daily cleaning; inside, the place is just as pristine. And everything is old-fashioned, from the excellent service to the rack of roast lamb, Stilton, and port at the end of your classic English meal. It is full of stockbrokers, bankers, and insurance magnates, and the wine list reflects its international clientele. ♦ British ♦ Lunch. Closed Saturday and Sunday. 3 Castle Ct (off St. Michael's Alley), Cornhill. 071/626.9710

**22 Lombard Street** In this, the center of banking, hang the medieval street signs banned during **Charles I's** reign. The king disliked them because they regularly fell from buildings, killing whoever happened to be standing or walking below. The signs were hung up again after 300 years for **Edward VII's** coronation. They're still here—the coronation never happened. Look for the giant gold grasshopper of old **Martin's Bank,** the castle of the **TSB (Trustee Savings Bank),** and even a gold cat and fiddle. A famous nursery rhyme about the street sign: "Hey diddle diddle/The cat and the fiddle/The cow jumped over the moon/The little dog laughed to see such fun/And the dish ran away with the spoon." ♦ Between King William and Gracechurch Sts

**23 The Monument** It is getting quite difficult to see things from The Monument, since the buildings surrounding it are now taller than this block of Portland stone. Built by **Sir Christopher Wren** and City Surveyor **Robert Hooke** between 1671 and 1677, The

Monument was commissioned by **Charles II** to "preserve the memory of this dreadful visitation" (i.e., the Great Fire). If the 202-foot column were laid down, it would touch the exact spot where the Great Fire began on 2 September 1666, in a baker's oven in Pudding Lane. ♦ Admission. M-F 9AM-6PM, Sa-Su 2-6PM 31 Mar-30 Sept; M-Sa 9AM-4PM 1 Oct-30 Mar. Monument St (between Pudding Ln and Fish St Hill). 071/626.2717

**24 Leadenhall Market** A very pretty place crisscrossed with glass-roofed alleys, the Leadenhall Market was built in 1881 by **Sir Horace Jones.** Highly decorated iron-and-glass facades cover what is essentially the only place in the City where Londoners can buy any food at all. Cheese, butter, meat, fish, eggs, plants, even books can all be purchased here. ♦ Gracechurch St

**25 Lloyds Building** If you liked his Pompidou Center, this building by **Richard Rogers** will amuse, as it is a much smaller version squashed into a confined space. Erected in 1986 around a central atrium and bedecked with oversize pipework, metal flooring, and glass, this zoo-style design allows the public to see the office workers busying about their day. The structure caused a huge controversy when it was completed, but it is a bold statement in a city packed with building blocks. ♦ Closed to the public. 1 Lime St. 071/623.7100

# TOWER HILL PAGEANT

**26 Tower Hill Pageant** To the west of the **London Tower,** just behind **All Hallows by the Tower,** stands what bills itself as "London's first dark ride museum," the Tower Hill Pageant. Run in conjunction with the **Museum of London,** the Pageant covers the 2,000-year saga of the City of London. Visitors take an hour-long ride in automated cars past scenes showing what life was like when the Thames reigned supreme, from its earliest Roman days right up to the Blitz. The attraction also includes a display of waterfront archaeology items dating from Roman, Saxon, and medieval times. ♦ Admission. Daily 9:30AM-5:30PM Apr-Oct; daily 9:30AM-4:30PM Nov-Mar. Tower Hill Terrace, Tower Hill. 071/709.0081; fax 071/702.3656

"You find no man, at all intellectual, who is willing to leave London. No, sir, when a man is tired of London, he is tired of life; for there is in London all that life can afford."

**Samuel Johnson**

**27 Tower of London** Though the crowds can be as thick and forbidding as the grayish-brown stone, this medieval monument (pictured above), with its displays of armor and exquisite **Crown Jewels,** must be seen at least once in a lifetime. Nine hundred years of fascinating, though brutal, history are embraced within these walls, and even though the tower's violent years are long past, an atmosphere of impending doom still lingers. The tower has been used as a royal palace, fortress, armory, treasury, and menagerie, but it is best known as a merciless prison. Being locked up here, especially in Tudor times, was tantamount to certain death. **Anne Boleyn, Catherine Howard, Lady Jane Grey, Sir Thomas More,** and **Sir Walter Raleigh** are but a few who spent their final days, and in some cases years, in the tower.

The buildings of **Her Majesty's Palace** and **Fortress of the Tower of London,** as it is officially known, reflect almost every style of English architecture, as well as the different roles the tower has played. **William the Conqueror** started the **White Tower** in 1078, and it was completed 20 years later by his son, **William Rufus (William II). Richard the Lionheart** strengthened the fortress in the 12th century by building a curtain wall with towers, of which only the **Bell Tower** remains. **Henry III** and his son **Edward I** completed the transformation into the medieval castle that stands today. The 120-foot-wide moat, now covered with grass, was kept flooded with water by a series of sluice gates until 1843; today, it serves as the village green for the 50 or so families who live on the tower grounds. Prisoners and provisions were brought in through the **Traitors Gate** when the Thames was still London's main highway. A gate in the **Bloody Tower** leads to the inner precincts. Once known as the **Garden Tower,** the Bloody Tower acquired its unpleasant name after the **Little Princes** mysteriously disappeared from it in 1485. Controversy still rages over whether **Richard III,** their uncle and protector,

had them murdered so he could secure the throne. Sir Walter Raleigh was a prisoner in the Bloody Tower from 1603 to 1616, and th is where he wrote *A History of the World.* Almost every stone in **Beauchamp Tower** contains desperately scratched messages from prisoners, pathetic reminders of those who perished. Nearby is the **Chapel Royal of St. Peter ad Vincula,** built in the 12th century and restored by **Henry VIII** in 1520 after a fire in 1512. The chapel is the burial place of the **Duke of Somerset, the Duke of Northumberland,** Anne Boleyn, Catherine Howard (two of Henry VIII's six wives), and Lady Jane Grey, all of whom were beheaded.

Glittering amid the historical doom and gloom are the **Crown Jewels,** the tower's most popular attraction. Dazzling and brilliant, almost breathing with fire, the spectacular collection far exceeds its reputation. The jewels were housed in **Martin Tower** until 1671, when the audacious **Colonel Blood** came very close to making off with them. The are now heavily guarded by yeoman warders in the ground-floor strongroom of **Waterloo Barracks,** known as the **Jewel House.** Here, robes, swords, scepters, and crowns adorned with some of the most precious stones in the world are displayed. Most of the royal regalia was sold or melted down after the execution of **Charles I** in 1649. Only two pieces escaped the **Anointing Spoon,** probably first used in the coronation of **King Henry IV** in 1399, and the 14th-century **Ampulla.** The rest of the collection dates from the restoration of **Charles II** in 1660.

**St. Edward's Crown** was made for Charles II, and has been used by nearly all of his successors, including **Queen Elizabeth II.** It weighs almost five pounds and is adorned with more than 400 precious stones. The priceless **Imperial State Crown,** originally made for **Queen Victoria,** contains some of the most famous stones in the world, including the 317-carat **Second Star of Africa** the **Stuart Sapphire,** and the **Black Prince's** balas ruby. Monarchs have worn this crown when leaving Westminster Abbey after coronation ceremonies, at the State Opening of Parliament, and at other state occasions. The exquisite **Koh-i-noor** diamond adorns th **Queen Mother's Crown,** made especially for the coronation of Queen Elizabeth II in 1937. But even grander is the 530-carat **Star of Africa,** believed to be the largest cut diamond which is on the **Sovereign's Sceptre.** Most spectacular of the many swords is the **State Sword,** decorated with diamonds, emeralds, and rubies that form the national emblems of England, Scotland, and Ireland.

The imposing Kentish and Caen stone walls of the **White Tower** dominate the Tower of London. Built in 1078 for William the Conqueror by a Norman monk, the walls are

15 feet thick at the base, 11 feet thick at the top, and 90 feet above ground level. In 1241, Henry III, finding comfort within such dimensions, added a great hall and royal apartments and had the exterior whitewashed, hence the name White Tower. Today, the tower houses the collection of **Royal Armories,** dating from the time it was the chief arsenal of the kingdom. The **Tudor Gallery** is the centerpiece of the collection. Here the personal armor of Henry VIII portray his massive presence more than any portrait ever could. On display are the armors made for foot combat when the King was young, slim, and charming, the famous ram's-horn helmet, and **King Henry's Walking Staff,** a spiked club with three gun barrels in the head.

**St. John's Chapel,** on the second floor of the White Tower, is one of the finest examples of early Norman architecture, with simple columns, roundheaded arches, and beautiful tunnel vaulting. It was here in 1503 that **Elizabeth of York,** wife of **Henry VII,** lay in state surrounded by 500 candles, and here that Lady Jane Grey prayed before her execution in 1554.

The tower's great sense of history and tradition lives on through ceremonies that have been performed virtually unchanged for centuries. Most famous is the **Ceremony of the Keys,** perhaps the oldest military ceremony in the world. Every evening at precisely 10 minutes to 10PM, the chief yeoman warder, wearing a large scarlet coat and accompanied by four soldiers, secures the main gates of the tower. As the clock strikes 10, a bugler sounds the Last Post. On 21 May of each year, representatives from Eton College and King's College, Cambridge, place lilies and white roses in the oratory of **Wakefield Tower,** where **Henry VI** was murdered in 1471, forever remembering him as the founder of these two great centers of academe. This ceremony is generally not open to the public. However, one tradition the public can see takes place only every three years (1993, 1996, etc): the **Beating the Bounds,** which marks the boundaries of the tower's liberties. It takes four hours on Ascension Day and, unfortunately, isn't very exciting to watch but might be interesting if you're passing by. The yeoman warder and choir boys go around to each marker and beat it with a willow stick to establish the boundaries. (They used to beat one of the boys, not the stone!)

Tradition continues with the daily feeding of the ravens who live within the tower walls. Since Charles II decreed there should always be at least six ravens at the tower, there have always been six with two reserves. In 1989, the tower managed to breed the birds successfully. Their wings are clipped to keep them here because legend has it that if they leave, the tower will fall and the monarchy with it. Watch out: ravens are much bigger than

crows and sometimes bite the ankles of unsuspecting tourists!

To attend the Ceremony of the Keys, write (suggesting alternative dates) to the Resident Governor, the Queen's House, HM Tower of London, London EC3N 4AB. It is very popular, but only 70 people are allowed to watch, so write as soon as you book your flight. The Jewel House is closed in January or February each year when the jewels are given a thorough cleaning. Call and check before visiting during these months. ♦ Admission. M-Sa 9AM-6PM, Su 10AM-6PM 28 Mar to 30 May; M-Sa 9AM-6:30PM, Su 10AM-6:30PM 31 May to 31 Aug; M-Sa 9AM-6PM, Su 10AM-6PM 1 Sept to 22 Oct; M-Sa 9:30AM-5PM, Su 10AM-5PM 23 Oct to 26 Mar. HM Tower of London. Tube: Tower Hill. 071/709.0765

**28 St. Katharine's Dock** London's Docklands had a proud heritage as working dockyards from the 16th century onward, but in Victorian times the area became poor, and crime was rife. During World War II, the Docklands was devastated by bombs and never fully recovered—until the mid-'80s when attempts were made to revitalize the area. St. Katharine's Dock was the pioneer of all Docklands redevelopment plans, and that is probably why it is the most successful; of course, having the tower nearby doesn't hurt! Perhaps it's because **Thomas Telford** designed this dock in 1828 that it is so lovely. One of the few docks with warehouses built close to the water, so thieving was minimal, bijou shops now flourish on the waterside. Sadly, large ships could never enter, and the docks failed, but today it's a thriving marina, playing host to the big oceangoing yachts of the wealthy. The dock has a collection of unusual ships moored here, a selection of shops and offices, including the **World Trade Centre,** and a riverwalk to the Tower of London. ♦ Tube: Tower Hill

Within St. Katharine's Dock:

**The Dickens Inn** ★$$ This rambling pub looks like it came from Disneyworld—meaning it's too authentic for words—yet it really is a converted 18th-century spicehouse that has been overhauled in the style of a 19th-century balconied inn. Inside, it's all wood tables and beams, and the most pleasant place for a drink in the whole of St. Katharine's Dock; the locals use it (always a good sign), and it fills up quickly on a Friday night. Upstairs, two restaurants offer a selection of grilled and fish dishes, but the ground-floor **Tavern Bar** is really the main attraction here. ♦ Pub ♦ Daily 11AM-11PM. 071/488.2208; fax 071/702.3610

**Nauticalia** Stop in here for seafaring gear such as captain's lamps, caps, spyglasses, scrimshaw, and other marine accessories. Avoid it like the plague, however, if you dislike brass! ♦ M-F 10:30AM-6PM; Sa-Su 10AM-6PM. 071/480.6805

**The Tower Thistle Hotel** $$$ Sandwiched between the Thames and St. Katharine's Dock with its colorful yachts and shops, the vast, zigguratlike Tower Thistle Hotel offers guests four-star accommodations right around the corner from that "other" tower. Bedrooms are plush, if somewhat unimpressive, and the hotel is designed more around the business executive than the tourist. **The Princes Room** (★★★$$$$) offers superb views over **Tower Bridge** and dishes up international cuisine, while the **Carvery** (★★$$) stays closer to home with traditional roast joints. **Which Way West Café** (★$$), serving food throughout the day, metamorphoses by night into a nightclub. ◆ 071/481.4575; fax 071/488.4106

**29 Tobacco Dock** After this Georgian tobacco warehouse was restored by **Terry Farrell,** boutiques, shops, and restaurants were invited into its yellow brick arches. The effort was successful only for a while, and today much of the complex lies vacant and abandoned. Still, Tobacco Dock does a decent trade in tourist season, largely because of the two replica 18th-century ships in its harbors: one is designed after the ship in **Robert Louis Stevenson's** *Treasure Island;* the other is a standard pirate ship. ◆ Between Pennington St and The Ornamental Canal

**30 Tower Bridge** London's most famous bridge (shown above) became a museum in 1982. The original hydraulic machinery that operated the bridge until 1976 is on display, along with exhibitions that explain the Victorian genius behind the design. Built in 1894 by **Sir Horace Jones** and **John Wolfe-Barry,** the Gothic towered bridge represents Victorian architecture and engineering at its best. The twin towers of steel encased in stone support the 1,000-ton weight of the bascules that were raised and lowered by hydraulic machinery located in piers at the base of the towers. At the peak of London's river traffic, and before steam replaced tall masts, the bascules rose as many as 50 times a day. Now they are operated by electricity and only open a few times a week. The glass-enclosed walkway, stretching majestically across the London sky 145 feet above the Thames, offers splendid views in every direction. From here you can step back and see the architectural variety of the city,

from the Portland stone office buildings on Tower Hill to the brick and concrete of the postwar rebuilding to the glass and steel of t last 20 years. The **Tower Bridge Museum,** located inside the bridge, recently installed a permanent, high-tech exhibition recounting the history and function of the bridge. ◆ Admission; last tickets sold 45 minutes before closing. Daily 10AM-6:30PM Apr-Oct daily 10AM-4:45PM Nov-Mar. Tower Hill. Tube: Tower Hill. 071/407.0922

**31 Butlers Wharf** Here, among the streets an alleyways, is the best place to capture the mood of the old docklands. The spices that were once shipped in from the Orient are still sold here, and until a year or two ago, hops could be smelled from **Courage's Brewery. Dickens** had Bill Sykes from *Oliver Twist* me his end on Shad Thames, which is now the home of glass-fronted restaurants.

Within Butlers Wharf:

**Le Pont de la Tour** ★★$$$ Sir Terence **Conran** seems to own everything 'round here This is his own smart-looking restaurant and bar that's got London talking, with wine by the glass and expensive food in the ultimate designer surroundings. Try the venison accompanied by beautiful roast parsnips. ◆ Modern British ◆ Lunch and dinner. Reservations recommended. 071/403.8403, 071/403.9403 (bar)

**The Butlers Wharf Chop House** ★★$$$ One of several riverfront restaurants in the Butlers Wharf development, the Chop House by far the most traditionally English in terms menu, despite all its chrome and glass. Try th smoked eel salad as an appetizer, or opt for th Whitstable rock oysters. Main courses includ roast lamb with mint and mustard crust, stea and kidney pudding, or turbot with watercress and braised lettuce. The fixed price lunch menu is well worth it, and daily specials are listed on the blackboard. This is a pleasant spot if you're looking for something slightly of the well-worn path. ◆ British ◆ Lunch and dinner; dinner only on Saturday; lunch only o Sunday. 071/403.3403; fax 071/403.3414

**31 Design Museum** The docklands development continues more successfully south of the Thames. Visit the Design Museu on Sunday, when London's designers have th day off to visit their shrine, built by—who else?—the king of designers, **Sir Terence Conran.** It's fun to spot them sporting design gear, designer husbands and wives, and, of course, designer children. The museum, on the other hand, is truly the *only* one of its kin in the world. Its **Review** gallery showcases international design, while the **Collection** shows design in its historical context. At the **Blueprint** (★★$$), you can gaze across a panorama of London as you sip mineral wate served from perfect blue bottles. ◆ Admissio

Daily 10:30AM-5:30PM. Butlers Wharf (off Shad Thames). Reservations: 071/378.7031. General information: 071/407.6261

**2 Bermondsey (New Caledonia) Market**
One of many London streetmarkets, this is for the dedicated bargain-hunter—you need to arrive by 6AM (flashlight in hand) to get the best deals. Antiques, objets d'art, and surprisingly tasteful bric-a-brac abound, along with the usual Toby jugs and pub mirrors. A lot of professional antiques dealers come here, though, so don't let them beat you to a purchase; don't forget to haggle, either.
♦ F 6AM-2PM. Bermondsey Sq. Tube: London Bridge

**3 Hay's Galleria** A yellow brick-built dock, now under a glass atrium, it's close enough to the City to be crowded during the day with bustling office workers rushing to the delis, sandwich bars, and pretty shops. In summer, they eat outside, so get here early if you want to do the same; you'll get a good view of the HMS *Belfast,* now a floating museum, from here. Although the Galleria's design is Georgian warehouse architecture, robust and hardworking, the refit has incorporated a charm the wharf must have lacked as a working dock. Watch out for **David Kemp's** *The Navigators,* a 60-foot-tall bronze moving sculpture with water jets and fountains. ♦ Tooley St

**4 The London Dungeon** Opposite the more refined pleasures of Hay's Galleria stand the gruesome delights of the world's first and only medieval horror museum—founded, as it happens, by a Chelsea housewife! Within its gloomy vaults beneath **London Bridge,** you can learn the finer points of hanging, drawing, and quartering, or how prisoners were boiled or pressed to death. Relive the Great Fire of 1666, and wander through the new "Jack the Ripper Experience" exhibit. Frankly, this puts the pricier **Madame Tussaud's** Chamber of Horrors to shame. But be forewarned: people *have* passed out in here, so it's *not* for the fainthearted. ♦ Admission. Daily 10AM-5:30PM (last entry 4:30PM) Oct-Mar; 10AM-6:30PM (last entry 5:30PM) Apr-Sept. 28-34 Tooley St. Tube: London Bridge. 071/403.0606

**5 The George** ★$ **Eisenhower** and **Churchill** drank beer here. As a child, **Charles Dickens** walked here every Sunday from Camden Town to visit his father in **Marshalsea Prison;** you'll even find the inn in *Little Dorrit.* This is an extraordinary survivor of bygone days, the last timbered, galleried inn in London, rebuilt in 1676. Before theaters like the Globe and the Swan were built, early plays were presented in these inns, with the "groundlings" standing in the courtyard and the wealthier patrons seated on the balconies; in summer, the show still goes on, so you can see some of **Shakespeare's** plays performed at one of his original venues. The food is tasty, the beer not so bad, and it's well worth the walk. ♦ Pub

♦ M-Sa 11AM-11PM; Su noon-3PM, 7-10PM. 77 Borough High St. 071/407.2056

**36 London Bridge** Imagination is required here, since "London Bridge has fallen down" time and time again. Twenty yards or so downstream was the site of the first wooden bridge to cross the Thames, built during the first century at the behest of Roman Emperor **Claudius.** A succession of wooden bridges followed until 1176, when **Peter de Colechurch** constructed a 10-arch stone bridge for **Henry II;** it was embellished with ramshackle wooden houses, and a few traitors' heads were spiked on for good measure. The heads were eventually removed, but the bridge remained until **John Rennie** erected a new one, 20 yards upstream, in 1831. This one was transported to Lake Havasu City, Arizona in 1971, when the present cantilevered affair was constructed.
♦ Between Duke's Hill and King William St

**37 Southwark Cathedral** This is the fourth church on this site and the earliest Gothic church in London. The oldest oak effigy, dating from 1275, is of a knight, ankles crossed, one hand on his sword, and even the ravages of time can't erase the eerie feeling that he's just fallen asleep. **John Harvard,** founder of Harvard University, was born in Southwark in 1607 and baptized here. The reconstruction in 1907 of the Harvard chapel was paid for by the university. Among those buried in the church is **John Gower,** known as the "first English poet" because he wrote in English, not French or Latin. The South Aisle features a **Shakespeare Memorial** and, every year on 23 April, a birthday service is held here in the Bard's honor. ♦ Free. Daily 9AM-6PM. Call ahead for times of services. Montague Close. 071/407.3708

**38 The International Shakespeare Globe Centre/Shakespeare Globe Museum**
Behind Southwark Cathedral, redevelopment hasn't entirely overtaken the ancient Georgian warehouses of Borough Market, where lorries laden with fruit and vegetables still draw up before dawn. This is how Covent Garden once looked. Four hundred years ago, this area south of the Thames was the haunt of **Shakespeare, Christopher Marlowe,** and other Elizabethan playwrights and their audiences. The Shakespeare Globe Museum and the **Rose Theatre Exhibition** explore the great playwright's links with this area and the start and growth of Elizabethan theater here at Bankside. The museum sells buttons, badges, and Shakespeare tea towels at reasonable prices—souvenirs for a good cause, as this is part of a massive educational charity project, born of the late American actor/director **Sam Wanamaker's** struggle of 30-plus years to reconstruct the Globe as Shakespeare knew it; you can see the site nearby. ♦ Admission. M-Sa 10AM-5PM; Su 2-5:30PM. 1 Bear Gdns, Bankside, Southwark. 071/928.6342

# Tooling along the Thames

The Thames is a river of infinite variety, embracing backwaters, islands, and changing landscapes. Some of the country's most spectacular monuments cling to its banks. Beginning in the limestone hills of the Cotswolds, the waterway twists and turns for 200 miles, making its way eastward until it loses itself in the sea. Though navigable as far west as Lechlade in Gloucestershire, the Thames seldom sees heavy traffic these days: cargo ships now use the deep North Sea port of Chatham, and most people and goods reach the capital via road, train, or plane. And while more than one Londoner has accused the modern city of turning its back on what was once its lifeblood, the positive side to the downturn in traffic is less congestion and pollution. A leisurely cruise along the Thames is finally enjoyable.

In its upper reaches west and southwest of London, the Thames flows past **Windsor Castle,** before moving on to the stately surroundings of **Hampton Court,** the oldest part of which dates from the 16th century. It winds its way through **Kingston-upon-Thames,** a medieval market town now more closely associated with upmarket suburbia, to **Teddington Lock,** which marks the end of the tidal Thames. From Teddington, the Thames flows north toward ancient and prosperous **Richmond,** passing the aristocratic 17th-century **Ham House** and the Palladian 18th-century **Marble Hill House,** with its beautifully landscaped grounds. Leaving behind its last trace of turbulence at **Kew Gardens,** the river flows toward the stone embankments that mark the start of central London.

Some of the city's most historic landmarks cast their reflections in its waters: the **Houses of Parliament,** the **Embankment, St. Paul's Cathedral,** and, of course, the **Tower of London.** Next come the **Docklands,** where continuing redevelopment makes it hard to imagine that **Charles Dickens** once set his novels in this district. Farther east, the waters lap the **Isle of Dogs,** where the huge, 800-foot **Canary Wharf Tower** dominates the landscape. The cognoscenti predict that this area will become the financial heart of London—especially now that work has started on a connecting tube line. In London, however, the historical still overshadows the modern, as when the masts of the *Cutty Sark* and **Christopher Wren's Royal Naval College** suddenly loom into view at **Greenwich.**

Finally, at **Woolwich Reach,** the huge and impressive **Thames Flood Barrier** stands guard, protecting the city from destructive, surging tides. At times, though, even the world's largest movable flood barrier fails to tame the river. After days of heavy rain, flooding still occurs in the reaches around Teddington and Kingston; park in the wrong place at Twickenham, and you will find your hubcaps immersed in water.

The best engineers have been able to do with the Thames is to cross it, beginning in the first century with a Roman structure located near the present **London Bridge.** Today, the Thames is spanned in 2 places, from the newest **Queen Elizabeth II Bridge** at Dartford, to the footbridge at Teddington Lock. A are road bridges; nine accommodate trains, and si. serve as footbridges (three of which are combined with rail bridges).

Apart from the car ferry at Woolwich, the only ferries across the Thames are from Ham House to Marble Hill House, and from the **Old Deer Park** in Richmond to **Syon Park;** both are skiffs that you must literally whistle up to take you from one side t the other (provided the ferryman is there in the firs place) for the grand sum of 25 pence.

While a walk on its bridges or banks certainly has i attractions—and it is possible, though not always pleasant, to stroll from **Lambeth Bridge** all the way to Southwark on the south bank—the best way to experience the Thames is to sail it (see **Westminste Pier,** page 28, for information about boating on the Thames). Cruise, if you can, at dawn, when the sun glints off the turrets of **Tower Bridge,** or at dusk, when the **Albert** and **Chelsea Bridges,** not to mention the **Embankment,** are lit up like in a fairy tale. Don't bother listening to the often inane commentary of the cruise operators; just relish the view of what was once the highway of kings and queens.

## Bests

### Elizabeth Harwood
Travel Writer

A room at **The Hyde Park Hotel** in Knightsbridge with a view over **Hyde Park,** my favorite London park. If you stay here you also get to see the splendid beasts of the **Household Cavalry** every morning (I was thinking of the horses, not the men!).

Lunch at **The Greenhouse,** the wonderfully English restaurant. Start with fillet of smoked haddock and Welsh rarebit, then order oxtail or salmon cakes as the entrée, and bread and butter pudding or hot apple fritters with vanilla ice cream and apricot sauce for dessert.

Tea at **Brown's Hotel,** the epitome of English elegance. Hot scones with raspberry jam and clotted cream.

Dinner in the most romantic restaurant in the world—**The River Room at the Savoy**—soft lights, gentle music, superb food, and exquisite views across the Thames.

In summer—a boat trip along the Thames. Maybe to the **Tower of London,** the most exciting way to arrive at **Traitor's Gate,** even if a little heady. Or, further east to **Greenwich** with its wonderful palaces and park, or maybe west to **Hampton Court,** the palace of **Henry VIII.**

A walk with my Doberman, **Simba,** through the beautifully landscaped park of **Kenwood House,** Highgate—the most glorious house in London, with the resplendent **Robert Adam** library and seven of my favorite **Gainsborough** paintings. In the evening, a symphony concert seated around the lake with the perfect accompaniment of nature—the croak of a frog, the quack of a duck.

A picnic in **Regent's Park** of caviar and poached salmon, with a glass or two of Napa Valley Chardonnay, followed by an open-air performance of *A Midsummer Night's Dream,* with the perfume of the wild thyme and sweet musk roses pervading the soft, balmy air.

A glass of Pimms at the **Royal Academy Summer Exhibition,** where the people and fashions are as intriguing as the paintings.

In winter—**The Sir John Soane's Museum** in Lincoln's Inn Fields, a veritable treasure trove of exquisite oddities, with wonderful **Hogarth** paintings and the **Sarcophagus of Seti I** from the Valley of the Kings in Egypt.

The **British Museum,** which never loses its charm.

Fish-and-chips from the **Sea Shell** in Lissom Grove, eaten off the Sunday *Times* newspaper, with a glass or two of champagne.

The view from the top of **Tower Bridge.**

A box at **Covent Garden** for the opera or ballet, with a smoked salmon sandwich in the interval.

Standing for 15 minutes in front of **Monet's** *Water Lilies,* at the **National Gallery.**

# Day Trips

For all its myriad sites and shops, London remains a city, with as much (or more) chaos and traffic as downtown Manhattan. And while most visitors agree that every British experience should start with the city, few ever make it beyond central London, let alone into the historic towns and villages that lie within striking distance. Just a couple of hours' drive can take you to the spires of **Oxford's** ancient university or to the Roman ruins of **Bath**. Faded Edwardian elegance resides on **Brighton's** south coast, while the mystery of **Stonehenge** remains unsolved on the Salisbury plain to the southwest. Closer to home, one can stroll about bohemian **Hampstead** (just a tube journey away) or trace part of Britain's maritime history at **Greenwich**. Those yearning for the full royal treatment may sail up the Thames to the **Hampton Court Palace**, home to kings and queens from **Henry VIII** to Georgian times. Allow a day or two for a jaunt into the stunningly verdant countryside, lest you miss out on the charms of rural England.

**1 Greenwich** Under **Henry VIII** (who was born here) and the **Tudor** royals, this Thames-side city was the center of the world, and it still possesses the confidence and grandeur befitting that position. **Greenwich Meridian** (zero-degree longitude) and **Greenwich Mean Time** are still the standards by which the world sets its measures, and the vistas, elegant buildings, and parklands recall the long-lost British Empire. The tall masts of the *Cutty Sark* (admission; M-Sa 10AM-4:30PM; Su noon-4:30PM. King William Walk. 081/858.3445), the last of the great 19th-century tea clippers that could sail 360 miles in a single day, loom over the city streets. Now drydocked near **Greenwich Pier**, the ship has been turned into a museum, as has the smaller *Gypsy Moth IV*

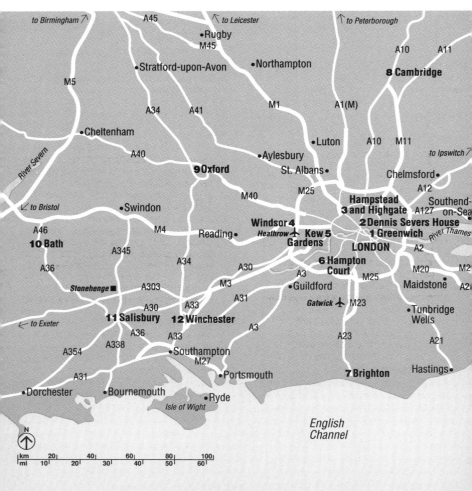

*Old Royal Observatory*

(admission; M-Sa 10AM-4:30PM; Su noon-4:30PM. 081/858.3445) nearby, which sailed around the world in 1966-67 with **Sir Francis Chichester** alone at the helm.

The domes and colonnades of the **Royal Naval College,** a feast of **Wren, Vanbrugh,** and **Hawksmoor,** preside magnificently over the River Thames. Inside the Naval College, the paintings of **Sir James Thornhill** (executed in 1727) line the walls of the **Painted Hall** (free; M-W, F-Su 2:30-4:45PM. 081/858.2154.) The chapel, opposite, was redone with intricate detailing after a fire in the late 18th century.

The **National Maritime Museum** (admission; M-Sa 10AM-5PM; Su 2-5PM. Rommey Rd. 081/858.4422), farther back from the river, houses the finest collection of globes in the world, along with marine paintings, navigational instruments, **Nelson** relics, and more than 2,000 model ships. The centerpiece of the museum is the pure and classical **Queen's House** (guided tours are offered every half-hour in summer; limited tours in winter; Sunday year-round, you can walk around on your own), designed by **Inigo Jones** in 1616-35. The great hall—a perfect cube—and the tulip staircase are both stunning.

From the Queen's House, pass through **Greenwich Park,** with its delightful flower garden, to the buildings of the **Old Royal Observatory,** designed by **Christopher Wren** for **Charles II** in 1675-76. Inside is a fascinating collection of telescopes and astronomical instruments. A river walk from the Naval College takes you to the extraordinary **Thames Flood Barrier,** constructed between 1975 and 1982 to the tune of £500 million and comprised of 10 enormous movable gates between river piers and abutments on either bank.

Two restored early Georgian town houses form the venue for a collection of largely European fans that date from the 17th century onward. The **Fan Museum** (admission; Tu-Sa 11AM-4:30PM; Su noon-4:30PM. 12 Crooms Hill. 081/858.7879) hosts specialist exhibitions such as "Fans and China Trade," an exploration of the links between fans and the silk and spice trade of the 17th and 18th centuries. The collection features more than 2,000 items.
♦ The best way to reach Greenwich is by riverboat. Boats depart from Westminster Pier (call 071/930.2062 for more information) every 30 minutes from 10:30AM to 5PM for the 45-minute journey. The last boat leaves Greenwich at 3:45PM in winter and 5PM in summer. Trains run from Charing Cross to Maze Hill every half-hour and take 20 minutes. The bus route to Greenwich is dreary, but buses 177 and 188 run between Greenwich and Waterloo Station, and the No. 1 goes to the Strand, making the journey in 35 minutes. If traveling by car, take the A200.

**2 Dennis Severs House** Ninety-seven candles light this old, dilapidated house, which has no electricity, running water, or bathrooms. The **Jarvises,** a Huguenot silk-weaving family, lived here from 1725 to 1919. Lovingly restored to its original condition by American Anglophile **Dennis Severs,** the house is wedged solid with bric-a-brac from the past three centuries. But this isn't a museum treat—Severs says that you use your soul, not your senses, when you visit his home and allow him to take you back two centuries. It is a unique experience. ♦ Steep admission. Open the first Sunday of each month and for pre-booked evening performances three nights a week. Book three weeks ahead from 9AM-12:30PM. 18 Folgate St, Spitalfields. 071/247.4013

**3 Hampstead** The centuries of London converge here—a must for architecture buffs—as houses and cottages of nearly every conceivable shape, style, and period ramble up and down these hills. Hampstead is one of the prettiest London villages, and its residents are wealthy enough to keep it that way. Above the village, close to **Jack Straw's Castle Pub,** are misty views of London to be glimpsed across **Hampstead Heath.** The heath has 802 vigorously preserved acres of grassland and woodland, providing great opportunities for exercise. For keen birdwatchers, 100 species are said to have been sighted here. There are plenty of walking and running trails, and for the brave at heart, the **Bathing Ponds** welcome open-air swimmers. Avoid the heath at night, however. Farther along the top of the heath is the **Spaniard's Inn** (★★$; Spaniards Rd and Hampstead Ln. 081/455.3276), an Elizabethan coaching inn and gateway to London rumored to have been a refuge for highwayman **Dick Turpin.** ♦ To get to the heath and Kenwood House, take the Northern Line to the Golders Green tube stop, then the No. 210 bus headed toward Finsbury Park. To start with the village, take the Northern Line to Hampstead and walk northeast. The British Rail station (North London Link) for Hampstead Heath is at the bottom of Parliament Hill. If you're traveling by car, take the A41 north from central London as far as Swiss Cottage, then the B511 from there to Hampstead.

On Hampstead Heath:

**Kenwood House** The grounds of Kenwood House, remodeled in 1767-69, are idyllic for picnics and for gazing across beautiful Hampstead Heath toward an ornamental lake and concert bowl where, most summer weekends, you can picnic to the strains of Vivaldi, Dvořák, and many others, with occasional fireworks displays for dessert. Inside is the **Iveagh Bequest of Grand Masters**—works by **Gainsborough, Reynolds,** and **Vermeer.** The tearooms are wonderful. ♦ Free. Daily 10AM-6PM Apr-Sept; daily 10AM-4PM Oct-Mar. Hampstead Ln. 081/348.1286

**Highgate Cemetery** Located to the east of the heath, the cemetery contains the haunting **Egyptian Avenue** dug deep into the ground and flanked by dark Egyptian columns—obelisks with catacombs built in between. At the top of the hill is the **Circle of Lebanon,** where catacombs surround you. Above the whole scene is a cedar of Lebanon like you've never seen before. **Christina Rossetti** is buried here; **Karl Marx** lies in the eastern cemetery. ♦ Admission. Daily 11AM-5PM; hourly tours year-round. Swain's Ln. 081/340.1834

In Hampstead:

**Keats' House** The English Romantic poet **John Keats** (1795-1821) lived at **Wentworth Place** from 1818 to 1820. Today, due in large part to American funds, the Regency house remains chock-full of his letters, manuscripts, books, and other memorabilia. In the garden, a plum tree grows on the site of the tree under which "Ode to a Nightingale" was supposedly composed. ♦ Free. M-Sa 10AM-1PM, 2-6PM; Su 2-5PM. Wentworth Pl, Keats Grove. Tube: Hampstead Heath Rail Station. 071/435.2062

**4 Windsor** Home to a magnificent park, a famous boys' school, and the largest castle in the world still occupied by royalty—**Windsor Castle** (admission; Daily 10AM-4PM Nov-Mar; daily 10AM-5PM Apr-Oct. 0753/868286 ext 2235), a royal residence for more than 900 years—Windsor lies on a pretty bend of the Thames just 21 miles east of London. **William the Conqueror** first built a round keep made of

timber in 1078, and over the centuries, monarchs have enlarged the castle and constructed new buildings. In the 1820s, **Edward IV** began **St. George's Chapel** (M-Sa 10AM-4PM; Su 2-4PM), a fine example of perpendicular architecture, with its elaborately carved stone vaulting. **Henry VIII,** his third wife, **Jane Seymour, Charles I,** and other monarchs are buried in the choir. Yet Windsor's ultimate accolade came in 1917 when **George V** declared that, henceforth, his family and descendants would take the surname Windsor. The **State Apartments,** used by the royal family when in residence, are decorated with paintings by **Van Dyck** and **Rubens.**

Within the same complex is **Queen Mary's** fabulous **Dolls' House,** designed by **Sir Edwin Lutyens** in 1921-24. Everything is a magical one-twelfth of life-size, with one-inch books by **Kipling** in the library. In 1992, while **Queen Elizabeth** looked on in sorrow as Windsor, her favorite castle, went up in flames, her son **Prince Andrew** became a vital link in a human chain that saved almost all the priceless paintings and art treasures from the fire. Only the structure of the **Great Hall** was badly damaged, and you can watch the painstaking restoration still in progress. In 1993, to help fund restoration, the Queen opened part of **Buckingham Palace** to the public for the first time ever. The **Great Park** at Windsor is as fascinating as the castle, with 4,800 acres of lawns, trees, lakes, herds of deer, ancient ruins, and **Prince Charles**—when he is playing polo on **Smith's Lawn.**

Across the cast-iron footbridge is **Eton College,** the best-known public school in Britain, founded in 1440 by **Henry VI.** It is best to visit the school during term time, when you can see the 1,200 students in their Eton wing collars and tails. Etonians exude an air of confidence that is quite unrivaled, and it is no surprise that 20 British prime ministers are among the alumni. Schoolyard and cloisters are open daily 2-5PM. Stay in Eton for lunch at the **Eton Wine Bar** (★★$$; 82-83 High St. 0753/854921).

*Windsor Castle*

The old town also has a museum of note: the **Household Cavalry Museum** (free; M-F 10AM-1PM, 2-5PM, Su 10AM-1PM, 2-4PM summer; M-F 10AM-1PM, 2-5PM winter. Combermere Barracks, St. Leonard's Rd. 0753/868222 ext 203) houses equipment and other items dating from the reign of **Charles II** to the present. Swords and uniforms are particularly interesting. ♦ Windsor is 27 minutes by train from Paddington (change at Slough) or 50 minutes direct from Waterloo. Greenline buses go from Hyde Park Corner (90 minutes) or Victoria Coach Station. Driving takes one hour; take the M4 to A308.

**5 Kew Gardens** What began as a hobby for **Princess Augusta**, mother of **George III**, back in 1759, has blossomed into the most famous collection of flowers and plants in the world. Kew Gardens is a botanical paradise of more than 300,000 varieties, set in 300 lush acres along the east side of the Thames. Officially called the **Royal Botanic Gardens**, it was given to the nation by the royal family in 1841 and is, for all its pleasure-giving, a scientific institution where plants are studied, classified, and cultivated. Kew Gardens offers a constantly changing display of flowers, as well as rock gardens, a stream with aquatic birds, a herbarium with more than five million varieties of dried plants, and stunning paths down to the river with a sublime view of **Syon House** across the Thames. Amid the greenery is an array of 18th-century garden follies designed by **Sir William Chambers** for Princess Augusta: classical temples, ruins of a Roman arch, a fanciful 10-story pagoda, and an orangery, now housing a shop and a restaurant.

The **Palm House**, with its sweeping curves of glass and iron, was built in 1844 by **Decimus Burton** and houses tropical plants from both hemispheres. All the greenhouses are masterpieces, as are the grand entrance gates on the corner of **Kew Green**, also built by Burton. Be sure to see **Queen Charlotte's Cottage** (admission; Sa-Su 11AM-5:30PM Apr-Sept) with its ceiling painted with summer flowers; the **Japanese Pagoda**; and, if you come in springtime, the **Rhododendron Dell**. The hurricanes of '87 and '90 have not affected this wonderful place too badly. The **Kew Gardens Gallery** (daily 9:30AM-3:30PM. 081/332.5618) has exhibitions all year round. ♦ Admission. Gardens: daily 10AM-sunset. Greenhouses: daily 11AM to a half-hour before sunset. The best way to get to Kew Gardens is either by riverboat from Westminster Pier or by tube on the District Line toward Richmond. Boats leave for the 90-minute journey at 10:15AM, 10:30AM, 11AM, 11:15AM, noon, 2PM, and 3PM; call 071/930.2062 for more information. Also, trains leave from Waterloo Station for Kew Bridge. If driving, take the A30. 081/940.1171

Near Kew Gardens:

**Maids of Honour** ★★$ Do try to visit Kew during the week, not just because it will be less crowded but because the best tea shop in the area is open! Maids of Honour is the original home of the tarts of the same name, and it was named after one of **Henry VIII's** maids of honor, who cooked such delicious pastries that he imprisoned her to ensure a constant supply. The recipe is still top secret. This quaint, rambling cottage is packed at weekends and is a must for cream teas in true British tradition. You'll need patience to queue for a seat, but you can also buy the cakes next door and eat alfresco in Kew Gardens itself. Book ahead for lunch. ♦ Cafe ♦ Lunch and afternoon tea; lunch only on Monday. 288 Kew Rd, Kew. 081/940.2752

**Kew Greenhouse** ★★$ Light and airy, the Greenhouse offers a good salad selection and excellent savory dishes such as vegetable crumble. Outside pavement seating is pleasant in summer. ♦ Cafe ♦ Coffee, lunch, and tea 9AM-6:30PM. 1 Station Parade, Kew. 081/940.0183

**6 Hampton Court Palace** Not really out of town but 15 miles down the road from London (and better still, up the river), Hampton Court Palace is a must as far as day trips go. The palace was begun in 1514 by **Cardinal Thomas Wolsey**, minister to **Henry VIII**. However, Wolsey's elaborately designed palace and lavish lifestyle made him fear the envy of his king—so in 1525 when Hampton Court was almost complete, he presented it to Henry VIII in return for **Richmond Palace**. Henry VIII added a moat, a drawbridge, and a tennis court, plus new royal lodgings, galleries, and chambers. His third queen, **Jane Seymour**, was married, gave birth, and died at the palace, and Henry lived there for a number of years with his sixth and last queen, **Catherine Parr**. **Elizabeth I** loved Hampton Court, and **Charles I** lived in it as King and as a prisoner of **Cromwell**.

When **William** and **Mary** came to the throne in 1689, they revamped the palace, with **Christopher Wren** and **Grinling Gibbons** in charge. The south front was severely damaged in a fire in 1986, but luckily, most of the paintings and art treasures were saved, and it has now been fully restored. Signs will help you find **Cardinal Wolsey's Apartments;** the **King's Dressing Room,** with works by **Holbein** and **Mabuse;** the **Great Hall,** which was the site of Henry VIII's famous banquets and performances of **Shakespeare's** plays by the Bard's company; and the lower **Orangery,** with the nine tempera paintings, *The Triumphs of Julius Caesar* (1485-92) by **Andrea Mantegna.** The 50 acres of landscaped gardens are absolutely beautiful and the maze is irresistible. ♦ Admission. M 10:15AM-6PM, Tu-Su 9:30AM-6PM

Mar-Oct; M 10:15AM-4:30PM, Tu-Su 9:30AM-4:30PM Oct-Mar. In summer, boats leave from Westminster Pier to Hampton Court at 10:30AM, 11:15AM, and noon; call 071/930.2062 for more information. The train from Waterloo Station takes 32 minutes. You can also hop a Green Line bus—Nos. 415, 716, 718, or 726. Allow an hour. To stay in one of the two self-catering apartments, contact the Landmark Trust (0628/825.925). 081/781.9500

*Royal Pavilion*

**7  Brighton**  The first place to stop in Brighton is the **Royal Pavilion** (admission; daily 10AM-5PM. Pavilion Parade. 0273/603.005), rebuilt between 1815 and 1822, by **John Nash** for the Prince Regent, who later became **George IV,** for £500,000 in real gold. Its great onion-shaped dome, huge tentlike roofs, and small ornate pinnacles and minarets are so reminiscent of a fairy-tale Indian mogul's palace that you almost expect to see elephants file past you carrying a rajah. Inside, it's pure chinoiserie, filled with the original ornate furniture and paintings that were chosen especially for this palace. A series of spectacular suites culminates in the banquet room with brilliantly colored, gilt-painted walls, and a ceiling like a huge palm tree with a bedragonned chandelier.

The rest of the town echoes the elegant proportions of Regency days with frequent and unexpected onion domes and roofs. For yet more inspiration, just behind the pavilion is the **Brighton Museum and Art Gallery** (free; M-Tu, Th-Sa 10AM-5PM; Su 2-5PM. Church St. 0273/603.005) with its award-winning Art Nouveau and Art Deco collections.

Brighton has two piers, but only the **Victorian Palace Pier** is open to the public and is a center of entertainment with its amusement arcades and "what-the-butler-saw" slot machines. It's well worth visiting during the week, but avoid the weekends as it's crowded with daytrippers. Don't wear yourself out walking on the pier, but continue on to **The Lanes**—17th-century redbrick streets full of tiny shops selling every kind of antique imaginable, a heaven for connoisseurs and browsers alike. Within the

Lanes, watch out for the **Lorelei Restaurant** (★★$$; 5 Union St. 0273/327177) for lunch; otherwise, there are some excellent alternatives a 10-minute walk away in **Kemp Town,** such as **Langan's Bistro** (★★★$$$; 1 Paston Pl. 0273/606933). Round the corner from Langan's is the popular and reliable **La Marinade** (★★$$$; 77 St. George's Rd. 0273/600992), or if you crave a cheap, Continental evening accompanied by the piano, a singing chef, and lots of laughter, the **Laughing Onion** (★★$; 80 St. George's Rd. 0273/696555) is for you. ♦ The nicest way to get to Brighton is by train, which takes 52 minutes from Victoria. Or by coach from Victoria Coach Station in 105 minutes. By car, take the A23 or M23; it takes well over an hour.

**8  Cambridge**  If you can manage only one excursion to the "palaces of privilege and academe," choose Cambridge. Established in the 13th century and a few decades younger than **Oxford,** it is architecturally more cohesive, more beautiful, and less interrupted by the city itself. Cambridge is located in a part of England called **East Anglia,** on the edge of the **River Cam,** and the back of the colleges face the river (hence the term "Backs"). The most interesting of the 29 schools at Cambridge are **St. John's Trinity,** founded by **Henry VIII; Clare; King's,** where the chapel has exquisite stained-glass windows, fan vaulting, and lofty spires; **Corpus Christi,** where the Old Court is worth visit; **Queen's; Peterhouse;** and **Jesus.**

The ideal time to visit is **May Week,** a 10-day period in June when graduating seniors receive their degrees. Festivities take place throughout the city, including a rowing competition on the Cam. Be sure to plan your day to include evensong at **King's College Chapel,** and however touristy it may seem, allow yourself to be punted on the River Cam along the Backs—it rivals the gondola in Venice in terms of sheer tranquility. Cambridge is not known for culinary achievement, but you can get a good pub lunch at **Free Press** (★★$; 7 Prospect Row. 0223/68337), which serves imaginative salads and excellent pies. **Browns** (★★★$$; 23 Trumpington St, opposite the Fitzwilliam Museum. 0223/461655) offers value for money in relaxed surroundings. Or go vegetarian opposite King's College at the **King's Pantry** (★★$$; 9a King's Parade. 0223/321551). ♦ Cambridge, 54 miles from London, can be reached by train direct from Liverpool Street Station in 75 minutes, by bus from Victoria Station in a little less than two hours, or by car on M11 to Junction 10 in 90 minutes.

| | |
|---|---|
| **Restaurants/Clubs:** Red | **Hotels:** Blue |
| **Shops/ ♠ Outdoors:** Green | **Sights/Culture:** Bla |

*Magdalen College*

**9 Oxford** The center of Oxford is dominated by the Gothic turrets, towers, and spires of its famous colleges, which have made this a university town since the 1200s. **Oxford University,** the oldest in England, is a collection of 30 colleges, all of which have unique charm. **St. Edmund Hall, Merton,** and **Balliol,** built in the 13th century, are the oldest of the colleges. **Magdalen,** pronounced "MADLEN," whose 15th-century tower was used by **Charles I** as an observation post during the siege of Oxford, has been home to student notables from the likes of **Cardinal Thomas Wolsey** to **Oscar Wilde.** Today, this is the central point of the May morning festivities, a medieval celebration. A visit during the academic year between mid-October and mid-May is most interesting; during summer holidays, the colleges are deserted or filled with American students. However, during summer, the buildings are open all day, while most of the colleges can only be visited in the afternoon during the school year.

Everyone goes to **Browns** (★★$$; 5-11 Woodstock Rd. 0865/511.995), and you'll soon see why. It's open daily for lunch, tea, and dinner, serving spaghetti, fisherman's pie, toasted sandwiches, and salads to starving students and tourists. For a more expensive but equally enjoyable dining experience, try **Gee's** (★★★$$$; 61A Banbury Rd. 0865/53540), where tasty pasta and salads line up alongside chopped steak on *ciabatta* bread with Swiss cheese. ♦ Oxford is 56 miles from London and can be reached by train from Paddington Station in an hour (trains leave hourly), or by bus from Victoria Station in one hour and 45 minutes. If you're driving, take the M40 (one hour).

**0 Bath** Elegantly proportioned Bath is as perfect as a novel by **Jane Austen,** who came here, sipped the water in the **Pump Room** (free; M-Sa 9AM-6PM; Su 11AM-5PM, Abbey Church Yard. 0225/444477), and captured its grace, elegance, and usefulness in *Northanger Abbey* and *Persuasion.* This Georgian city of terraces, crescents, and squares is the most famous spa in England and worth a visit for its warm springs, Roman ruins, glorious architecture, and gentle Austenesque atmosphere. The Romans, nostalgic for the warm waters of home, founded Bath in AD 43 and stayed for four centuries. But it wasn't until the 18th century, when luminaries such as **Gainsborough, Queen Victoria,** and **Lord Nelson** were regular visitors, that Bath became a fashionable spa town. The Roman baths, among the most striking ruins in Europe, are still the city's major attraction. Excavations nearby have unearthed relics ranging from coins to a sacrificial altar. You can sample water from the fountain in the Pump Room, which **Charles Dickens** said tastes like warm flatirons. The Georgian perfection of the town is largely the work of two 18th-century architects—a father and son, both named **John Wood.**

As for the modern architecture, well, close your eyes. After its heyday in the 18th century, the city went downhill. But the last two decades have brought new life to Bath. Today, Londoners come here as much for the city's renewed cultural life as for the waters. If you're interested in art and antiquities, do not miss the **Holbourne Museum** (free; M-Sa 11AM-5PM, Su 2:30-6PM Feb-Dec; Tu-Sa 11AM-5PM, Su 2:30-6PM Nov to Easter. Great Pulteney St. 0225/66669), which houses one of the largest collections of silver in the country, along with porcelain and paintings by **Turner, Stubbs,** and other major British artists.

One of Bath's greatest achievements is the renovation of the **Theatre Royal** (box office: M-Sa 10AM-8PM. Saw Close. 0225/448844), which hosts some of the country's top productions before they move on to London. Near the top of Bath's major shopping street, **Garlands** (★★$$; 7 Edgar Buildings on George St. 0225/442283) is a popular place to eat lunch—every day except Monday, when they're closed. Try a simple salad of red mullet or go for something more substantial like their *salmon au beurre blanc,* or duck with orange and Dubonnet. On Mondays, try **Circus** (★★$$$; 34 Brock St. 0225/330208), another excellent, French cafe-style restaurant offering dishes such as grilled goat cheese with roasted peppers. Hotel meals are more expensive but both the **Queensberry** (★★★$$$; Russell St. 0225/447928) and the **Royal Crescent** (★★★$$$; 16 Royal Crescent. 0225/319090) are recommended for their excellent cuisine. ◆ Bath is 116 miles from London and can be reached in 70 minutes by high-speed train from Paddington Station, by bus from Victoria Station in three hours, or by car, from the M4 to Junction 18 to A46 and A4, in two hours.

**11 Salisbury** Wiltshire's country town of Salisbury, 83 miles from London, rests on a plain where the rivers Nadder and Bourne flow into the Avon, quietly expressing the calm beauty of this charming medieval town and its famous cathedral. Salisbury is lucky: it's too far from London for commuters, rather poorly served by British Rail, and is now bypassed by major roads. As a result, the old city center is virtually intact, utterly charming, and well worth a wander round. Salisbury's other major attraction is its convenient location, just 10 miles from **Stonehenge,** one of the most important prehistoric monuments in Europe.

Immortalized by **John Constable,** classic **Salisbury Cathedral,** consecrated in 1258, is the perfection of English cathedral architecture, made even more beautiful by its majestic spire (circa 1320) rising above the water meadows beside the Avon. The painting by Constable can be seen at the **Victoria & Albert Museum** if you can't make this trip. At 404 feet high, it is the tallest spire in England, enchanting the eye with its deceptive lightness—the 6,400 tons of stonework put such a strain on the four load-bearing columns that they are slightly bent. The Avon marks the western side of the cathedral's grounds, and a 14th-century wall of stone from **Old Sarum,** part of the city that was razed in 1331 to provide building materials for the **Cathedral Close,** borders the other three sides. The interior of the cathedral is not as breathtaking as the exterior, due in part to the ruthlessness of **James Wyatt's** renovations (1788-89), in which he removed the screens and chapels and rearranged the monuments in rows. Happily, the restoration by **Sir Gilbert Scott** in 1859 minimized some of the damage. The cathedral contains tombs of the Crusaders and those who died at Agincourt. Other treasures

include exquisite lancet windows with patchworks of glass from the 13th and 15th centuries and a 14th-century wrought-iron clock that was restored to working order in 1956, and is now possibly the oldest working clock in the world. The **Cloisters** and the beautiful, octagonal **Chapter House,** built from 1364 to 1380, were modeled after **Westminster Abbey.** Many of the cathedral's treasures are displayed in the Chapter House, including one of four existing copies of the **Magna Carta,** brought here for safekeeping shortly after 1265. The Cathedral Close contains the medieval **Bishop's Palace and Deanery.** Also in the Close and open to the public are **Malmsbury House,** built in 1327 and restored in 1749, and the 18th-century **Mompesson House.**

For lunch, try the first-floor eatery **Harper's** (★★$$; 7 Ox Row, The Market Sq. 0722/333118). They serve simple, delicious English cooking, including a tasty beef casserole with herb dumplings. A couple of miles west of Salisbury and easily reached by bus or car is the splendid **Wilton House** (admission; M-Sa 11AM-6PM; Su 1-6PM Apr Oct. 0722/743115), the home of the **Earl of Pembroke** for more than 400 years, with 17th-century staterooms by **Inigo Jones.** The incomparable art collection includes 16 **Van Dyck's,** which are hung in the famous double-cube room (60 feet long by 30 feet high and 30 feet wide) where **General Eisenhower** planned the Normandy invasion. Wilton House is also home to 7,000 model soldiers. Buses leave for Wilton House every half hour and arrive in 18 minutes; cars take the A30. ◆ Salisbury is 83 miles from London and can be reached by way of a picturesque railway journey, leaving from Waterloo Station every hour and arriving in Salisbury 90 minutes later. There are two bus trips daily from Victoria Coach Station that take three hours, but the bus service in the afternoon from Salisbury is often at awkward times—take the train! The station is a 10-minute walk from the center of Salisbury. If you're driving, take the M3 and the A30.

Near Salisbury:

**Stonehenge** Ten miles northwest of Salisbury, on the A345, this great, historic structure is one of the oldest and most important megalithic monuments in Europe, dating from between 1850 BC and 1400 BC, although the earliest signs of the Stone Circle date back to the Bronze Age, circa 3500 BC. Though the fence around Stonehenge, added for its own protection, makes it look like a captive animal and takes away the initial impact, the sight of the long, eerie collection stones is still breathtaking, and the way the monument interacts with the sun on certain days of the year is astounding. The stones are arranged in four series within a circular ditch 300 feet in diameter (see above right). The

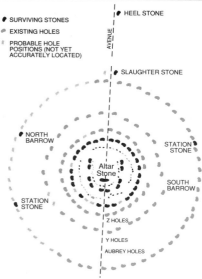

- ● SURVIVING STONES
- ◐ EXISTING HOLES
- ○ PROBABLE HOLE POSITIONS (NOT YET ACCURATELY LOCATED)

HEEL STONE

AVENUE

SLAUGHTER STONE

NORTH BARROW

STATION STONE

Altar Stone

SOUTH BARROW

STATION STONE

Z HOLES

Y HOLES

AUBREY HOLES

Stonehenge plan showing the solstitial alignment of the axis of symmetry

outer ring, with a diameter of 97 feet, is a circle of 17 sandstones connected on top by a series of lintel stones. The second ring is of bluestones, the third is horseshoe shaped, and the inner ring is ovoid. Within the ovoid ring lies the **Altar Stone,** made of micaceous sandstone. The great upright **Heelstone** is along the **Avenue,** the broad road leading to the monument. Some of the stones, weighing up to four tons each, have been shown to come from the **Preseli Hills** in Wales, a distance of some 135 miles. Stonehenge was at one time believed to be a druid temple, a theory contradicted by the fact that the druids didn't arrive in Britain until circa 500 BC. In 1963, British astronomer **Gerald Hawkins** theorized that Stonehenge was a huge astronomical instrument used to accurately measure solar and lunar movements as well as eclipses. Avoid Stonehenge for the two weeks preceding Midsummer's Day, when it becomes a battleground between thousands of travelers, latter-day hippies, and legions of police.

**12 Winchester** This is the ancient capital of England, graceful and unspoiled, and a perfect trip to combine with **Salisbury** and **Stonehenge,** only 20 miles away. Winchester was the capital of England for nearly 250 years, from 829 until the **Norman Conquest,** when the Normans gradually moved the capital to London. **King Alfred the Great** reigned here from 871 to 899, during the invasion of the Danes, and developed Winchester into a great center of learning. The picturesque **High Street,** the center of the city, is lined with a charming medley of buildings dating from the 13th century. Near the end of the street is the **Great Hall** (1235), all that

remains of **Winchester Castle,** demolished in 1644-45. An early fake Round Table of the legendary **King Arthur** stands in the hall, which was the scene of many medieval parliaments and notable trials, including that of **Sir Walter Raleigh** for conspiring against **James I.**

The beautiful early Norman **Winchester Cathedral** is the longest Gothic cathedral church in Europe (556 feet), made to seem longer by its height (78 feet). The best view of the cathedral is from **Magdalen Hill,** the approach road to Winchester from the east, which emphasizes its setting in the city. Begun in 1079, consecrated in 1093, and partially rebuilt in 1346-66, it contains a wealth of treasures, most striking of which are the seven richly carved chantry chapels. **Bishop Wykeham's Chantry,** in the west end of the nave, contains an effigy of the great builder, statesman, and founder of nearby **Winchester College,** one of the oldest public schools in England, dating from 1382, and of **New College,** Oxford. On the opposite wall are a brass tablet and window dedicated to **Jane Austen** (1775-1817), who is buried here. The bronze statues of James I and **Charles I** are by **Hubert Le Sueur** (1685).

Under the organ loft in the north transept is the **Chapel of the Holy Sepulchre** (12th century), with superb wall paintings (circa 1170-1205) of the *Life and Passion of Christ.* The oak screen separating the choir from the nave is by **Sir Gilbert Scott,** and the magnificent stalls (1305-10), with their misericords carved with human, animal, and monster motifs, are the oldest cathedral stalls in England, except for some fragments at Rochester. The **Library,** over the passage between the south transept and the old **Chapter House,** was built in the 12th century and reconstructed in 1668. It contains 4,000 printed books and rare manuscripts, the most important of which is the *Winchester Bible* (12th century), one of the finest medieval manuscripts.

For great views of the cathedral while you eat, go to **Nine the Square** (★★★$$$; 9 Great Minster St, the Square. 0962/864004). If you walk about a mile south of the cathedral, you will come upon the ancient **St. Cross Hospital,** where the "wayfarer's dole" of a horn of beer and a portion of bread—once a handout to the needy—is still offered to visitors. If you're feeling a good deal wealthier than this, then **Lainston House** ($$$; Sparsholt. 0962/863588) makes a charming place for an overnight stay. Surrounded by beautiful parklands, the House has 38 luxurious rooms and a 12th-century chapel to boot.

♦ Winchester, 65 miles from London, can be reached by train from Waterloo Station in 90 minutes, or by buses leaving Victoria Coach Station every hour, a two-hour journey. By car, take the M3 and A33.

# History

| EVENT | | MONARCH |
|---|---|---|
| Julius Caesar invades Britain | **BC 55-54** | |
| Roman Conquest of Britain by Emperor Claudius. | **AD 43** | |
| London is destroyed by Queen Boadicea. | **61** | |
| First London Bridge is built. | **100** | |
| Roman army withdraws from Britain to defend Rome from the Goths. | **410** | |
| The Vikings invade Britain and create havoc, sacking London as well. | **842** | |
| | **871** | **Alfred the Great** (871-899) |
| Alfred the Great occupies London. | **886** | |
| | **925** | **Athelstan** (924-40) |
| Canute captures London. | **1016** | **Canute** (1016-35) |
| | **1042** | **Edward the Confessor** (1042-66) |
| Consecration of first Westminster Abbey. | **1065** | |
| William the Conqueror crowned at Westminster Abbey. | **1066** | **House of Normandy** <br> **Harold** (1066) <br> **William I** (1066-87) |
| Fire destroys most of the City and St. Paul's Cathedral. | **1086** | **William II** (1087-1100; probably murdered) |
| White Tower is completed. William II begins to build the Great Hall at Westminster. | **1097** | |
| | **1100** | **Henry I** (1100-35) |
| | **1135** | **Stephen** (1135-54) |
| | **1154** | **House of Plantagenet** <br> **Henry II** (1154-89) |
| Construction begins on London Bridge, the first stone bridge, completed in 1290. | **1176** | |
| | **1189** | **Richard I (the Lionheart)** (1189-99; killed in battle) |
| London establishes rule by mayor. | **1192** | |
| | **1199** | **John** (1199-1216) |
| King John signs the Magna Carta at Runnymede. | **1215** | |
| | **1216** | **Henry III** (1216-72) |
| First Parliament is summoned; English state begins. | **1265** | |
| Consecration of present Westminster Abbey. | **1269** | |
| | **1272** | **Edward I** (1272-1307) |
| Old St. Paul's Cathedral is completed, half as tall as the present building. | **1280** | |
| | **1307** | **Edward II** (1307-27; murdered) |
| | **1327** | **Edward III** (1327-77) |
| Edward III claims the French throne and the Hundred Years War begins. | **1337** | |

| Event | Date | Monarch / House |
|---|---|---|
| Westminster becomes regular meeting place of Parliament. | **1338** | |
| Black death strikes Europe; about half of London's 50,000 citizens die. | **1348** | |
| | **1377** | **Richard II** (1377-99; deposed and murdered) |
| Wat Tyler's Peasant Revolt. | **1381** | |
| | **1399** | **House of Lancaster.** **Henry IV** (1399-1413) |
| | **1413** | **Henry V** (1413-22) |
| Henry V's victory at Agincourt. | **1415** | |
| | **1422** | **Henry VI** (1422-61; deposed) |
| Joan of Arc is burned. | **1431** | |
| War of Roses begins. | **1455** | |
| | **1461** | **House of York** **Edward IV** (1461-83) |
| Caxton's printing press is set up near Westminster Abbey. | **1476** | |
| Princes probably murdered in the Tower. | **1483** | **Edward V** (1483; probably murdered **Richard III** (1483-85) |
| Accession of Henry Tudor. | **1485** | **House of Tudor** **Henry VII** (1485-1509) |
| Henry VIII builds St. James's Palace. | **1509** | **Henry VIII** (1509-47) |
| Fall of Thomas Wolsey. | **1530** | |
| Henry VIII moves into York Place (renames it Whitehall) and takes over Hampton Court. | **1530 cont.** | |
| Henry VIII's Reformation; dissolution of the monasteries, including Westminster Abbey. | **1533** | |
| Henry VIII divorces Catherine of Aragon. | **1534** | |
| Anne Boleyn is executed at the Tower of London. | **1536** | |
| Jane Seymour dies while giving birth to Edward VI. | **1537** | |
| Henry VIII marries Anne of Cleves. | **1540** | |
| Catherine Howard is executed in Tower of London. | **1542** | |
| Henry VIII proclaims himself King of Ireland. | | |
| Henry VIII marries Catherine Parr. | **1543** | |
| | **1547** | **Edward VI** (1547-53) |
| Mary marries Philip II of Spain and reinstates Catholicism. Citizens are martyred at Smithfield. | **1553** | **Mary I** (1553-58) |
| Elizabethan Age begins (45 years). | **1558** | **Elizabeth I** (1558-1603) |
| Mary, Queen of Scots, flees to England (executed 1587). | **1568** | |
| Royal Exchange is set up. | | |

| | | |
|---|---|---|
| Shakespeare arrives in London. | **1585** | |
| Spanish Armada tries and fails to invade Britain. | **1588** | |
| Wood from theater in Shoreditch is used to make the Globe of Bankside. | **1598** | |
| | **1603** | **House of Stuart**<br><br>**James I** (James VI of Scotland; 1603-25) |
| Guy Fawkes tries to blow up Parliament in Gunpowder Plot. | **1605** | |
| Pilgrims sail on *Mayflower* and settle in New England. | **1620** | |
| Inigo Jones' Banqueting House is completed. | **1625** | **Charles I** (1625-49; beheaded) |
| Covent Garden is laid out. | **1631** | |
| Quarrels between Charles I and Parliament lead to Civil War between the Royalists and Parliament. King is forced to leave London. | **1642-46** | |
| Charles I is executed at Banqueting House. | **1649** | |
| | **1653** | Commonweath: **Oliver Cromwell**, Protector (1653-58) **Richard Cromwell**, Protector (1658-59)<br><br>**House of Stuart** (Restored) |
| | **1660** | **Charles II** (1660-85) |

| | | |
|---|---|---|
| Great Plague; 100,000 die. | **1665** | |
| Great Fire destroys half of London; 9 die. | **1666** | |
| Christopher Wren designs and builds St. Paul's and 51 London churches. | **1670-1723** | |
| | **1685** | **James II** (1685-88; deposed and exiled) |
| Glorious Revolution. William and Mary come to the throne. | **1689** | **William III** and **Mary II** (joint monarchs 1689-1702) |
| Bank of England founded. | **1694** | |
| Whitehall Palace destroyed by fire. | **1698** | |
| | **1702** | **Anne** (1702-14) |
| | **1714** | **House of Hanover**<br><br>**George I** (1714-27) |
| | **1727** | **George II** (1727-60) |
| | **1760** | **George III** (1760-1820) |
| Dr. Johnson's Literary Club is founded. | **1764** | |
| Royal Academy of Arts is founded. | **1768** | |
| The Adelphi is built by Robert and John Adam. | **1772** | |
| America declares its independence from Britain. | **1776** | |
| Lord Nelson dies at the Battle of Trafalgar and is buried in St. Paul's Cathedral. | **1805** | |

| | | |
|---|---|---|
| Charles Dickens born in London. | **1812-70** | |
| Gas lighting is installed on Piccadilly. | **1814** | |
| Wellington defeats Napoleon at Waterloo. | **1815** | |
| John Nash lays out Regent's Park, Portland Place, Regent Street, and the Mall. | **1816** | |
| | **1820** | **George IV** (1820-30) |
| National Gallery is founded. | **1824** | |
| First police force is founded. | **1829** | |
| First London bus. | | |
| | **1830** | **William VI** (1830-37) |
| Charles Barry and Augustus Pugin start the Houses of Parliament; completed in 1860. | **1835** | |
| London University receives Royal Charter. | **1836** | |
| Buckingham Palace becomes permanent residence of the sovereign. | **1837** | **Victoria** (1837-1901) |
| London's first passenger railway opens, running from Southwark to Greenwich. | **1838** | |
| Nelson's statue is erected in Trafalgar Square. | **1843** | |
| Brunel's Rotherhithe Tunnel (the first under the Thames) is built. | | |

| | | |
|---|---|---|
| British Museum is built on grounds of Montagu House. | **1844** | |
| Great Exhibition in the Crystal Palace at Hyde Park. | **1851** | |
| First mailbox on corner of Fleet and Farringdon streets. | **1855** | |
| Tooley Street fire; worst since 1666. | **1861** | |
| Opening of first underground railway. | **1863** | |
| Victoria proclaimed Empress of India. | **1887** | |
| Jack the Ripper strikes in Whitechapel. | **1888** | |
| Creation of London County Council, giving the city a comprehensive government for the first time. | **1889** | |
| First electric railway tube, from the City to Stockwell. | **1890** | |
| Tower Bridge, with double drawbridge, is opened. | **1894** | |
| Westminster Cathedral built. | **1895** | |
| Queen Victoria's Diamond Jubilee. | **1897** | |
| | **1901** | **House of Saxe-Coburg** |
| | | **Edward VII** (1901-10) |
| First fleet of horseless carriages. | **1905** | |
| | **1910** | **House of Windsor** |
| | | **George V** (1910-36) |

| | | |
|---|---|---|
| World War I; London is damaged from Zeppelin air raids. | **1914-18** | |
| Women win the right to vote. | **1918** | |
| General Strike. | **1926** | |
| | **1936** | **Edward VIII** (1936; abdicated) |
| | | **George VI** (1936-52) |
| World War II; the Blitz; St. Paul's stands among ruins. | **1939-45** | |
| Rebuilding of London. | **1945-55** | |
| Festival of Britain. | **1951** | |
| South Bank is built as culture center (Royal Festival Hall). | | |
| | **1952** | **Elizabeth II** (1953-present) |
| Post Office Tower is built. | **1963** | |
| New London Bridge and new Stock Exchange completed. | **1973** | |
| National Theatre is built. | **1976** | |
| Museum of London opens. | | |
| Silver Jubilee of Queen Elizabeth. | **1977** | |
| Margaret Thatcher becomes first female prime minister. | **1979** | |
| Royal wedding of Prince Charles and Princess Diana. | **1981** | |
| Barbican Centre opens. Thames Barrier completed. | **1982** | |
| Greater London Council abolished. | **1986** | |
| The Times is the first newspaper to move to the Docklands. | | |
| Museum of the Moving Image and Bank of England Museum open. | **1988** | |
| The Daily Express is the last newspaper to leave Fleet Street. | **1989** | |
| Introduction of Poll Tax in England. | **1990** | |
| Margaret Thatcher, Britain's first woman prime minister, deposed. | **1991** | |
| The Prince and Princess of Wales separate. | **1992** | |
| The Duke and Duchess of York separate. | | |
| Princess Anne remarries. | | |
| John Major becomes prime minister. | | |
| Fire at Windsor Castle. | | |
| Canary Wharf Tower completed, Britain's highest building at 800 feet. | | |
| Women are ordained into the Anglican priesthood. | **1993** | |
| IRA attacks London's financial district. | | |

# Index

# Index

# Index

## Restaurants

Only restaurants with star ratings are listed at right. All restaurants are listed alphabetically in the main (preceding) index. Always call in advance to ensure a restaurant has not closed, changed its hours, or booked its tables for a private party. The restaurant price ratings are based on the average cost of an entrée for one person, excluding tax and tip.

★★★★ An Extraordinary Experience

★★★ Excellent

★★ Very Good

★ Good

$$$$ Big Bucks ($20 and up)

$$$ Expensive ($15-$20)

$$ Reasonable ($10-$15)

$ The Price Is Right (less than $10)

**Page**     **Entry #**     **Notes**

# Credits

*Writer/Researcher* **Jamie Ambrose**
*Assistant Researcher* **Elvned Jones**

## ACCESS®PRESS

*Managing Editor*
**Linda Weber**

*Project Editor*
**Lisa Zuniga**

*Staff Editor*
**Karin Mullen**

*Assistant Editor*
**Erika Lenkert**

*Editorial Assistant*
**Karen Decker**

*Contributing Editors*
**Jeff Campbell**
**Stacey Colino**
**Charlotte Knabel**
**Jean Linsteadt**
**Antonia Moore**

*Editorial Consultant*
**Rebecca Forée**

*Proofreaders*
**Susan Charles**
**Elizabeth Ferguson**
**Denise Lawson**
**Bennett N. Miller**
**Julie Powell**

*Word Processor*
**Jerry Stanton**

*Writers/Researchers*
*(previous editions)*
**J. Abbott Miller**
**Joan Plachta**

*Design/Production Manager*
**Cherylonda Fitzgerald**

*Designer*
**Barbara J. Bahning Chin**

*Maps*
**Teresa Conniff**
**Kitti Homme**
**Patricia Keelin**
**Jesse Kline**

*Cover Photograph* ©
**Stuart Watson**

*Printing and Otabind*
**Webcom Limited**

**ACCESS**®PRESS does not solicit individuals, organizations, or businesses for inclusion in our books, nor do we accept payment for inclusion. We welcome, however, information from our readers, including comments, criticisms, and new listings.

**Printed in Canada**

*King's College, Cambridge*